SALEM COLLEGE
LIBRARY

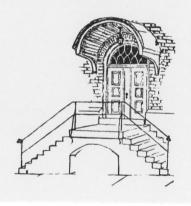

Partisans and Poets explores the popular poetries that interacted with American political culture during World War I. Studying the interplay between poets, political groups, and social transformation, the book draws upon archival materials to examine poetry used by the Woman's Peace Party, the Industrial Workers of the World, the National Association for the Advancement of Colored People, and the Vigilantes, a patriotic writers' syndicate. Van Wienen describes how poetry in mainstream newspapers and major-press anthologies bolstered dominant, nationalist ideologies and demonstrates how pacifist and socialist verse mobilized minority groups contending for hegemonic power. While recovering the work of many forgotten modern poets – women, blacks, pacifists, patriots, and radicals – *Partisans and Poets* asserts that wartime poetry engaged in complex negotiations with specific and often dangerous political and historical circumstances.

CAMBRIDGE STUDIES IN AMERICAN LITERATURE AND CULTURE

Partisans and Poets

CAMBRIDGE STUDIES IN AMERICAN LITERATURE AND CULTURE

Continued on pages following the Index.

Partisans and Poets

THE POLITICAL WORK OF AMERICAN POETRY IN THE GREAT WAR

Mark W. Van Wienen
Augustana College, South Dakota

CAMBRIDGE
UNIVERSITY PRESS

Published by the Press Syndicate of the University of Cambridge
The Pitt Building, Trumpington Street, Cambridge CB2 1RP
40 West 20th Street, New York, NY 10011-4211, USA
10 Stamford Road, Oakleigh, Melbourne 3166, Australia

First published 1997

Printed in the United States of America

Library of Congress Cataloging-in-Publication Data
Van Wienen, Mark W.
Partisans and poets : the political work of American poetry in the
Great War / Mark W. Van Wienen.
p.   cm. – (Cambridge studies in American literature and
culture)
Includes bibliographic references and index.
ISBN 0-521-56396-8 (hardback)
1. American poetry – 20th century – History and criticism.   2. World
War, 1914–1918 – Literature and the war.   3. Politics and literature –
United States – History – 20th century.   4. Literature and society –
United States – History – 20th century.   5. Political poetry,
American – History and criticism.   6. War poetry, American – History
and criticism.   I. Title.   II. Series.
PS310.W679V35   1997
811'.5209358 – dc20   93-15653
                                                                            CIP

A catalog record for this book is available from the British Library.

ISBN 0-521-56396-8 Hardback

For Anne

Contents

Illustrations

Acknowledgments

I am deeply indebted to a host of teachers, colleagues, friends, and family members for their contributions to the making of this book. Cary Nelson was a generous mentor from my first year of graduate school, through my dissertation, which he directed, and on to the publication of the book, which sprang from the dissertation. The book owes much to his intellectual influence and professional example. Many thanks are due Janet Lyon, Robert Dale Parker, and Jack Stillinger, invaluable dissertation committee members and mentors at the University of Illinois at Urbana-Champaign. George Hendrick helped with my work on Carl Sandburg, the American poet whose writing on World War I first caught my attention. Meaghan Morris, quite fortuitously a visiting professor at the university in the spring of 1990, gave early impetus to my work on food conservation poetry, which was to become the germ of both the subsequent dissertation and this book. The later development of *Partisans and Poets* was catalyzed by the encouragement and close scrutiny of Barbara Hanrahan, Susan Schweik, Alan Wald, and a Cambridge reader known to me only by a wonderfully incisive, constructive report. For shepherding my manuscript through the process of review, final revisions, and production, I am grateful to Eric Sundquist, general editor of the Cambridge Studies in American Literature and Culture, to Cambridge editors T. Susan Chang and Anne Sanow, to editorial assistants Emily Shelton and Lisa Stollar, and to copy and production editor Mary Racine.

The curators, staff, and researchers of several special collections were principal collaborators in *Partisans and Poets*. Much that is original in this study must be credited to the following collections and their guardians: the University Archives and the Rare Book and Special Collections Li-

brary of the University of Illinois at Urbana-Champaign; the Rare Book
Room of the University of Virginia; the Swarthmore College Peace Collection, and especially curator Wendy Chmielewski; the Archives of Labor and Urban Affairs at the Reuther Library, Wayne State University,
with special regard for research archivists Raymond Boryczka and Warner
Pflug and the staff who assisted me during my week-long stay; the Rare
Book and Special Collections Library at the University of Michigan, and
particularly researcher Ed Webber; the Library of Congress Manuscripts
Division; and the Rare Books and Special Collections Library at Princeton University and archivist Margaret M. Sherry.

From day to day and month to month, my work depended upon free
access to various general collections and interlibrary loan services, and
upon the unstinting generosity of many librarians. Thanks to the Fintel
Library of Roanoke College, Salem, Virginia, and kudos to Fintel librarians Rebecca Heller, Pat Scott, Julie Beamer, and Tom Davidson; the same
to the University of Southern Maine library and to the endlessly resourceful Cassandra Fitzherbert and Mary Beth Gendron. My appreciation, as well, goes to the libraries of the University of Illinois at Urbana-
Champaign, especially their reference librarians; the Alderman and
Clemons libraries of the University of Virginia; the Newman Library at
Virginia Polytechnic Institute and State University; and the McConnell
Library of Radford University, Virginia.

For financial assistance I thank the Graduate College of the University of Illinois for a Dissertation Research Grant and the Henry J. Kaiser
Family Foundation for a Research Travel Grant to the Wayne State University Archives of Labor and Urban Affairs. I also thank Nancy Simmons
and Virginia Tech's Center for Interdisciplinary Studies for their assistance
in the final stages of this book's formation.

Portions of the book have previously appeared in *Modern Fiction Studies* and *American Literary History*. For their contracts reverting copyright
to the author, I thank the Purdue Research Foundation, publisher of
"Women's Ways in War: The Poetry and Politics of the Woman's Peace
Party, 1915–1917" (*Modern Fiction Studies* 38.3 [1992]), and Oxford University Press, publisher of "Poetics of the Frugal Housewife: A Modernist
Narrative of the Great War and America" (*American Literary History* 7.1
[1995]).

Thanks are due the following copyright holders for permission to
reprint the illustrations listed: Bettmann Archive, for "Defenders of
Antwerp – Belgians behind Their Intrenchment of Sheaves Defending
One of the Roads Leading to Fort Waelhem," photograph by Underwood

and Underwood. *The Crisis Magazine,* for "These," illustrated poem by Lucian Watkins, *Crisis* 15.4 (February 1918): 185. *New York Times* Pictures, for "The White Ships and the Red," poem by Joyce Kilmer illustrated by R. G. Russom, *New York Times* May 16, 1915, picture section: 1. Walter P. Reuther Library, Wayne State University, for three items: "It's So Different in America!" cartoon by Ralph Chaplin, *Solidarity* July 28, 1917: 1; "One Half Million Free Advertisements Boosting the I.W.W.: Stickerettes Designed by Ralph H. Chaplin," advertisement in *Solidarity* November 20, 1915: 4; and "When Block Meets Block," cartoon by Ernest Riebe, *Solidarity* September 5, 1914: 1. Underwood Archive, San Francisco, for "Peace and War," photograph by Underwood and Underwood published as "Reaping and the Digging of Trenches Going on Side by Side," *New York Times* September 6, 1914, picture section: 7. Peter Viereck (legatee of the George Sylvester Viereck estate and author of *Archer in the Marrow: The Applewood Cycles, 1967–1987* [New York: Norton] and *Tide and Continuities: Last and First Poems, 1995–1938* [Fayetteville: University of Arkansas Press]), for "Germany: Defender of Civilization against the Barbarian Host," cartoon by S. Helmholz Junker published in *Fatherland* 1.7 (September 23, 1914): 11. Washington State Historical Society Library for "You Join the I.W.W.," stickerette reproduced from *American West* 5 (January 1968): 21.

My thanks to the Academic Affairs Library, University of North Carolina at Chapel Hill, for making available its originals of the war posters "Britons: Join Your Country's Army!" by Alfred Leete and "I Want You for U.S. Army" by James Montgomery Flagg.

A number of friends and colleagues helped to sustain my intellectual and emotional energies throughout this project: while I was at the University of Illinois, these people included Brian Daldorph, Jacqueline de Vries, Hester Furey, Timothy S. Jones, James Postema, and James D. Sullivan; at Roanoke College, Pamela S. Anderson, Gary G. Gibbs, Michael Hakkenberg, Michael A. Heller, Katherine Hoffman, and Sangeeta Tyagi; at Virginia Tech, Thomas Gardner, Lillian S. Robinson, Leonard Scigaj, and Nancy Simmons; and at the University of Southern Maine, Richard Abrams, Lucinda Cole, Eileen Eagan, Diana Long, Dianne Sadoff, and Richard Swartz.

For their unstinting support throughout this project, I owe much to my family. My parents, William and Margaret Van Wienen, have been generous and constant in their backing. Thanks to my sister, Marcia, and brother-in-law, Mark Van't Hof, who have been good friends as well as kindred spirits in their love for literature and language. Thanks are also due my cousins Greg and Jolynn Van Wienen, who in June 1992 contributed an afternoon of literary-historical research at the Michigan State University library. I am grateful for the bountiful spirit and sense of history provided by my grandparents Peter and Martha Van Wienen. Grandma recollects many of the political figures and popular songs featured in this study, and then some. Grandpa tells how, upon entering high school, he requested instruction in the native language of his mother, who had died in his childhood. Problem was, his mother was German, and he entered high school in 1917. The teacher not only denied his request, but made him an object lesson for his classmates. I have often thought about that story, told to me early in my research: I have been charmed by my grandfather's schoolboy trust in American tolerance and fair-mindedness in 1917 and inspired by his sense of humor so much in evidence in the 1990s.

My children, Nathaniel Peter and Miranda Catherine, whose due dates gave extra starch to certain important deadlines, have provided daily doses of love, diversion, and perspective. Anne Windholz, spouse and fellow scholar, has sacrificed more for this project than any other person or institution. She has subsidized my labors by more grants-in-time and grants-in-aid than I can count. She has heard my deliberations and inspirations; read, commented on, and proofread innumerable manuscript drafts; shared all that has gone into this book and all that has gone on in the meanwhile. I thank her heartily.

Introduction

PARTISAN POETICS, CIRCA 1914

I N the Swarthmore College Peace Collection, there are two and a half file boxes of miscellaneous "peace poetry" sorted alphabetically by author – the productions of hundreds of "peace poets." Judged by dates of publication and historical references in the poems, virtually all were written in this century, most date from before 1940, and the greater share were produced in the years during and immediately after World War I.[1] In the Labadie Collection at the University of Michigan and the archives of the Industrial Workers of the World at Wayne State University, there are likewise reams of verse published in pamphlets, broadsides, privately printed books, mass-circulation songbooks, and union newspapers from early in the century. Especially in the period from 1914 to 1918, scores of these poems declare the coming of a great "class war" and denounce the "capitalist war" in Europe. Any American library founded before the Great War, whether university, college, or municipal, holds dozens of anthologies and single-author collections containing Great War poetry; in large collections hundreds can be found. Most, and essentially all from the period 1917–18, proclaim their support for the great "War against War" or America's "Crusade for Democracy." The back issues of U.S. newspapers from the Great War period reveal yet another major source of war poetry, for at that time nearly every newspaper in the country printed at least one poem per day, and during the war this poetry increasingly addressed the conflict in Europe. Some newspaper poetry was circulated around the country through press syndicates, and at least one of these, the Vigilantes, was formed during the war exclusively for the purpose of distributing patriotic editorials and poetry for newspapers. These releases are extant by the hundreds in the archives of cofounder

1

Hermann Hagedorn at the Library of Congress, and they can be found in numerous papers under the byline "the Vigilantes."[2] In conducting my research seventy-some years after the end of the Great War, I even found first editions of war poetry in commonplace antique stores, titles such as *A Book of Verse of the Great War, Spirit of Democracy,* and *History and Rhymes of the Lost Battalion.*[3]

To grasp the significance of these poetries whose artifacts are so abundant, varied, and forgotten, we need to imagine a very different poetry-producing and poetry-reading culture than the one we are accustomed to in the late twentieth century. To begin with, many of these poems were written by amateur poets – people who may have read, written, and published poetry regularly but who did not or could not take poetry to be their occupation. In part because writers had primary roles besides that of poet – they were wives, housewives, journalists, editors, manual laborers, and political activists, and tended to see these roles as being at least as important as the role of poet – the poetry they produced typically attempted less to build up the cultural capital of poetry per se than to use poetry's cultural authority in specific, often explicitly political ways. Many of these amateur writers wrote with apparent disregard for the craft of poetry; any critic today who might remark that much of the poetry considered in this study is "bad poetry" has been preceded by many such critics during the period under discussion. An editor at the *New York Times* complains of poetry written in the war's first week, "Not since the loss of the Titanic have the mails brought to *The Times* office such numbers of metrical offerings as they have since Europe took up arms – and not since then, either, have the offerings so clearly proved how much besides a thrill of heart and mind is required for the production of verse which can be called even tolerable."[4] Yet because of this very fact, that just about anyone might consider himself or herself fit to write poetry and even called upon to write it, poetry in the 1910s enjoyed a popularity and status as social currency that it has never achieved through the modernists' professionalization of poetry writing and the New Critics' professionalization of poetry criticism. Poetry was read by many people, in many venues, for many different purposes: not only published in books and literary periodicals, but printed in "ladies'" magazines and daily newspapers; not only read in private, but recited in public spaces and sung en masse by large groups; not only for the sake of contemplation, but for protest, political persuasion, and mobilization; certainly not for the "poem itself," but for worldly purposes lying beyond the poem. The various American poetries of the 1910s, and specifically the poetry of

1914–18 that addresses the world war, can be understood adequately only if we recognize their authors' political objectives and audiences. We can read these poems productively only when we recognize their complexity as political texts: their work as self-conscious (as well as unconscious) agents of ideological production, inscribing and interrogating various cultural and political formations of the Great War era; their constructive rapport with their audiences, particularly partisan audiences inclined to act on their injunctions; in short, the ways they helped form, shape, speak to, and speak on behalf of political collectives.

I

Partisan debate characterized American poetry from the beginning of the war, well before U.S. policy was closely entangled with European wartime politics. When, for example, Ernst Lissauer's "Chant of Hate against England" ("Hassgesang gegen England") was published in the *New York Times* of October 15, 1914, the event stirred up a ferocious exchange: first on the *Times* editorial page, subsequently across the range of American publications. Beatrice Barry's pro-English "Answering the 'Hassgesang'" was published in the following day's edition, a feat which required that the poem be composed and delivered to the editor's desk in the few hours between the appearance of the morning paper and the afternoon deadline for the next day's edition. Lissauer's poem had criticized England's colonial power and wealth as indications of moral corruption and hubris:

> Take you the folk of the Earth in pay,
> With bars of gold your ramparts lay,
> Bedeck the ocean with bow on bow,
> Ye reckon well, but not well enough now.[5]

Barry's reply emphasized the invasion of Belgium as a greater moral stain:

> French and Russian, they matter not,
> For England only your wrath is hot;
> But little Belgium is so small
> You never mentioned her at all –
> Or did her graveyards, yawning deep,
> Whisper that silence was discreet?[6]

On the next day, the *Times* printed "Another Chant of Hate" by Rosalie Moynahan, which applied the criticism of Britain's imperialism to

Ireland: "Ireland or Belgium – dare you say / Whose wrongs cry loudest this Judgment Day, / *ENGLAND?*"[7] Barry provided a rejoinder to this poem too: "The Crucial Moment," printed in the October 20 edition of the *Times.* A fourth poem published in the *Times* on October 21, "Motherhood's Chant" by McLandburgh Wilson, proposed that all sides in the conflict were committing atrocities, particularly against womanhood. By the end of 1914, the "Hassgesang" had been transformed from a particular poem giving rise to a volley of poetic exchanges to a veritable subgenre. *Contemporary War Poems,* one installment of a bulletin series published by the Carnegie Endowment for Peace, reprinted nearly the whole sequence from the *Times* in its December 1914 issue, excluding only Barry's second rejoinder. On May 30, 1915, Frank L. Stanton, the regular poetry columnist for the *Atlanta Constitution,* published a poem itself entitled "'The Song of Hate'" which critiqued the poetic form. Another anti-English, Irish nationalist entry, Charles J. O'Neill's "Ireland's Chant of Hate," was published in the April 21, 1915, edition of the *Fatherland,* an American journal dedicated to "Fair Play for Germany and Austria-Hungary." "France's Hymn of Hate" by Jules de Marthold appeared on the cover of the *New York Times* magazine section for the Fourth of July 1915. When on New Year's Day 1916 *Solidarity,* the eastern organ of the Industrial Workers of the World, published Harry McClintock's "Hymn of Hate" against American capitalism, the poem was simply applying to the class war the same rhetoric on display in the respectable *Times.*[8] By the time of U.S. intervention, the "Hymn of Hate" – the most common translation of the German original – could refer to a whole class of intensely partisan poems being published in the newspapers. The *New York Call* of February 10, 1918, describes the war poems in other newspapers as "perhaps not exactly 'Hymns of Hate,' [but] certainly not love songs."[9] By June 11, 1918, editors at the *New York Times* had apparently gone to work constructing a retrospective literary history of the genre, identifying and reprinting Georg Herwegh's hundred-year-old poem, "Ein Lied des Hasses," a rallying song for an 1818 rebellion against autocratic authority in Baden, Germany.[10]

If political debates carried on in "Hymns of Hate" and other partisan poetry had been limited to disagreements among individual poets or circumscribed by distribution through literary journals, it would be difficult to argue that they were representative of American culture and more difficult still to claim some formative role for poetry in American society. Poetry emerges, however, as an important site for the production of ideology in the war years when we recognize poetry's status as a popular genre and the growing popularity of war poetry as the war proceeded. At the same time that *Poetry,* the most widely circulating magazine touting the "new poetry," could count a few thousand subscribers and the circulations of other little magazines such as the *Little Review* numbered in the hundreds,[11] newspapers across the United States were printing at least one poem per day on their editorial pages, whether by staff poets, freelancers, or amateurs. In the *New York Times,* which relied on outside contributors (though the repeated appearance of certain authors suggests there were editorial favorites), at least one poem appeared on the editorial page in 97 percent of its printings during the war years. Other papers were less punctilious but nevertheless ran a greater total number of poems: in 1917 and 1918 the socialist *New York Call* included poems on its editorial page 92 percent of the time, and on those days when poetry appeared the paper averaged nearly three poems per issue. Gauged by the same measures, war poetry was also assuredly popular, and increasingly popular through the war. If we define war poetry as any verse addressing patriotism or military affairs, or making reference to events, government agencies, or persons connected with the war, we find that between August 1914 and March 1917, the period of U.S. neutrality, 47 percent of the poems published in the *New York Times* were war poetry; from April 1917 to November 1918 fully 83 percent were. Few other newspapers published as high a percentage of war poems as the *Times,* yet a spot survey of five papers – the *Atlanta Constitution, Boston Globe, Chicago Tribune,* and *Los Angeles Times,* in addition to the *New York Times* – indicates they were all publishing significant quantities of war poetry, quantities recorded in the following table as a subset of total poems published:

	May 1915	June 1917
Atlanta Constitution	11/73, or 15%	34/101, or 34%
Boston Globe	19/138, or 14%	37/95, or 39%
Chicago Tribune	5/30, or 17%	32/67, or 48%
Los Angeles Times	10/34, or 29%	41/63, or 65%
New York Times	29/48, or 60%	28/30, or 93%

The *New York Times* stands out as the most aggressive champion of war poetry during U.S. neutrality, even though it published a moderate number of poems overall compared with the *Boston Globe,* which had a Sunday poetry section, and the *Atlanta Constitution,* which ran a daily poetry column. The *Chicago Tribune,* reluctant to publish war poems during the period of U.S. neutrality, increased its number of war poems sixfold after intervention, and the *Boston Globe* eventually outdid even the *New York Times* in its editorial support for war poetry, for the one poem that appeared on the *Globe* editorial page Monday through Saturday was, by June 1917, *always* related to the war effort and was specially designated by icons of American flags either framing the poem or clustered around its title.

Some of the same patterns characterize other periodicals and the book trade. During the 1910s poems were printed regularly in magazines as varied as the *Ladies' Home Journal, McClure's,* the *Atlantic Monthly,* the *Crisis,* and the *Masses* – and often prominently as well: while some poems filled spaces at the ends of feature stories and between advertisements, others were given a full-page spread with illustrated borders. According to figures compiled by James Hart – whose thirty-year-old dissertation on American Great War poetry provides a mine of bibliographic and statistical data – war poetry appeared regularly in all five of these magazines, plus the *Century, Collier's, Dial, Good Housekeeping, Harper's,* the *Literary Digest,* the *Nation,* the *North American Review, Outlook,* the *Saturday Evening Post, Scribner's,* the *Woman's Home Companion,* and some sixty other American periodicals of various circulations (319–22). Hart's bibliography shows that books of poetry comprised a surprisingly high percentage of total books published: 265 out of 8,563 titles published in 1914, or 3 percent; 383 out of 7,686 published in 1918, or nearly 5 percent (270). Meanwhile, collections of war poetry, whether books by individual authors or anthologies by many authors, were published in ever greater numbers: from 17 percent in 1915 (50 out of 291) to more than 45 percent in 1918 (174 out of 383) (Hart 270–71). Alan Seeger's *Poems* was the first of several best-selling books of war poetry. Seeger, a Harvard graduate who volunteered with the French Foreign Legion in 1914, was killed in action on the Fourth of July 1916.[12] *Poems* appeared posthumously and sold rapidly: four printings were made and some 11,500 copies were sold within six months of its December 1916 publication date; four more printings and nearly 13,000 additional copies were run in the next six months; by the end of the war 28,375 copies of *Poems* had been printed, and the book stayed in print until the middle of World War II, totaling 38,495 copies.[13] War-poetry anthologies, of which more than 90 were published during the war (Hart 317), sold with similar success. Frank Foxcroft's *War Verse,* published in 1918, went through seven printings in one year.[14] George Herbert Clarke's *A Treasury of War Poetry,* first series, went through sixteen printings between 1917 and 1920 for a total of 42,000 copies.[15]

Just what does the popularity of war poetry mean? It certainly indicates that nonmodernist poetry, including poetry in the genteel tradition so often characterized as oblivious to worldly concerns, was in fact widely construed as a medium for representing and debating the war, its impact, and responses to it. It also suggests that individual writers and groups could expect a significant proportion of Americans to be accustomed to reading poetry, and to reading poetry as a forum for serious discussion on social and political issues. Beyond these assertions, we must be cautious of generalizing about how poetry's popularity functioned ideologically and politically. It is one thing to say that writers and editors used poetry, deliberately and habitually, to politick and proselytize; it is quite another to describe the relationship of this poetry to dominant American ideology. The *New York Times*, as we have seen, took the lead in demonstrating how poetry might be used to distill and broadcast particular responses to the war. After the sinking of the *Lusitania* on May 7, 1915, the *Times* commissioned one of its staff, Joyce Kilmer, to write a poem denouncing the German action. The result, Kilmer's "The White Ships and the Red," appeared, elaborately illustrated, on the cover of the *Times* magazine section for Sunday, May 16 (Figure 1).[16] As if to leave no doubt about the paper's attitude toward the event, elsewhere in the same edition were published nine other poems that alternately mourned the disaster and condemned the Germans as its sole cause.[17] While we can see, retrospectively, that Kilmer's poem and the others in the *Times* were at work constructing the dominant ideology that was eventually to bring the United States into war, it was by no means assured at the time that the United States would in fact involve itself politically and militarily in the European war. The major publishers were, to be sure, very much linked to the nation's most powerful intellectual and economic classes, centered as they were in the Northeast, especially New York, and run by managers, editors, and writers predominantly white, Protestant, male, and middle to upper class. Moreover, in spite of its regionalism, the publishing industry's networks of distribution were national in scope, so that the northeastern presses were well positioned to propagate nationalist and expansionist ideology to the masses. It was not entirely clear, however, that publishers favoring the Triple Entente and intervention had a firm grip on the popular mood until February 1917 (when Alan Seeger's *Poems* began to sell off the shelves and the Germans resumed unrestricted submarine warfare). If we consider the popularity of individual texts as a kind of barometer of popular opinion – a national poll before polling became a profession and an institution – we can see the precariousness of writers' and publishers' aspirations to project their identifications and ideologies onto

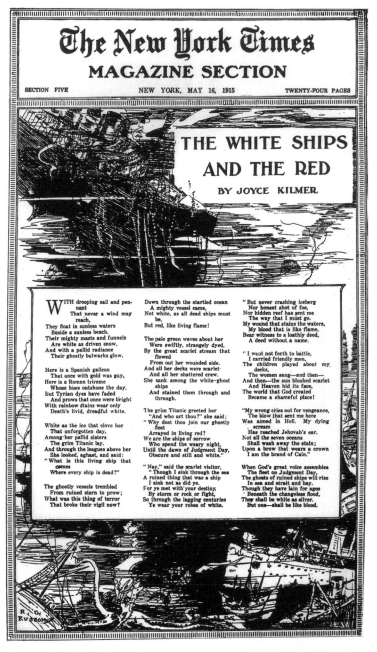

Figure 1. "The White Ships and the Red." Poem by Joyce Kilmer, illustration by R. G. Russom. Cover of *New York Times Magazine* May 16, 1915. By permission of *New York Times* Pictures.

the nation. Dependent upon, if not responsive to, a national market, the pro-Allied, interventionist-leaning publishing industry could hardly be certain whether it was in the vanguard when the pacifist song "I Didn't Raise My Boy to Be a Soldier," released in January 1915, sold 650,000 copies within three months and went on to become one of the best selling songs for all of 1915.[18] In contrast, Edith Wharton's *Book of the Homeless,* published by Charles Scribner's in January 1916, sold fewer than 3,000 copies.[19] The publishing industry had the cultural and institutional power to speak to – and even to some extent for – America, but consumers and readers might still choose whether or not to hear what Charles Scribner's Sons and the *New York Times* wanted to tell them.

Publishing institutions worked in tandem with other institutions, especially public education, to promote a conservative social order. But these social formations were built and maintained not automatically, but by the concerted efforts of many people tacitly agreeing to operate according to their strictures, and these strictures and social formations might be questioned and tested rather than simply adhered to. It was in the institution of education that most Americans alive during the Great War would have learned how to read poetry and understand its cultural significance.[20] Stressing the spiritual and moral edification of poetry and teaching through rote memorization and recitation, American primary schools constructed poetry as a discourse for discovering moral truth and as a practice demanding the subordination of the readers' minds to that of the poet.[21] Furthermore, this encounter with the great mind of the poet was mediated through an educational hierarchy emanating patriarchal order and authority: a hierarchy with the great poets (almost always male) positioned at the top; just below them, college educators writing textbooks and "manning" the teachers' colleges; next, primary-school administrators (again, usually male) overseeing day-to-day operations in the schools; and further down, primary-school teachers (mostly female), who by their deference to the masculine authorities above them modeled submissiveness for the students at the bottom of the chain of command. In effect, poetry as it was employed in the schools taught children to be dutiful citizens and compliant industrial workers.[22] Meanwhile, books designed for home consumption sought to continue poetry's moralizing and socializing influence outside of school and beyond childhood education. In Burton Stevenson's *The Home Book of Verse,* a massive anthology first published in 1912 and repeatedly reprinted during the next twenty-five years, the contents are divided not by author but according to subject matter and mode (e.g., "The Duty of Children," "The Irony of Love,"

"The Changing Year," and "The Conduct of Life").[23] By compiling a huge number of poets and poems (more than 1,000 poets and over 3,700 poems) that address a comparatively small number of explicit themes, many with moralistic overtones, Stevenson contributes to a construction of poetry as a discourse of moral and philosophical guidance: a chorus of voices, both venerable and contemporary, that comprise the wisdom of the ages. As the school environment stressed personal morality and individual responsibility rather than political action or social change, so anthologies like Stevenson's emphasized the enduring monuments of poetic achievement and, as well, the tempering of great art's passion with the "sweetness" and "chastity" of "humbler" verse.[24]

Yet by helping to make poetry a viable popular genre and by instituting poetry within the realm of moral choice and social responsibility, American educational, publishing, and media institutions founded not only a discourse of social control but also a potential discourse of dissent and resistance. Even if the schools sought to establish the Poet and the Poem as nearly unattainable ideals, they provided the opportunity for all students to claim competence as readers of poetry. Furthermore, the variety and sheer volume of poetry used both in the classroom and in anthologies such as Stevenson's (not to mention the daily poem in the newspaper, often submitted by a reader) must have had a democratizing effect on the *writing* of poetry: if the thousand-plus contributors to *The Home Book of Verse* can be poets, why not me too? Furthermore, once poetry was defined as a field of social and moral practice, it was not so difficult for writers, publishers, and even political activists to connect poetic production to a more comprehensive program of social action. Thus, while the tendency of poetry education may have been regressive, the habits of poetry reading taught in the public schools offered a ready means of idealizing and propagating virtually any cause, whether conservative, progressive, or radical.

Thus, for any American institution or reading context in which poetry appears, in general, to work conservatively and hegemonically, it is possible to locate instances of political resistance and subversion. Take, for example, the schools. While in the first two years of the war many states instituted educational programs emphasizing patriotism and readying boys for military service, other school districts stressed internationalism, pacifism, and something bordering on socialism. In May 1915, President Wilson proclaimed "A Mothers' Day Dedicated to Peace," merging the Mother's Day holiday with another celebration, a May "Peace Day" commemorated annually in many American schools since 1905, the opening year of the Hague conference on international peace. From the beginning of the war up to the U.S. intervention, the president of the New York City Board of Education endorsed a pacifist stanza written by Katherine Devereux Blake for use in the public schools. Blake's stanza, set to the tune of the "Star Spangled Banner," shows how the definition of "Americanism" was up for grabs before the U.S. intervention:

> O say can you see, you who glory in war,
>   All the wounded and dead of the red battle's reaping?
> Can you listen unmoved to their agonized groans,
>   Hear the children who starve, and the pale widows weeping?
>   Henceforth let us swear
>   Bombs shall not burst in air,
> Nor war's desolation wreck all that is fair,
>   But the star spangled banner by workers unfurled
> Shall give hope to the nations and peace to the world.[25]

While demonstrating the respectability of pacifism early in the war, the song also points to the potential for pacifist subversion in the schools later on, even after the U.S. declaration of war. Whether or not this pacifist – and socialist – stanza of the national anthem was used in schools after the U.S. intervention, some New York schools apparently persisted in commemorating Peace Day even after the declaration. The May 18, 1917, edition of the *New York Call* reported that "at least 15 New York City schools" planned to observe the event, although that year they had not received any instructions from school authorities to do so.[26] Thus, school peace programs and the poetry comprising many of them, which would appear at first glance to be cultural forms contained by patriarchal norms and authority, could become in some New York schools occasions for dissent, with their effects felt not merely in the education of the next generation but also in the present political landscape.

Elsewhere poetry became even more than a vehicle for political debate and dissent. In the Industrial Workers of the World (IWW), poetry and songs became the foundation for group identity. IWW songs, collected and carried by workers in the union's famous, pocket-size "Little Red Song Book," also became on many occasions the very utterances for which Wobblies were arrested, as throughout the western United States they fought for the right to organize on the streets by staging "free-speech fights" in which not only oratory but singing were punished as disorderly conduct.[27] Group singing of Wobbly songs became the practice through which the IWW demonstrated its unity. On November 5, 1916, during the IWW's rancorous fight to organize among striking workers in the Everett, Washington, lumber mills, 250 IWWs boarded the passenger ferry *Verona* bound from Seattle to Everett. At Everett they were met at the dock by the sheriff and a group of deputized townspeople; the IWWs crowded on the deck sang "Hold the Fort" as they prepared to disembark:

> We meet today in Freedom's cause
>   And raise our voices high;
> We'll join our hands in union strong,
>   To battle or to die.
> [*Chorus*] *Hold the fort for we are coming,*
>   *Union men be strong.*
> *Side by side we battle onward,*
>   *Victory will come.*[28]

The band of deputies opened fire, and amid the volleys and panic that followed, five Wobblies and two deputies were killed.[29] The lyric alone caused no riot. But sung by 250 IWW agitators as in one voice, the song together with its singers posed a threat. The lyric was significant both for the deputies, who apparently found its defiant performance threatening, and for the IWWs singing it, whose actions bore out the song's boast and pledge "to battle or to die." Here, in dramatic tragedy, was acted out the role of lyric and song in shaping a collective consciousness and collective action.

Few instances of partisan poetry in action are as vivid as the *Verona* incident. But poetry was routinely called upon for public occasions (as well as in printed publications) to sum up a polemical stance, to elicit an emotional response favorable to one's point of view, or to call upon the authority of the poet. When U.S. Senator John Sharp Williams quoted a war poem in a May 1918 Senate debate, he was not only making use of what he took to be an apt expression of U.S. unity under arms:

> And here's to the Blue and Gray as one,
>   When we meet on the fields of France;
> May the spirit of God be with us all
>   As the sons of the Flag advance.[30]

By indicating that the author of the poem, George Marrow Mayo, was a naval enlisted man, Williams was also calling upon the authority of a war participant and a common citizen to represent the unanimity of the American people. When in 1918 perennial Socialist presidential candidate Eugene Debs was arrested for speaking out in defense of fellow So-cialists, then jailed and charged with obstructing the draft,[31] the defen-dant's closing statement to the jury called upon the authority of one of the great genteel poets of America, James Russell Lowell, as Debs re-cited:

> He's true to God who's true to man;
>   whenever wrong is done.
> To the humblest and the weakest,
>   'neath the all-beholding sun.
> That wrong is also done to us,
>   and they are slaves most base,
> Whose love of right is for themselves
>   and not for all the race.[32]

Of course, the authority of the speaker – in this case both a speaker and a reader of poetry – mattered as well as the poet's. Debs's assertion through Lowell's poem, that the United States was neither a unified society nor a just one, whether in war or in peace, was seen as simply too dangerous coming from a public figure who had polled nearly a million votes as a Socialist presidential candidate in 1912. Debs was convicted and sen-tenced to ten years in prison.

James Russell Lowell's advocacy for the humble and weak, as well as Debs's, points to the fact that American society in the first decades of the twentieth century was dominated more by progressive ideals than by con-servative ones (albeit with considerable debate over what "progressive" meant). As for the pacifist programs and poems in the schools, one might as readily argue that the Peace Day commemorations of 1917 marked simply a continuation of a pacifist tradition dating back over a decade, and arguably over many decades; it was the militarist and nationalist school programs of 1917 and 1918 that subverted the "truer" American tradition of pacifism. Even the parodic songs of the IWW and their protest tactics, which seem to strike so blatantly at the heart of the status quo, were themselves the products of specifically American industrial conditions and American poetic traditions of mimicry – traditions evi-dent in the incessant recycling of the "Hymn of Hate" as well as in Blake's pacifist "Star Spangled Banner." Clearly, then, the social hegemony that emerges in the United States during the Great War, characterized by a strident and expansionist nationalism abroad and an often intolerant po-litical conservatism at home, was still very much a work-in-progress throughout the period – and, indeed, hegemony is *always* a work in progress. Consequently, the specific social groups and texts in which patriotic culture was nurtured, and through which intervention finally became a national imperative, must be subjects of this study coequal with pacifist and radical groups and texts. For hegemonic formations are not by any means static, fixed, and impersonal, but are created by human agents who are no less resourceful and cunning than the "subversives" – whom we call subversive, in fact, not because their position need permanently be fixed as marginal but because we recognize in hindsight that theirs was, for a particular historical moment, the losing struggle.

So Debs's poetic resourcefulness, calling on the shade of James Russell Lowell, was quashed not only by the stern, seemingly impersonal dictates of the courts that sentenced him, but by the shrewdness of a patriot such as Senator Sharp who recognized the authority of a virtually anonymous enlisted man and part-time poet. The swagger of the IWW was matched by the brazen assurance of the mother who, once persuaded by her son to let him enlist, went around parlors up and down the eastern seaboard challenging other mothers to press their boys into patriotic service. On January 27, 1918, a letter from Mary Thomas Raymond appeared in the *Times* under the heading "History of a Poem. 'The Volunteer's Mother' Has Helped in Recruiting." As Raymond explains, in the summer of 1917 her son, recently graduated from Princeton, asked her permission to volunteer for the army air corps; she resisted, at least until her son showed her a poem by Sarah Benton Dunn originally published in the *Times* on July 3, 1917, which he said "'tells the whole story of our lives, mine and yours, mother.'"[33] Raymond's conversion took place when she saw the poem, whose moment of crisis arrives when the mother, having raised her son to become a pillar of masculine virtue and respectability, recognizes what this upbringing demands of him – and her – in time of war:

> And yet – but now – my well-beloved son,
> For your perfection can I pay the price?
> Or would I have you play the coward's part,
> With selfish, shriveled soul too small to dwell
> Within so fair a frame? Is that my choice?
> I sought the best! Shall I be satisfied with less?[34]

"I read the poem," Raymond recounts; "I recognized that his desire was the result of his upbringing, so he is now 'Somewhere in France.'" This incident in itself suggests the way that certain readers – a well-educated, upper-class reader, in this case – responded to genteel newspaper poetry with enough high seriousness to base potentially life-or-death decisions at least in part on the poetry's argument and sentiment. But what is more, the mother's testimony about her subsequent employment of the poem offers additional evidence about how poetry could be used in the service of an emerging nationalist hegemony:

> I write this letter to ask you to place before your readers again those beautiful verses, and that Sarah Benton Dunn, the author, may know what a power for recruiting among mothers she has sent forth. I carried copies of it while traveling last Summer from the Canadian border down to quaint old Waynesboro, Ga. I have read it scores of times – to mothers whose hearts were already strangled with grief for the boy who had gone away, to mothers whose sons were soon to be called, to pampered and selfish mothers, to a negro charwoman whose two sons had gone, and to one slacker's mother! And no matter where I've read it tears have come to the eyes of those who heard, and comfort to aching hearts was given, for, after all, different though our ways of doing it may be, every mother believes that in rearing her son she has always "sought the best."[35]

Even as it marks class and regional differences and prejudices – "quaint old Waynesboro, Ga." and "different though our ways of doing it may be" – the passage implies and demands a solidarity among American mothers, American locales, ethnicities, and classes that transcends those differences. The vehicle for transcending those differences, tellingly, is a poem, constructed in the genteel tradition as the medium of just such transcendent value. By Raymond's testimony, the acts of reciting, hearing, and sharing the poem "The Volunteer's Mother" provided the occasion for building unanimity for the U.S. war effort (as indeed also did the testimonial in the *Times*). Through local, informal gatherings, the patriotic war poem promotes the kind of group self-definition and unity needed to delineate a "patriotic" citizenry and mobilize the nation for war.

Raymond's case, like the others, illustrates the prominence of poetry in American public life. Her quotation of Sarah Benton Dunn, like Debs's quotation of James Russell Lowell, underscores the embeddedness of poetry within American culture and, at the same time, the distinctive cultural authority of poetry as a genre. Whereas both romantic and modernist conceptions of poetry and the poet stress that separation from culture, not embeddedness, creates authority by establishing the author as disinterested, my opening examples of partisan poetry exhibit quite the contrary possibility: that it is close interconnection with a historical moment and a social group which produces critical as well as social power. Poetry's supposed "uniqueness" as a genre, its relative autonomy from other forms of discourse, may indeed allow for a transference of cultural authority from, say, the high-art poetry of James Russell Lowell to the *New York Times* poem "The Volunteer's Mother," and even from these mainstream texts to Katherine Blake's pacifist version of the "Star Spangled Banner" and the IWW's "Hold the Fort." And yet there are surely as many differences among these poems as there are similarities, so much so that I cannot pretend to identify a single alternative to modernist poetry – for example, "the genteel" – which serves to circumscribe the poetic forms and practices abounding in the United States during the Great War. Rather we must speak of alternative *poetries*, plural; my term "partisan poetry" does not identify a particular style or form but rather a rhetorical stance, and a relationship with an audience and with particular social formations. Dominant ideologies may mark a genre, poetry, as a repository for "higher authority" or "ultimate ideals." But it remains for particular groups of readers and their social and political practices actually to confer that authority and produce such ideals. After all, Blake's "Star Spangled Banner" would not necessarily captivate a hearer with a vested interest in arms manufacturing just because it was written in a familiar poetic and patriotic form. Even more starkly, the lyric "Hold the Fort" did not hold cultural power except when sung en masse at a specific political rally, by a group of IWWs determined to act on its injunctions. But once mobilized, that cultural power did in fact have to be acknowledged and dealt with by the posse waiting at dockside, however differently that power was interpreted by them.

Ultimately, the central assertion of this study is not just that American popular poetries and poetry-reading cultures opened up the possibility of using poems politically, or even simply that all American poetries, like the moralistic poetry taught in the schools, were always already political, but further that at a number of junctures during the Great War, poetry did in fact fulfill a self-consciously political, and politically transformative, role. For this to happen, poetry and poets needed more than a popular audience used to reading their work as social and political commentary. They also needed to be connected to some audience for whom politics mattered: a collective group with some degree of ideological and social consistency, and also a group willing to act on such poetic utterance as spoke to and for their causes. As with Antonio Gramsci's "organic intellectual" and his or her class, the relationship between a political poet and his or her group must be dialogic, for the poet not grounded in the experience, the struggles, and the convictions of his or her group can neither represent its perspective accurately nor mobilize the group effectively.[36] The same applies to the position of the reader, who needs alternative reading communities and institutions, not just the possibility of reading differently because one isn't always "at school," in order to develop reading practices that provide authentic political alternatives to the dominant culture. During the Great War, collectives that provided this kind of forum for political poetry included various partisan organizations, among them political-action associations, political parties, labor unions, citizens' leagues, and writers' groups. Of these, my focus will be on the following: the Woman's Peace Party, founded in January 1915 and within months the most prominent pacifist group at the vanguard of an extensive peace movement; the Industrial Workers of the World, the radical union organizing among unskilled workers in the nation's most exploitive industries and a group virtually eliminated from U.S. politics for its antiwar stance; the Vigilantes, a writers' syndicate that during the intervention solicited and distributed patriotic poetry to newspapers throughout the country; civilian poets and editors who, in publishing poetry favoring the war effort, found their group identity within the nation and particularly in wartime agencies such as the U.S. Food Administration; and the National Association for the Advancement of Colored People, which even as it criticized the racist imperialism of the warring European nations sought to use the U.S. war effort to win equal rights for African-Americans. For all of these groups, poetry in various forms was used to define partisan positions, to enunciate difference from dominant cultural formations, to proselytize among potential recruits, and to urge political action. In short, poetry was used as a medium for partisan-political organization and mobilization. Just how poetry was deployed in these explicitly political ways varied considerably, but of course it is this variety which augurs that "political poetry" was not so much a specialized subgenre or an extraordinary application of poetic practice as a wide range of poetic strategies that were widely available in American culture of the 1910s.

II

In *Partisans and Poets* I have set out to tell a story, or really a set of connected stories, about American literary and political history during the Great War. The urgency in telling them consists, I believe, in their having largely slipped out of our cultural memory of the early twentieth century. At the same time, a study such as this touches on a number of fields of critical inquiry, literary and otherwise, and so it is also important to set the stage for my narrative by foregrounding some of the intellectual traditions in which this narrative participates, whether antagonistically or sympathetically, and in so doing to spell out the issues it seeks to address. Specifically, there are four areas of inquiry that I see as integral to this project: first, a historical narrative of the American experience of the Great War that stresses the distinctiveness of the United States from Europe and the importance of homefront policy and politics, both as catalysts of U.S. involvement in Europe and as cultural "battlegrounds" in themselves; second, debates in American literary history and criticism about the meaning of "modern" literature, in which the entangling of modern literary history with modernist aesthetics has resulted in an emphasis on experimental modernism and the near obliteration of alternative literary traditions preceding and coexisting with it; third, debates about war literature and the "war text," in which traditional criticism focusing on the sites of the battlefront and the soldier-poet has been challenged by feminist work emphasizing interdependence between the battlefront and homefront, the soldier and the civilian; and fourth, ongoing discussions of hegemony and resistance, in which Althusserian Marxists stressing the formative power of ideology over human subjectivity have been challenged by proponents of Antonio Gramsci who stress that alternative political blocs with their own semiautonomous ideologies can actively contest dominant formations.

It is first necessary to ground this study in the history of the Great War, where it is most crucial to distinguish between the war as experienced in Europe and in the United States, for differences of geography and national politics produced very different conditions. Unlike the European combatants, the United States had various social and political options – a wide, even bewildering, range of concrete choices and progressive, conservative, and radical groups all with some leverage in national politics. Most clearly absent from the immediate American experience of the war is the discourse of national necessity that in August 1914 drove Austria-Hungary, Serbia, Russia, Germany, France, Great Britain, and Belgium into the war in quick succession. When, in 1917, arguments were made that it was "necessary" for the United States to enter the war, those arguments had to be made on very different grounds than among the European countries in 1914. In 1914, to all but the most confirmed Europhiles in the United States the war meant not the collapse of Western civilization but the inevitable dissolution of corrupt Old World culture. At first, even the German violation of Belgian neutrality, though considered outrageous by many, was seen by most not as a cause demanding condemnation of Germany, retribution, and U.S. intervention, but as one event among many confirming the general degradation of Europe's political and social systems. Contrary to latter-day legend, American politicians and citizens were aware of the probable material consequences of fighting in Europe; the atrocious casualties that had beset all combatants from August 1914 onward were known. Indeed, in the fall of 1914 virtually no one saw any national interest in getting involved in the European war. In 1916 Woodrow Wilson ran a winning reelection campaign based on the slogan "He kept us out of the war."[37] That within a month of Wilson's second inaugural the United States had declared war, in spite of two and a half years of national debate that had seemed to confirm U.S. neutrality, is decidedly bizarre and demands explanation. So does the fact that America proceeded in its war to make the world "safe for democracy" by suppressing freedom of speech, imprisoning dissenters, and promoting political conformity.[38]

The United States entered the war out of neither expediency nor necessity. Woodrow Wilson and his lieutenants declared the war to be a conflict of ideals and ideas, and in fact America's decision to intervene – as well as its subsequent mobilization – was intensely and even uniquely ideological. The battlefield situation and America's strategic relationship with the European combatants changed little between 1914 and early 1917 – save that the United States had profited economically and politically from remaining neutral.[39] Although Germany's resumption of unrestricted submarine warfare, announced in February 1917, threatened American citizens traveling to Europe as well as American trade with Great Britain and France, the United States could readily enough afford to lose some of its trade, and North America seemed secure from German invasion.[40] German submarine warfare hardly demanded a massive intervention of the kind begun in April 1917; it provoked intervention only because certain powerful Americans – and a powerful matrix of American ideologies – said it ought to. We can see such an ideological system at work in Carl May's seminal *The World War and American Isolation,* whose reading of Wilson's second inaugural address is instructive:

> The one hope of preserving a world in which America's peculiar values could thrive lay in a settlement that averted future wars, and such a peace could be achieved only if the United States exerted the influence to which her power and virtue entitled her. The President asserted, in other words, that a policy which sacrificed America's

prestige and moral reputation would mortgage the welfare and happiness of generations yet to come.[41]

According to May, the war was fought for "America's peculiar values," "the influence to which her power and virtue entitled her," and "America's prestige and moral reputation" – not for immediate national defense or territorial gain, but for more abstract notions of honor, virtue, and rightful power. Without necessarily being self-conscious about the significance of the terms – he was, after all, writing in the 1950s at the height of the Cold War – May reveals the ideological underpinnings of America's war declaration.

The construction of American ideology during the Great War had consequences not only for international policy, but also for homefront politics and society. Progressivism had been the dominant political currency since the turn of the century. While, to be sure, the Democratic variant of progressivism was limited by the power of southern conservatives in the party and the Republican variant was colored by the jingoist nationalism of Theodore Roosevelt, the trend in federal policy before the war had been toward greater protection of labor and consumers, less collusion with capitalists and producers, and increased openness to new approaches toward social and political problems.[42] Whether the nation went to war or not, and how it conducted its mobilization, had much to do with the fate of progressivism as a political idea. Furthermore, under the umbrella of "progressive" reform movements were many different organizations and proposals that had their own histories and peculiar courses to travel through the maze of wartime politics. The women's suffrage campaign was nearing its goal after nearly seventy years of politicking. The pacifist movement in the United States – itself a separate progressive cause – seemed, by its popularity in 1914 and 1915, to offer suffragists the historical opportunity they needed. Peace was clearly better than war; women were deemed to be pacifists; so what better way to guarantee national peace in a democracy than to give women votes? – thus went the popular ideology, which suffragists stood ready to exploit whether or not they fully embraced it. But all too soon, the rise of militarism and "reasonable preparedness" in 1916 posed dilemmas for pacifism and suffrage alike, and particular difficulties for those women and men who were ardently committed to both.[43] The Socialist Party of America and radical labor organizations such as the Industrial Workers of the World seemed in 1914 to be on the rise, whether by demonstration of national prestige (Debs's respectable showing in the 1912 presidential election), by organizational strength (100,000-plus members in the SPA and IWW at some time in the decade), or by successful local actions (the IWW's strikes and free-speech fights). These organizations were also philosophically opposed to nationalist wars, regarded as an outgrowth of international capitalism that would always be more destructive of labor than of capital. This opposition was to spell their downfall, to mark the ascendancy of more conservative trade unions and especially the American Federation of Labor, and to bring legal restrictions on speech and action that shaped American culture at large as well as limiting possibilities for labor activism and radical politics.

Another factor influencing the American wartime experience was the presence of many millions of ethnics, many of them from Central Europe and Ireland. These populations at first helped maintain momentum toward strict U.S. neutrality, but later seemed to demand that America's war overseas be conjoined with a homefront battle to suppress undesirable ethnic identifications – 100 percent Americanism. Between 1900 and 1914 some 9.5 million immigrants entered the United States, and roughly one-third of the total population of 99 million were immigrants or the children of immigrants;[44] large sections of most cities were dominated by languages, ethnic identities, and cultures other than English and Anglo-Saxon. These ethnic communities had considerable power in American politics – realized to differing extents by different groups. While German-Americans were fractured more than other ethnics by differences of class, religion, and geography,[45] they still wielded considerable cultural power: 2.5 million German immigrants lived in the United States and an additional 8 million people were German by lineage.[46] The National German–American Alliance, an association of some 10,000 clubs, claimed as many as 2 million members; and German readers could choose from some 532 periodicals in their native language.[47] The potential power of German-Americans and of other ethnics – especially the Irish – unenthusiastic about siding with the Triple Entente served to stir up and justify xenophobia and forced assimilation. The war also put tremendous cultural and political pressure on African-Americans. The National Association for the Advancement of Colored People, founded in 1909, sought to create a nation-wide political organization for the 10 million Americans of African descent; its organ, the *Crisis,* edited by W. E. B. Du Bois, and dozens of black newspapers cultivated political consciousness and leadership. The war presented risks for black Americans – that suspicion of ethnic minorities would extend to America's largest racial minority. But it also promised some opportunities – that

African-Americans could by their service as American citizens gain leverage for demanding their rights as citizens. Even in this, however, the war mobilization presented further dangers, for African-Americans took the chance that their labor might yet again be appropriated for the nation's cause without recognition or remuneration. During the neutrality period, troops conducted two major military ventures south of U.S. borders that suggested minimal regard for the condition and rights of people of color. In 1915 the United States began its occupation of Haiti, which was to last for the next ten years (with little success at putting down resistance in the countryside), while in 1916 the punitive march against Pancho Villa made Mexico a drill field for General Pershing and an American Expeditionary Force just months before Pershing and another AEF were bound for France.[48]

That the particular historical events outlined here cannot be explored with the relatively narrow range of texts now within the canon of modern American literature is, I think, fairly evident. As my opening sample of poetry suggests, however, there were poems published in newspapers, magazines, and anthologies that do comment on them. Yet there are considerable critical obstacles to simply diving into an analysis of these poems, and these difficulties have to do with placing American partisan poetry of the war in some relation to the dominant paradigm for early-twentieth-century writing – modernism, and particularly modernism as defined by a select avant-garde of formally and linguistically experimental writers. Upon closer examination, there appear to be two key issues here: the first having to do with literary history, the second with modernist aesthetics. On the matter of literary history, I would state simply that we cannot claim to know the literary history of the United States during the 1910s without examining the various poetries engaging with the Great War. Since the war is supposed to lie at the very fulcrum of modernism, unless we examine these poetries we cannot yet claim to know modern American poetry in all its complexity.[49] The critics who have reified the literary history of the period into a lopsided contest between experimental modernist poetry and traditional, genteel verse have simply ignored the variety of poetry lumped together under the non-modernist, "genteel" heading. This point is made forcefully by Cary Nelson at the outset of *Repression and Recovery;* in many ways, the present study might be seen as working to discover some of the poetries that Nelson argues are obscured by the modern–genteel binarism: some of the "other vital poetries and other engaged audiences for poetry [that] were also at work. . . . black poetry, poetry by women, the poetry of popular song, and the poetry of mass social movements."[50] In response to Frank Lentricchia's characterization of the poetic traditions that preceded and coexisted with modernism, "the big blank of American poetic history,"[51] I argue along with other revisionist literary historians and critics: we cannot pretend to offer a literary history of modern American poetry when we treat those poems that seem to us unreadable as if they had never been written.[52]

The second issue, the aesthetics of modernism, is of course very much behind literary historians' contempt for premodernist and nonmodernist poetry. Lentricchia is perfectly frank about how his aesthetic predilections inform and restrict the literary history of modernism that he writes in *Modernist Quartet:* a contribution on "modern American poetry" originally solicited for the Cambridge History of American Literature was narrowed down to a "modernist quartet": Robert Frost, Wallace Stevens, Ezra Pound, and T. S. Eliot. Lentricchia reports: "My taste is hopelessly canonical. And for this taste of mine I offer no apologies."[53] Of course, for most readers Lentricchia's taste needs no apology, for it is very much in accord with the twentieth-century verdict on poetry of the 1910s, rendered in the canon of modern poetry and literary histories of the period alike. While I cannot beg the question of literary value as Lentricchia does – cannot entirely dodge the question that would never be asked of Lentricchia regarding Frost, Stevens, Pound, and Eliot, "But is their poetry any good?" – I can, to begin with, insist on some advantage in describing some of the "other" modern poetries that Lentricchia and others make a point of omitting as uninteresting or insignificant.[54] How do we know these poetries are unimportant without investing any effort in seeing how they might be culturally, historically, or aesthetically valuable? Like Lentricchia, I cannot shut off aesthetic taste – indeed I would not want to, for aesthetics has everything to do with the success of political rhetoric and political poetry alike. But at the same time, I have consciously chosen to be guided primarily by a historical and political narrative: American poetry's engagement with the phenomena of the Great War and the uses of that poetry by particular political groups of the same period. I began not with the modernist canon but with whatever poetry I could find in the anthologies, magazines, and organizational archives of the 1910s, and then sought to discover how these poems responded to, represented, and shaped America's experience of the Great War.

I imagine that such a move, taking, as it were, a hard left turn into literary and cultural history rather than staying on the straight path of aesthetic appreciation, will not satisfy all readers of this study. To those who do not want to change the subject, who persist in asking, "But is the poetry any good?" I would ask in return, *good for what?*[55] Answering this question demands an analysis of the contexts in and for which texts are produced, an analysis of the social situations in which texts are situated. As Barbara Herrnstein Smith emphasizes, we must ask to what *use* a work of art is put in a particular society, or what function it serves in a given context, before we can determine whether it is valuable. Defined in terms of speech-act theory, we must consider not only the performance of *locution* – how a "grammatical utterance" is produced within a particular formal network, whether linguistic or literary – but also the act of *illocution* – the purpose of that utterance within a social situation.[56] The modernist poem, whether the lyric or the long poem, emphasizes the act of locution itself (by its concern with style, formal and linguistic experimentation, the "play" of signification) and thereby invites inspection as a self-contained linguistic construct, however dialogic, fragmentary, or indeterminate its effects. In contrast, partisan-political poetry foregrounds acts of illocution, not least because its primary functions include those not customarily privileged in the production and reception of poetry: "directives" – injunctions to an audience to *do* something; "commissives" – commitments that the *author* will do that thing; and, occasionally, "declarations" – statements that in themselves comprise actions.[57]

While in the 1910s as today the genre of poetry inevitably constructed the poetic persona as an autonomous individual, and her or his program as romantic, inspired utterance, the performance of that utterance invited the participation of the audience: either simple assent, the immediate motive for much newspaper verse; or concrete action, the case for much poetry published as government or party propaganda and especially for poetry used in public performance or as part of mass meetings. Almost as important for the formation of group solidarity was the way partisan poetry could function as a pledge of the author's commitment and loyalty – and here authorship might be construed broadly to include not only the originating author of a text but also subsequent reciters, publishers, and readers. Even when a pledge of loyalty was reneged on by the original author, the performative act of pledging could be recycled by the group, through re-publication or rereading of the poem. Finally, in certain contexts the recitation or publication of a poem became an action in and of itself: the massed singing of "Hold the Fort" by the Everett Wobblies contributed to, if it did not itself comprise, the provocation that led to their massacre and martyrdom, while under the regimes of wartime mobilization many kinds of dissenting poems became defined

as acts of treason, in themselves illegal and punishable by jail. Even regarding the speech-act of *representation,* the most obvious of the functions
of conventional literary work, we must note a difference between the customary purposes of literary texts and those of partisan texts. For while
literary texts typically declare their status as "fictions" – their distinction
from commonplace texts of fact and practical functionality – war poems
were introduced into contexts where their truth claims could and would
be tested in proximity to more conventional texts of historical "fact" –
newspapers, public oratory, government propaganda – so that partisan poetry not only tested the conventional distinctions between "serious" and
"fictional" discourse, but also entered into explicit argument, refutation,
and rebuttal regarding representation of the "facts."[58]

The connection of partisan-political texts with immediate political
struggles and historical events means, finally, that partisan-political poetry flies in the face of several bedrock conceptions of artistic achievement,
including originality, atemporality, and poetic craft. In formulating an
ideologically and politically feasible agenda, poets often outlined singularly "unoriginal" positions, following the general ideological and political critiques of the groups with which they were affiliated (McClintock's
"Hymn of Hate" offers a distinctively radical, IWW analysis; McLandburgh's "Motherhood's Chant" allies itself with the women's peace movement). To some extent, then, the poetics of partisanship is one of close
imitation and repetition. Responding to day-to-day developments in
American society, partisan poems were also highly topical and ephemeral. Political effectiveness demanded that poets respond swiftly and surely
to daily developments in political, military, and economic affairs, assisted
by daily and weekly publications consistently distributing their work.
Consequently, they often wrote with haste, using traditional forms or
even, as in the case of the "Hymns of Hate," borrowing or parodying individual lines, tropes, or entire stanzaic patterns; timeliness was the leading feature of these productions, not necessarily formal innovation or
polish. Given these qualities, it would not be surprising if some readers
find it difficult to see in the partisan poetry of World War I a tenable aesthetic alternative to modernism. But if not, it remains possible to recognize that the functions of political verse demand a distinct kind of poetics and to see in this poetry the outlines of a writing practice more engaged
with contemporary culture and politics than that offered during the same
period by the modernists, and particularly a collectivist, activist poetics
offering a clear alternative to their individualism and aestheticism.

Modernism is not the only literary-critical legacy with which this study must grapple. While the academy scarcely acknowledges the mass of American poetry written in response to the Great War, it has certainly not ignored war literature, having established the subgenre of war poetry and defined a considerable number of writers as "war poets." In other words, we again confront the problem of the canon - a canon of war poetry well established in the American literary academy. For World War I, this canon suggests that poetry by a select few British soldier-poets (chiefly Edward Thomas, Edmund Blunden, Robert Graves, Siegfried Sassoon, Wilfred Owen, Herbert Read, David Jones, and Isaac Rosenberg) supply the only adequate account of modern realities – especially the specifics of mass, industrialized warfare.[59] For British soldier poetry, too, a foil is provided, homefront patriotic poetry, so that the cultural value of soldier poetry might be constructed in terms of a dualistic opposition: the truth of the front, known only to the soldiers who fought there, as opposed to the falsity of the rear and the homefront, accepted out of convenience by civilians and outright duplicity by commanding officers and propagandists.[60] In *The Great War and Modern Memory,* Paul Fussell argues categorically, "Even if those at home had wanted to know the realities of the war, they couldn't have without experiencing them: its conditions were too novel, its industrialized ghastliness too unprecedented. The war would have been simply unbelievable."[61] Thus, he offers an interpretation of soldier poetry as a disjunction between two generations of (male) writers while stressing the primacy of front-line combat experience. Fussell actually goes a step further, to define the Great War not simply as a rite of initiation for innocent young men, but as *the* initiatory rite into the modern world, so that British World War I poetry becomes not only the starting point for a canon of war literature that is decisively opposed to war, but also the origin of modernism. "I am saying," Fussell writes, "that there seems to be one dominating form of modern understanding; that it is essentially ironic; and that it originates largely in the application of mind and memory to the events of the Great War."[62]

Fussell in effect asserts that the experiences of women and civilians on the homefront are less "real" and less "modern" than those of soldiers on the front lines; Fussell's account of modern war literature, like those of many other critics, boils down to an epistemological privileging of a particular male perspective over the perspectives of women, male civilians, and children. This is the central critique of the war-poetry canon and of traditional war-poetry criticism made lately and repeatedly by feminist critics and bibliographers, and it is this critique that underlies my turn toward the poetry and politics of the homefront.[63] The first and most basic claim of feminist scholars is that critical work must be done to describe and analyze women's wartime realities – experiences and perspectives that have been occluded by the critical attention directed toward the experience of men at the battlefront. Within this project, women are discovered to be active agents supporting – or resisting – the national mobilizations that undergird nationalist wars; women, like men, are complicit in and responsible for the war text.[64] The material contributions of women are indispensable to a nation's capacity for war making, whether that means manufacturing bombs, knitting socks for the "boys over there," raising sons to be soldiers, or, for that matter, bearing children who might someday be soldiers. Having rediscovered the active contributions of women to the war-making power of the state, however, we are struck all the more powerfully by the way ideological production in wartime denies the independence and power of women on the homefront: indeed, the fundamental structure of military conflict depends upon the gendered binary of an interior, precious, vulnerable "motherland" that must be defended, defined by an exterior, rigid border – a "marked" territory – which sets off the front line of that defense. The second kind of intellectual work done by feminist scholars involves, therefore, a working out of the theoretical implications of women's erasure from the war text, of the rigid gender binaries that structure nationalist conflicts, and of the cultural or political work possible when gender analysis is brought to bear on the "art" of war.[65] Jane Marcus's "Corpus/Corps/Corpse: Writing the Body in/at War" critiques the valorization of Great War literature by men, "not simply [to] valorize the feminine over the masculine war narrative" but so that the recovery of the "lost voices" of women writers might destabilize the conventions upon which war making depends.[66] Susan Schweik argues that masculine–feminine binaries "conceal other gulfs and fissures *within* these categories."[67] In other words, Schweik's analysis points to the ways in which the divide between the "masculine" battlefield and the "feminine" homefront conceals the other kinds of social and political struggles that, I will argue, were particularly contentious and pivotal in the United States during the Great War: differences among women over self-definition, political goals and tactics; differences between the upper and middle classes and working-class people, between white "native-born" Americans and black and ethnic Americans, between well-heeled northeasterners and majorities in many parts of the South, Midwest, and West.

The soldier-poet may expose the reality of the front, but undivided attention to the soldier-poet and the battlefield conceals the reality of the homefront. And the homefront is important, even more important than the battlefield, because it is there that the cultural energies – political imperatives, social needs, psychological desires and fears, even military necessities – needed to go to war and stay there are defined and maintained. These are the cultural, ideological, and political dimensions of war making that feminist critics take as their focus and that traditional, masculinist critics have all too often obscured. It must be noted, at the same time, that feminist war critics and traditional soldier-poet critics share more in their critical motives and in the social situation of their subjects than might be first apparent. Their motive, in short, is protest against war. The male soldier-poets, and still more the maimed and killed soldiers who so often provide the material for their poems, are hardly more empowered than the dutiful, patriotic women of the homefront. Soldier-poets such as Wilfred Owen and Siegfried Sassoon can be among the most devastating critics of patriarchy.

In either case, however, we must ask what is meant by "protest" and what is wanted by it. By and large, feminist and masculinist critics of poetry would like the work of their subjects, and their own work as critics, to comprise an *effective* protest: to begin some kind of social movement that will end war, or at least make it less likely, and even somehow to create a better society. Jon Silkin's account of Isaac Rosenberg's poetry, for example, asserts that "anger and compassion are merged, with extreme intelligence, into an active desire for change, a change that will re-align the elements of human society in such a way as to make it more creative and fruitful."[68] But Silkin's claim that Rosenberg's poetry "*will* re-align the elements of human society" amounts to simple wishful thinking. Whatever the intellectual grasp and poetic craft of poets such as Rosenberg, Owen, and Sassoon, they never were able to construct an effective resistance against World War I, largely, I would suggest, because they lacked the material and political resources to do so. Rosenberg and Owen did not have significant numbers of their poems published until after their deaths and after the war; their protest against the war was largely a private, personal affair.[69] Owen's case illuminates, rather, the way an individual's protest is overwhelmed by the institutions of the military and the nation, and contained within the value systems of heroism, stoicism, and self-sacrifice on which the war machine runs. After a period of hospitalization for nervous exhaustion, during which he met Sassoon and was transformed into a "protest poet," Owen dutifully returned to his officership in France and fought with distinction, winning a Military Cross in one action and being killed in another, a week before the Armistice.[70] Siegfried Sassoon *did* have his antiwar poems published during the war, and he stated his views publicly in the hope that he would be court-martialed and thereby draw attention to his protest. But instead, fellow soldier-poet and officer Robert Graves contrived to have Sassoon examined by a medical board, which declared him a victim of shell shock and ordered hospitalization.[71] Like Owen, he returned to the front, serving from February 13 until July 20, 1918, when one of his own men accidentally shot him, though not fatally, in the skull.[72] Even if we emphasize the ways in which Owen and Sassoon were not altogether solitary, individual geniuses, but rather members of a community of antiwar protesters, civilians as well as soldiers, it remains difficult to see in their work the grounds for effective protest. Elizabeth Marsland argues that Sassoon and other dissenting poets developed into "protest poets" when they established relationships with civilian pacifists, so that their protest emerged out of a kind of political coalition between soldiers and a select audience of civilians. Yet Marsland's argument, like Silkin's, seems naive in its willful optimism: "The failure to reach a mass audience was no handicap to the poets. Their work was designed (both as text and as commodity) to appeal to a small and sympathetic group of readers, and 'the truth' would be spread as the circle expanded gradually through personal or semi-personal contact."[73] Quite the contrary, I maintain that the marginality of antiwar poetry, its inability to reach a large audience, represents not only a handicap but indeed marks the failure of war opposition in England. In an age of mass propaganda and state control of war industry, a "gradually expanding" circle of antiwar advocates will not be sufficient to alter the nation's course.

Feminist theory offers much more insight than does traditional criticism about the power of collective ideologies and the recalcitrance (and the flexibility and durability) of state institutions. Yet the analyses of Schweik and others continue to emphasize the situation of individuals responding to and criticizing the war system, not those collectives that shape the war system and those that might actually dismantle it. Schweik's *A Gulf So Deeply Cut* analyzes ideological concealments in World War II by showing how the poetry of Gwendolyn Brooks, Muriel Rukeyser, Mitsuye Yamada, and others works to deconstruct American nationalism. Marcus in fact valorizes political collectives, including working-class collectives and the politics of the English suffragists,[74] yet "Corpus/Corps/Corpse" by and large illustrates the general tendency of cultural work on nationalism and militarism to trust that deconstruction in itself, the destabilizing of the gender categories that undergird the war system, will be enough to disable it. But there remains a distinction between analyzing the war text – deconstructing dominant texts, providing alternative perspectives on war through rediscovered texts – and theorizing how the dominant, hegemonic institutions and ideologies which make war possible and "necessary" might actually be changed. Further still, there is the real work of actually altering those structures. Institutions and ideologies are collectively formed; they can be transformed only through political and social collectives, which means, in effect, that studies which see war resistance as dissent, protest, conscientious objection, or subversion sketch out intellectual and political preliminaries, at best. These discourses are important, certainly; I shall argue that when the state's power becomes pervasive, as it certainly was during the World War I mobilization, the only course left for dissenting groups is subversion, often carried out on a local or even personal level. When, however, the subject of subversion becomes the sole focus of discussions of social and political discourse, these projects risk remaining locked in a valorization of individuality and of the stylish, localized gesture, meanwhile ignoring the larger collective discourses of civil society and allowing the power of the state to run on unexamined and unchecked.

To analyze the collectives that undergird the power of states to make war and, as well, those that make the progressive transformation of society possible, I have drawn upon work done by theorists in the Marxist tradition. Some of the key concepts to be drawn from this tradition surround the terms "ideology" and "hegemony": the former receiving its definitive elaboration in the work of Louis Althusser, the latter in the writing of Antonio Gramsci. Ideology, for Althusser, interpenetrates both institutions and human subjects. Ideology consists of the unspoken assumptions and "common sense" that permeate a society, in spite of differences of gender, religion, occupation, class, and so on; it is crucial not simply insofar as shared social assumptions tend to maintain social order in the present, but also because it leads to the reproduction of the existing modes of production, nurturing precisely the kinds of willing, compliant subjects needed for the maintenance of social institutions: "In other words," Althusser writes, "the school (but also other state institutions like the Church, or other apparatuses like the Army) teaches 'know-how,' but in forms which ensure *subjection to the ruling ideology* or the mastery of its 'practice.'"[75] Social institutions that contribute to the reproduction of the status quo Althusser divides into two kinds: the "Repressive State Apparatus," or "RSA" (the "official" government, including courts, the police, legislative assemblies), and "Ideological State Apparatuses," or "ISAs" (civil society, including schools, religious institutions, political parties, unions, and mass media) (142–45).[76] For Althusser, subjectivity is ideological through and through – "individuals are always-already interpellated by ideology as subjects" (176). The importance of Althusser's formulation consists in his challenge to free agency. He demands that we consider the power and pervasiveness of ideology in determining social subjectivity, and thus also the power of state institutions to reproduce their power, to maintain the hegemony of the existing social order, and to protect the privilege of those classes already benefiting from that order. To theorize about any possibility for social transformation, Althusser's formulation seems to demand that ideologies and their corresponding state apparatuses be contested at many different sites of struggle in order for relations of power to be significantly altered: they must be resisted collectively, if they can be at all.

The problem with Althusser's scheme consists precisely in the difficulty of imagining how social institutions might be overturned, changed, or even challenged: individual subjects and collective institutions alike seem too immersed in dominant ideologies to gain any critical purchase to question them. Althusser's insistence on the overdetermination of social apparatuses has the effect of construing all subject positions as equally permeated with ideological construction, thereby rendering all subjectivities and all forms of ideology virtually interchangeable. He writes, for example, "As the formal structure of all ideology is always the same, I shall restrict my analysis to a single example, . . . that of religious ideology, with the proviso that the same demonstration can be produced for the ethical, legal, political, aesthetic ideology, etc." (177). One result of this startling view is that it becomes possible, apparently, to analyze an entire social system by synecdoche: any small part of society adequately represents the whole. But if ideology is in fact dispersed evenly throughout a cultural formation, then it appears as though all members of a society will always reproduce the dominant social formations, whether they are of the exploited classes or those enjoying the benefits of the prevailing system ("capitalists," "managers," "functionaries" [133]). From Althusser's later account of the way ideologies are socially produced, not merely given, his assertion that "ideologies are not 'born' in the ISAs but from the social classes at grips in the class struggle" (186), it is apparent that he differentiates between the experiences and ideological formations pertaining to a particular class, but his conception of ideology as always imaginary and delusional does not seem to provide terms for making this difference politically effective and socially transformative.[77]

The problem of how, in a society immersed in ideology, an exploited class might recognize its position as such and fashion an effective strategy for claiming power is the central concern of Antonio Gramsci. Gramsci, an Italian communist who was a political prisoner under Mussolini's dictatorship and died in prison in 1937, developed his political theory in meticulously kept notebooks, published as *The Prison Notebooks* in the 1970s and taken up by Marxist thinkers as an alternative to Althusser. "Hegemony" is Gramsci's term for that cultural formation that succeeds in directing social activity toward its own maintenance, which includes the organization of social ideology so as to reproduce its power. Unlike Althusser's account of hegemony, with its RSA and ISAs, Gramsci's concept emphasizes that dominant ideology permeates society to differing degrees depending on the class position of the person in question. Indeed, there are ideologies specific to the various social groups, so that ideology is not, as in Althusser, necessarily alienating to one's class identity and class interests. Hegemony is not a steady state under which a single, monolithic ideology dominates all social thought, but consists rather in the co-optation and orchestration of various class ideologies by a dominant ideology and a dominant class – or, more likely, a kind of alliance among dominant classes. So hegemony is a constantly shifting terrain, described by Gramsci as a "war of position" or a "war of maneuver" (depending on the circumstances of the case). Gramsci's insistence on the relative autonomy of class positions within a society is crucial, for it allows him to assert a difference in perception and interest (which in turn permits one to allow for the possibility of conscious, directed political strategy) without denying that ideology is a pervasive fact of social life. Thus, Gramsci distinguishes between intellectuals who are "functionaries," "the dominant group's 'deputies' exercising the subaltern functions of social hegemony and political government" (12), and intellectuals who are "organic," "who come into existence on the same industrial terrain as the economic group [the proletariat]" (18). Gramsci's "organic intellectuals" gain critical purchase on dominant ideological formations precisely to the extent that they remain connected with their class. But dominant ideology and working-class ideologies are, of course, not transparent or immediately known, so that in Gramsci's conception there is real intellectual work to be done: certain ideologies are "more active and organic" than others; some will advance the cause of society's marginalized

groups, others will not; and it is the job of intellectuals to distinguish between these. This conception, despite its emphasis on analysis, remains
stubbornly antielitist. First, the intellectual is an exceedingly broad cate-
gory for Gramsci, including "all members of a political party" (16), so
that anyone is at least potentially an activist-intellectual. Second, because
hegemony is defined and maintained by multiple ideologies and institutions, it remains necessary to mobilize alternative politics through large
masses of people, and therefore intellectuals' close association with the
masses is crucial.[78]

How do these concepts work themselves out in American politics and
poetry of the Great War period? My critique of protest poetry has probably already made clear enough why a fairly strong sense of ideology
seems warranted: simply put, in wartime, ideologies identifying an unstinting war effort with national pride and self-identity were over-
whelmingly pervasive. This was the rule in the European nations from
the start of the war; the United States followed suit when it entered the
war in 1917. At the same time, we do well to bear in mind Gramsci's assertion that hegemony is a constant cultural and political struggle, for the
particular consequences of the Great War seem much more inevitable and
determined in retrospect than they were in the process of determination.
Gramsci's formulation of hegemony seems to fit the American context
even more closely, for as I have already argued in my general sketch of
America's Great War history, the protracted period of neutrality brought
intense, fundamental ideological and political struggle regarding the nation's response to the war. If it seems to us that America's growing assurance as an international power impelled it toward war, and if it seems,
too, that the dominant economic, cultural, and ethnic classes demanded
a U.S. alliance with Britain and France, we must also grapple with the fact
that the United States kept out of the war for more than two and a half
years, and on several occasions during that period it appeared that pacifism defined America's dominant ideology – and women its leading political agents! Finally, Gramsci's account of the "organic intellectual"
makes a connection to the narrative I have to tell and to my way of telling
it through the work of partisan-political poetry and poets. On the one
hand, my case for poets' and poetry's engagement with ideological and
political work must always be limited; poets are not the only possible organic intellectuals – indeed part of the story that Gramsci would tell about
them, and that we must also, includes the ways in which most poets
are traditional intellectuals and therefore ideological "functionaries" –
and poetry is only one of many possible sites for articulating ideological

resistance, enunciating alternative subject positions, and politicizing the masses according to those positions. On the other hand, Gramsci's organic intellectual seems to describe the many poets in this study who not only addressed immediate political and historical issues in their poems, but also chose to affiliate themselves with political parties and worked to make their poetry speak in the interest of those groups. I came to Gramsci's notion of the organic intellectual relatively late in the development of this study; it now seems to me to affirm my decision, made early on, to seek out specifically partisan sites of poetry publication and, thereby, to pursue work produced not by modernist poets or soldier-poets, but by partisan poets.

III

While this book is in one sense about the variety of American poetry during the Great War – a variety extending beyond even the most expansive notions of modernism – it is also centrally about social and political strategy during the Great War, and this emphasis is explained by my earlier point – that what counts in the constitution and cultural power of these forms of "partisan poetry" is not their status as poetry per se, but their placement within the ideologies and political practices of particular groups. Therefore, the story told in this book does not focus on "literary history" so much as on political history; it does not follow trends or innovations in stylistics except where these show changes in cultural formations and political stances; it does not examine the work of the individual author as such, but rather the production of groups of writers, editors, and activists – and in most cases the "group" is formally constituted as a political party or other collective organization.

I shall begin with two groups situated at nondominant sites within American culture – the Woman's Peace Party and the Industrial Workers of the World – which, nevertheless, in the preintervention period were able to contend with more entrenched, traditionally dominant social factions. Chapter 1 examines the women activists who in 1914 and early 1915 led the American peace movement; it focuses on the activities of the WPP, which, by its deployment of essentialist notions of pacific femininity, organized a large number of women, and even the country at large, behind the banner of peace and which, in support of this movement, employed traditional, largely genteel notions of poetry as a medium for moral persuasion and social idealization. The chapter concludes with an analysis of a particular poetry reading and political rally held in

Detroit in the fall of 1915, an event organized by WPP members but not endorsed by the national WPP leadership. The rally, which sought to forge a pacifist political alliance with working-class Americans, revealed the limitations of a peace movement based on conventional femininity, for in spurning the rally the national WPP showed itself unable either to link women's pacifism with other forms of antiwar resistance or to embrace forms of poetry demotic enough to connect with an audience beyond women's clubs and existing activist groups.

Chapter 2, considering the IWW, proceeds to one of the groups whose poetics and politics, though resolutely opposed to nationalist wars, were incommensurable with the women's peace movement. While the WPP treated poetry as a source of high moral authority and, by and large, high seriousness, the IWW's art and politics alike were marked by parodic play and suspicion of moralistic pronouncement. For its offenses against cultural norms, the IWW was thought subversive of U.S. institutions and American common sense; yet this perception – held by IWWs themselves as well as their opponents – is laced with irony, for the IWW's poetic mimicry and recycling of popular songs were common practices in mainstream newspaper verse, and the industrial conditions that enabled the IWW's growth were integral to American capitalism.

From the WPP and IWW, the narrative in Chapters 3 and 4 turns to the coalition of political groups and interests that came eventually to define the direction of American policy – in homefront politics as well as abroad. While within this coalition the patriarchal northeastern establishment constituted the most powerful bloc, it relied heavily on the consent and collaboration of other groups – some of them among the most marginal in American society. Chapter 3 examines the interplay between the white establishment, represented by Anglophile book publishers and the war-poetry anthologies they published beginning in 1916, and African-American intellectuals, particularly W. E. B. Du Bois and the activists and writers of the *Crisis*. I argue that a cultural and racial ideal – white Anglo-Saxon Protestantism – lies at the core of American identification with the Triple Entente, as I find the white, English-speaking soldier (and, increasingly, the English soldier-poet) to be a primary locus of American identification with England and its war cause. But running parallel to this was another set of identifications by black Americans, as represented and led by Du Bois: first, an identification with black and brown colonials coming to the rescue of their white colonizers and, second, an identification with black Americans who had made notable careers in the U.S. military. So while the ideals (and the social pressures) bringing black and white Americans toward the war were very different, privileged whites and virtually disenfranchised blacks were uneasy, unequal, but very much cooperating partners as, in 1916 and 1917, the United States prepared for war.

Chapter 4 examines the partnerships that American women and ultrapatriotic organizations, specifically the writers' syndicate called the Vigilantes, formed with the wartime state. While still popularly regarded as natural pacifists, in 1917 women were called upon to play essential roles in the war effort, particularly in the wartime conservation programs overseen by Herbert Hoover and the U.S. Food Administration. The traditional symbolic power of women as life givers and nurturers was connected, through Food Administration propaganda and privately produced "food poetry," to the necessary wartime tasks of decreased home consumption and increased home production of food. Women were thus transformed from essential pacifists to essential cogs in the war machine. Meanwhile, the Vigilantes not only distributed poetry and editorials supporting the government's food conservation propaganda; they helped to transform the meaning and direction of the war effort from a "Crusade for Democracy" abroad to a crusade to eliminate dissenting groups and to turn back progressive reform at home. A patriotic writers' guild, national press syndicate, and reactionary political organization all in one, the Vigilantes adapted a range of poetry styles, from the high genteel to comic light verse, to the purposes of a national movement toward political conservatism and jingoism.

Chapters 5 and 6 consider the plight of dissenting groups after the U.S. war declaration, when pacifists and radicals, far from playing a formative role in the nation's political culture, were reduced to subversion or simply a struggle for personal survival. Chapter 5 returns to the poetic and political work of the Woman's Peace Party and the Industrial Workers of the World, this time under the repressive conditions of 1917 and 1918. Only the New York branch of the WPP remained active in 1917, but it underscored its public opposition by publishing a fortnightly journal, *Four Lights: An Adventure in Internationalism,* which mixed both formal and free verse with short prose squibs and political cartoons. The *Four Lights* editors and contributors reveal the increasing sophistication of the feminists who remained active in the antiwar movement, as much of the writing in the magazine draws attention to the necessity of *constructing* women's pacifist identities, not simply assuming them as given. At the same time, however, *Four Lights* satire and criticism of women participating in war work – many of them former allies and WPP members –

propelled the more conservative members of the New York WPP to eliminate funding for the magazine; it died of self-censorship. The Socialist Party, the IWW, and others on the Left were dealt with by the federal government, which revoked their mailing rights and prosecuted party and union leaders for sedition. In September 1917 all of the leaders of the IWW were arrested; in the summer of 1918 they were put on trial, with the most important venue being Chicago, site of the IWW's national headquarters. There the IWW's famous poetic ingenuity was stretched to new limits, for the poetry introduced as evidence against them was reinterpreted by Wobblies on the stand as the writings of liberal reformers, not the rants of saboteurs and revolutionaries. If the IWWs revealed the flexibility of poetic discourse under the pressure of possible conviction, so did the court, which found more than a hundred union members guilty of over a hundred counts of sedition each.

With political repression of this kind becoming the central fact of existence (or nonexistence) for dissenting political groups, my narrative turns, in Chapter 6, to the ways in which resistant discourses and political collectives survived. Drawing upon the theoretical work of Michel de Certeau, I argue that resistance was kept alive through local, often highly secretive, sometimes nearly invisible forms of subversive practice and writing. This subversion could often take place even among groups that were, by and large, supportive of the war effort; accordingly, I return to dissent among the ranks of African-Americans and to resistance among women and working-class people against the government's food conservation regimen. Several black metropolitan newspapers called for a much more qualified endorsement of the war effort than the one given by Du Bois and the *Crisis*. And even in the pages of the *Crisis* and other patriotic periodicals can be found poets who demand democracy at home as well as abroad, and even a soldier-poet who praises the mutiny of black soldiers at their camp in Houston, Texas – men who placed their race pride ahead of their loyalty to country. Similarly, the grandiose rhetoric of the Food Administration provided plenty of fodder for poetic satire, whether that satire was published in socialist papers like the *New York Call,* which continued to go to print and be distributed locally despite losing its mailing rights, or in periodicals including the *Detroit Labor News* that otherwise held to the patriotic party line. It was even possible for resistance to be kept alive when committed radicals and pacifists, unassimilated "foreigners," and other disaffected Americans continued simply to read food conservation poetry and other patriotic literature subversively. The resources of food poetry became – I argue in the conclusion – part of a subcultural discourse of resistance keeping nondominant political options and identities alive for later decades and later opportunities for hegemonic struggle.

My study proceeds chronologically, moving from the early successes of American pacifism to the later dominance of repressive and conservative political forces, and also dialectically, exploring interconnections between dominant and nondominant groups as well as debates within organizational factions. At the same time, this book focuses on particular poems and their constitutive practices, making poetry the primary media for analyzing American culture during the Great War. If such a procedure sounds unduly limiting to political and cultural analysis, I might gesture toward something I have been arguing, and should soon be all too apparent: the pervasive application of poetry to political struggles during the period. If partisan-political analysis seems unliterary or antiliterary, I must emphasize yet again that the value of poetic production consists not in its "literariness" per se, but in the social uses to which poetry is put by groups of readers and writers. When poems are quoted in the literature of political parties, when they are written expressly for party publications, and when they set forth political agendas or ideals, how can politics and partisanship not be central categories of "poetic" understanding? If poems prove useful in analyzing the structures of political domination and repression, and if they provide new possibilities for describing potential alliances among nondominant groups – here most prominently between women's groups and labor organizations – do we really want to gainsay the value of such a critical practice?

1

"I Didn't Raise My Boy to Be a Soldier"

THE WOMAN'S PEACE PARTY AND THE
PACIFIST MAJORITY

WHILE American newspapers described the beginning of the European war with various measures of horror, disgust, and fascination, activist American women took to the streets almost immediately to declare their opposition to any U.S. involvement. The first American demonstration against the war, held on August 19, 1914, was organized by women, fifteen hundred of whom marched down New York's Fifth Avenue to the beat of muffled drums.[1] Because the largely conservative peace societies predating the war declined to engage in partisan politics when war actually came, groups formed in direct response to the European conflict came to the forefront, and leading this emerging peace movement were women. In January 1915, discussions among women active in the suffrage movement, in social work, in prewar peace societies, and even in genteel social clubs led to the formation of the Woman's Peace Party. Having drafted Jane Addams as national chair, the party soon became the leading voice of pacifism in the United States as it built a membership of some 40,000 in its first, tumultuous year.[2] The WPP established itself internationally as well when in February 1915 it sent a delegation including Addams, Emily Balch, and Alice Hamilton to the international women's peace conference convening at the Hague.

In the cultural and political struggle over America's response to the Great War, women largely defined the terms of the debate from August 1914 until May 1915 and the sinking of the *Lusitania*. Their success may be attributed to the wide prewar organization of women in societies and political lobbies, to the consensus among these women and the public at large that they, as women, were essentially pacifist, and to activist women's ability to identify their perspectives with popular opinion and the public good. Also notable is a tradition of feminist intellectuals and activists who conceived of pacifism both as a fundamental attribute of women's nature and as a largely untapped resource for social progress: Jane Addams's *Newer Ideals of Peace* (1907), Charlotte Perkins Gilman's *The Man-Made World* (1911), and Englishwoman Olive Schreiner's *Women and Labour* (1911) all argue that if women were given an equal share of power in the affairs of society and nation, domestic and international peace would become far more prevalent.[3] Of course, an argument that demands increased social status for women by stressing gender difference is a risky one. This kind of dilemma was typical of the women's peace movement, for even as women's leadership in the peace movement foregrounded questions of gender, that leadership also forced into the open contradictions among women about their identities and their corresponding public roles. Victorian and still very current conceptions of the "woman's sphere" stipulated that women were natural pacifists and, by implication, natural advocates of peace, but also construed women as submissive by nature, less suited to public advocacy than to moral influence exercised through domestic responsibilities or nonpartisan philanthropy. At the same time, suffragists, then launching their final campaign for the vote, had for seventy years campaigned on the basis of equality between the sexes – the fundamental personhood and citizenship of women on equal terms with men.[4] Women's pacifism is everywhere marked by these contradictions, which appeared not only between feminists and nonfeminists, but also among woman's sphere adherents over the appropriateness of public advocacy for "ladies" and among feminists over the relative importance of antiwar activism as opposed to suffrage campaigning. The popularity of pacifism in the United States allowed women to salve over these differences for a time and offered them also the opportunity to appropriate a wide variety of antiwar slogans, statements, and literature and to claim those texts as supplying a pacifist mandate. This kind of assertive appropriation and inclusion, one of the keys to early success, proved, however, to be a precarious art of cultural negotiation. Grown accustomed to using the WPP as a kind of conduit for pacifist sentiment, providing a context in which pacifist ideas and pacifist-leaning associations were embraced, and cultivating an image of themselves as servants of a popular will inclined toward pacifism, the leaders of the WPP were confounded when the national popularity of pacifism waned. Having gathered together so many members with such diverse ideological underpinnings, the WPP never had the power to practice anything like party discipline. And when pacifist radicals sought, beginning late in 1915, to organize a more durable, wider antiwar coalition, cultivating ties with antiwar labor organizations and radical political groups, they were abandoned by the middle- and upper-class women whose antipathy for war was matched by an antipathy for radicalism.

Poetry – particularly genteel poetry – was one of the few modes of public pronouncement that permitted women an active role, and accordingly the WPP used poetry extensively. Of course, genteel poetry was itself marked by the kind of problematic gender politics that always threatened the WPP from within. Some WPP activist-poets adopted the genteel conceptions prominent in the schools, which dictated that poetry was predominantly a discourse of personal improvement, of individual moral and spiritual edification rather than a discourse of political mobilization. In taking this approach, these writers risked limiting the public authority they might claim as women. Others, many of them younger activists, sought to locate in their poetry a more forthrightly political version of genteel poetic authority and, in the process, risked losing the readership and political support of women in the former camp. Perhaps the majority of WPP poets and activists negotiated some course in between, asserting both the uniqueness of women's pacifist perspective and the importance of women's pacifist activism – a strategy no less troubled than the others given how this internalized, within women themselves, the social and political contradictions of their role as the pacifist conscience of the nation.

I

Olive Tilford Dargan's "Beyond War" appeared in *Scribner's* in the month of the WPP's founding, January 1915. Later in the year it was reprinted as a broadside that the WPP distributed.[5] The poem, like the WPP itself, vacillates between a confidence in the inevitable, steady progress of civilization and an imperative that progressive people must act immediately to save civilization from destruction.[6] It bears close analysis for the way it enacts this vacillation and, no less, for the way it describes the kind of activist role for pacifist poets that the WPP's practice was to illustrate repeatedly. This poem, consisting of three sections and twenty-two stanzas, describes women's wartime tribulations early on, in the second and third stanzas of the first section. True to a traditional conception of female stoicism in face of war, however, the poem ostensibly *dismisses* women's sufferings as a good reason for mourning:

'Tis not that brides shall turn to stone,
    And mothers bend with bitter cry
    Cursing the day they did not die
When daring death they bore a son,
    And waifs shall lift their thin hands up
    For famine's empty cup;

'Tis not that piled in bleeding mounds
    These fathers, sons, and brothers moan,
    Or torn upon the seas go down
Glad that the waves may hide their wounds;
    Not that the lips that knew our kiss
    Are parched and black . . .

Written from the point of view of women, the stanzas describe feeling-
ly the pain of losing a loved one in war, to some extent belying the poem's
claim that these losses are unimportant in comparison with other "higher" concerns. Nevertheless, the poem does argue that a calamity greater
than physical death is "That thou must pause, O vaulting Mind, / . . .
Pause, stricken by the spear of one, / The savage thou hadst left behind."
    This "vaulting Mind," the progress of human consciousness and soci-
ety, is seemingly the hero of Dargan's poem. Indeed, the second section
of "Beyond War" concludes hinting that in the future the war's destruction might be put in the perspective of some larger spiritual development
– "Let reckoners to come outrun / This unstaunched loss." While this
section as a whole seems to hold little hope for reckoning such a gain –
"Dumb until then, / We wet Eternity with tears; / The aching score is
hers" – Dargan's form follows less closely the pattern of an argument than
that of a sonata, so that, like a sprightly closing movement, the third section affirms the ultimate triumph of progress. The progress of "Mind"
must reassert itself, being in Dargan's view a natural force that exerts itself as surely as the earth's motions:

Tho' now at final Autumn seem
    Our world with blood and ashes wound,
    Unfaltering Spring shall choose her ground;
Man shall rebuild with bolder dream,
    The god astir in every limb,
    And earth be green for him . . .

Although not absolutely blind to the suffering of war, Dargan apparently finds progress so attractive as an ideal that she seeks any way to salvage
it. Further, Dargan's assertion of progress may actually be a politically use-

ful idealization, for without an optimistic interpretation of general history – some god like "Progress" on the side of right – women's lack of practical political power could readily lead to despair about ever challenging militarism.

But in spite of its relentless optimism, "Beyond War" finds it necessary to criticize the nationalist causes that led so many to die. The second section of the poem debunks nationalist appeals vigorously:

> For "honor" lift we dripping hands.
>   For "home" we loose the storm of steel
>   Till over earth Thy homeless reel.
> For "country!" – Thine are all the lands.
>   We pray, but thou hast seen our dead
>   Who knew not why they bled.
>
> So warm were they, with destinies
>   Like straining stars that lustrously
>   Bore Goethes, Newtons not to be.
> ("Long live the king!") So warm were these
>   That dropped, and the cold moon alone
>   May count them, stone by stone.

Although the third section's logic seems to dictate that progress is inevitable, the section also prescribes a political role for poets who would reinstate progress: "O Brothers of the lyre and reed, / Lend not a note to this wild fray, / . . . Cast here no song, like flower prest / To Slaughter's seething breast." Dargan's argument against patriotic poetry, like the whole of "Beyond War," evinces tension between a triumphant ideal and an as yet imperfect achievement of it. Dargan announces that war, being a relic of humankind's lower nature, is a degraded, barbaric theme for poetry. Yet in the midst of a world war Dargan must acknowledge that war has not entirely lost its appeal, so poets should refuse to write pro-war poetry in order to prompt people finally to reject war:

> Long gone the warrior's dancing plume
>   That played o'er battle's early day;
>   Now must his song be laid away,
> Child-relic, that was glory's bloom;
>   And Man who cannot sing his scars,
>   Is he not done with wars?

"Beyond War" holds two competing views of pacifist activism in an uneasy balance. On the one hand, Dargan suggests that the logic of peace is irresistible, implying that a civil, dignified expression of women's wartime interests would persuade the European governments to end the carnage, or at least would keep the United States from joining in. On the other hand, Dargan's poem clearly speaks out against existing nationalist ideals and condemns government indifference toward the war's victims. She construes poetry, in short, as a form of political action. She visualizes poetry both narrowly, as the verse written by "Brothers of the lyre and reed," and broadly, as the rhetorics and ideologies by which people "sing of their scars" and thereby justify wars. Although poetry is a literary genre, poems can also spur ideological transformation even as ideology conditions poetic possibilities.

At its best, this was the view of poetry and of textuality generally that informed the WPP's work, even when its poetry was genteel in form and diction – as it typically was. In one of her contributions to *Women at the Hague,* Jane Addams herself shows an understanding of how the conditions enabling warfare were not unalterable facts, but rather were narrativized through nationalist and militarist ideologies. When European women and men believed their states' invocations of a national emergency, and accepted as necessary the loss of their material well-being and their lives, they were not only victims of unfortunate circumstance. They were also victims of nationalist fictions of the sort Addams identifies in the words of a "young German":

> "I happen to live near the line of Schleswig-Holstein. I am told the men of Schleswig-Holstein are my brothers, but my grandfather before me fought them. I do not know whether they are my brothers or my grandfather's enemies; I only know I have no feeling for them different from that I have for men living farther north in Denmark itself. The truth is that neither to my grandfather nor to me do the people of Schleswig-Holstein mean anything; that he hated them and that I love them are both fictions, invented and fostered for their own purposes by the people who have an interest in war."[7]

The young German's speech relativizes the version of "truth" then prevalent in European affairs and opens up, in turn, the possibility for other forms of truth – including feminist, pacifist truth – which might alter the conditions that initiated and later perpetuated the war. Criticism like this and poems such as Dargan's worked to deconstruct the ideologies of national defense, reasonable preparedness, and so on that make war seem a "natural" or necessary national policy.

Such deconstructive effects in the texts of WPP activists and poets were, it should be clear, local and selective within WPP literature. To put the matter another way, the WPP's subversion of nationalist ideologies did not lead to a wholesale undermining of all positions of moral and political authority; rather, it was practiced strategically to open a space in which women's values and politics – whether feminine or feminist – might be constructed. We may thereby distinguish it from what appears to be the practice of some modernists, whose general subversion of moral and cultural authority included undercutting one's own authority.[8] In this regard the poets of the WPP adopted the moral authority and, with it, the oracular voice of the genteel tradition. With few exceptions, the personae of their poems appear convinced of the pacifist truth they speak. This unseemly moral certainty may explain why these poems have been so thoroughly neglected by literary historians. But the poems' certainty represents one of their chief political advantages, as their authors sought to proclaim a pacifist politics and mobilize Americans under its banner. And we should not assume that the absence of self-questioning implies a lack of craft or sophistication in the poetry. Especially when we can place these poems within their political contexts, the accomplishment of many of them emerges as a complex negotiation between dominant and emerging cultural domains, involving the reinterpretation of patriarchal poetic and cultural traditions, and the rearticulation of those traditions to a pacifist politics and still-emerging antiwar coalitions. For poet-activists of the WPP, operating within an organization fractured by ideological and practical differences, articulating a cohesive pacifist position became especially perplexing; a straightforward rendering of the party's pacifist dogma was impossible, simply because there was no one, unifed party position to occupy. The challenge became all the more demanding when, as in mid-1915, it was necessary for the party to forge alliances with groups outside the WPP's original constituency.

II

In the war's opening month, it appeared that women's pacifist voices would be readily heard and that no new antiwar organizations would be needed, for Americans recoiled in horror from the European war and U.S. newspapers seemed largely open to the poetry of antiwar protest. The *New York Times* had given favorable coverage to the August 29 peace parade; its editorial quibbled only that the women's complaint against war was universally shared by Americans: "There is no class that needs to be impressed by the strength of the essential anti-war cause; there are no converts to be made, as in political campaigns, no 'doubtful vote' to attract, no opponents to cow."[9] In August the *Times* editorial page published several antiwar verses by women: Marguerite Merington's "The Call to the Colors," Clara Davidson's "The Cry of the Women," Edith Thomas's "Princes and War," and Caroline Russell Bispham's "Peace and War."[10]

It soon was clear, however, that American pacifism could not be a wholly spontaneous movement, and women could not depend on mainstream papers such as the *New York Times* to convey their message. First, the newspaper's day-by-day, blow-by-blow coverage of the war provided a narrative more fascinating than repellent, as page 1 documented the Germans' steady advance across Belgium and northern France and page 2 illustrated that advance with maps updated daily. Readers were invited to see the war as a titanic contest and to pick sides in that contest. (Belgium, disappearing further and further under the heavy line of German occupation, was the immediate popular choice as the underdog.) Second, in an instrument of masculine authority such as the *New York Times,* the one forum in which women's voices could be distinctly heard was the poem featured each day on the editorial page – meaning that poetry was an especially important genre for women, but also that women's scope for advocacy in the mainstream press was extremely limited. Third and decisively, supposedly impartial newspapers such as the *Times* could not be counted on to serve the interests of pacifism consistently; indeed, they could not be trusted to represent any peace movement or women's movement equitably. The paper continued to print some poems by pacifist women throughout the fall, but at the same time it demonstrated that condemnation of the war could be used in a variety of ways. Rudyard Kipling's "For All We Have and Are," published on the front page on September 2, 1914, directs that condemnation not so much at war itself as at the "foe." His poem is a cry for international mobilization against Germany: "Once more it knits mankind; / Once more the nations go / To meet and break and bind / A crazed and driven foe." Furthermore, Kipling's opening stanza uses a perceived threat to feminine, domestic spaces defined by home and children to justify a war of national defense: "For all we have and are, / For all our children's fate, / Stand up and meet the war; / The Hun is at the gate." The *Times* was far from innocent in legitimizing Kipling's argument. The *Times* editors indicated their judgment that the poem's plea was worthy as well as newsworthy by the prominence of the poem's layout, framed by a box in the upper right-hand corner of the front page and afforded a headline – "Rudyard Kipling

Calls to Britons to Stand up and Meet the War."[11] In a tribute to Kipling's poem included on the next edition's editorial page, the *Times* congratulated the author for his worldwide influence, as his patriotic verses "in a single day have reached and been read by more millions of people around this earth than any other poem written since the dawn of history." Of course, even as such wide influence was supposed to demonstrate the "Spartan strength and intensity" of Kipling's verse, it also reflected favorably on the efficiency of modern communications and, just as important, the availability of pro-British news outlets in the United States and throughout the world. The achievement of Kipling's "great poem" thus depended heavily upon the *New York Times* and other sympathetic papers.[12]

The pro-Allied partisanship of the *Times* and other papers made obvious the need for dependable vehicles for pacifist ideas. The institution of the WPP itself filled this need by providing a visible, formal structure for expressing the pacifism of American women as well as of American citizens generally. The WPP addressed the lack of reliable networks for pro-peace information and ideas by printing and distributing its own newsletters, lists of pacifist literature, broadsides, and booklets. Pacifist poems appeared prominently in all of these media. WPP literature and, particularly, WPP poetry constructed two different, if not wholly distinct, audiences: one, a popular audience inclined to accept women as pacifist but not always willing to accept them as the primary leaders of a pacifist movement; and another, a private audience more likely to support both women's rights and women's authority to speak and act publicly. To the second audience, more strongly confirmed in its pacifism, we turn first, for they speak most directly to the aspirations of the activist, feminist women at the core of the WPP.

Pacifist poetry that circulated among WPP members and party patrons negotiated the dilemma of women's activism and their supposed "natural" reticence by providing a forum for women to assert their public, political authority, but at the same time limiting that forum to a like-minded, private readership. Pacifist poems printed in broadsides, folders, or booklets circulated by mail could hardly expect a mass audience of the kind reached by the *Times*. The WPP poets could count on a sympathetic audience, however, since these items were available principally on request.[13] For pacifist poets, this private audience provided room to test pacifist ideas and to speculate about political strategy. WPP publication of broadsides and booklets fulfilled the charter of the WPP Arts Committee to encourage "Artists, Musicians and Writers to productions promoting peace" by establishing an audience for writers who otherwise might be reluctant to write propagandistic poetry.[14] For their readership, these pacifist poems offered a space to suspend the standards of "factual" representation that applied to the journalistic prose of WPP pamphlets and to imagine those alternative, peace-loving worlds they hoped to realize in the present, bellicose one.

Florence Wilkinson's "The Fighters" was "presented by her to the Peace Party" according to a prefatory note and was in turn distributed by the WPP Arts Committee. It is one of many poems that present – and represent – the activist pacifism and feminism to which most WPP leaders ascribed, even when they were not able to persuade the WPP membership at large to adopt these attitudes. In particular, Wilkinson's poem attempts to debunk the conception of defensive war described, among other places, in the opening lines of Kipling's "For All We Have and Are." Without questioning the bravery of soldiers fighting to defend their homelands, "The Fighters" asserts that they are mistaken in believing women support them in their wars:

> You who are fighting for your honor,
> For your future,
> For your existence, –
> You who think that you are fighting for all these things,
> And for us,
> (Or who think not at all!)
> We are they whom you love and cherish,
> Whom you have left behind,
> Whom you have stripped of everything,
> Having robbed us of our sons
> And of the hope of Mary,
>   Oh, brave fighters.
> We are singing to you from our graves,
> And from our sterility,
> And from our outraged viriginity [sic];
> You are fighting against us, brave fighters.[15]

While the poem continues to visualize men as "fighters," it reminds them of their roles as husbands and fathers. If women must keep removed from politics, the poem implies, men ought likewise to eschew politics and its last resort, military conflict. But since men have already committed themselves to war, women ought to be permitted entry into political life. Thus, the poem goes on to introduce women to the spheres of social and political action outside the home, where they will join the survivors of war:

> When the fight to kill is ended
> You will begin another fight,
>   You, brave fighters,
> The few that are left of you,
> And the fight will be for us,
> Not against us,
> And oh, the up-hill work of the world
> After the Fight to Kill is done,
> When we begin the world's real work,
>   We, brave fighters.

Men can work with rather than against women, but the balance of power is shifted so that women – "We, brave fighters" – take the leading role.

Other poems circulated by the WPP envision even more ambitious imaginary projections, where the empowerment of women extends to the creation of a matriarchal society. One example is "Woman's Armaments" by Mina Packard, dated January 7, 1915, and distributed as a broadside by the WPP. The poem uses its epigraph, "If this war lasts one year, it will cost fifteen billion dollars," to inspire a phantasmagoric daydream and, in turn, a fantasy question: what would women do with 15 billion dollars?

> If I were sitting out of doors
>   Beneath the deep blue sky,
> And a great bank should fly along,
>   And leisurely pass by,
> And drop right down into my lap,
>   With nothing to explain,
> A fifteen billion dollar bundle,
>   Just like a drop of rain,
>
> What do you think that I would do
>   With such a roll of money!?[16]

Put in these reduced terms, the answer seems clear: the female speaker would "buy some shoes and stockings / For every foot that's cold!"; would "fill all empty stomachs / With all that they could hold"; and "would do so many things / Some folks would call me 'funny.'" If such philanthropic zeal sounds bizarre, the poem suggests that its readers consider the results when the money is "used the other way" – not for a generous social welfare program but for the systematic prosecution of war:

> It makes the baby faces
> So pale; and scared; and white!
> It makes the boys, so young and fair,
> We taught should never fight,
>
> Go out to kill! and scatter blood
> And brains upon the dirt!
> Till those fair lithesome bodies
> Lie still! and cold! inert!

The poem's presentation of war is, by virtue of its melodramatic punctuation, very nearly "funny," yet details like "brains upon the dirt" make clear that the business of war is hardly comic. At the poem's close, Packard issues a challenge to let women have a chance to manage the affairs of state:

> Just give a woman power and see
> How she will heed the calls,
> To hand out earthly comforts
> Instead of cannon balls!

Ultimately the poem envisions a woman's republic, where men are simply deposed from power. While perhaps only a minority of WPP members were able to contemplate overturning the existing order, the party's drive for political influence in fact amounted to just this assertion: Let us run the country. We can show you how it's done.

Writing to an audience likely to be committed to feminist pacifism, poets like Wilkinson and Packard postulated alternative realities where all women could be counted on to be thoroughgoing pacifists and where women would control political institutions. Such idealizations, while not necessarily palatable to a national audience or even to all WPP members, offered the WPP's leaders an ideological framework and a telos – a vision – that could help them carry on their more mundane, day-to-day organizing. In public, the WPP showed a less feminist, more pragmatic face.[17] The group incorporated into its membership virtually any women's organization willing to proclaim its interest in peace, regardless of that group's previous agenda or political tactics. Therefore, in one organization the WPP brought together suffragists, women active in women's clubs and prewar peace organizations (including antisuffragists), political conservatives, progressives, and radicals. This kind of confederation was possible largely because most of these groups believed, in early 1915, that pacifism was a popular cause which would bolster the reputation of their own favored agendas (Steinson 6). At the same time, the WPP founders thought the union workable because, presuming that women were pacifistic *by nature,* they saw pacifism as a cause uniting all women (Degen 40). Rather than being a recipe for disharmony, the alliance of existing women's groups, whether they had been initially organized to lobby for prohibition or to win votes for women, seemed simply the most economical way to create a large political organization united against war. The WPP leadership as well as its general membership brought together a broad spectrum of America's most influential women, immediately establishing the women's peace movement as a national and international force. The party leadership reads like a Who's Who of American Women: national "chairman" was Jane Addams; "vice chairmen" were Anna Garlin Spencer, Mrs. Henry Villard, Mrs. Louis F. Post, and Mrs. John Jay White; the secretary was Lucia Ames Mead. The famous suffragists Mrs. Pethick-Lawrence of England and Rosika Schwimmer of Hungary were honorary members. And the "Co-Operating Council" drew prominent women from seventeen different women's organizations: suffrage leaders Carrie Chapman Catt and Anna Howard Shaw joined with temperance activist Anna Gordon; leaders of Catholic and Jewish women's organizations were brought together, along with Mrs. Booker T. Washington, president of the National Association of Colored Women; the president of the Daughters of the American Revolution and a former president of the General Federation of Women's Clubs were included with the president of the National Woman's Trade Union League and the director of Women's Work in the National Socialist Party.[18]

By including leaders from most women's groups, the inaugural convention sought to represent the women's peace movement as a wide, popular movement already in existence. Likewise, while poetry mailed to individual party members idealized women's activism as an international movement with the potential to overturn patriarchal authorities, WPP poetry read or distributed at public functions emphasized the party's connection to an utterly respectable tradition of American pacifism. At the heart of this conservative application of poetry to politics is the influence of the genteel tradition among American audiences, particularly among the women who made up the bulk of the WPP membership. In conservative versions of the genteel tradition, women were counted a receptive audience to the moral and social work of poetry, but the canonical poets who defined the highest moral and social ideas were virtually all men. In nineteenth-century educational theory, the moral refinement and elevation ascribed to the study of poetry were the peculiar endowments of women, ideally suiting them for the education of children both at home and at school; but women teachers were nevertheless expected to teach the great male poets and were, furthermore, to work under the supervision of male school administrators.[19]

Thus, the bibliographies of peace literature that the Arts Committee compiled and distributed not only sought to establish pacifism as a well-established precept of democracy and, indeed, an ideal for centuries of artistic achievement; they also presented a version of pacifism enunciated largely by men. The WPP's widely advertised production of Euripides' *Trojan Women* was meant to stress the venerable antiquity and universality of the pacifist cause and even a long-standing tradition of women's pacifism. The play was billed in the WPP's "Preamble and Platform" as a "protest against war made by women three thousand years ago and never surpassed in beauty and poignancy, [which] relates our protest to that of women of all ages."[20] But that "women's protest" was, of course, written by a man in a society where women were denied education and basic rights.

"Peace Day," which had been celebrated by pacifist-minded Americans for ten years, was for 1915 merged with the national holiday Mother's Day: "A Mothers' Day Dedicated to Peace." The event provided an ideal occasion for stressing connections between femininity, pacifism, and Americanism. Indeed, "Suggestions and Bibliography for Program for Peace Day, 1915," a pamphlet compiled jointly by the Arts Committee and the Chicago Peace Society, points out the national, decade-old tradition behind the peace "holiday": "For more than ten years May 18th has been observed in the schools of this country as Peace Day, in commemoration of the opening of the First Hague Peace Conference, May 18, 1899."[21] Thus, the very history of the event helped to connect the substantial tradition of peace diplomacy at the Hague with the conference of women recently concluded there.

Nevertheless, the WPP Arts Committee's programs for Peace Day seem so intent on displaying the respectability and venerability of American pacifism that women's distinctive perspectives on war are essentially absent. In the WPP Arts Committee's "Suggestions" for peace programs in the schools, only one female poet, Elizabeth Barrett Browning, is featured, while five male poets are included – Englishmen Richard le

Gallienne and Alfred Lord Tennyson, Americans Vachel Lindsay, Wittier, and Longfellow. "Peace Day: May 18, 1915," also published by the WPP Arts Committee, quotes extracts or complete poems by English poets Swinburne and Alfred Noyes, Americans Edwin Markham and Longfellow, and German poet Franz Karl Ginzkey, as well as a passage from Isaiah.[22] The program also quotes prose fragments from Frenchmen Victor Hugo and Jean de Bloch, U.S. presidents Washington, Madison, Jefferson, and Wilson, and, incredibly, the Union Civil War general Sheridan. Women's voices are represented only through excerpts from an oration by Jane Addams and from anonymous letters by a Swiss woman and by a group of German and Austrian women.

Arguably, even as the WPP relied heavily upon the writings of men, it demonstrated the power conferred by controlling the context surrounding given texts, or managing the sites of their cultural production. The peace programs and meetings organized by the WPP seem to demonstrate that the present political affiliation of a poet did not necessarily matter; what mattered more was whether a poem could be contextualized in a way that enabled a particular audience to understand it as pacifistic. Among work by men and nonpacifists, the WPP typically injected materials that were distinctively pacifist, internationalist, and even feminist. In the "Peace Day" program, for instance, the letters from German and Swiss women indicate the WPP's emphasis on sisterhood and motherhood as the practical and moral foundation for the peace movement; the German "open letter" to the women of England expresses the hope that their common bond as women will work to unite the nations: "There glows like the dawn of a coming better day the deep community of feeling of many women of all nations."[23]

From the perspective of organizational effectiveness, there can be nothing objectionable about the WPP's pervasive use of materials produced by male authors or authors who did not necessarily share the WPP's political objectives. But a much greater difficulty arose when the WPP organizers indiscriminately culled materials that did not deal realistically with the intractability of the present war and, hence, the tremendous obstacles facing the peace movement. Such texts not only neglected women's unique, critical perspectives on war; they also offered a passive, nearly apolitical version of pacifism that had little chance for success. Even a paragraph offered by Jane Addams, quoted from *Newer Ideals of Peace,* simply assumes the ultimate triumph of peace ideals. Her concern is not with elucidating specific principles for gaining that triumph, but with speculating on the emotional response of people to the end of warfare:

"The final moral reaction may at last come, accompanied by a deep re-morse, too tardy to re-claim all the human life which has been spent and the treasure which has been wasted, or it may come with a great sense of joy that all voluntary destruction of human life . . . [has] become a thing of the past."[24] Other selections convey a somewhat clearer sense of the present emergency. A quotation from Edwin Markham's "Peace" at least describes the terrain of the European war:

> Peace, peace, O men, for ye are brothers all –
> Ye in the trench and on the shattered wall.
> Do ye not know ye came
> Out of one Love and wear one sacred name?

But Markham's plea emphasizes brotherhood and "Man" far too much for the poem to stand as a formulation of women's peace ideology.[25] Even more problematically, the poem printed on the top of the first page of the "Peace Day" program, Alfred Noyes's "The Dawn of Peace," appears to be completely, blissfully ignorant of the entrenched militarism and na-tionalism underlying the European war. This poem takes for granted the achievement of world peace to a degree approached by few poems writ-ten by WPP members. One stanza of Noyes's poem invokes progress as the pacifist's sure hope, adopting reassuring images of natural order as its conceit:

> Voices, confused and faint, arise,
>   Troubling their hearts from East and West.
> A doubtful light is in their skies,
>   A gleam that will not let them rest:
> The Dawn, the dawn is on the wing,
>   The stir of change on every side,
> Unsignalled as the approach of Spring,
>   Invincible as the hawthorn-tide.[26]

While it is true that many conservative WPP members shared Noyes's tendency to see peace as ascendant and, therefore, to downplay the ne-cessity for vigorous political action, this was precisely the problem, for any confidence in the quiet influence of pacifist women was soon to prove misplaced.

Other meetings in which the WPP participated seemed even less like-ly to advance pacifism. Held on March 6, 1915, and sponsored by the WPP and the Pennsylvania Arbitration and Peace Society, a "Meeting for Constructive Peace" included the songs "America" and the "Recessional" by Kipling. By featuring well-known American pacifists Jane Addams and Rabbi Stephen Wise as speakers, the program provided a context in which the phrase "Long may our land be bright / With freedom's holy light," from "America," might be understood as an effusion opposing the growth of militarism and the coercive state apparatus of a militarist regime. At least, the presence of the song on the program helped connect the peace movement to American patriotism. The inclusion of Kipling's "Recessional" is more troubling and problematic. Its invocation of divine sanction for imperialism seems nearly as insuperable as it is insupportable. In the context of the peace meeting, some lines might be understood as a plea for divine forgiveness for the folly of war:

> For heathen heart that puts her trust
> In reeking tube and iron shard –
> All valiant dust that build on dust.
> And guarding calls not Thee to guard –
> For frantic boasts and foolish word,
> Thy mercy on Thy people, Lord.[27]

But Kipling's poem holds out the possibility that if a nation does "call Thee to guard," God will bless a "godly" defense of this kind. It in fact hints at the conceptual framework for a just, defensive war. Do several hundred American pacifists singing this song really remake it as a pacifist anthem? More likely, the presence of Kipling – sweet singer of the Boer War, imperialism, and Britain's 1914 call to arms – undercuts the status of the meeting as a pacifist gathering.[28]

III

The tentativeness of much WPP propaganda might not have seemed to matter in early 1915. The organization of the WPP had seemed a necessity given the pro-Entente partisanship of many in the eastern establishment, in the press, and in and close to government (e.g., former president Theodore Roosevelt, ambassador to England Walter Page, Woodrow Wilson's confidant Edward House). But at this time, the arguments of the more conservative and optimistic members of the WPP appeared persuasive, as they suggested that women could keep the United States out of the war – and perhaps even effect a resolution of the conflict – without practical control in the state, but rather through moral and ideological conviction exercised by the popular will. This is one view suggested in *Women at the Hague,* a book coauthored by Addams, Emily Greene

Balch, and Alice Hamilton that recorded their experiences as WPP delegates to the 1915 international women's peace convention. WPP leader Emily Greene Balch asserts: "Never again must women dare to believe that they are without responsibility because they are without power. Public opinion is power; strong and reasonable feeling is power; determination, which is a twin sister of faith or vision, is power."[29] Because women can make their influence felt through public opinion – indeed, they seem to be the special guardians of it – Balch suggests that women do not need political, institutional power. They need not even lobby for it, apparently. Such optimism may well have seemed quaint, or hopelessly Pollyannish, by the time of *Women at the Hague*'s publication in 1916. But Balch's formulation of women's democratic power seemed much more realistic in the first months of 1915, at a time when the WPP appeared to have plenty of reason for optimism. Not only was the organization a success in its membership growth and its mobilization of women's clubs, but evidence of a popular American pacifist movement seemed to be everywhere.

Among the indications that a mass peace movement was afoot in the United States was the huge popularity of Piantadosi and Bryan's song "I Didn't Raise My Boy to Be a Soldier." The fact that its release coincided with the WPP's founding convention, and that it sold 650,000 copies in the first three months of 1915, seemed to indicate that the WPP's voice and the nation's were as one. There was a remarkable coincidence between the position of the WPP and the views set forth in "I Didn't Raise My Boy to Be a Soldier." Sung to a rollicking, music-hall tune seemingly out of keeping with its somber theme, but very much in sync with its points of reception in music halls and parlors, the song is best known for its chorus:

> I didn't raise my boy to be a soldier,
>   I brought him up to be my pride and joy,
> Who dares to place a musket on his shoulder,
>   To shoot some other mother's darling boy?
> Let nations arbitrate their future troubles,
>   It's time to lay the sword and gun away,
>   There'd be no war today,
>   If mothers all would say,
> "I didn't raise my boy to be a soldier."

The poem evokes the international sympathy common in WPP literature, the sense that a mother instinctively empathizes with the suffering of another nation, however foreign its people or hostile its government. It hints at the importance of education, seeming to assume that a boy raised by a peace-loving mother could go to war only under compulsion. It also shares the WPP's advocacy of negotiation and, perhaps most important, shares the belief that women could, if united, bring the war to a halt. Finally, the second verse of the song argues, like Wilkinson's "The Fighters," that war necessarily destroys women's lives and work: "What victory can cheer a mother's heart, / When she looks at her blighted home? / What victory can bring her back / All she cared to call her own[?]"[30]

"I Didn't Raise My Boy to Be a Soldier" helped make the pacifist movement a hard, quantifiable political reality to be reckoned with. The song and its pacifist philosophy had vocal detractors, but all conceded that the song reflected a broad pacifist movement in the United States. The *Literary Digest* evaluated the song's popularity critically, citing English sources who "wonder[ed] how America can be so sunk in pacifist conviction as to elevate such a ditty as 'I didn't raise my boy to be a soldier!' into a song of nation-wide popularity." One Englishman, the *Digest* observed, "found it sung wherever he traveled in America." A correspondent of the London *Daily Mail* believed that "behind the sentiments exprest in the ditty there is rallied . . . a force of American opinion such as has never yet in any country been devoted to the cause of peace – peace at any price, peace regardless of justice and national dignity and rights." Yet another writer, from the London *Spectator,* could recognize the song's appeal even while deploring its pacifism: "There is a terrible, triumphant crash about that last line. . . . With a good tune it must be invincible. But what are we to say of the political faith behind this verse of captivating ugliness? It is surely an appallingly unforeseeing faith, even a mad one."[31]

The song spawned poetic imitations and parodies as well – again a tribute to the widespread perception that it represented American attitudes accurately. Gerald G. Lively's "'Twas You Who Raised Your Boy to Be a Soldier," published in the *San Francisco Bulletin* on June 5, 1915, augments the pacifism of the original song by challenging mothers to examine their child raising critically: "You lifted him when soldiers passed your way. / You first gave him a gun . . . a book of 'heroes' . . . the box of wooden soldiers . . . the little sword of tin." The poem bids mothers, "Take down the general's picture in the parlor, / Tear down the gaudy butchers from the wall"; for as things now stand, "'Twas you who raised your boy to be a soldier, / And mothers, you are paying for your sin."[32]

As matters fell out, the sudden flaring of American pacifism, of which the phenomenon of "I Didn't Raise My Boy to Be a Soldier" was a reflection, contributed to its implosion. As we have seen, peace groups such as the WPP welcomed virtually all joiners. Even had they not, pacifism became so popular that many activists saw it as the means to attain their favored reform or to air their own specific grievances. The women's suffrage movement, particularly the National American Woman Suffrage Association led by Carrie Chapman Catt, provided a large share of the WPP's feminist activists, but for many suffragists, having worked so long for the vote, antiwar activism was secondary; peace activism became a potential vehicle, and seemingly a promising one, for finally winning women's suffrage. More notoriously, the pacifist movement provided a context for D. W. Griffith and other unreconstructed southerners to reappraise the War between the States, suggesting that the earlier war was no more justified than the Great War and, further, that its consequences – Emancipation and Reconstruction – had been catastrophic to a genteel, idyllic southern culture. In cinematic terms, Griffith's *The Birth of a Nation* successfully portrays the Ku Klux Klan as the savior of the nation reunited by the Civil War.

As important as the disunity and occasional disreputableness of the pacifist movement, however, was the way in which the success of the peace movement galvanized its opposition. The backlash against "I Didn't Raise My Boy to Be a Soldier," while it shows the "threat" posed by American pacifism, reveals as well the strength of the pro-British, pro-preparedness lobby in the United States. Former president Theodore Roosevelt was the most powerful and indefatigable of Allied supporters; in headlines of April 1915, he singled out the women's peace movement for attack, declaring it " 'Silly'. . . . 'Illogical,' 'Futile,' 'Hysterical,' 'Base,' and 'Cowardly.' "[33] Meanwhile, for every approving imitation of "I Didn't Raise My Boy to Be a Soldier" there were scores of scornful parodies to come. In 1915 and 1916, the musical sequel "I Did Not Raise My Girl to Be a Soldier's Bride" was countered by "I Didn't Raise My Dog to Be a Sausage" and "I Did Not Rear My Boy to Be a Coward." Twelve musical sequels were published in 1917 and four in 1918, and all these later titles implicitly criticize the pacifist sentiment of the original song: among them, "I Didn't Raise My Boy to Be a Molly-Coddle," "I Did Give My Boy to Uncle Sam," and "I Wish I Had a Thousand Sons to Fight for U.S.A."[34] Printed poems responded to "I Didn't Raise My Boy" with ridicule as well. One called "M.O.R.C.," published in *Detroit Saturday Night* and reprinted in *Western Medicine,* scorns as effeminate the kind of pacifist upbringing that the original song advocated:

They didn't raise their boy to be a soldier;
They much preferred to raise him as a pet,
They didn't want him taught
How these naughty wars are fought,
And the using of a gun and bayonet.
. . . .
So he lived a life of peaceful vegetation
On a ladylike, inconsequential plan,
Full of happiness and joy,
Mamma's perfect little boy
Till the guns commenced to shoot and war began.[35]

In effect, the poem accepts the WPP's linkage between femininity and peace in order to exploit cultural associations between effeminacy and weakness.

As British commentary reprinted in the *Literary Digest* indicates, "I Didn't Raise My Boy to Be a Soldier" and the substantial peace movement that lay behind it kept the Allies from taking American sympathy for granted; it helped strengthen ties between (apparently) besieged interventionists in the United States and those overseas who most wanted them to succeed. A further indication of Allied concern is an Australian reprinting of an American poem, "I Did Not Raise My Boy to Be a Soldier," which by its title makes its criticism of Piantadosi and Bryan's original and its satire of contemporary American politics unmistakable. First published in the *New York Evening Sun* on July 31, 1915, the verse's republication in the *Syndney Journal* on August 25, 1916, testifies to a persistent – and internationally recognized – link between Piantadosi and Bryan's "I Didn't Raise My Boy" and pacifist politics in the United States. The poem visualizes a matriarchal republic similar to Packard's in "Woman's Armaments":

And the women were strong in that land;
They were eloquent women, they ruled the State;
They were capable women and eloquent, lenged [sic] fate
With arguments fate could never withstand;
Out of their world-old night they had fought
Their way to a place in the light; they had wrought
Mightily, gallantly, till they were free,
And they ruled with the men in equality;
They were capable women and eloquent,
Sublte [sic] and strong in argument;

So they made it the law: NEVERMORE
Shall the men of our land be bred to war.[36]

To this point, the poem seems, indeed, to describe quite accurately the aspirations of the women's peace movement generally and the WPP specifically. The poem essentially tells a parable of the United States. Such a wealthy, peaceful, and progressive country, where women's leadership and women's pacifism have triumphed, will suffer disastrous consequences, the poem predicts. As the story goes, "There waxed elsewhere, on the brutal earth, / A clan . . . / Who dwelt in the dale of an earlier day, / . . . [and fell] on this land of the peaceful talk / With the sudden wings of the swooping hawk." The men of the pacifist country, "Untrained, . . . to war unbred, . . . could only bleed, and they valiantly bled"; the women "saw their homes go up in smoke" and were enslaved "under an alien yoke." The paranoia of such predictions speaks to the consternation, not only in segments of U.S. society but also in the British Commonwealth, over the apparent strength of American pacifism. The poem also foreshadows the kind of alarmist rhetoric that was to prove effective as the pro-interventionist lobby in the United States found its voice and its constituency.

When, on May 7, 1915, the British liner *Lusitania* was sunk with 128 Americans lost, advocates of military preparedness and intervention were ready to exploit the event systematically.[37] In contrast, the WPP, which had based its calculations on a demonstrated American predisposition toward pacifism, was not well equipped to counter advocates of a naval and military buildup when Americans' lives seemed in imminent danger. When in April Roosevelt had derided the women's peace movement in the press, many Americans would have agreed with the WPP retort, which called Roosevelt a "Barbarian";[38] the *Lusitania* incident and unrestricted submarine warfare made them more inclined to consider Roosevelt's hawkish position. In the American popular imagination, unrestricted warfare in the Atlantic moved the war closer to the United States.

But we need not suppose that public opinion turned away from pacifism inevitably. One important factor in the decline of pacifism was, rather, that the WPP and other peace organizations were not well suited to organizing Americans into an active, mass political movement, and their preparedness foes were.[39] The WPP was itself not especially unified: chapters held widely varying ideals and strategies; individual chapters were not obliged to follow the WPP national leadership; few had a strong commitment to public agitation. By counting affiliated organizations as part of the party apparatus, the WPP was able to claim a large membership almost immediately. Marie Degen cites membership figures of 40,000 in January 1916 and 20,000 in December 1917 (156, 203). But these numbers include the membership of scores of affiliates who pledged only sympathy for the WPP's peace making, not necessarily cooperation with the national directives of the party. Among the 165 groups that Degen counts, fully 132 were affiliates with this kind of tenuous link to the party (156). Furthermore, Steinson has argued that organizers were able to establish active WPP branches in only a handful of cities: chiefly, San Francisco, Philadelphia, Chicago, St. Louis, Washington, D.C., New York, and Boston (117–20). In these branches the number of participating members was modest. The Boston branch, second in size only to New York, totaled just 2,500 in 1915 (Degen 62). At a later, more difficult period, March 1917, the New York branch could count just 1,600 members.[40] Membership rolls for other branches reveal still smaller numbers: 604 in Washington, D.C.; 182 in Chicago; 32 in Washington State.[41] Whether nationally or locally, the WPP simply did not constitute a mass political organization. Rather, its active members formed a vanguard group with a membership base among well-educated, well-to-do, socially elite women, predominantly from the Northeast.

Even among those women who were activists – those who believed political change could be worked only through institutional power, and not simply by popular opinion or moral conviction – the genteel affiliations and aesthetics of the WPP hampered their populist appeal. The WPP failed to organize war-wary Americans in part because its propaganda was never suited to engaging and empowering women outside of educated, middle- and upper-class society. Even while preparedness advocacy and pro-Allied propaganda grew more populist, many WPP propagandists were hindered by the constraints of "good breeding," which even in propaganda demanded decorous, correct performance of productions aspiring to high art. While public schools sought to teach the virtues of genteel, refined art, Americans' poetic tastes proved far more varied and somewhat less fussy. The gap between WPP propaganda and most American audiences is apparent, for instance, in the stylistic differences between "I Didn't Raise My Boy to Be a Soldier" and the song version of "The Five Souls," a favorite publicity vehicle for the party that was based on a lyric by English author Anthony Ewer (published originally in the London *Nation* of October 3, 1914). "I Didn't Raise My Boy" was set to a sprightly melody and *marziale* (martial) tempo; it was appropriate for noisy music halls, where its catchy tune was easily carried by impromptu or amateur performance and its insistent beat demanded audience attention. In contrast, "The Five Souls" was set to a slower, statelier Allegretto from Beethoven's Seventh Symphony. The Beethoven melody was suitably dignified for a lyric that decried the war's reckless destruction, but it also placed high demands on its performers, as its main theme developed through insistent repetition and gradual modulation. Its opening musical phrase, which repeats the same note ten times consecutively, varying only the rhythm, demands particularly skillful execution. The song, in short, did not lend itself to popular performance and, indeed, was not initially designed for it. Rather than being released through the distribution network of a music publishing company, "The Five Souls" was printed at the request of the WPP, and then only in March 1915, after the Fuller Sisters had begun their WPP-sponsored tour of the United States.[42]

The song was not entirely ineffective as propaganda, despite Degen's preference for the WPP production of *The Trojan Women*, "doubtless a more effective contribution of the women to both art and peace" (59). There seems no reason to doubt the proficiency of the Fuller Sisters' recital of this piece or of the "old folk songs of War and Peace" that rounded out their program.[43] And Ewer's lyric demonstrates quite powerfully the essential similarity and emptiness of all the European combatants' rationales for going to war, as the stanzas represent, in turn, the voices of working-class men from Poland, Austria, France, Germany, and England who answered the call to arms and were killed in the war. The sameness of the various national rallying cries is underscored by the common refrain ending each man's story: "I gave my life for freedom, this I know: / For those who bade me fight had told me so."[44] For an American reader, the piece demonstrates the virtual equivalence of all the rhetorics of just war, the rationales of the Allies as well as those of the Central Powers. The English justification for the war – "There came a sudden word of wars declared, / Of Belgium, peaceful, helpless, unprepared, / Asking our aid" – sounds little different from the German one:

> I owned a vineyard by the wooded Main,
> > Until the Fatherland, begirt by foes
> > Lusting her downfall, Called me, and I rose
> Swift to the call and died in fair Lorraine.

The logics vary slightly, to be sure, but both boil down to an empty, rhetorical *"freedom,"* and both are successful only because the soldiers meekly believe what their nations' propagandists tell them.

"The Five Souls" arguably met with some success precisely because the WPP did maintain considerable control over the contexts in which the song was performed. Like Euripides' play, the song and the Fuller Sisters' tour featuring it are mentioned in essentially all of the WPP listings of peace programs.[45] To an extent, as the WPP provided the venues in which the song was heard, the song's message became identified with the WPP's political and ideological perspective. The WPP Chicago chapter, for instance, directly supervised programs that included the song "at Hull House, in churches, and at mass meetings in theatres." The song's structure, allotting one stanza each to fallen soldiers of Poland, Austria, France, Germany, and Great Britain, also readily permitted additional stanzas depicting other victims of war. One extant version is dedicated to "The Conscientious Objector":

> I was a soldier of the Prince of Peace,
> "Thou shalt not kill" is writ among his laws.
> So I refused to fight, and for this cause
> Myself was slain – 'Twas thus I gained release.
> I gave my life for freedom – this I know;
> For he for whom I fought has told me so.[46]

An addition such as this permitted the WPP to connect its own agenda of pacifism to a version of "freedom" radically opposed to that of nationalist rallying cries – which in Ewer's stanzas betray the "five souls."

Still, the song confirms what the party's distinguished but relatively small membership already suggests: that the WPP catered to well-educated "society" women, who would be most impressed by the adaptation of a classic Beethoven theme and the musically sophisticated, correct presentation of the Fuller Sisters. In contrast, there were virtually no productions aimed at a wider popular audience, no upbeat, tuneful songs such as "I Didn't Raise My Boy to Be a Soldier." At bottom, however well conceived and well received its pacifist critique, the WPP needed members to act on that critique; and rather than building and mobilizing their ranks, at the time of the Fuller Sisters tour many WPP members were beginning to reconsider their initial enthusiasm for the peace movement.

IV

Already by mid-1915, women's pacifism in the United States had reached a crisis. The peace movement had been founded on an uneasy truce between conservative moralists who stressed women's essential submissiveness and domesticity as the foundation of pacifism, and feminist activists who seized upon women's pacifism as a tactical political advantage as much as an unalterable fact. Now unanimity between the groups rapidly deteriorated. Moral influence had obviously failed to keep the nation on a pacifist course, and as popular support for pacifism faded, only a minority of WPP members were willing to commit themselves to public antiwar agitation. By the fall of 1915 preparedness measures were supported by the Massachusetts branch, which had the wealthiest and most conservative of the WPP memberships, including many antisuffragists (Steinson 121–24). Meanwhile, in the latter months of 1915 Carrie Chapman Catt, chair of the National American Woman Suffrage Association, had come to believe its alliance with pacifists would hurt rather than help the suffrage cause, and thereafter the Association did little to support the WPP.[47]

The WPP had to determine whether it could continue to constitute itself, and act, as a national political organization or whether it would be forced to occupy a minority and merely dissenting position. The WPP had been formed as a coalition of women's societies united only by the supposition that all women were naturally pacifist. Now the organization needed to form other coalitions – or at least to cultivate new members – in order to confront the aggressive political campaign being staged by preparedness advocates. In early 1915, a conservative agenda had dominated the public programs of the WPP, even as a more activist, feminist strategy was outlined privately in party mailings. In mid-1915, the WPP needed to adopt a more confrontational public image and politics. In this, the party's hope lay not only in articulating a version of pacifism that might gain support among potential allies and the public, but also in describing a pacifism that moderate WPP members – including the national leadership – could continue to support. The greatest test of party solidarity was to come when members inclined toward radical politics sought to include working-class interests and groups within the WPP's agenda and its antiwar coalition.

The WPP had opportunities to create such a coalition. A link between women's pacifism and socialism, the two causes politically and ideologically most resolutely opposed to war, held the greatest potential. Such an alliance, unfortunately, could not readily be countenanced by the moderate, progressive, middle- and upper-class women who continued to fill out WPP memberships and held positions in the national leadership. Both the potential and problems of a socialist-pacifist alliance are illustrated amply in the poetry readings given by WPP activist Angela Morgan in

Detroit in November 1915. Morgan's readings especially lend themselves to analysis because they are well documented by the separate file on Morgan in the Swarthmore College Peace Collection; they are also crucial because of their close relation to a pivotal moment in the peace movement, the formation of the ill-fated peace mission backed by industrialist Henry Ford.

In October 1915, WPP member Rebecca Shelly went to Detroit, hoping to gain financial support for a neutral peace conference from Henry Ford, who on August 22 had pledged half his fortune to bring an end to the war (Steinson 76). In Detroit Shelly planned a mass rally, whose success she saw as crucial for gaining Ford's backing. Joining her was poet Angela Morgan, who had met Shelly when they served together on the WPP delegation to the women's peace conference at the Hague (Steinson 75), and also Louis Lochner, an aggressive advocate of neutral mediation. The activities of these three youthful organizers were not, however, supported by more senior pacifists.[48] For his efforts to secure Ford's support for continuous neutral mediation, Lochner was expelled from the American Peace Society, a conservative organization founded before the war.[49] Likewise, unwilling to risk public controversy and preferring to work through private contacts, WPP national chair Addams disapproved of Shelly's scheme.[50] Barbara Steinson writes that "Addams not only declined to attend the Detroit meeting but also denied Shelly any personal endorsement."[51] Thus, the Detroit rally placed Morgan and Shelly at the lunatic fringe of the women's peace movement, for they risked breaking entirely with the moderate elements of the women's peace movement and, as the WPP national leadership saw matters, risked losing the public influence the party exercised through private contacts and behind-the-scenes negotiation.

But while Shelly, Morgan, and Lochner employed tactics more public and confrontational than most WPP members were willing to endorse, their peace rally showed above all the value of collaboration – not only with fellow pacifists, but also with the popular press and with people not formally affiliated with any pacifist organization. In eventually persuading Henry Ford to back plans for a neutral conference, Shelly relied heavily on the charismatic Rosika Schwimmer, a well-known Hungarian suffragist and pacifist. It was Shelly who initially convinced Schwimmer to come to Detroit and speak at the peace rally (Steinson 77–78); Schwimmer remained in Detroit for two weeks following the November 5 rally and at last persuaded Ford to give his support (Degen 130–31). Meanwhile, as the Detroit rally succeeded indirectly in gaining Ford's financial and personal backing, it also showed how a mass meeting that was well publicized could project the peace cause as a national, grass-roots political movement. Coverage in Detroit newspapers established the rally as purposeful and popular, and Detroiters did their part in making the meeting a success simply by turning out in impressive numbers. One reporter stressed that the audience, which "nearly filled the auditorium of the Detroit Board of Commerce," consisted "of citizens, not of officials":

> People of different European descents, with men of Revolutionary ancestry, Irish-Americans, Canadian-Americans, German-Americans. The vice presidents of the meeting included men and women whose sympathies have been rather pro-British and others whose sentiments have been pro-German. They were brought together in a pro-Peace meeting.[52]

Just as crucial as a large, diverse attendance and sympathetic reporting of the local meeting was the newspapers' assertion that a national antiwar drive was under way. "National Campaign to Open in Detroit Tonight," a Detroit paper declared, accepting without question Shelly's claim that, on the following Monday, ten thousand meetings would be held in support of neutral mediation. The same newspaper announced that Governor Ferris of Michigan "has joined the governors of Kansas, Kentucky, North Dakota, Vermont, Wyoming and other states" in urging President Wilson to sponsor a neutral conference.[53]

So too, Angela Morgan's contribution to the peace rally was not inconsiderable. Though she was by no means a renowned poet, she was in all likelihood better known than her associate Shelly. In the fall of 1914 she had published a collection, *The Hour Has Struck (A War Poem) and Other Poems,* which set her forward as a commentator on the war. When after the Hague peace conference she and Shelly had gone to Germany to inspect wartime conditions there, Morgan's comments seem to have been reported more extensively in the press than Shelly's, and she returned to the United States as something of an authority on the wartime sufferings of German women.[54] While the *Detroit Free Press* does not mention Shelly in its report on the rally, it hails Morgan as the "noted peace poetess of New York."[55] In addition to her personal experience in Germany, the fact that she was recognized as a poet seems to have heightened her authority as a spokesperson for the peace movement, so that her readings were seized upon by the newspapers as an occasion crystallizing the purpose and significance of the entire rally. To one reporter, Morgan's "The Hour Has Struck" seemed to express "the keynote of the whole meeting, a meeting of action rather than sentiment."[56] The *Detroit Times* especially praised "Battle Cry of the Mothers," which Morgan delivered "with great eloquence and feeling."[57]

Reporters were impressed by Morgan's appearance as well as her eloquence. The *Times* remarked on "her Greek costume enhancing her beauty of face and form";[58] another Detroit newspaper described Morgan as a "stately young woman in a Greek gown, her black hair bound with a fillet."[59] Such commentary on Morgan's "sex appeal" – sexist remarks in news articles describing the appearance of no other rally participant – also seems to indicate a purposeful bit of role playing by Morgan. First, her Grecian costume – which may seem to us an absurdity – invoked, to an audience raised on school poetry recitations, the classical tradition, the disinterested elevation, and therefore the moral authority of poetry. Second, by costuming herself so as to emphasize her femininity, Morgan implicitly linked her presentation to conservative dogma about the essential pacifism of women, thereby stressing her authority to speak pacifist truth. Her poetry emphasizes, as well, the hard, practical experience that authorizes women's protest against war. In "Battle Cry of the Mothers," Morgan uses women's suffering as the basis for decrying as inadequate the nationalist justifications for war offered by state leaders:

> Governors! Ministers! You who prate
> That war and ravage and wreck must be
> To save the nation, avenge the state,
> To right men's wrongs and set them free –
> You who have said
> Blood must be shed
> Nor reckoned the cost of our agony –
> Answer us now! Down the ages long
> *Who has righted the mother's wrong?*
> You have bargained our milk, you have bargained our blood,
> Nor counted us more than the forest brutes;
> *By the shameful traffic of motherhood*
> *Have you settled the world's disputes.*[60]

Besides her classical, feminine garb, the rhymed and metered lines of Morgan's poetry conform to a respectable genteel poetics. Like virtually all visions of women's pacifism from early in the war, "Battle Cry of the Mothers" sees women as united in war opposition. At the same time, however, the declarations of Morgan's poetry form a bridge between conservative poetic traditions and the populist, dissident motive apparent in Shelly's organization of the peace rally. It articulates women's solidarity against war as politically charged, a militant movement that will rise in opposition to patriarchal war policies:

> Warriors! Counselors! Men at arms,
> You who have gloried in war's alarms,
> When the great rebellion comes
> You shall hear the beat
> Of our marching feet
> And the sound of our million drums.
> You shall know that the world is at last awake –
> You shall hear the cry that the mothers make –
> You shall yield – for the mother's sake! (*U* 46)

Unlike more conventional public programs sponsored by the WPP – including most of the Peace Day events – and, indeed, at variance with the patriarchal organization of a genteel poetry education, Morgan speaks from a position of female authority rather than adopting men's perspectives on peace.

Furthermore, the poems Morgan read at the Detroit rally imply an alliance of women's and men's efforts to secure peace, emphasizing that responsibility to agitate for peace is shared by both. "The Hour Has Struck" affirms women's solidarity, but the poem also implies an identification between the mothers' cause and that of common people, whether male or female: *"Yet none have answered for the people's tears."* In the poem's conclusion, it is mothers' pain that renders action imperative, but *all* people must act:

> A Monster sprawls upon the breast of Time –
> To question or to hesitate were crime,
> While o'er those awful battlefields of hate
> The mothers gaze, too late!
> It is the world-command, God's judgment call,
> Greater than all.
> *The hour is here for the immortal deed;*
> *For huge, majestic action we have need –*
> *Now let the people stand – and take great heed!*[61]

In order to confront the patriarchal "Beast" of war, Morgan's rhetorical strategy employs the ultimate patriarchal gesture – the appeal to "God's judgment call." Yet Morgan implicitly looks beyond an essential divide between violent masculinity and pacific femininity: in terms of politics, she combines feminist pacifism with working-class activism.

Morgan goes still further, to define this politics as oppositional to the existing U.S. policies of declared neutrality (which, according to the Wilson administration, ruled out participation in mediation efforts) and undeclared favoritism toward the Allies. At a time when the WPP leadership urged caution in confronting the government and some chapters were moving toward support of government policy, Morgan defines an agenda for American women and the American state that goes well beyond passive and partial neutrality. In one stanza of "Battle Cry of the Mothers," European women beseech American women to intervene in the cause of peace: "O, women! You who are spared our woe, / . . . Will you dumbly stand / In your own safe land / While our sons are slaughtered and torn? / . . . Will you join our battle cry with might, / Will you fight the mother's fight?"(*U* 45).

The third poem on the program, "To America," makes a broader accusation, not only chastising American women for remaining inactive, but charging the United States with complicity in the European slaughter. In a press article describing Morgan's travel in Germany, Morgan had recalled the words of a German woman that questioned the sincerity of U.S. neutrality: "'How can you talk peace to us?' she asked, 'when you are sending ammunition from America that is putting out the eyes of our sons?'"[62] "To America" seconds this accusation: "Yea, all have sinned, America, / We, too, are slayers of the slain." The poem portrays Europe's suffering as Christ's, so that the crime of American arms dealers becomes a transgression against universal humanity: "And thinkst thou thy prayer avails / Because thou did'st not draw the sword? / . . . America, thy protest fails. / . . . 'Tis thou hast shaped the nails / That pierce the Savior's hands." This "Humanity beseeches" America to remake itself as the savior, not the tormentor, of Europe: "Be thou the saviour of all lands; / Wash thou the stain from off thy hands / And set the nations free!" (*U* 47–49).

The populist and oppositional politics of the Detroit rally and Morgan's poetry continued to be shunned by the national leadership of the WPP. Without official backing and financial support from the WPP, Shelly and Morgan were pressured into ever more radical tactics. On Friday, November 5, the *Free Press* had reported that ten thousand peace meetings were planned for Monday, but in fact Shelly had no money to coordinate or even to communicate with so many organizations. Driven by necessity, on Saturday Shelly announced a street rally where Morgan would again read "Battle Cry of the Mothers" and where Shelly proposed to raise $10,000. The *Detroit Times* reported, "Unless the money is raised promptly, the effort must be abandoned, Miss Shelley [*sic*] says."[63] The money could not, in fact, be had at the street meeting, but the fund-raising plan was not abandoned; when Schwimmer gained Ford's support, she persuaded his wife to buy $10,000 worth of telegrams requesting that women's groups in turn telegram Woodrow Wilson to call for mediation (Degen 123–24). By November 26, when Schwimmer and another representative of European women visited Wilson, twelve thousand telegrams had reached the White House, each declaring, "We work for peace. The mothers of America pray for it" (quoted in Degen 124). Even this success failed to impress the national WPP leadership. On the contrary, subsequent events related to the Ford peace mission made Jane Addams and the other party leaders all the more reluctant to run their organization on "nerve and brass tacks," as Shelly herself described the Detroit venture (quoted in Steinson 77). When, as a publicity stunt, Ford chartered a "Peace Ship" to transport the American peace delegates, the press recruited for the trip found much to ridicule in the small and factious group of peace activists on board, the "secretive and authoritarian behavior" of delegation leader Schwimmer, and the many hangers-on with no evident interest in pacifism (Steinson 77–78). For the future, Addams entirely ruled out the possibility of using newspaper coverage to publicize the women's peace movement, and most elements of the WPP grew ever less likely to court popular sentiments or to hold large public demonstrations.[64]

Activists such as Morgan and Shelly showed how the WPP might broaden its political base and make use of the mass media. But Addams and the rest of the national leadership, influenced by the Ford Peace Ship debacle, refused to condone more confrontational, more public political tactics. In doing so, the national leaders effectively chose to abdicate, for they were choosing to abandon the WPP's aspirations to being a national political organization. When they chose not to work with the press anymore, they perhaps spared themselves embarrassment. But they also abandoned a crucial conduit between their movement and the larger American audience that they had hoped to engage – and that in the spring of 1915 they had plausibly claimed to represent. It was the successful manipulation of the press and the rhetoric of patriotism that was to bring success to the interventionist camp; it is not entirely clear why the support of the press and the meaning of patriotism could not also be fought for by the WPP. The course taken by Shelly, Lochner, and Morgan in Detroit was much riskier than the behind-the-scenes influence and negotiation that Addams preferred, but it is difficult to see how the Detroit strategy of mass meetings and rapprochement with a working-class politics would have yielded less success than the more decorous course taken by Addams.

In 1915 the WPP had an opportunity to situate itself as a pivotal force in U.S. politics. Sometime in that year, too, that opportunity was lost. It is tempting to suggest that Addams and the other national leaders were merely products of their genteel, middle-class upbringing, were effectively bound to a nonassertive, pacific version of femininity, and so to excuse them for lacking boldness.[65] On the other hand, it is possible to conceive of the opportunities of 1915 not so much as events to be passively reacted to or against, depending upon one's socialization, as situations to be actively chosen – and to choose such charged, politicized situations meant to embrace a new role and identity. Certainly, Angela Morgan seems to have had a flair for self-promotion that suited her for pressing the agenda of the WPP as well. A journalist by profession, Morgan also actively pursued a vocation as a public performer and interpreter of poetry; before the war she perfected her oratory at the nationally known conference grounds at Chautauqua Lake, New York. But she needed the right historical moment, and the right organizational framework as well, to become the voice of an emergent alliance of workers and women. Later in her career, and in fact later in the war, she did not again find the context needed for making her poetry and her personage work for political change. By the end of the war, she was more likely to lend her voice to a variety of public ceremonies celebrating the status quo. She read her poem "The Unknown Soldier" over his tomb in Arlington National Cemetery. Later, a radio broadcast transmitted her reading of a poem helping to dedicate the "Will Rogers Shrine to the Sun" in Colorado Springs, Colorado (also a shrine to himself; Rogers is buried there). In 1933, when she was poet laureate of the General Federation of Women's Clubs, that group dedicated her poem "When Nature Wants a Man" to President Roosevelt.[66] While these may have been contexts where Morgan continued to make her poems occupy a public, social role, they were hardly as politically risky or potentially transformative as her readings in Detroit in November 1915.

As Morgan's moment to articulate the direction of a popular pacifism came and went, so too did the WPP's chance to establish a broader coalition – and counter the ever-widening sphere of preparedness organization. Pacifist activism had only begun, but among the WPP memberships only the New York branch led by Crystal Eastman would later make a significant contribution to the peace movement. Other, mostly smaller and more disciplined groups were now to take the lead. These groups, however, never had much chance to present themselves as a large popular movement; this the WPP had briefly been able to do. Also absent in these organizations was the impulse and the strategy, demonstrated in some WPP poems, of bridging the chasm between respectable, genteel progressivism and grass-roots activism.

2

"The New Society within the Shell of the Old"

WOBBLY PARODY POETICAL AND POLITICAL

The "Hymn of Hate" published on New Year's Day 1916 in *Solidarity*, the eastern organ of the Industrial Workers of the World, describes the coordinates of a cultural struggle quite distinct from those described by either pacifist activists or advocates of military preparedness. The rhetoric of Harry McClintock's "Hymn" likewise marks a difference from most other forms of American cultural production, particularly the genteel:

> We hate you! D'amnyou! hate you! we hate your rotten breed.
> We hate your slave religion with submission for its creed.
> We hate your judges. We hate your courts, we hate that living lie,
> That you call "Justice" and we hate with a hate that shall never
> die.
> We shall keep our hate and cherish our hate and our hate shall
> ever grow.
> We shall spread our hate and scatter our hate 'till all of the
> workers know.
> And The Day shall come with a red, red dawn; and you in your
> gilded halls,
> Shall taste the wrath and the vengeance of the men in overalls.[1]

McClintock's version straightforwardly adopts the virulent rhetoric of Ernst Lissauer's "A Chant of Hate against England" and some of the other hymns of hate, but it directs that rhetoric away from the national military conflict in Europe and toward a class war at home. The binarism of military aggression versus just defense, or of militarism versus pacifism, is replaced by the binary of the working class versus the propertied class. If

73

the antagonism channeled from the world war to the class war was immense and menacing to most Americans, it was no more than the reflection and refraction of hatreds stirred up by the militarists and capitalists themselves. But because the poem's rhetoric challenges the fiction of a unified, homogeneous nation, even threatening to seek the destruction of the nation from within, the poem pronounces goals more ideologically and politically destabilizing than any external threat.

That the IWW's agenda and methods were also at odds with those of the Woman's Peace Party may be evident from the distinctly ungenteel diction in the first line of the "Hymn of Hate" or in the poem's fundamental contempt for American, which is to say capitalist, "Justice." Another way of drawing the contrast between the IWW and WPP (and the IWW and middle-class America) is to consider the Wobblies' version of "I Didn't Raise My Boy to Be a Soldier," titled "Harvest Song 1915" and written by IWW editor, artist, and poet Ralph Chaplin.[2] Other than the fact that the suggested tune is the same, "Harvest Song" does not so much imitate or satirize the original as offer a radical alternative to both pacifism and militarism. The poem makes no reference whatsoever to the European war:

> The Wobbly is the boy to reap the harvest –
>   The only one prepared to do it right.
> The cockroaches and the hogs who'd like to starve us,
>   Will give us what we want or fade from sight.
> The wooden sabot is the proper method
>   To make them run their hold-up at a loss;
>   Each Sizzlook of a boss
>   Gets "next" and comes across; –
> The Wobbly is the boy to reap the harvest![3]

This version of "I Didn't Raise My Boy to Be a Soldier" asks a very different question of a very different audience: not, what is a mother's patriotic duty to her country? – but, what is the worker's task in the class war? Furthermore, in contrast to the WPP – which pointedly did not use "I Didn't Raise My Boy to Be a Soldier" in its organizing, which sought instead to use genteel forms to address Americans – the IWW positioned itself in a closer relationship with American popular culture by using the tune to begin with. To be more precise about the IWW's relationship with popular culture, however, it is important to note that this particular IWW song also sets itself apart from popular *mass* culture. "Harvest Song 1915" suggests that the IWW sought to construct a distinct American *subculture.*[4] Note the song's peculiar jargon, including such terms as "cockroaches," "hogs," and "Sizzlooks" to refer to the capitalist bosses. These terms treat the property-owning classes with obvious and unqualified derision and indicate the exploited working classes as the poem's primary audience, so that the song works to construct workers as a subculture for which jargon of this kind is a common language. Another, even more puzzling bit of jargon, the "wooden sabot," indicates the mode of labor agitation that the IWW endorsed to make the boss "come across" with concessions. The term alludes to the supposed origin of the word "sabotage": that once, a French worker, disgusted with being exploited, threw his wooden shoe (*sabot,* in French) into a piece of machinery, thus "sabot-aging" it.[5] Specifically, then, the "wooden sabot" – among IWWs more commonly Anglicized as simply "wooden shoe" – denotes the various methods of industrial sabotage both threatened and actually used by the IWW, ranging from physical destruction of machinery to a work slowdown, "bum work for bum pay."

The IWW not only confronted Americans with the nation's class diversity and social inequality; the union also conceptualized class division as an opportunity to be exploited as much as it considered it a problem to be solved. It was this radical antiestablishment stance that lay at the root of the middle-class public's revulsion toward the union and that, in wartime, seemed to demand the union's suppression by the state. But insofar as the IWW took no particular action to impede the war effort – in spite of threatening a general strike – the IWW's suppression also demonstrates as clearly as anything else that the war in the United States was as much about domestic politics and power as it was about international policy. The IWW never did more than threaten war resistance, and only occasionally directed its attention to the European war or the U.S. intervention per se. The IWW was inimical not because it threatened to succeed in altering war policy, but because it was in fact succeeding in altering domestic politics: union membership was to leap from sixty thousand in the summer of 1916 to a hundred thousand a year later, and wartime demand and wartime profits made it possible for the union to gain concessions from employers, especially in the harvest fields of the Middle West. The IWW had to be suppressed as "unpatriotic" in large part because the union, nourished by uniquely American labor and industrial conditions, was becoming too much of an all-American success.

This contradictory relationship between the IWW and American society and culture can be located in the IWW's production and practice of poetry and songs as well. The IWW's frequent borrowings from Amer-

ican cultural forms – especially from religious hymnody and popular
songs – were irreverent, expressing the voices of the dispossessed. Between 1914 and 1917, IWW writers prophesied that the war would bring
down world capitalism and leave the IWW's one big union in its place.
Union visionaries saw the IWW as the framework for a self-conscious,
egalitarian society that would emerge from the ruins of an unreflective,
exploitive one. Yet the relationship between the IWW and American culture was not merely antagonistic; it was dialogic as well. The IWW did
in fact grow in power as the war in Europe continued, but not at the expense of American capitalism; both the IWW and its capitalist adversaries
benefited from increased wartime demand for American products. Even
the IWW's parodic and supposedly subversive uses of culture were surprisingly imitative. The poetics of appropriation – borrowing, mimicry,
parody – was, as we have seen, the very hallmark of popular poetry as
represented in newspapers. Ideologically, too, IWW writers and organizers may have ridiculed the languages of patriotism, religion, and militarism, but in Wobbly songs and poems they simultaneously reintroduced
languages of power and loyalty. In effect, even as the IWW transformed
popular idioms to speak for the underclass, the group's compulsive recycling of American culture belied later denunciations of the group as "un-
American."

I

The IWW came to war opposition early, yet the union's identity as an
implacable opponent of war was created not so much by any official antiwar policies as by the IWW's rhetoric idealizing class warfare and also
by the distorted image of the union offered up by those who wanted the
union suppressed. To be sure, the IWW, founded in 1905, had long been
on record as opposed to national wars.[6] But the IWW never took up war
opposition as its primary cause, nor was it categorically opposed to violence, since its own theory of class war, its advocacy of industrial sabotage, and its hopes for revolution presupposed the necessity of conflict
and the destruction of property, if not bloodshed (martyrdom figures significantly in IWW literature; murder does not). "Should I Ever Be a Soldier" by Joe Hill, first published in the fifth edition of *Songs of the Workers,* roughly a year before the war began,[7] might serve as a kind of radical
socialist prequel to "I Didn't Raise My Boy to Be a Soldier." Like the
1915 song, it argues against national militarism; unlike it, Hill's lyric endorses another kind of militancy – in the labor movement.[8] Hill urges
his readers to withhold their loyalty from American society as presently

constituted – "Don't sing 'My Country 'tis of thee.'" Instead workers should pledge allegiance to industrial radicalism:

> Should I ever be a soldier,
>   'Neath the Red Flag I would fight;
> Should the gun I ever shoulder,
>   It's to crush the tyrant's might.
> Join the army of the toilers,
>   Men and women fall in line,
> Wage slaves of the world! Arouse!
>   Do your duty for the cause,
> For Land and Liberty.

This chorus offers class war as the justifiable, even necessary, alternative to national defense. Exhibiting the IWW's habit of co-opting nationalist rhetoric – "Land and Liberty" – to suit its own purposes, the stanza transfers the language of military organization from the realm of national banners to that of international socialism's "Red Flag." The song's final stanza insinuates, further, that the armaments supposedly needed for national defense against external enemies are more likely to be employed in internal battles against the laboring classes:

> Why do they mount their gatling gun
>   A thousand miles from ocean,
> Where hostile fleet could never run –
>   Ain't that a funny notion?
> If you don't know the reason why,
>   Just strike for better wages,
> And then, my friends – if you don't die –
>   You'll sing this song for ages.[9]

A year before the war, Hill, like many Europeans and other Americans, could not predict the sudden, extensive use of the European nations' arsenals against one another. But in wartime, state militias and paramilitary groups would also mete out brutal and sometimes bloody repression of the IWW, and this Hill could foresee given the IWW's repeated "peacetime" confrontations with armed Pinkerton guards and militiamen controlled by business owners.[10]

Because of its view that international warfare could not be effectively confronted without doing away with the very idea of the nation-state, the IWW condemned the war but did not agitate against it per se. Whereas politically active women swiftly organized the WPP and agitated for a negotiated armistice, the IWW simply noted that national wars were inevitable under capitalism and that therefore it would be futile to protest the war by dealing with existing governments.[11] The union opposed the war only insofar as it intensified the exploitation of workers and distracted the laboring masses from their ultimate aim of social revolution. Therefore, IWW publications adopted an attitude that was at the same time passionate and thoroughly cynical. Late in August 1914, *Solidarity* printed Ralph Chaplin's "Slaves, to the Slaughter," a poem that presents succinctly the IWW's views of capitalist wars and class wars. It brims over with antipatriotic scorn for the nationalist (and in the IWW's view, distinctively *capitalist*) war being waged in Europe:

> The drums roll forth their summons,
>   The war-like bugles thrill,
> From here and there and everywhere
> The slaves are given arms to bear –
>   Some other slaves to kill.
>
> Each one must do his "duty" –
>   Must find warm blood to spill;
> For "wrong" or "right," with dread or spite,
> Although HE has no cause to fight;
>   It is HIS MASTER'S WILL.

Capitalist wars compel wage slaves to kill fellow slaves while risking their own lives and attaining no practical benefits. In sharp and favorable contrast, Chaplin places class warfare, in which workers establish their solidarity with others of their class and, though they risk their lives in the process, stand to win their freedom, "A world to gain and fill." So the final stanza proclaims:

> Unite! unite! for your own fight,
>   You slaves of shop and mill,
> How much better far such battles are
> Than all the streaming ways of war
>   Where slaves fight slaves to kill![12]

In their derision of the capitalist war and their foolish European comrades who had mobilized for it, IWW propagandists in the union newspapers evinced also an underlying confidence that the war had demonstrated beyond doubt the monstrosity of industrial capitalism and that, because of this demonstration, the workers of America would recognize the folly of letting national loyalty supersede class solidarity. A September 5, 1914, editorial in *Solidarity* decried the "sinister, cold-blooded, 'un-

Figure 2. "When Block Meets Block." Detail from cartoon by Ernest Riebe, *Solidarity* September 5, 1914: 1. By permission of the Archives of Labor and Urban Affairs, Wayne State University.

sentimental' capitalists" who manipulated their "crowned puppets" to precipitate war and their "slaves" to sacrifice themselves for the sake of economic expansion. This, however, was the behavior expected of capitalists. What *Solidarity* found most disgusting was that the laboring classes forming the bulk of the armies were "WILLING victims," deluded by "patriotism . . . inbred through thousands of generations." For such powerful delusions, the editorial declared the only possible remedy to be unbridled ridicule: "The mass of slaves . . . may be moved to some extent by a realization of how foolish they appear in the eyes of their enlightened fellow workers."[13] As a specimen of this ridicule the editorial directed attention to a cartoon on the paper's front page, "When Block Meets Block," in which compliant wage slaves wearing military garb and "blockheads" assault one another while pealing out patriotic banalities such as "Hurrah for English Supremacy!" "For God and Tzar," and "Hoch Der Kaiser!" (Figure 2).[14]

The IWW regarded the delusion of European workers and the treachery of the ruling classes as far more profound than the WPP was willing to admit. Although certain WPP activists were to be successful in allying the women's movement with the labor movement, the gulf between the bourgeois WPP and the proletarian IWW made any rapprochement between these groups unimaginable. Yet union organizers apparently shared with Jane Addams and other WPP leaders the relatively optimistic assumption that the masses could be educated to see the war's absurdity. The bizarre cartoon and its accompanying editorial comment stress that wage slaves in Europe are probably irremediable "blockheads." But the editorial also holds out the possibility that some workers, particularly American workers and certainly Wobblies, will recognize their foolishness. A poem by Charles Ashleigh in the October 31 *Solidarity* offers up an "Anti-Militarist" who resists the national call to arms and recognizes his class responsibility:

> The thrill of a myriad war lusts beats upon me;
> The churning of a million passions is abroad.
> I will not cast myself into this frenzy.
>
> I will be a rock of irony.
> I will be a rain of pity.
> I will be a wind of scorn.
>
> My arm is strong to destroy, but I withhould [*sic*] it;
> I will destroy only that which stands
> in the way of our red redemption.[15]

Although in 1914 the IWW might reasonably have been wary that "myriad war lusts" would boost American militarism, the occasion of the war also appears to have provided IWW propagandists with a perfect lesson in the evils of capitalism. Though European laborers and socialists had proved all too susceptible to nationalist appeals, the calamity resulting from their war participation seemed to guarantee that American workers would be wiser.

IWW writers such as Ashleigh seem to have welcomed the world war as a kind of overture to the coming class war. While this particular attitude was distinctive to the IWW, the union's economic and class interpretation of the European war can otherwise be found in the writing of American analysts from across the political spectrum. Wobbly contempt for the delusion of the European participants likewise points to similarity to rather than difference from the perspective of other Americans. In *The War in Europe,* a book speeded to press in the fall of 1914, Harvard professor Albert Bushnell Hart finds age-old "racial" antagonisms to be at the foundation of the Great War. While Hart's emphasis on cultural and ethnic divisions is distinctly at odds with the IWW's analysis, which saw these as superimposed upon economic and class forces, Hart's perspective accords with the IWW's in other ways. He suggests, for instance, that war might have been averted if more democratic, popular governments had been in place in England as well as in Germany, Austria-Hungary, and Russia.[16] Furthermore, although presumably the racial hatreds whipped up in Europe would threaten the integrity of America's polyglot culture, Hart repeatedly emphasizes the threat of the war to U.S. trade and commerce. Americans throughout the economy are threatened, Hart remarks: "The great wheat farmer and the cotton planter look doubtfully across the sea. The banker who is ready and anxious to finance their shipments finds his capital dormant because of the lack of ships." Hart's conclusion that "aside from personal sympathies, the United States is mightily moved by the disturbance in commerce" is entirely consonant with the IWW's view of America's interest in the war.[17] Elements of the IWW's perspective can be found elsewhere in the productions of the conservative, predominantly northeastern intellectual and publishing establishment. Clarence W. Barron, author of a 1915 study of the war's causes, *The Audacious War*, is no socialist; his concern is mainly over tariffs and international trade. But in his chapter "Tariffs and Commerce the War Causes," he, like socialist analysts, sees economic rivalry – and chiefly, unequal economic competition between Germany and Russia – as the underlying cause of the European war.[18] So too, in 1916, Newell Dwight Hillis's *Studies of the Great War* cites German militarism as the immediate cause of the war ("the nation that first sent out her armies was Germany"), but it sees as the underlying cause Germany's "problems of expansion" – namely, problems of economic expansion, international trade, and colonization.[19]

While even conservative commentators noted the importance of economic competition in the European conflict, progressive and left-leaning intellectuals and artists joined the IWW and other committed radicals in examining class issues in the war. *Contemporary War Poems,* an anthology published in December 1914, appeared as part of a periodical series begun in 1907 by the American Association for International Conciliation, a relatively conservative organization espousing the pragmatic internationalism favored by certain financiers, lawyers, and intellectuals.[20] It was hardly a publication in which one would expect to find a radical critique of capitalist war. Yet the charge leveled most frequently by the writers of *Contemporary War Poems* is that the war is being fought on the battlefields by working people with nothing to gain from it, while kings and capitalists who stand to profit remain safely at home. Christopher Morley's "Peasant and King," speaking from the perspective of Europe's peasantry, castigates the governments and monied interests, charging that war "is *your* game: it was none of our choosing – / We are the pawns with whom you have played." The poem promises retribution: "when the penalties have to be paid, / We who are left, and our womenfolk, too, / Rulers of Europe, will settle with you."[21] Morris Ryskind's wickedly satirical "Who Dies if England Live?" holds forth on a similar theme, extemporizing on the following newsclipping that forms its epigraph: "LONDON, Sept. 3. – England, ready for a staggering blow on publication of the government casualty list, heaved a sigh of relief when it was found that so few of the noble families had been affected. *The Mail.*" Ryskind's response is three stanzas in the following vein:

> Ten thousand Tommy Atkinses went forth into the fray;
> Ten thousand stalwart Tommies who gave Death their lives for pay.
> But still we sing, "God Save the King," and thank the Fates of War:
> *For Viscount What-the-Who's-This hasn't even got a scar.* (*CW* 25)

The *Masses,* a regular publisher of poetry, was a forum more closely tied to the American Left. But in its poetry especially, it showed a surprising eclecticism; the editors' preference for genteel over free-verse forms and their acceptance of nature lyrics as well as social critiques suggest the variety of sentiments and perspectives that the *Masses* intellectuals assumed to be assimilable to the Left. Striking, however, is the degree to which class analyses of society and of the war are held in common throughout the range of political perspectives represented in *Masses* poems – including some verses that suggest or openly declare the most bourgeois of sentiments.

For instance, the November 1914 *Masses* published Margaret Widdemer's "God and the Strong Ones," a poem that would seem unsuitably bourgeois for its references to God as the champion of the laboring classes. Within a few years, Widdemer would be publishing patriotic material through the Vigilantes.[22] But in 1914 her poem demarcates strongly both class oppositions and class warfare, as she describes the oppression of workers by their masters:

> "We have made them fools and weak!" said the Strong Ones;
> "We have bound them, they are still and deaf and blind,
> We have crushed them in our hands like a heap of crumbling sands,

> We have left them naught to seek or find:
> They are quiet at our feet!" said the Strong Ones,
> "We have made them one with stone and clod;
> Serf and laborer and woman, they are less than wise or human – "
> **"I can raise the weak,"** saith God.[23]

Widdemer's perspective is not altogether what we would expect in a Left journal. As opposed to the IWW's delight at any opportunity to bully the master class, she appears to consider class relations from the perspective of the "Strong Ones," permitting their panic to dominate the poem's description of class warfare:

> "They will trample us and bind!" said the Strong Ones:
> "We are crushed beneath the blackened feet and hands!
> All the strong and fair and great they will crush from out the
>   State,
> They will whelm it like the weight of sands –
> They are witless and are blind!" said the Strong Ones,
> "There is black decay where they have trod –
> They will break the world in twain if their hands are on the
>   rein["] –
> **"What is that to me?"** saith God.

The IWW – and other radicals, too – would see the laborer's work, however crushing and inadequately rewarded, as ennobling. Widdemer's attitude appears more ambivalent: she sees the working classes as exploited and demeaned but gives no indication that their experience has done anything more than brutalize and embitter them. Yet in spite of Widdemer's reluctance to identify with and valorize the masses, her poem operates on the same premises that underlay the IWW's conception of class war: the working classes and the owning classes are fundamentally divided; the owners necessarily seek to exploit the workers; and the workers will inevitably – and justly – rise up and overthrow them.

Other poems, articles, and cartoons in the *Masses* postulate the interconnections between nationalism, militarism, and capitalism that were basic to American socialists' criticism of the war. But again, these critiques fit no typical ideological or poetic scheme; not all urge political agitation, as the IWW's poetry typically did, and not many fit the social-realist dogma that has come to be associated with Left literary production. Published in the December 1914 issue, Charles Wood's "King of the Magical Pump" uses a fable in rollicking light verse to describe the connection between autocratic government and militarism. The poem depicts a despot whose consumerist whims run ragged the masses of laboring "Chumps" who, for a pittance, run the kingdom's manufacturing "Pump":

3.

It pumped up his prunes and his new pantaloons
    And it pumped up his bibles and beer;
    His tribal old bibles and beer:
    For palaces, chalices, garters or galluses,
    Or jeans for his queens or his Julias and Alices,
The King of the Chumps, he just went to the pumps
    And whatever he wished would appear.

4.

And the Chumpetty-Chumps who were pumping the pumps
    Which pumped up these thing-a-mum bobs,
    These thing-a-mum, jing-a-mum bobs,
    They humped it and jumped it and pumpetty-pumped it
    And fearfully, tearfully liked it or lumped it;
While the King in his glee hollered: "Bully for Me!
    Ain't you glad that I gave you your jobs?"

Conditioned by the habits, superstitions, and fears that have kept them subservient – and exploited – vassals "for ages," the "Chumpetty-Chumps" can only say "A prodigious, religious 'Amen'" in praise of their king's beneficence. Wood's poem, then, postulates not only a classic Marxist split between a propertied, consuming class and a producing class, but also a Marxist concept of ideology in which the producers are deluded into accepting the very values of private ownership and deference to authority that underlie the system oppressing them.[24] When the manufacturing "Pump" overproduces and workers are laid off, the king decides upon a military adventure as the way to renew production and a national emergency as the way to precipitate such an enterprise. He reasons, "The lesson this session of business depression / Points out beyond doubt is that foreign aggression / Has caused a big slump in the work of the pump – / So up, men, and after your foes!" Just as bizarre as the king's logic, however, is the crazed response of the worker-citizens, who "in joy and in laughter" go off "To fight for country and King" (like the massive British volunteer army). The king of the "magical, tragical pump" is, of course, the only one who gains by the workers' pain, mutilation, and death. But the conditions underlying peacetime and wartime industry are the same; either way, "An oodle of boodle he's got by his noodle / And umpty-nine Chumpties he's fed with flapdoodle − / For we live for a thingum and die for a jingum / In the Kingdom of Chumpetty-Chump."[25] Wood's poem thus suggests, like the IWW's analysis, that there is only a difference of degree, not of kind, between the oppression of workers in wartime and that of workers in peacetime.

The most conservative of socialists, though they differed substantially from their radical counterparts in the IWW, could agree on its analysis of the European war. Carl Sandburg, for instance. Since 1912 Sandburg had not kept up his membership in the Wisconsin Social-Democratic Party, a party already on the right wing of the Socialist Party of America.[26] Yet in "Ready to Kill," a piece from his 1916 collection, *Chicago Poems,* Sandburg expresses revulsion for the destructive trade of soldiery and admiration for the constructive work of industrial labor. Encountering "a bronze memorial of a famous general / Riding horseback with a flag and a sword and a revolver on him," he had wanted to "smash the whole thing into a pile of junk" − at least unless honorary bronzes were also erected of "the farmer, the miner, the shop man, the factory hand, the fireman, and the teamster, / . . . the real huskies that are doing the work of the world, and feeding people instead of butchering them."[27] Sandburg's poem depicts not just a generalized dismay over the high cultural standing of military heroism, but a disgust for militarism that is grounded in a specific U.S. locale − Chicago's Grant Park. Another of his *Chicago Poems,* "Wars," indicates a socialist distrust for national wars and faith in class wars, while suggesting that the present European war is of the former type:

> In the old wars kings quarreling and thousands of men following.
> In the new wars kings quarreling and millions of men following.
> In the wars to come kings kicked under the dust and millions of
>   men following great causes not yet dreamed out in the heads of
>   men.[28]

Facilitated by the scope of the modern nation-state and the efficiency of industrial technology − "long-range guns and smashed walls, guns running a spit of metal and men falling in tens and twenties" − the "new wars" such as the current European conflict are more contemptible than the old feudal conflicts involving "clutches of short swords and jabs into faces with spears." For Sandburg and others across the socialist spectrum, warfare ideally should involve the deposing of kings and the struggle to establish a progressive society – in short, the class war. These are the "wars to come."

II

Given the variety of Americans who opposed war and whose analysis of the war did not differ substantially from the IWW's – those associated with the progressive movement as well as those affiliated with Left politics – the fact that the IWW was singled out as the most obnoxious and threatening of dissenters demands explanation. Between 1914 and 1916, the European War often seemed remote, or at least peripheral, to IWW interests. IWW organizers and presses focused on improving the wages and shortening the hours of unskilled, mostly western workers in the mining, farming, and logging industries – only occasionally launching squibs against the capitalistic European war and the profits American businesses were drawing from it.[29] *Solidarity* printed a number of poems explicitly condemning the European war in the fall of 1914 (one in August, three in October). But in all of 1915 it printed just three – one a reprint of a poem by William Lloyd Garrison, the other two by John Kendrick. In the same year, the WPP and its pacifist allies were making use of numerous poems that criticized warfare generally and the policies of the warring nations particularly. Rather than agitating against warfare, writers of the IWW were more likely to use the rhetoric of warfare to suit the union's own purposes; characteristically, the IWW reinterpreted the language and popular culture of patriotism, militarism, and even pacifism to apply to the union's industrial struggle.

Precisely because the IWW did not take war opposition to be its raison d'être, class solidarity and economic common interest promised to make the organization more sturdy than the coalition of peace societies that had collapsed when members' social and economic identifications – and, in the case of the suffragists, political goals – were threatened by continued war opposition. Meanwhile, as the IWW downplayed its criticism of capitalist wars, it profited economically and politically from the growth of American industry brought about by increased demand from Europe. It is one of the sharpest ironies of U.S. wartime politics that the IWW, dogmatically opposed to capitalist wars, should have prospered from what was effectively a wartime economy in the United States between 1914 and 1916. Taking advantage of a heightened demand for farm labor precipitated by increased agricultural production in 1915 and 1916 (a circumstance brought on largely by the wartime needs of the Allies), the

IWW organized western agricultural workers with great success; the Agricultural Workers Organization, a local of the IWW, expanded to 20,000 by the fall of 1916, leading the growth of the IWW as a whole from 40,000 in 1916 to 100,000 in 1917 (Dubofsky 316, 349). The IWW's success came just as other, more moderate socialist political parties were slightly declining – the Socialist Party of America had experienced its high-water mark of 118,000 members in 1912 and was down to about 80,000 in 1917.[30] Besides agricultural laborers, the IWW was most active and successful among workers in copper and coal mining and in logging, industries that, for a variety of reasons – the irregularity of work, the large number of unskilled laborers – were among the most exploitive (Dubofsky 345–46). They were also among the most crucial war industries. Melvin Dubofsky explains: "American and Allied soldiers could not fight without food; without lumber, the military could not house recruits, transport them across the ocean, or challenge German pilots for control of the skies; without copper, production of military-related hardware was hampered and wire essential to battlefield communication lines was impossible to obtain" (359). If workers producing these commodities were mobilized for the IWW's class war, America's mobilization for the international war in Europe could falter.

What is more, by 1916 the IWW had repeatedly demonstrated its adeptness at self-promotion. The trial and execution of Joe Hill provide perhaps the best-known example of how the IWW was repeatedly able to exploit the wrongful arrests, imprisonments without charges, and vigilante lynchings that IWW members endured. In the hands of IWW publicists, journalists, songwriters, and poets, these incidents became flashpoints in the class struggle. Between January 1914, when Joe Hill was arrested on murder charges, and November 1915, when he was executed, Hill was transformed from a migrant worker and "Little Red Song Book" contributor to an internationally recognized martyr of the class war.[31] As Dubofsky argues, the process by which Hill became an IWW martyr depended, first of all, on polarization between the reactionary Utah press and other presses: the former seemed to believe that innuendoes about Hill's affiliation with the (supposedly) violent, anarchist IWW were the easiest way to condemn him; partly as a result, the latter found in Hill's case the perfect archetype for capitalism's injustice and labor's patient struggle, and it orchestrated an international publicity campaign that established the myth (309–10). So the IWW made the Hill imprisonment a publicity triumph by working the mainstream "capitalist" press as well as the labor press. Just as national WPP leaders were deciding the press could not be useful to dissenting movements, the IWW, a far more radical group, was able not only to create controversy in the conservative press but also to construct popular opinion favorable to its cause through newspapers with more progressive or leftist leanings.

Hill, though not a union organizer, was the most frequently published songwriter and poet in the IWW, and he played his part as IWW saint superbly. While in jail he wrote a series of letters that, as a commentator in the *Industrial Pioneer* later wrote, "show that peculiar spirit which enabled Joe to bear up so well under the enormous strain, while all the forces of both sides of the struggle were being marshaled – one to take his life, the other to save him."[32] On the night before his execution, Hill reportedly telegraphed a martyr's final words to IWW general secretary Haywood: "Good-bye, Bill. I will die like a true blue rebel. Don't waste any time mourning. *Organize*" (quoted in Dubofsky 311).[33] The IWW did mourn Hill, but true to Hill's last wishes, the union employed its mourning and memorials to recruit and mobilize union members. Hill was buried in Chicago next to the Haymarket victims, thus establishing his high rank in the pantheon of radical martyrs. Hill's memorial service, held in Chicago's West Side Auditorium on November 25, 1915, included his songs "The Rebel Girl," "There Is Power," "Stung Right," and "Preacher and the Slave," and on the backside of the program was printed another Hill lyric, "Workers of the World, Awaken," which envisioned the workers' paradise that could be established on earth if only they would act decisively and unanimously:

> Workers of the World, awaken,
> Rise in all your splendid might;
> Take the wealth which you are making,
> It belongs to you by right.
> No one will for bread be crying,
> We'll have freedom, love and health,
> When the grand Red Flag is flying
> In the workers' commonwealth.[34]

With poems of this kind, plus speeches by Haywood and other union leaders, Hill's funeral became an IWW rally sacralized by Hill's martyrdom and focused by his songs. Reprinted after Hill's death in the ninth edition of *Songs of the Workers*, in the tenth edition (the "Joe Hill Memorial Edition"), and indeed in most subsequent printings, "Workers of the World, Awaken" joined other Hill songs in the IWW repertory and, with the others, gained in authority as the legend of Hill's martyrdom grew.

The IWW was a tangible threat to the U.S. government, and especially to any nationalist, authoritarian enterprise such as war mobilization. In 1916 and 1917, the union was arguably larger, bolder, and more unified than any other likely opponent of war. But we should not exaggerate the practical power of the IWW, although both the IWW and the state, each for its own reasons, did precisely that. In spite of the IWW's many poetic and musical celebrations of sabotage, the actual manifestations of the practice appear to have been few. Dubofsky points out that in the IWW's federal trials in 1918, "hard as they tried, state and federal authorities could never establish legal proof of IWW-instigated sabotage" (163). In his 1948 memoir, *Wobbly,* Chaplin insists that the forms of sabotage used in the United States by the IWW consisted primarily of the "sitdown and slow-down strategies,"[35] or, as he put it in the Chicago IWW trial, "Sabotage means good pay or bum work," but doesn't "involve the destruction of property."[36]

At bottom, the IWW's threat to the United States was deeply ideological, shaped by IWW rhetoric and poetics as much as by practical organization. To be sure, organization and ideology were closely intertwined in the IWW. The IWW was unique in its reliance on poetry as a tool for indoctrination and socialization into its organization: a worker's first encounter with a union organizer would most likely include his or her rendition of selections from *Songs of the Workers,* the union's famous "Little Red Song Book"; and singing from the pocket-size book became standard fare at IWW meetings and gatherings.[37] But the IWW's threat of sabotage seems to have loomed much larger as a rhetorical and ideological construct than as an immediate physical danger. Even while Chaplin testified in court that the IWW did not incite the physical destruction of property, he held forth enthusiastically on the language of sabotage and its rhetorical and practical effects. Explaining the symbolism of the black cat, Chaplin's own peculiar figure for sabotage incorporated in many of his drawings, he remarks that sabotage is "a bluff or scare" to frighten the boss: "You know if you saw a black cat go across your path you would think, if you are superstitious, you are going to have a little bad luck. The idea of sabotage is to use a little black cat on the boss" (7711). To whatever degree IWW members practiced sabotage, it was the threat as much as the act of sabotage itself that constructed the power Wobblies hoped to wield in American industry and society – even as it was the constant, apparent menace of sabotage that was the basis of the government's and the public's paranoia about the IWW.

Ideologically, sabotage was so contrary to America's reverence for – and legal protection of – private property, that the IWW could be readily cast as un-American, however homegrown were the industrial conditions enabling the union to thrive. Sabotage – the subversion of capitalism from within – effectively set the pattern for IWW propaganda as well as its agitation. But literary sabotage, much like its material counterpart, was as much constructive as it was destructive. IWW writers parodied the languages of patriotism, religion, and militarism but at the same time adopted them for their own use. Similarly, IWW organizers mimicked the methods and organization of capitalist corporations, government apparatuses, commercial advertisers, and religious institutions – which is to say that they ridiculed them at the same time they adapted them to the IWW's own aims. The resulting "perversion" of American culture might be regarded as all the more empowering to workers, and all the more disturbing to the propertied classes, because of its origin within America's social and cultural boundaries. Even before the United States intervened, the IWW had in effect already committed intellectual and cultural treason by its use of literary resources for "disloyal" purposes.

The IWW's version of piracy is clear in virtually any poem written about the war or, more precisely, in any poem that transmutes the terms of American war debate into the lingo of class war. In the summer of 1916, the U.S. Congress was debating preparedness; the National Defense Act, which it passed and the president signed into law, instituted the Council for National Defense and moderately increased the size of the standing army.[38] The IWW's answer to the preparedness debate was Ralph Chaplin's "Preparedness," which appeared in the June 24, 1916, *Solidarity*. First, three stanzas repudiate all nationalist appeals for loyalty: "For freedom die? . . . Defend the Flag? . . . Protect our land?" Workers cannot conceive of these under the present system, for they have no freedom except to starve, they have been gunned down by armed men flying the flag, and they live in a land owned by a few "thieves on high." They can conceive, however, of striking down the present order. In its fourth and final stanza, the poem demonstrates that the IWW offered up not only cynicism about nationalist ideals, but also commitment to its own ideals:

> Resist the foe, we shall! from sea to sea
>   The lewd invaders [sic] battle-line is thrown;
>   Here is our enemy and here alone –
> The Parasite of world-wide industry!
>   His wealth is red with mangled flesh and bone.
> Resist the foe, ah, crush him utterly –;
>   Resist the foe . . . . . . ?[39]

Rejections of national idealization are followed by an idealization of class warfare that echoes the zeal of the patriot.

Also appearing during the summer, Victor Basinet's "A Song of Preparedness" portrays a similar dichotomy between the irrational appeals of nation and the compelling appeal of class. Basinet first undercuts various national calls to battle by casting them in nakedly brutal terms: a man of draft age is urged to "prepare to kill, who [sic] you never saw"; a mother who "At the risk of life . . . [has] birthed a son" must "prepare for the Sacrifice, – food for a gun"; a "youth" can hope to experience "blood and rape and the jingo song"; and a "Maiden" must "Fling love dreams to Hell," for "Your duty's a war bride – war brides must breed." The reasonable alternative to these degrading, irrational demands of the nation-state is the liberating imperative of working-class solidarity. Throughout the poem the "Man," the "Woman," the "Youth," and the "Maiden" are all addressed in the singular, as "worker!"; in the poem's penultimate stanza, these different personalities realize their collective identity in that epithet:

> Workers; Workers!
> Life of the race – prepare!
> For the Red Revolt – 'tis marked by Fate,
> That slaves must themselves emancipate –
> Prepare!

Basinet's final stanza, which sketches the fate of the "Masters; shirkers! / Damned of the race," is just as unequivocal as the preceding stanza's affirmation of revolution. It does not waver in its confidence that the workers' revolution will radically level society, while it delights in the possibility that the bosses should have to do the same kind of hard labor they previously meted out to their "slaves": "prepare! / To wipe from your greasy cheeks, that smirk – / To strip to your hides, you bums – and work!"[40]

As we shall see in the next chapter, pro-war English and American poetry anthologized by the major New York publishers was effective as propaganda partly because it professed to stand above politics. In contrast, the IWW poetry published in *Solidarity* served up revolutionary propaganda forcefully and unabashedly. The rhetoric of IWW songs is distinctive in American poetry; the permeation of poetry and song throughout its subculture and its practice as an organization is unique. Comparing the IWW's practice with that of the anthologists, however, it is difficult to say which is more and which less "American." Even in the most general terms, the idea of an anthology as a disinterested presentation of the "best" poetry on a particular subject was in no way traditional; Alan Golding notes, for instance, that American anthologies from before the revolution were consciously used as instruments for proclaiming particular cultural and political agendas.[41] Is the "Little Red Song Book" perhaps more American than the purportedly apolitical anthology? The *Solidarity* editorial policy of publishing one or two poems in each issue can be located in many metropolitan, "capitalist" papers; any number of newspapers – the *Boston Globe*, the *Atlanta Constitution* – typically ran far more.[42] Newspaper verses like Chaplin's "Preparedness," referenced by the popular melodies they could be sung to, were unique insofar as they worked in tandem with the IWW *Songs of the Workers*, so that the union papers *Solidarity* and the *Industrial Worker* functioned as supplements updating the Wobbly repertoire to keep it abreast of current labor struggles. But the kind of imitation and parody practiced by IWW writers – though fundamentally and uniquely constitutive of their work – was also practiced throughout popular culture with both poetry and song lyrics, as we have seen exhibited in the numerous sequels to "I Didn't Raise My Boy to Be a Soldier" and "A Chant of Hate against England." IWW newspaper verses not set to a tune frequently employed rhyme, repeated choruses, and insistent parallelism, making them suitable for the street-corner rant of Wobbly organizers and the group recitation of IWW members. Yet as Salvatore Salerno points out, IWW soapboxing found its counterpart in the street-corner rallies of the Salvation Army and other religious (and, indeed, political) groups. Salerno writes that IWW songs offered "parodies of the Christian religious hymns used by the Salvation Army who frequently occupied street corners in the same locality used by I.W.W. soapboxers."[43] And of course, the kinds of diatribe and idealization offered in IWW poetry were commonplace in the national and religious languages they pirated.

In one sense, the "conventionality" of Wobbly forms served to highlight ideological difference with mainstream American culture: IWW rhetoric insists on clear demarcations between capitalism and socialism, a pure dichotomy between "us" and "them." This radical difference of perspective was politically useful not only because it designated a specific class enemy and demanded class solidarity in turn, but also because it helped deconstruct the ruling ideologies that threatened to keep the working classes perpetually subordinate. That is, while for the ruling classes ideological construction can, and to a significant extent *must be*, covert, for the working classes ideology must be exposed for its delusions and therefore must be dealt with more self-consciously. Thus, "subversive" IWW rhetoric, politics, and practice come closer to getting to the bottom of American traditions and institutions than do the popular conventions and "common sense" from which they sprang. The IWW grew and flourished in the most exploitive material conditions, even as its verse and songs adapted the forms and practices of popular culture – religious and patriotic culture, particularly – which were most responsible for ideological "false consciousness." The IWW did not have to be silenced because it lied about America, but because it spoke the lived experience of many workers. Their accounts of capitalist exploitation and worker disenfranchisement were the "truer" accounts of American culture, politics, and popular literary form.

III

As we have seen, the IWW not only practiced subversion but also sought to offer a constructive alternative to present society. In other words, it entered into hegemonic struggle even as it engaged in subversion. When the United States went to war in 1917 and the actions of a few union leaders, notably Ralph Chaplin, exposed the IWW to the charge that it advocated sedition, it is not always clear whether the IWW was trying to subvert the government and sabotage industry or whether it was simply competing with them. Beginning in 1915 and 1916, when Ralph Chaplin was an illustrator in the IWW's Cleveland headquarters, he designed a variety of "stickerettes" – colorful gum-backed stamps that combined artwork with IWW slogans and poetry. Some took particular aim at capitalist wars. The large stickerette concluding "Young Man, Don't Be a Soldier – Be a Man" was a reprint of an antienlistment squib said to be written in 1911 by Jack London.[44] According to Chaplin's trial testimony, "ten to twenty thousand" copies of this stickerette were printed "very early in 1916" and most had been distributed by July 1916 (7702). Indeed, its appeal to soldiers not to enlist was marked by the same antagonism between capitalism and socialism that had from the beginning been fundamental to IWW philosophy: "The 'good' soldier never tries to distinguish right from wrong. He never thinks, never reasons; he only obeys. . . . All that is human in him, all that is divine in him, all that constitutes a man has been sworn away when he took the enlistment oath."[45] The government's case against the IWW was based on its quotation of this kind of propaganda, which was loathsome to the state not so much because it promoted opposition to the present U.S. policy as because it encouraged opposition to virtually any policy of the state (except perhaps its self-abolition).

Chaplin's propaganda was repeatedly cited to back sedition charges against the IWW, since Chaplin had not only produced antiwar stickerettes, cartoons, and poems appearing in *Solidarity* but also edited the newspaper during 1917. More than those of other IWW writers and organizers, Chaplin's various productions as IWW editor, poet, and artist did tend toward confrontation over the issue of the U.S. military buildup and intervention. "The Deadly Parallel," a comparison between the antiwar position of the IWW and the pro-war stance of the American Federation of Labor, was printed on the front page of the March 24, 1917, *Solidarity.* Below the IWW's "Declaration" and AFL "Pledge Given," reprinted in their entirety, *Solidarity* presented another comparison, between the working classes of Europe, who eagerly supported their countries, and the AFL, which now was offering its support: a table of European casualties lists an Allied figure approaching 6 million and a German tally nearing 3.5 million; the column's final lines declare these casualties "a monument to the national patriotic stupidity of the working class of Europe!" and ask pointedly, "Who will be to blame if the workers of America are betrayed and led into the bloodiest slaughter of history?"[46] Printed roughly ten days before the U.S. war declaration, the column advocated, "in time of war, the general strike in all industries." In this case, as in others, IWW rhetoric (or Chaplin's rhetoric) was not matched by union action. After the United States intervened, the IWW did not call a general strike. Still, in the July 28 issue of *Solidarity* Chaplin did print an editorial column, "Were You Drafted?" which spelled out "where the IWW stands on the Question of War" and particularly on the question of the draft.[47] In July the IWW board had convened and, over the objections of Chaplin and a few other leaders, had decided not to issue any official proclamations on the war; Chaplin, however, feeling that the IWW board "owed" its membership at least "some kind of statement" (7778), went ahead anyway to publish his editorial on "where the IWW stands." Its conclusion could be readily construed as direct opposition to the draft, punishable under the Espionage Act: "*All members of the I.W.W. who have been drafted should mark their claims for exemption, 'I.W.W.: opposed to war.*'"[48]

Under the circumstances obtaining by mid-1917, the practical effect of Chaplin's rhetoric had become unimportant, for the Espionage Act, passed in June 1917, treated seditious rhetoric and seditious activity as equivalent. Although active opposition to U.S. war intervention was never in itself an objective of the IWW, at the time of the declaration of war the Wobblies found themselves right in the middle of the wartime mobilization and demands for absolute loyalty to the nation. Although most IWW members were in fact less outspoken than Ralph Chaplin, few members of the IWW were prepared to give such loyalty, for the IWW's principle of organization (indeed, its name) and its socialist agenda were fundamentally antinationalist. Even so, the profound Americanness of the IWW remains a paradox at the union's very core, a central feature of its rhetoric and of its rhetorical appeal even when Wobblies denounced U.S. militarism most vociferously. The Wobblies did not so much subvert American narratives and ideologies as rewrite them with itself, the "one big union," as the leading player. The revulsion of the state and middle-class polity toward the IWW is a perfectly understandable reaction to the IWW's supposed perversion of the American story. But given the IWW's borrowings from and contributions to American culture, it remains a deep irony that the IWW should come to be labeled and suppressed as "un-American."

The IWW was in certain ways trying only to emulate the success of American businesses. While its rhetoric was flamboyant and revolutionary, its practice tended not so much toward inciting immediate, violent revolution as toward claiming a niche for itself within industry and unionism. IWW demands for the disenfranchised workers it represented amounted, typically, to claims on a fair measure of the value of their labor. The IWW's stickerettes suggest this kind of similarity between the IWW and business. The stickerettes were fairly straightforward political advertisements. They parodied and simultaneously adapted ingeniously the tactics of mass commercial advertising, though it may be difficult to tell in this case whether the IWW was leading or following the trend toward incorporating visual and poetic art in advertisements. In 1917 and 1918, the U.S. Food Administration was to apply the techniques of modern advertising to the wartime regulation of food production and consumption. Advertising slogans were pitched by "four-minute men" who spoke at the intermissions of movies and shows; they were proclaimed in posters; they were stamped or printed on sheet music.[49] But since 1915 this kind of mass political advertising had already been employed through the IWW stickerettes.

Chaplin testified that his idea for the stickerettes had in fact been inspired by commercial advertisements of a similar kind: "posterettes," which were stamps "printed in pretty colors" and used for the purpose of "advertising different mercantile concerns and different products and things of that sort" (7699). As Chaplin recalled, he had known of "no big mercantile concern that . . . ever carried on an advertising campaign through this medium on a large scale," and so he decided:

> I would get up a few of these representing the main principles of the I.W.W., so as to put them out to the members of the organization in different parts of the country, so that they could see just exactly what it was the I.W.W. stood for. In other words it is an advertising publicity campaign for the organization; that was the thing that I had in mind when I made the drawings. (7699)

In fact, from the first time they were mentioned in union literature, the stickerettes were billed as the IWW's answer to mass advertising: the November 20, 1915, issue of *Solidarity* introduced them with the heading, "ONE HALF MILLION / FREE ADVERTISEMENTS BOOSTING THE I.W.W." (Figure 3). The magazine notice for the stickerettes itself exemplified two of the most basic advertising gimmicks: the product giveaway – "free advertisements" – and the appeal to originality – "You Will Want to Be First to Use These 'Silent Agitators.' " Below, the notice went on to explain how the stickerette advertising was to work:

> Let one of these persistent, thought compelling designs do for you what a long argument oft times fails to accomplish. Reach a thousand workers where only one was possible. . . . A single design gives more information about the I.W.W. than will stick in the mind of a worker hearing snatches of a dozen average talks on Industrial Unionism. Each subject is better than another, and there are eleven of them.[50]

The stickerettes were intended to influence their audience through skillful design rather than rational argumentation, and to recruit new union members en masse by flooding the market with publicity rather than by personal contact with individual workers.

Stickerettes mark the union of the laboring masses as, at the same time, an agency of mass advertising. In their form, then, the stickerettes were highly ambiguous cultural artifacts. They might be seen as potentially subversive either of the capitalist society from which the original advertising concept had been pirated or of the revolutionary union the stickerettes sought to popularize. Yet we need not read the stickerettes' negotiation between revolutionary unionism and market capitalism strictly as a relation of subversion. While the stickerettes' advocacy of sabotage, "abolition of the wage system," and "good pay or bum work" may have

Figure 3. "One Half Million Free Advertisements Boosting the I.W.W.: Stickerettes Designed by Ralph H. Chaplin." Advertisement, *Solidarity* November 20, 1915: 4. By permission of the Archives of Labor and Urban Affairs, Wayne State University.

been inimical to American capitalism, these positions were not necessarily incompatible with profitable commerce and certainly not with justice in class relations. The style of Wobbly art might similarly be read as entering into dialogue with mainstream cultural productions, honoring as much as ridiculing them by imitation. One stickerette design, for example, mimics a British army recruiting poster. A watercolor of Lord Kitchener points outward at the observer; Kitchener is used, literally, as an icon, as the picture stands for the grammatical subject completed by the predicate "Wants You"; the framing text hails "Britons" to "Join Your Country's Army!" (Figure 4). The poster later became the pattern for perhaps the most famous recruiting poster ever drawn, James Montgomery Flagg's version of Uncle Sam bearing down on the onlooker, captioned, "I Want YOU / for U.S. Army" (Figure 5). The IWW version was an intermediate manifestation of the design, postdating the Lord Kitchener poster, predating the Uncle Sam one. Simpler in its presentation, the IWW stickerette depicts only the outward-pointing finger and the imperative "You / Join / the / I.W.W." (Figure 6). While the relation between the military recruiting posters and the IWW stickerette can be read as subversive, it is also possible to read these artifacts as advertisements directed at a particular group of consumers – some segment of the body politic – and

Figure 4. "Britons: Join Your Country's Army!" Poster by Alfred Leete ($29\frac{1}{2}''$ × 20"). Black-and-white illustration and lettering, "[Kitchener] Wants You"; red lettering above and below. From the copy in the Bowman Gray Collection, Academic Affairs Library, University of North Carolina at Chapel Hill.

competing for the brand-loyalty of those consumers. That the IWW and the U.S. military were both angling for absolute consumer loyalty made the competition especially fierce, but not entirely different from the relationship between business competitors.

Other stickerettes aim, like modern advertisements, to shape consumer consciousness by ridiculing a consumer with undesirable tastes and habits, hoping to construct their audience into this miscreant's inverse, a group of political consumers attuned to the demands of a revolutionary con-

Figure 5. "I Want You for U.S. Army." Color poster by James Montgomery Flagg ($39\frac{1}{2}''$ × 30″). From the copy in the Bowman Gray Collection, Academic Affairs Library, University of North Carolina at Chapel Hill.

sciousness. One stickerette satirizes a "Scissorbill," who may have been a responsible worker by capitalist standards but was defined by Wobblies as a worker lacking class consciousness. "The Scissorbill's Prayer," illustrated with a pug-nosed, potbellied man kneeling and looking heavenward, reads as follows:

Now I get me up to work
I pray the Lord I may not shirk
If I should die before the sun
I pray the Lord my work well done
     (P.S. O Lord, give me my reward in HEAVEN!)[51]

Figure 6. "You Join the I.W.W." Stickerette by Ralph Chaplin (3″ ×
2¼″). Black and red on white. By permission of the Washington State Historical Society, Tacoma, copy from *American West* 5 (January 1968): 21.

The "Prayer" parodies the mentality of the blindered, dutiful American
worker who would never think of seeking the reward for his labors on
earth. Although this parody effectually ridicules the Protestant work eth-
ic as well as home-spun religion, it also potentially appeals to such American ideals as self-improvement and Yankee shrewdness.

The intermixture of verse and visual design in the IWW's stickerettes
singles them out as relatively sophisticated "commercial" art. The stickerettes offer a tangible link between poetic language and advertising slogans – a concrete connection between registers that literary criticism customarily separates by a wide margin, if it even bothers to acknowledge
advertising materials as texts worth examining. But like any effective advertisement, the stickerettes directed attention not to their own materi-
ality but to the reality and desirability of the product advertised. However arresting the IWW stickerettes might be formally, their fierce advocacy
of revolutionary unionism constantly mitigated against any reaction like
aesthetic contemplation, as did the Wobbly practice of pasting them in
places where the stickers themselves would do the work of sabotage. The

stickerette advertisement in the inside back cover of *Songs of the Workers*, ninth edition, hinted at the possibility of using stickerettes to "use a little black cat on the boss": the notice claims they were "designed especially for use on the job and on the road," "publicity agents that work everywhere and all the time," and "just the thing to wise up the slave, jolt the scissorbill and throw the fear of the O.B.U. [One Big Union] into the boss."[52] So while Chaplin's stickerette picturing a black cat set in relief against a red moon is strikingly drawn, its being pasted up around a factory, or, as Chaplin suggests in trial testimony (7759), on the handle of a farmer's pitchfork, would be more inclined to embolden workers and annoy or even frighten their bosses than to provoke aesthetic admiration.[53] To heighten this effect, the stickerette's message echoes conventional warnings like "Beware of Dog" or "Danger: Extremely Flammable": "BEWARE" is printed on the top of the sticker, "SABOTAGE" on the bottom. Between each of these warnings and the black cat positioned at the center of the sticker Chaplin offers some fine print detailing the terms and the duration of the sabotage threat: "Good Pay or Bum Work // We Never Forget." Another stickerette proclaiming a similarly threatening strategy pictures a factory wheel with "SLOW DOWN" printed within. Below, the sticker offers a verse justifying and explaining the slowdown strategy: "The hours are long. / [T]he pay is small / So take your time / And buck them all."[54]

In the spring of 1917, more than a year after the first large printing of stickerettes, the IWW initiated a publicity campaign spearheaded by a mass printing even larger than the first. Thus, at about the time the U.S. government's wartime agencies and mobilization propaganda were being put in place, the IWW began its own publicity campaign aimed to mobilize workers in the cause of revolutionary unionism. But again, the IWW's strategy looks as much like head-to-head competition – however misguided – as subversion of the U.S. government. Indeed, given that the IWW's membership continued to grow in the summer of 1917, union leaders, though they recognized the IWW's minority status in American society, would not necessarily have been inclined to act as a disempowered, dissenting minority, one poaching at the edges of a hegemonic state. In March *Solidarity* announced: "Stickeretts [*sic*]. One million of them, black and red, new impressions, fifteen designs (four new ones)."[55] When these were quickly sold out, another 3 million were to be printed for distribution before May Day. During about the same period, approximately 65,000 foreign-language stickerettes were produced.[56] Stickerette mania grew so intense that a poem in *Solidarity*,

"Stick 'Em Up," dubbed May Day "Stickerette Day." Set to the popular tune of "Stung Right," the lyric concisely summed up the dual function of the stickerettes – to intimidate the bosses and to exhort the workers:

> Now all the bosses and their stools will think they're out of luck
> To see the spots of black and red where Stickerettes are stuck;
> And after they have scratched them off and shook their fists and swore
> They'll turn around to find again about a dozen more.
>
> Upon the back of every truck, on packages and cards,
> Upon the boats and in the mines and in the railroad yards,
> From Maine to California and even further yet,
> No matter where you look you'll see a little Stickerette![57]

As a poem, set to a tune, that advertised stickerettes, "Stick 'Em Up" indicates the three basic forms of poetic propaganda used by the IWW: song, printed poetry, and stickerette art. With these three genres drawing upon and infiltrating American culture, the IWW could reasonably claim to have occupied ground at the center of that culture and might plausibly lay claim to a leading role within the labor movement.

That the IWW's art and political culture were read in 1917 and 1918 as subversive – indeed, that they continue to be read almost exclusively as revolutionary and countercultural – is to some extent a function of the IWW's inflammatory rhetoric. (Though read in the context of commercial advertising, the IWW's promises to overturn the established order are hardly less exaggerated than the claims for various patent medicines, ointments, and yeast cakes.) But this reading of the union stems as well from the construction of the IWW as a dangerous, seditious organization that was promulgated by the state and its interventionist allies. The IWW's growing strength put the union on a collision course with American capitalist institutions and, thus, also squarely in the path of U.S. war mobilization and wartime vigilantism. So did the IWW's blatantly antiwar propaganda. Yet the union was singled out for wartime suppression not simply because it posed some material threat to society, but also because of the symbolic challenge it posed to capitalism and militarism. The war did not demand the dismantling of the IWW; rather, it provided a convenient opportunity for suppressing an increasingly powerful, nettlesome voice speaking for the most oppressed of America's workers.

3

The Barbarians at the Gate
THE SOLDIER-POET AND THE GREAT
WAR IN BLACK AND WHITE

MY argument has asserted that certain groups which in retrospect appear marginal and dissenting in American culture, specifically the
Woman's Peace Party and the Industrial Workers of the World, were in
fact pivotal in politics and very much within the mainstream of cultural
production. This does not mean that the WPP or IWW was dominant in
society, but these groups were active in shaping politics in the United
States, and indeed contributed to defining the conditions under which
they were later to become very marginal indeed. In the period from August 1914 to April 1917, American society moved toward involvement in
the European war by lurches, not by a straight, swift, unchecked march,
and this was the case largely because no one social group, no one class interest, directed society and policy unilaterally.[1] American culture, always
composed of multiple centers and competing interests, consisted at this
time of a variety of especially conflicted struggles and of coalitions that
were only very loosely defined and constantly shifting. Political, class, ethnic, and racial minorities had considerable leverage in these struggles and
coalitions; they had opportunities to redraw the cultural and political map
in their favor, even while their interests and loyalties constantly remained
at risk of appropriation by groups and interests that, though not fully
hegemonic, remained more dominant politically.

In 1914 white, northeastern, middle- and upper-class Americans comprised the most culturally and politically privileged groups in the nation,
but they constituted neither an outright political majority nor an undis-
puted ruling bloc. The most Anglo- and Francophilic of Americans, they
were the most eager to support the Triple Entente against Germany, but
other Americans had to be persuaded of the necessity of taking a more

active role in the war. The German U-boat campaigns contributed to that end, especially when, as in the May 1915 sinking of the *Lusitania,* American lives were lost. But just as crucial was a redefinition of America's self-interest in global, rather than hemispheric, terms and an assertion of national identity and destiny as closely connected with the fate of Western European civilization. In effect, America's connection to the Great War was based on both a cultural and a racial ideal. The contradiction that Germany, historically at the center of that ideal's formation, was being targeted as its nemesis did not particularly matter. What mattered was the fact that Western superiority, morally and culturally, was being exposed as a sham, and its world superiority politically and practically seemed threatened by dissolution from within. Americans had to be made to care more about the incipient demise of European culture, and one way of accomplishing this feat was to disseminate its cultural artifacts and "values" more broadly, to propagate the sense of impending risk for those artifacts and values, but also to offer up a highly selective version of that cultural history so as to invoke sympathy toward Belgium, France, and Great Britain and antipathy toward Germany and Austria-Hungary. This was the set of tasks taken up by the northeastern publishing establishment, which found in war-poetry collections and anthologies precisely the kind of tangible cultural artifact that might persuade readers they shared a priceless cultural heritage with the Allied countries, and a heritage that demanded armed defense by the United States. In particular, this conception of a shared and embattled culture came to be embodied in the anthologized English soldier-poet as the number of England's war dead grew into the millions, as its soldier-poets (and soldier-poet martyrs) accumulated, and as these soldier-poets became known to American readers by means of a common language and a common racial identity.

Embracing such an identification with England's culture and its soldiers was, of course, more difficult for some American groups than others. German-Americans of recent migration to the United States certainly found such a move agonizing, if not impossible. Given that the cultural identity Americans were asked to assert was particularly European, perhaps even more problematic was the situation of African-Americans, who had been enslaved and were still oppressed by uniquely European and American institutions. Yet African-Americans did give their loyalty to the American state in time of war, led in large part by W. E. B. Du Bois's editorializing in the *Crisis,* the fast-growing organ of the National Association for the Advancement of Colored People. They did so for a variety of reasons: because they sought to strengthen their claim on democracy at home by fighting for democracy abroad; because in embracing certain ideals (including "democracy," but also "beauty"), they sought to claim the rights corresponding to those ideals; and because the values of martyrdom and heroism embodied in the soldier-poet were by no means simply immanent in the white, English soldier-poet, but were uniquely developed in black American culture as well. African-Americans had their soldier-poets too, both soldiers in the fight against racism and soldiers in the U.S. Army, and the two types reinforced each other and asserted an ideal of heroic masculinity readily assimilable to the general war mobilization.

I

At first there were few Americans, either the powerful or the disempowered, who saw any reason for the United States to get involved in the European war. *Contemporary War Poems,* the first anthology of war poetry to appear in America during the war, gives some sense of how drastically politics and society – or at least the balance of power within them – would have to change for intervention to take place. As we have already noted, the American Association for International Conciliation, backed by the Carnegie Foundation, did not represent an especially activist or progressive political coalition: it was a loose assemblage of financiers and lawyers who saw international peace as good for their business. Yet the Association's anthology suggests that in 1914 American poets writing about the war were universally appalled by the European war and were opposed to U.S. intervention. We have already noted the considerable number of poems in the collection offering economic – and class – arguments about the war's origins and continuation. Introducing the collection, John Erskine argues that the roughness of its verses results from the barbarity of the war, whose shock would not yet permit writers to describe it in refined aesthetic forms: "When we have become hardened to this war or have got further away from its horrors," Erskine remarks, "we may begin to make literary use of them, but at present, it seems, the poets and their readers think it a kind of sacrilege to convert any of this stupendous misery to the purposes of art."[2] Erskine believes that the collection as a whole asserts each individual's freedom to refuse participation in the war, supporting "the right of the common man to enjoy life, peace and safety" and likewise "woman's right to decide whether she will pay the penalty that war always exacts of her" (*CW* 6).[3] If the Association's membership did not match its poets in antiwar fervor, the previous publishers of the poems certainly indicate something of the breadth of antiwar sentiment among American periodical presses: the *Bookman, Outlook, Nation, Independent, Columbia Jester,* and *San Francisco Bulletin;* the *Boston Globe* and *Evening Transcript;* the *New York Times, Tribune, Globe, World, American, Evening Journal, Evening Sun,* and *Evening Post.* Poets appearing in the collection include some of the best-known writers of the period, among them Conrad Aiken, Percy MacKaye, Clinton Scollard, and Edith M. Thomas.

The selections in *Contemporary War Poems* not only describe war's cost for women; some even declare support for women's pacifist activism. Edith Thomas's "We Mourn for Peace" conveys utter scorn for patriotic slogans of whatever kind: "Your 'Glory' is to us but venomous breath! / A-near our hearts your 'causes' do not lie – / Nor one, nor other, O ye warring States!" Going further, the poem unmasks the complicity demanded of women in conducting war, pledging that women will never cooperate:

> And we are they whom ye shall ask in vain,
> In home's dear covert to remain –
> Praying at home – yet serving still your needs,
> Yielding to you our sons, our brothers and our mates –
> We mourn for World-Peace slain –
> We mourn – but oh, not that alone!
> A heresy through all our ranks is blown:
> The order old is changing – shall not come again;
> No more shall tender cowardice restrain,
> The "Call of Country" shall betray no more,
> To trick our tears in bravery of a smile,
> Gazing upon the glittering file
> Of those that march away to war (so fain!) –
> Of whom what remnant shall their fate restore? (*CW* 20)

Written "For the Peace Parade, August 29," Thomas's poem describes the feminist rationale that underlay the subsequent organization, in January 1915, of the Woman's Peace Party. Another poem, "Woman and War" by U.S. Army captain W. E. P. French, though not directly linked to political activism, is just as fierce as Thomas's poem in its denunciations of the powerful and its defense of the marginalized. The poem describes the response of a woman whose son has been killed in battle, who directs blame toward the leaders of her own country, asking bitterly, "What have I done to you, Brothers, – War-Lord and Land-Lord and Priest, – / That my son should rot on the blood-smeared earth where the raven and buzzard feast?" She insists that her son "was slain for your power and profit – aye, murdered at your behest," while deriding the patriotic rhetoric that would conceal their crime: "You prate of duty and honor, of a patriot's glorious death, / Of love of country, heroic deeds – nay, for shame's sake, spare your breath!" (CW 16).

If, however, the writers in Contemporary War Poems are united in their outcry against the war, some of their protests are clearly grounded in discourses that might, in time, be used to construct an alliance with one or more of the combatants. For example, even as "Woman and War" claims women's moral authority to denounce war, the author's status as a soldier adds further credibility to the poem's account of war. But, of course, the military was not, and never has been, the most likely place to find opponents of war and critics of patriotism. Matching the antiwar soldier-poet French, for example, was "Uncle Sam's Soldier-Poet, Capt. Steunenberg, Famous in the Army," as he was hailed in the New York Times on October 25, 1914. George Steunenberg, an Idahoan who had served and risen in rank in the Spanish-American War, wrote poetry that was decidedly ungenteel and even antiestablishment, and that otherwise reflected American nativist and antiprogressive prejudice. His poem "The Feline Curse of Leavenworth," satirizing an army attempt to rid Camp Leavenworth of thousands of cats (forty thousand in the poem), finds offense in women's reform as well as government meddling in Cuba:

> Send 'em back to Boston, that highly favored land,
> Where maiden girls are plentiful and cats are in demand;
> Give the Yankee maids a chance to turn 'em into pets,
> Or ship 'em all to London to repel the suffragettes;
> Send 'em 'round the earth to conquer all creation;
> Chase 'em down to Guthrie town to tackle Carrie Nation;
> Or, if you can persuade 'em all to take the right direction,
> Drive 'em down to Cuba to control the next election.
> Bad cats, mad cats, reveling in scraps;
> Send 'em to the Golden Gate to scare away the Japs;
> For how could old Kuroki ever gain a footing there,
> With all the cats of Leavenworth a-clawing at his hair?[4]

While catching the antiprogressive spirit that was soon to dominate U.S. politics, Steunenberg also seems to have been in the vanguard regarding American attitudes toward Germany. As the Times reports, publication of Steunenberg's poem "The German Trained Army of the Turks" two years before had "caused, it will be remembered, a racket in diplomatic circles that almost equaled that created by the lamented Admiral Coghlan's world-renowned 'Hoch der Kaiser.' " Steunenberg's political gibes earned him an official reprimand from the chief of the army, Major General Leonard Wood, and kept the poem out of Steunenberg's soon to be published collection, *Songs of a Soldier,* because, the *Times* says with a gibe of its own, "the Kaiser might consider its publication a violation of neutrality."[5] Not only American newspaper editors but anthologists were soon to discover the cultural authority of anti-German soldier-poets, and they found a ready supply in English soldier-poets who had the advantages both of sharing a common language with most Americans and of remaining, by a vast majority, staunchly patriotic.

The kind of discourse about race, cultural value, and national politics suggested in Steunenberg's poem was also described in *Contemporary War Poems.* In "The Mad War," Richard Butler Glaezner does not hesitate to assign blame to the national leaders who formed the fateful alliances leading to world war. He finds horrible incongruity in comparing the immediate origin of the war – "one man, one man, was slain – / No more a man than you or I" – with the worldwide consequences; he implores, "Must nations suffer murder's stain, / Millions be made to die?" But the lines that follow, even as they criticize the war policies of both sides in the conflict – the tragedy of inflexible alliances, the blasphemy of Christian "just wars" – also seem grounded in views that presume the superiority of Caucasians over Asians:

> One group of three who fraternise
>   To-day, though once close locked in hate,
> To thwart another three must rise,
>   All blaming all on Fate.
>
> Christians, they prate of "Triplices"
>   As if of pledges made to God.
> What is the Trinity to these
>   Who trample life roughshod?
>
> The civilised! The civilised! –
>   Smug irony of modern cant!
> Culture so blind, self-idolised,
>   The East may well supplant. (*CW* 9–10)

"The East" has not supplanted the West, but with the Russian and Japanese War of 1905 in the background, the poem suggests that the East should be considered a serious threat to the West's world domination. From this racist vantage point, is not some form of Western alliance based on common religion, culture, and race in sight? For more than one American writer, race and politics were aligned, and could be mapped geographically proceeding from east to west, with the feudal oligarchies of the East on one end of the political spectrum, the constitutional monarchies of Europe in the center, and the democratic institutions of America on the progressive end. At the time *Contemporary War Poems* was published, this political, racial, and geographical continuum marked off the United States as uniquely enlightened and all countries across the Atlantic Ocean, to the east, as corrupt and backward. In "America" Conrad Aiken describes Europe's resort to military might as a "murderous shadow" that blocks out the sun, a "sick and fetid wind . . . from the stale tenements of the east." Aiken fears not only contagion from across the ocean but also, more alarming, complicity from within the United States to "prove us brother to the beast" (*CW* 33). Yet Aiken's two key metaphors warning against involvement in Europe – contagion and familial relations – would soon be used to justify that involvement, as American sympathizers with Britain, France, and Belgium were to claim *they* were the democracies that faced a contagion from *their* east, while claiming too that America owed fidelity to those countries as a brother, nephew, uncle, or child (the terms are almost always specifically masculine).

Still further, construction of the United States as morally and politically superior, even as it construes Europe as corrupt, might offer it up as a kind of international champion of justice and democracy. To Percy MacKaye, a well-known dramatist and poet,[6] the European war was the result of political and social institutions that had long been girding for it. In his sonnet "Destiny" he writes that "Europe acts to-day / Epics that little children in their play / Conjured, and statesmen murmured in their creeds; / In barrack, court and school were sown those seeds." The sestet, offering American democracy as antidote to this militaristic system, sees European-style military preparedness as precisely antithetical to that democratic system:

> Mock, then, no more at dreaming, lest our own
> Create for us a like reality!
> Let not imagination's soil be sown
> With armed men but justice, so that we
> May for a world of tyranny atone
> And dream from that despair – democracy. (*CW* 22)

The poem is explicit about the diametrical opposition of militarism and preparedness. But once such an opposition is undermined by the "commonsense" assertion that democracy must be defended, the poem's positioning of America as a world ideal of justice and democracy might – and did – contribute to an assertion that America must make the world "safe for democracy."

That such a change could be worked in a few years or even a few months is amply demonstrated by the changing commitments of a number of writers involved in the production of *Contemporary War Poems*. By 1917 MacKaye reversed his earlier warning against involvement in Europe, publishing "The Battle Call of Alliance" in the *New York Times* on May 6, 1917, and the book *Roll Call: A Masque of the Red Cross* in 1918. Scollard proclaimed his pro-Allied sympathies sooner, publishing *Italy in Arms, and Other Poems* in 1915, *Ballads: Patriotic and Romantic* in 1916, and *Let the Flag Wave, and Other Verses in War-Time* in 1917.[7] During the war Thomas published thirty-nine poems in the consistently pro-Allied *New York Times,* and her poetry collection *The White Messenger, and Other War Poems,* published in the fall of 1915, already included anti-German diatribes alongside her pacifist writing from the first months of the war.[8] All three of these writers also appeared in the Vigilantes' inaugural poetry collection, *Fifes and Drums,* published in June 1917. Even John Erskine, so passionate in his denunciation of the war when introducing *Contemporary War Poems,* gave wholehearted support to the war effort when the United States intervened. In 1918 and 1919, he served with the American Expeditionary Force as chairman of the Army Educational Commission, and in 1919 worked as well as educational director of the AEF university at Beaune, France.[9] Unlike members of radical organizations and persons of foreign birth, these writers, upstanding citizens of Northern European descent, were never subject to coercive public or government pressure to alter their early antiwar attitudes. They became avid supporters of the war as a consequence of less overt pressures and seemingly free, individual choices. In large part, the country's preparedness debate took place in the context of these kinds of subtle ideological (often conceived of as personal) impulses, which transformed well-educated Americans' perceptions of the war, its main participants, and their relationship with those participants.

II

The issues of race and cultural allegiance that were to provide the grounds for U.S. intervention were obviously approached very differently by

African-Americans. For W. E. B. Du Bois and the NAACP, then in its
first decade of existence, the ideologies of imperialism and racist hatred
were perfectly obvious in the conduct of all the European combatants.[10]
With a circulation of some 25,000 to 30,000 by the fall of 1914, averag-
ing more than 30,000 in 1915, the *Crisis*, edited and often largely authored by Du Bois, provided an ample vehicle for addressing black America – not as a mass-circulation magazine, but as a political magazine
rivaling the largest socialist periodicals in subscriptions.[11] Seldom did the
NAACP find itself precisely in step with public opinion among white
Americans. While Du Bois, in his November 1914 *Crisis* editorial, declares his sympathy for England and France, he argues that all the European combatants are to blame for the conflict, based on a shared history
of economic exploitation of non-European colonies. "To-day civilized
nations are fighting like mad dogs," Du Bois writes, "over the right to
own and exploit . . . darker peoples." Even Belgium, whose "rape" served
as the pivot for turning American opinion against the Central Powers,
did not escape Du Bois's censure: "Belgium has been as pitiless and grasp-
ing as Germany and in strict justice deserves every pang she is suffering
after her unspeakable atrocities in the Congo."[12] Events that shook the
confidence of contributors in *Contemporary War Poems* – their faith in the
total superiority of European civilization – served to vindicate Du Bois
and other African-Americans in their long-standing criticism of European imperialism and exploitation. Much like American socialists, Du
Bois saw in the Great War the confirmation of all that he and other critics of race in the United States had declared about the economic and social inequities of Western civilization.

Du Bois's criticism was enunciated from a position even more marginalized than that of the socialists, but it was also a more equivocal position, both because he saw the war as the proving ground for people of
color and because his admiration for Western culture was profound and
acknowledged. From the very opening days of the war, Du Bois and other commentators in the *Crisis* saw great significance in dark-skinned soldiers from the colonies arriving in Europe to fight in the interests of their
colonizers. Never mind that their exploits were seldom acknowledged or
that Europe saw its colonial subjects as repaying a debt of gratitude for
the gift of civilization; Du Bois and other *Crisis* contributors found the
power of the non-European world everywhere manifest. Featured in the
November 1914 *Crisis* was a two-page illustration of French Senegalese
troops in review; below the original, paternalistic caption, "Out of Africa
Have I Called My Son," was added the *Crisis*'s gloss, "Black Soldiers from
Senegal Fighting to Protect the Civilization of Europe against Itself."[13]

A photograph in the next month's edition makes essentially the same point. A black rifleman from Congo is pictured before a group of white women, the spiked helmet of a German officer in his hand, and below is the caption "A Black 'Heathen' of the Congo, fighting to protect the wives and daughters of the white Belgians, who have murdered and robbed his people, against 'Christian' Culture represented by the German trophy in his hand!"[14] The following month offered a still more telling demonstration of the significance of the black man in the war. The two-page illustration in the January 1915 *Crisis*, a reproduction of Paul Thiriat's painting *The Desperate Attempt of General von Kluck to Break the Allied Line on the Marne*, featured Senegalese troops taking a leading role in throwing back the Germans at the famous battle.[15] For Du Bois, such martial accomplishment held out the tantalizing promise of African-Americans proving themselves by acts of patriotic heroism, made all the more outstanding by the fact that white American society had done little since Reconstruction to merit such allegiance. While Du Bois sharply criticized the European powers, his adulation of French colonial troops fighting on the Marne dates from the period when the intellectuals and poets of *Contemporary War Poems* were decrying the bloodbath on the Western Front.

Reports of black soldiers distinguishing themselves – and being killed – among the ranks of the Triple Entente provided the groundwork for African-Americans to identify with the Western alliance of Britain, France, and Belgium. Meanwhile, homefront politics provided other reasons for black Americans to be disposed toward the Allied cause. Theodore Roosevelt, an early champion of intervention, was remembered as the president who had invited Booker T. Washington to the White House, and his version of progressive Republicanism was viewed as more supportive of black civil rights than was the Democratic regime of the neutral Woodrow Wilson, who was beholden to southern Democrats and was Virginia-born himself. When provided with a prerelease screening of D. W. Griffith's *Birth of a Nation*, the unprecedentedly popular film of 1915 that shamelessly linked pacifism with a defense of the ante bellum South and the Ku Klux Klan, Wilson had remarked, "It is like writing history with lightning. And my only regret is that it is all so terribly true."[16] Wilson's remarks, widely publicized by Griffith, gave the film instant visibility and helped to get it past censors wary of its racism. The NAACP, on the other hand, immediately denounced *Birth of a Nation* and made its suppression an organizational priority rivaling its campaign to end lynching.

As if it were not enough for certain partisans of neutrality to adopt racist interpretations of U.S. history – indeed, to call into question the validity of the war that emancipated the slaves – the colonial soldiers dying in France were being viciously slandered from another quarter. In the German-American monthly the *Fatherland,* editor George Sylvester Viereck sought, in the opening months of the war, to exploit U.S. racism by making precisely the point being made by Du Bois – that black troops played a considerable role in the battles of 1914. But that which Du Bois saw as a source of race pride Viereck cast as an object of racist scorn. "We and the World," a poem by Hanns Heinz Ewers translated from the German, argues that it was Germany, not the Triple Entente, which was beset by aggressive, superior military forces. Not only was Germany surrounded in Europe, Ewers claims; it was also being threatened by France's and England's African colonials:

> With Sengalese [*sic*] Negroes, oh shameful time!
> The Frenchman supports his troops.
> With the desert's outcasts, the earth's slime
> With them and others to boot;
> And out of Britannia's gigantic lap
> Forth come the Negro, the Hindu, the Jap;
> And as the English bagpipes play
> Five hundred million slaves will prey
> Upon one and crave for the loot.[17]

This was published on September 23, 1914, among seven other stanzas emphasizing the perfidies of Germany's European neighbors. As if to emphasize that the racism in Ewers's poem was the rule rather than the exception, the *Fatherland* provided an illustration two pages later in which a female figure, "Civilization," is being defended by spike-helmeted German soldiers against "Mongol," Indian, and African soldiers.[18] While Helmholz Junker's cartoon contains a species of imperialist critique, as the colonials are being (literally) whipped and prodded into battle, the polarity of white civilization versus colored barbarism is its central organizing principle, and its most prominent stylistic feature is racist caricature (Figure 7). Later the *Fatherland* tried to mobilize opinion against Great Britain and France on the basis of their colonial exploitation rather than through an identification between the Allies and their "barbaric" colonials. But the best that pro-Germanists seemed able to do on the issue of race was to let English critics of Anglo imperialism do the talking for them. Frank Harris, an English expatriate, concludes in his *England or Germany – Which?,* published in 1915, "Ever since the iniquitous South

Figure 7. "Germany: Defender of Civilization against the Barbarian Host." Cartoon by S. Helmholz Junker, *Fatherland* 1.7 (September 23, 1914): 11. By permission of Peter Viereck.

African war I have felt that England's success and England's material prosperity taken together with her low spiritual ideal constitute the gravest danger to the cause of civilization in the world!"[19] In its November 4, 1914, issue, the *Fatherland* reprinted a nineteenth-century poem by the English politician Henry Labouchere, radical M.P. from 1865 to 1880. "Where Is the Flag of England?" finds the Union Jack wherever there is exploitation, want, and death:

> . The Maori, full of hate, curses
>   With his fleeting, dying breath,
> And the Arab hath hissed his curses
>   As he spat at its [the flag's] folds in death.

The hapless fellah hath feared it
  On Tel el Kebir's parched plain,
And the blood of the Zulu hath stained it
  With a deep, indelible stain.[20]

This stanza could have appeared in the *Crisis* as well as the *Fatherland*.[21] But following on the heels of "We and the World," its accompanying cartoon, and indeed similarly offensive poems and cartoons published on October 21 (Frederick Martens's poem "A White Man's War" and the cartoon "Recruits of English Culture"),[22] the advocate of "Fair Play for Germany and Austria-Hungary" revealed its defense of exploited minorities as the most cynical and self-interested of political strategies. To the extent that the *Fatherland* represented German-Americans' attitudes toward black Americans — and the magazine, boasting a readership of 100,000 in the fall of 1914, certainly purported to be representative[23] — it is not difficult to see why black intellectuals might identify with France and England, which, though they exploited black troops' labor, did not vilify them. Given the economic and political disenfranchisement black Americans endured at home, it is possible to see the appeal of standing on equal footing with white Europeans — and white Americans — on the battlefields of France.

It may not be surprising, then, that the first poetry anthologist to posit a link between American and English interests in the war was a black American, William Stanley Braithwaite, the son of West Indian immigrants and an editor at the *Boston Transcript*.[24] Beginning in 1913, Braithwaite edited a yearly anthology of magazine verse, a practice he would continue through 1929.[25] Unlike better-known (but less widely distributed) imagist and avant-garde collections, Braithwaite's anthologies are eclectic, reflecting not only the coming of "new poetry" but also the continuing cultural influence of the genteel. Braithwaite's collections engage directly with the relationship between culture and the world war. His *Anthology of Magazine Verse for 1915* published war poems eulogizing the dead and condemning Germany's misdeeds, including "The Pyres" by Hermann Hagedorn, soon to be founder of the Vigilantes, "Sing, Ye Trenches" by Helen Coale Crew, "The White Ships and the Red" by Joyce Kilmer, "The Return of August" by Percy MacKaye, and "Battle Sleep" by Edith Wharton. Other war poems in Braithwaite's 1915 anthology included Ridgely Torrence's "A Vision of Spring," James Oppenheim's "The Laughters," Josephine Preston Peabody's "Harvest Moon, 1914," E. Sutton's "The Wind in the Corn," and Amy Lowell's

"The Bombardment."[26] Of these, only Percy MacKaye's and Joyce Kilmer's entries explicitly declare their partisanship for the Allies, but none are explicitly opposed to war, and taken together the selections establish the Great War as an important theme for serious (anthologized) American poetry.

Even as Braithwaite was setting the pattern for poetry anthologies to come, by the time his *Anthology of Magazine Verse for 1916* was published, he knew himself to be part of a growing consensus among eastern intellectuals about the justice of the Allied cause. In supporting Germany, Frank Harris and George Viereck stood virtually alone; Professor Hugo Münsterberg, author of *The War and America* (1914) and *The Peace and America* (1915), was perhaps the best known of a handful of German-American university professors who defended Germany's war policy.[27] Historical and political analyses favoring the Triple Entente, if not favoring U.S. intervention, were the main stock in trade of the established northeastern publishing houses. H. G. Well's 1914 book *The War That Will End War* supplied the phrase that would become one of President Wilson's chief rallying cries in 1917,[28] and Wells's books in support of England were published and distributed in the United States throughout the war. Still more important was the impressive but often erroneous *Alleged German Outrages,* compiled by the English Bryce Committee and, at the prompting of the British propaganda ministry, published in 1915 by the American firm of Macmillan.[29] These books by English authors were soon joined by many written by Americans: in 1914, Albert Bushnell Hart's *The War in Europe,* the first book-length study to urge military preparedness in the United States; in 1915, Newell Dwight Hillis's *Studies of the Great War,* Clarence W. Barron's *The Audacious War,* and Edward Van Zile's *The Game of Empires: A Warning to America;* and in 1916, Robert Herrick's *The World Decision.*[30] The increasingly strident advocacy of these "studies" is suggested by Van Zile's chapter headings, including "The Immorality of Weakness," "Valor Versus Avoidance," and "The Religion of Steadfastness," or by Herrick's verdict on the peace movement: "Americans, having evaded the responsibility of pronouncing a decisive moral judgment on the rape of Belgium, the sinking of the *Lusitania,* and the extermination of the Armenians, play the buffoon with women's peace conferences, peace ships, and endless impertinent peace talk."[31] Thus, even as Braithwaite sought to represent the best of American magazine verse by featuring war verse and especially verse favoring the cause of England, France, and Belgium, his anthology of 1915 is representative of the partisan and interventionist sentiments coming to dominate attitudes among America's political and intellectual elite.

Braithwaite's *Anthology of Magazine Verse for 1916* offered further evidence – and support – for that trend. Although the anthology was not dedicated exclusively to war verse (a fifth of the poems, approximately, address topics related to the war), Braithwaite credits the war with having catalyzed an intellectual and poetic renaissance:

> I believe that inscrutably and mysteriously the forces which a generation have been preparing for the present European war, have also by an unusual combination of spiritual circumstances brought about the renaissance of poetry in both England and America. The fermentation of national affairs has always antedated the spiritual flowering. The evidence that the two are related shows in the fact that around the pivot of a war in which the conscience of the world is brought to judgment a vigorous and productive creative era prevails.[32]

Braithwaite's argument here seems to run as follows. First, Braithwaite recognizes positive consequences arising from the war: he sees an intellectual, moral, and aesthetic renewal, and for proof he submits a book of "first-rate poetry." As such, it stands as a beginning refutation of the isolationists and pacifists who would say nothing good comes of war. Second, Braithwaite redefines the war in moral and spiritual terms, about which "conscience" can render an unambiguous verdict. The great European war, he indicates, offers one of those rare conflicts where "the social mind of the most intellectual portions of the human race" is forced "to decide between advocates that [seek] to rule through one or the other forces of tyranny or liberty."[33] Third, Braithwaite makes it perfectly evident which nation involved in the present conflict advocates liberty: England – the one that along with the United States had experienced a "renaissance in poetry."

Given that Braithwaite seems to have been the first American critic to include war poetry in a substantial anthology – to bestow upon it the laurel of literary accomplishment as well as the mantle of historical significance – we might see Braithwaite's work as far more influential than has been previously allowed. Certainly Braithwaite was not first to put forward the notion that the Great War might stimulate artistic production; for one, Brander Matthews had suggested it in the *New York Times* of September 13, 1914.[34] But David Perkins discounts Braithwaite's importance overmuch when he emphasizes the conventionality of Braithwaite's work, describing his views on poetry as "genteelly conventional to a remarkable degree" and his verse as "often whimsical, sometimes vaguely mystical, and usually insipid."[35] Even if Braithwaite's poetic taste and critical perspective are highly derivative, Perkins overrates the cultural power of innovation and underrates that of convention – to say nothing of the potential influence in editing a major poetry anthology yearly for fifteen years, as Braithwaite did. In any case, as an anthologist and poetry editor Braithwaite was at least as much an arbiter of poetic conventions as he was an amanuensis. And if Braithwaite appears to accept "white" aesthetic standards too readily, we must remember that his affiliation with black culture and politics was also firmly established. W. E. B. Du Bois lionized him as one of the "talented tenth" whom he enjoined black readers to emulate. In a March 1915 editorial, Du Bois directs aspiring poets to examine one of Braithwaite's anthologies to study the craft of poetry; in August 1915 he is a contributor to a series of articles supporting the women's suffrage movement (the only poet included); and his verse appeared regularly in the pages of the *Crisis*.[36] Recognizing the early identification of Du Bois with black soldiers fighting for France, and noting too the explicitness of German racism against those soldiers, we can make a case that Braithwaite, Du Bois, and black attitudes about the war established a dialectical and constructive relationship with the evolving American sympathies for the Triple Entente.

III

The kind of rhetorical exercise Braithwaite offers in his introduction defines a commonplace mode for war-poetry anthologies of 1916 through 1919. Braithwaite's rhetoric, it must be noted, suppresses racial difference and struggle much more completely than does Du Bois's, which focuses on the African identities of some of the soldiers fighting in France. Race difference within American society, and between Europe and its colonies, is effectively displaced by a form of ethnic and national antagonism toward Germany – an antagonism that is also racial insofar as the Germans come to be known by the sinister, ethnically indeterminate designation "Huns." This transformation of race difference, a signal feature of Braithwaite's strategy, is also central to the work of the white anthologists following him. Through their anthologies, U.S. participation in the Great War became a matter of national destiny and responsibility: a matter of destiny because America's democratic heritage supposedly placed it on a collision course with autocratic Germany; a matter of responsibility because vigorous America seemed the only resource capable of saving Western civilization from the "Hun" onslaught. But furthermore, pro-Allied anthologies not only linked U.S. interests with those of the Allies, but also merged America's cultural identity with the identities of Britain and France, so that American poets and editors professed to be swayed not so much by Allied appeals from "over there" as by the inner promptings of their own conscience and being. War-poetry anthologies, which increasingly became soldier-poetry anthologies, offered an outlet for American poets to express their kinship with Britain, France, and Belgium; they also provided tangible evidence of a shared culture – books of poems written in a language and a literary tradition shared with England. In this merging of Anglo and American identities, race reemerges with the effect of excluding black Americans, once again, from full American citizenship.

The poems in pro-Allied anthologies were hardly less polemical than those in *Contemporary War Poems,* a slim pamphlet of sixty pages; they were, however, packaged in hardbound volumes of hundreds of pages, merchandise that by its weight, price, and workmanship proclaimed a substantial heritage and, at the same time, offered a collective opinion on the war that by its unanimity would appear to be a national consensus. Their editors professed, like anthologists before and after, that the books offered the best poetry available, not merely the best of one particular style or perspective. Such claims could only make the poems' nearly univocal endorsement of the Allies all the more persuasive. This is, indeed, the claim of J. W. Cunliffe in *Poems of the Great War,* the first hardbound anthology from an American press dedicated exclusively to war poetry (Macmillan, in 1916): "While poetic merit has been, of course, the paramount consideration, I have endeavored to exercise a catholic judgment, and to give fair representation to various schools of thought and expression as well as to the various phases of the War."[37] But from the start Cunliffe's collection tilts toward the Allied cause; even the book's organization necessarily suggests a particular alignment of nations. The table of contents divides the poems into five national groups: Australia, Canada, India, the United Kingdom, and the United States. Titles in the first three sections indicate the absolute loyalty of Britain's crown colonies to their motherland: "Australia to England," "Australians to the Front," "Canada to England," "To Shakespeare, 1916," "Mother of Nations," "India to England." Most remarkable, given the colonial subjection of India, is the solidarity proclaimed by Nizamat Jung: "Thine equal justice, mercy, grace

/ Have made a distant alien race / A part of thee." Jung's "India to England" concludes:

> They, whom thy love hath guarded long;
> They, whom thy care hath rendered strong
>   In love and faith,
> Their heartstrings round thy heart entwine,
> They are, they ever will be, thine
>   In life – in death. (GW 140–41)

Given these sentiments and the book's organization, *Poems of the Great War* takes on the character of a British anthology that happens to include poems by England's "offspring" nations, including "adopted" India.

Jung's attitude, like Braithwaite's, suggests that ideologies of cultural value, even when explicitly grounded in white, European traditions, could readily enough be assimilated by nonwhite colonized citizens. In one way or another, people of color also saw their identities and interests as defined by the European culture being threatened by the "Huns." We need not automatically take this as a matter of Marxist "false consciousness," for citizens of color, whether black Americans or Indian subjects of Britain, recognized all too clearly their own marginality and the political risks that would accompany dissent. This is not, of course, to say that a more radical race critique of the nation-state would not be useful; such a critique was (and is) certainly necessary for African-Americans as a group to challenge white supremacy. In Cunliffe's *Poems of the Great War*, it is left to a white writer, Karle Wilson Baker, to raise the issue of race prejudice. Baker's "Unser Gott," one of a few dissenting poems in the collection, not only interrogates the just-war rationales that mobilized the European combatants but also, by exploring racial tensions along the color line between black and white Americans, threatens to undermine the relatively stable, homogeneous national identity needed, practically and symbolically, for the United States to intervene in the European war. The poem does not entirely question the anti-German premise of most poems in the book; as the poem's title implies, it takes Germany as its chief negative example of myopic nationalism:

> THEY held a great prayer-service in Berlin,
> And augured German triumph from some words
> Said to be spoken by the Jewish God
> To Gideon, which signified that He
> Was staunchly partial to the Israelites. (GW 11)

Unlike virtually every other poem in the collection, "Unser Gott" recognizes how nationalist prayers to a Judeo-Christian God exclude non-Western, non-European perspectives. The narrator's declaration that "we have all made our God too small" turns toward unusually frank self-examination:

> (Yet it is hard
> To make Him big enough! For me, I like
> The English and the Germans and the French,
> The Russians, too; and Servians, I should think,
> Might well be very interesting to God.
> But, do the best I may, my God is white,
> And hardly takes a nigger seriously
> This side of Africa. Not those, at least
> Who steal my wood, and of a summer night
> Keep me awake with shouting, where they sit
> With monkey-like fidelity and glee
> Grinding through their well-oiled sausage-mill –
> The dead machinery of the white man's church –
> Raw jungle-fervor, mixed with scraps sucked dry
> Of Israel's old sublimities: not those.
> And when they threaten us, the Higher Race,
> Think you, which side is God's? Oh, let us pray
> Lest blood yet spurt to wash that black skin white,
> As now it flows because a German hates
> A Cossack, and an Austrian a Serb!) (13)

The self-examination is limited. While operating through a distinct persona, the poem does not altogether undermine the malicious racial stereotypes suggested by comparing Christian African-Americans to monkeys and by portraying the blacks in his neighborhood as thieves. Perhaps most invidious of all is the speaker's apparent wish that black skin might not yet be purified and, below this, the implication that black skin somehow *needs* purification. Yet in spite of its continuing racist assumptions, the poem does raise the issue of race in ways that destabilize the Eurocentrism and self-righteousness of American responses to the war.

In the wider context of the anthology, however, the inclusion of a poem such as Baker's seems principally to signify an editorial open-mindedness that is nevertheless overwhelmed by a poetic consensus focusing on the European theater and largely accepting the premise that a close, familial relationship exists between the United States and England (rather

than between, say, the United States and West Africa). Scores of poems
by American authors articulate such Anglo-Americanism. Elizabeth
Townsend Swift's "From America" straightforwardly proclaims the superiority of the English perspective over the American. American ethnic
diversity seems in the poem to comprise a national weakness, a plurality
of perspectives needing to be sublimated to a purer, less conflicted attitude and identity:

> We who are neutral (Yet each lip with fervor
>   The word abjures):
> Oh, England, never name us the time-server!
>   Our hearts are yours:
>
> We that so glory in your high decision,
>   So trust your goal;
> All Europe in our blood, but yours our vision,
>   Our speech, our soul! (*GW* 252)

Few poems in Cunliffe's collection are so willing to submit absolutely to
England's will. Yet with few exceptions in the rest of the collection,
American independence of mind does not involve criticism of the conduct of Britain or its allies; it consists merely in an ability to identify with
all the different Allied countries. Most prominent is U.S. support for
France in poems like "Vive la France!" "Honor to France," "O Glorious
France," and "The American Volunteers." Marie Van Vorst's "The American Volunteers," like Swift's "From America," scorns America's neutrality: "NEUTRAL! America, you cannot give / To your sons' souls neutrality. . . . // Neutral! We who go forth with sword and lance, / A little
band to swell the battle's flow, / Go willingly, to pay again to France /
Some of the debt we owe" (*GW* 273). Another obvious object of sympathy – and occasion for moral outrage – was the plight of Belgium.
Reginald Wright Kauffman offers a poem about Belgium titled "The Nations' David" (142) and Marion Couthoy Smith provides another called
"Heart of All the World" (242), while Edith Wharton's "Belgium" declares the country, though "homeless," "The home of all that makes [great
nations] great" (285).

Even as the American selections in Cunliffe's collections depict U.S.
citizens and writers with their gaze directed outward and across the sea,
devoutly desiring a wider role in the world and especially in the war to
save European civilization, many of the British poems look back across
the Atlantic, where they hope to forge an alliance with the United States

and even aggressively lobby for it. "Neutral?" by Harold Begbie appeals "To the Humanity of America," challenging Americans to condemn Germany's assault on Belgium. Begbie asserts that Belgium's destruction can be avenged by British military forces. No Americans will have to die for Belgium's sake, but he urges the United States to take the side of freedom and justice:

> We ask not that of all your hosts
>   One man, one sword be sacrificed:
> Your cousins guard these ancient coasts,
>   Your kinsmen charge this Antichrist:
> But we expect your mighty voice
>   With judgment through the world to run,
> O land of freedom, make your choice,
>   Are you for Belgium or the Hun?

Begbie appeals to America as a family member, he flatters the American sense of justice and legacy of freedom; at the same time he attempts to reduce the war to a conflict between good and evil, so that if Americans fail to stand up for Belgium they will be shamed even by their children: "Your children judge you if you stand / In hearing of the Belgian cry, / Not only with the folded hand, / But with the cold, averted eye!" (*GW* 15–16).

Begbie's propaganda operates through a direct appeal to American ideals and a dogmatic assertion about the justice of Britain's cause. Its categorical moral pronouncements, along with its high diction, point to a variety of poetics held in common with the American genteel tradition – and widely accepted by American readers. But Cunliffe's *Poems of the Great War* are not all genteel, even as they are not all as openly propagandistic as Begbie's. Certain poems reflect the literary affiliations between American and British modernist writers, and these modernist productions would presumably have appealed as well to cultural elites identifying with the new art and the new poetry. Richard Aldington's "War Yawp," while avoiding an explicit appeal for American sympathy, employs a casual, loose free verse to forge cultural identity between England and the United States. If the regular rhyme and meter, and the moral appeal, of Begbie's poem comprise a version of genteel propaganda, the free verse, puckish wit, and pragmatism of Aldington's poem exhibit a strain of modernist propaganda. Like Begbie's "Neutrality?" Aldington's poem asserts a familial relationship between the two countries:

America!
England's cheeky kid brother,
Who bloodily assaulted your august elder
At Bunker Hill and similar places
(Not mentioned in our history books),
What can I tell you of war or peace?
Say, have you forgotten 1861?
Bull Run, Gettysburg, Fredericksburg?
Your million dead?

But unlike Begbie's poem, Aldington's is lighthearted and honest enough to admit past and present differences between the two countries. Whereas Begbie focuses on the moral weight of America's "mighty voice," Aldington is more pragmatic, recognizing the kid brother's experience in his Civil War. He declines to assign moral or spiritual value to the conflict: *"D'you know what it's all about? / Let me whisper you a secret – we don't."* Yet the speaker's confidentiality and casualness work to establish the American reader's trust, as does his self-assurance: *"And so here we are, / And we're going to win . . ."* (*GW* 3).

Aldington's poem moves on to aesthetic concerns, confiding to the reader as one artist to another:

And after all it will be more fun afterwards –
More fun for the poets and the painters –
When the cheering's all over
And the dead men buried
And the rest gone back to their jobs.
It'll be more fun for them to make their patterns,
Their word-patterns and color-patterns.
And after all, there is always war and always peace,
Always the war of the crowds,
Always the great peace of the arts. (4–5)

Aldington, an associate and sometime rival of Pound, stipulates the kind of divide between high art and mass politics that was characteristic of high modernism. He also anticipates art's transcendence beyond war. Yet his vision of art contributes to the British propaganda machine, for he tames the brutality of war with good humor and the promise of an artistic renaissance (Braithwaite's argument, basically). What is more, having distinguished between the "poets and painters" and the "crowds," he likens England to the former group:

The little rock-citadel of the artists
Is always besieged;
There, though they have beauty and silence,
They have always tears and hunger and despair.
But that little citadel has held out
Against all the wars of the world –
Like England, brother Jonathan.
It will not fall during the great war. (6)

Not only is England by suggestion the "citadel" where "peace, beauty and silence" can take refuge; it is also the "little citadel" surrounded, starved, and despairing – threatened, seemingly, by the "war of the crowds." Aldington's poem then makes a case for the supremacy of art and of England, but at the same time his imagery intimates that England is besieged and might be willing to accept help from its plucky "brother Jonathan." Thus, Aldington, while avowedly interested primarily in the arts, does in fact forge a cultural, political, and familial compact between modernists in America and Britain. Modernism, supposedly an international movement including Germany and Austria-Hungary, becomes in Aldington's verse a politically interested alliance foremost between the British and American powers.

As the divergent examples offered by Begbie and Aldington illustrate, writers and editors could merge America's interests and identity with those of the Allies in a variety of ways. Edith Wharton's *Book of the Homeless,* published in 1916 by Charles Scribner's Sons, marks perhaps the most ambitious – and most elitist – attempt by a book to forge cultural ties between neutral America and the Allies at war.[38] The collection consisted of poetry, prose, art reproductions, and even musical scores by artists, essayists, and politicians of the Allied countries and the United States; it offered a kind of Allied VIP benefit for the homeless of Belgium, who received the proceeds administered through the "American Hostels for Refugees" and the "Children of Flanders Rescue Committee."[39] The book mixes the most direct propaganda urging U.S. war involvement with seemingly apolitical artworks. Theodore Roosevelt's introduction directly appeals to Americans' sense of responsibility: "The part that America has played in this great tragedy is not an exalted part; and there is all the more reason why Americans should hold up the hands of those of their number who, like Mrs. Wharton, are endeavoring to some extent to remedy the national shortcomings."[40] Elsewhere in the collection English critic Edmund Gosse writes on "The Arrogance and Servility of

Germany," American essayist Agnes Repplier demonstrates in "The Russian Bogyman" how Germany's barbarity far outstrips Russia's, and Belgian writer Maurice Maeterlinck proclaims in "Our Inheritance" the martyrdom of his country's war dead. The book also contains straight-forwardly propagandistic poems by writers as well known as Laurence Binyon, Thomas Hardy, Edmond Rostand, W. D. Howells, and George Santayana. On the other hand, some of the poetry and much of the art-work in the book seem to be simply testaments to the high culture be-ing threatened by German conquest. Poems serving this purpose include Rupert Brooke's "The Dance," whose only apparent connection with the war is its author's identity as a fallen soldier-poet, and Emile Verhaeren's "The New Spring," which simply registers the poet's impression that spring will never again bring life to the war-torn world. There is also mu-sic by Igor Stravinsky and Vincent d'Indy, and reproductions of artwork by Monet, Sargent, and Rodin. The design of the book itself suggests not a propaganda tract but an art book: the page format is large ($11'' \times 8\frac{1}{2}''$), some paintings are reproduced in color, and a sheet of tissue paper be-tween the pages protects reproductions of drawings and paintings. Al-though Wharton wrote translations of the French pieces, the originals appear also.[41] Other features of the book's publication suggest the price-less heritage represented (and threatened) and also the narrow, elite audi-ence to which the book was directed. The book's market was limited: its one printing of 3,300, run in January of 1916, did not sell in its entire-ty. Priced at five dollars a copy, it was clearly not designed for mass con-sumption; indeed, the regular print run was supplemented by an addi-tional 125 copies bound as "deluxe" editions and 50 bound as "grand" editions, priced at twenty-five and fifty dollars respectively.[42] At these prices, Scribner's was clearly trading on the prestige of its editor to sell the book and was targeting a well-heeled audience. For this limited au-dience – but also, perhaps, for those who could not afford the book but noted its publication – the book's price and rarity reinforced the pre-ciousness of the (white) Western culture represented therein.

IV

Personal identifications with Western culture, the Allied war effort, and even the "rape" of Belgium were negotiated much more readily by white Americans than by blacks. Though Braithwaite was able, in his writing anyway, to suppress or transmute racial difference, this was not a rhetor-ical and ideological move easily made by black intellectuals. For Du Bois and the NAACP, the way to supporting America's war effort was never straight. Time and again the *Crisis*'s attention to issues of race brought it to question the virtues of American democracy. Du Bois criticized as racist the U.S. invasion and occupation of Haiti initiated on July 28, 1915. In September Du Bois suggested that the government institute a biracial commission to oversee the restoration of peace in Haiti and to guarantee that the United States "will always respect her political integrity."[43] In October Du Bois charged that the United States had in fact violated Haiti's political integrity, having "made a white American Admiral sole and irresponsible dictator of Hayti," and he denounced "uninvited American intervention, the shooting and disarming of peaceful Haytian citizens, the seizure of public funds . . . and the pushing of the monopoly claims of an American corporation which holds a filched, if not fraudulent railway charter."[44] Du Bois declaimed, "SHAME ON AMERICA!"

But while Du Bois was criticizing U.S. military incursions into the affairs of nonwhite nations, U.S. military involvements overseas were providing career opportunities for black servicemen in the armed forces. The *Crisis* of January 1916 introduced Major Charles Young with a photograph and a biographical note stating that Young "was a Major in the Spanish War . . . and has seen military service in Haiti, the Philippines, and Liberia."[45] In the issue of March 1916 Young was announced the winner of the second Spingarn Medal, awarded each year to an African-American of distinction in his or her profession.[46] The monthly NAACP report in the *Crisis* claimed that "[black soldiers'] service during the Spanish War and since has shown our colored troops to be infinitely better fitted for service in our tropical dependencies than white troops."[47] During the U.S. military incursion into Mexico, which began in February 1916, the debacle at Carrizal made heroes of the 80 black troops who, though faced by some 120 Mexican soldiers, obeyed orders to charge the Mexican lines and then stood their ground in the ensuing firefight. Two of the 3 white officers in charge were killed, as were 8 of the "Buffalo soldiers" of the Tenth Cavalry; in addition, 9 black soldiers were wounded and 22 taken prisoner.[48] Even as Du Bois criticizes the expedition generally, he praises the black soldiers involved in the Carrizal combat: "a glory for the Mexicans who dared to defend their country from invasion and for Negro troopers who went singing to their death. And the greater glory was the glory of the black men, for Mexicans died for a land they love, while Negroes sang for a country that despises, cheats and lynches them."[49]

Despite Du Bois's and others' fundamental convictions about Ameri-

can racial injustice, military actions such as Carrizal, where black soldiers
fought and were killed under the U.S. flag, seemed to offer some tangible hope for recognition in dominant white society. Soon after the skirmish, on June 30, 1916, the *New York Times* printed a poem by Charles
T. Dazey, "At Carrizal," which celebrated the black soldiers' heroism, so
that a poem about black soldiers was one of the earliest pieces of the Great
War period to memorialize American military dead. The poem provides
a kind of affidavit about the valor of black soldiers. Following its epigraph, "'Captain Morey says his negro troops faced death singing,'" are
lines focusing on the question "How did they die in that far land, / . . .
Those men whose fathers bore the brand / That marked the southland
slave?" The answer:

> Betrayed, outnumbered, still they fought
>   To their heroic end,
> And smiled at death, and bravely sang,
>   As welcoming a friend.
>
> The strange, wild music of their race
>   With mellow, low refrain,
> From cabin homes, from rice-land swamps,
>   In memory swells again.
>
> But never such a song rang out
>   As when they faced the foe,
> And, singing, charged from trench to trench,
>   And gave him blow for blow!
>
> And in the annals of our land,
>   Long as our flag shall wave,
> That song will show that men are men,
>   Though children of the slave.[50]

The poem confirms certain white stereotypes about blacks – "the strange,
wild music of their race" – but it pointedly resists others, particularly the
assumption that blacks would, when facing combat, "like recreant cow-
ards, weep, / Or vainly seek to fly." The very music that in its original
black social contexts was strange to the white listener becomes incom-
parably glorious in the context of a national military adventure. The message seems clear: by giving their allegiance first to the nation rather than
to the race, black Americans can be admitted to an equal relation with
white society (or, more insidiously, black Americans cannot gain respect

by defiance against racist American society, but only by soldierly self-sacrifice in the service of an imperialist and racist agenda carried on elsewhere). Either way, the poem points beyond the skirmish at Carrizal, for the charges "from trench to trench" indicate the tactics and topography of the Western Front more than the ambush at Carrizal, where the combat involved no in-depth trench defenses and a brief firefight rather than a pitched battle.[51]

Major Charles Young, the ranking black officer in the U.S. armed services, was regularly featured in the pages of the *Crisis* after his Spingarn award. Comments on his receipt of the award credited his military service as proof of a black man's ability to serve as an officer.[52] Young's promotion to lieutenant colonel was reported in the *Crisis,* as was his service in the military expedition into Mexico; later there appeared a picture of Young in conference with Generals Pershing and Bliss "Somewhere in Mexico," a picture of Young's children, and an article on how they had escaped the German advance through Belgium, their residence while he served in Liberia.[53] Young's celebrity status provided him with a platform for his own views. While willing to be used as a symbol of the advancement of his race, Young could not brook criticism of the state he served. The May 1916 *Crisis* reprinted two news stories sympathetic to an eleven-year-old black boy in Des Moines who refused to salute the flag and was punished by school authorities for it. One reported, "The voice of little Hubert Eaves, with the prophetic instinct of Hannah's sons, rings over this land: 'I will not salute your flag, for there is no God in it.' And these ringing words presage the awakening *of a people who will no more be slaves.*"[54] Young's rejoinder to these stories, published in the August issue, puts the weight of his authority as a soldier and a black celebrity – status provided, in part, by the *Crisis* – fully behind U.S. military preparedness and 100 percent loyalty:

> This Eavesism has done us no good as a race, nor has it done the country at large any in this time of need of preparation for its defense. . . .
>
> The old toast of the army and navy should be that of every true American today: "Our country may it ever be right, but right or wrong our country." . . .
>
> The best soldiers of the Tenth Cavalry have bidden me say that they find God in the fold of the flag and delight to salute and protect it. They bid me say again that Eavesism does no good; that it cools our friends and heats our enemies.[55]

Young's equation of loyalty with military preparedness was not necessarily in accord with the views of Du Bois, who referred to Young's letter as "interesting" and in the March *Crisis* had asked whether "there is any 'preparedness' for Christianity, for human culture, for peace or even for war, that is more pressing than the abolition of lynching in the United States."[56]

From the beginning of the war, the *Crisis* had developed two lines of analysis in response to the war, each of which bordered on contradiction: the magazine had extolled the heroism of colored colonial troops fighting in Europe while denouncing European colonialism, and it had campaigned for equal treatment for African-American soldiers while opposing American militarism. The possibility that these multiple lines of argument might lead to indecision, and even to the state's co-opting of African-American energies and interests, was not entirely lost on Du Bois, who in May 1916 had commented that "in America, in Europe and in Africa black men are fighting for the liberty of white men and pulling their chestnuts out of the fire. One of these bright mornings black men are going to learn how to fight for themselves."[57] But the problematic position of the NAACP regarding black military service and militarism was not brought into the open until the emergence of Major Young, who by his success in the armed forces became not only a black hero but also a highly visible advocate of 100 percent black loyalty. The situation escalated to a full-blown crisis of black intellectual and political leadership when, in February and March 1917, it became clear that the United States would intervene in the European war. The NAACP had demanded that the expanded peacetime army include four new regiments open to blacks, two of infantry and two of artillery;[58] now with war and a greatly expanded army coming, and with blacks likely to be conscripted, a shortage of black officers to command black conscripts was certain. In response, NAACP chairman of the board Joel Spingarn proposed the formation of a segregated training camp for black officers. In the *Crisis* of April 1917, anticipating the declaration of war, Du Bois threw his full support behind the camps, arguing that segregated camps were better than no camps at all, insofar as black officers in charge of segregated regiments were preferable to white officers. Black intellectuals opposed to segregated training camps and segregated units were misled, Du Bois argued, by the perception that armed service would be voluntary; the *Baltimore Afro-American,* the *Chicago Defender,* the *New York News,* and the *Cleveland Gazette,* Du Bois wrote, "assume a choice between volunteering and not volunteering. The choice will be between conscription and rebellion."[59]

Colonel Young's endorsement of the camps was far less agonized and equivocal; his response entirely jettisoned civil rights activism in favor of patriotic idealism:

> Let us do nothing to divide our people in this hour of our country's trials; neither let our work be negative nor reactionary but constructive. THIS PLAN OF DR. SPINGARN'S IS CONSTRUCTIVE, AND I HOPE IT WILL MEET WITH THE BEST OF RESULTS. When the storm is past we can take up the idealism of the cause. . . .
>
> May there be in this case no Achilles sulking in his tent. Such actions "cool our friends and heat our enemies," do no good, and are not in the line of strict loyalty to the flag.[60]

Published in the "Looking Glass" column of the May 1917 *Crisis*, Colonel Young's declaration is seconded by similar comments quoted from the *Louisville Courier-Journal* and the *Washington Bee*. For every African-American leader demanding the NAACP's resistance to the war mobilization, there seems to have been another urging the organization's cooperation.

During the war Du Bois did not altogether abandon the *Crisis*'s responsibility to speak out against racism. When in July 1917 the East St. Louis riot left thirty-eight blacks dead and more than six thousand homeless,[61] the *Crisis* responded with a twenty-page investigation, including dramatic pictures of burned-out black homes, which ran in the September issue. When in August soldiers of the 24th Infantry division, reacting to a wrongful arrest of one of their number, assaulted a police station in Houston, leaving sixteen whites dead and eleven wounded, Du Bois wrote an editorial in the October *Crisis* that pointed out the aggravating circumstances of extreme racist treatment in Houston and denounced the summary execution of nineteen soldiers from the offending unit.[62] But homefront racism and violence, and the misadventures of black soldiers, did not dampen Du Bois's support for the war effort; his hopes for the salvation to be worked by black soldiery now became the central theme of his writing. Du Bois's most outrageous statement of patriotism, the "Close Ranks" editorial of July 1918, is a declaration of allegiance strikingly similar to Colonel Young's of May 1917: "Let us, while this war lasts, forget our special grievances and close our ranks shoulder to shoulder with our own white fellow citizens and the allied nations that are fighting for democracy. We make no ordinary sacrifice, but we make it gladly and willingly with our eyes lifted to the hills."[63] It is possible Du

Bois wrote the editorial under the impression that he himself was about to become a military man. He wrote it immediately after he had agreed to accept a captain's commission in the U.S. Army's Military Intelligence Branch. David Levering Lewis argues, in fact, that Du Bois had agreed to trade his influence as the most respected black American leader, quid pro quo, for an influential military posting: "What he wrote was in large part written in order to consummate the bargain."[64] Amazingly, that position in Military Intelligence would have had as its assignment the elimination of "Negro subversion."[65] As it happened, Du Bois's previous reputation as an agitator led to his being denied the captaincy, so he provided his propaganda appeal for loyalty without gaining the promised commission.

Du Bois's nearly unqualified embrace of American patriotism in time of war was, to many black intellectuals, not only inexcusable but inexplicable. It is my contention, quite to the contrary, that Du Bois had been among the first Americans to forge a strong identification with the soldier, and among the first to celebrate military heroism, and so it should not be surprising that the U.S. military expedition to France – in which black Americans were early participants – should have won his approval. Thus, to the issue of political strategy – the expanded role Du Bois hoped African-Americans and the NAACP might assume by their participation in a patriotic coalition – we must add a consideration of ideology. Du Bois, Braithwaite, and Young were involved in the formation of an ideal of masculine heroism and martyrdom that articulated a patriotic American identity masking racial difference (indeed, they were arguably in the vanguard of that formation).[66] This does not mean that race difference was transcended: the treatment of black soldiers in the U.S. Army was different from that of whites, and in fact, it seems clear that Du Bois's military ideal was distinctively black, while those of white Americans could be more straightforwardly Anglo-Saxon or Gallic. Yet under the pressure of wartime coercion and the apparent demands of political strategy, the military ideals were parallel enough to bring Du Bois to announce the suspension of the NAACP's race activism for the duration of the war.

V

While in 1916 and 1917 Du Bois was striving to achieve some balance between lobbying for African-American interests and celebrating the patriotic contributions of black soldiers, other writers and editors were plowing ahead with the less complicated task of encouraging white, often Anglo-Saxon Americans to identify with white, Anglo-Saxon Britons.

Poetry anthologies were becoming crowded with soldier-poets, deceased soldier-poets, poets memorializing deceased soldiers, and poets explaining the "necessity" of additional deceased soldiers. American readers were thus brought to the most riveting, heart-wrenching situation in war literature — the death of a comrade, child, father, or lover — from a strictly Allied perspective. J. W. Cunliffe's identification with a Canadian officer, a friend killed on the Western Front, and his hallowing of the English war effort were fairly characteristic:

> If undue prominence seems to be given to what may be called [the war's] more personal aspects — the spirit of sacrifice and devotion which inspired men and women to give themselves and those dearest to them to a great cause — I must plead in excuse that during much of the time of the preparation of this volume my mind was full of the memory of my friend Lieut.-Col. G. H. Baker of the 5th Canadian Mounted Rifles, who fell in command of his battalion during the third battle of Ypres on June 2, 1916. (*GW* v–vi)

His collection offers a variety of elegaic poems by British writers, including Herbert Asquith's "The Fallen Subaltern," Laurence Binyon's "For the Fallen," and Walter de la Mare's "How Sleep the Brave."[67] Besides these, it offers English patriotic poems focusing on the valor and sacrifice of British soldiers: Rupert Brooke's "The Soldier," Julian Grenfell's "Into Battle," Thomas Hardy's "'Men Who March Away,'" and Charles Sorley's "All the Hills and Vales Along."[68] This preponderance of soldier poetry and poetry about dead soldiers, types of poetry that Cunliffe admits might be given "undue prominence," was soon to become the norm in American anthologies. In E. B. Osborn's *Muse in Arms,* for instance, the "List of Authors" is highlighted by crosses placed next to soldier-poets killed in battle (seventeen out of fifty-two in the collection).[69] This particular practice is unusual, but others that emphasize the "ultimate sacrifice" made by so many British soldiers can be found in virtually every collection, whether of soldier or civilian verse. George Herbert Clarke's *A Treasury of War Poetry,* first published in 1917, includes a section of twenty-nine poems by "Poets Militant" (i.e., soldier-poets), a group of five poems about "The Wounded," and twenty poems dedicated to "The Fallen." By the second series of the *Treasury,* a wholly separate selection of poetry published in 1919, the number of poems by "Poets Militant" had swelled to forty-two, those about "The Wounded" remained constant at five, while those about "The Fallen" had increased to thirty-six.[70] In both collections, the two largest sections consist of the poems composed by soldier-poets and those dedicated to the war dead. Frank Foxcroft's *War Verse* (1918) notes the proximity of death to the enterprise of war-poetry publication, as Foxcroft notes in his preface: "In not a few instances, the poems, when printed, have borne, under the name of the writer, the inscription 'Killed in action, _____' which has given the lines the peculiar poignancy of a message from a man who has fought his last fight, and has done it without fear or faltering."[71]

Human impulses to pay homage to the dead hardly seem objectionable. It is notable, however, how soldiers killed in battle were used both to compel interest in various war-poetry anthologies and to legitimate the ideologies that they represented. By dying while in uniform, poets like Rupert Brooke and Alan Seeger became obligatory selections for such anthologies; as martyrs they gained lasting symbolic power. Brooke's death came to signify, in later criticism, the passing of an age-old heroic tradition in English poetry.[72] Alan Seeger was, at least for a generation, the one outstanding American soldier-poet of the war.[73] His "I Have a Rendezvous with Death" was the one non-British poem to appear in *From the Front: Trench Poetry* (1918), and the first book of American soldier poetry, Herbert Adams Gibbon's *Songs from the Trenches: The Soul of the AEF* (1918), was dedicated to Alan Seeger, "The First American Soldier Poet who gave his life in France."[74] Seeger was also important for the emergence of soldier poetry in American presses because his posthumous *Poems,* intensely partisan on behalf of the Allies, compiled sales figures which demonstrated that propaganda by soldier-poets could be commercially profitable. Published in December 1916, Seeger's *Poems* got the jump on other books of soldier poetry and never looked back: by the end of 1917 it had gone through seven printings and sold 21,275 copies; it added two more printings and another 6,100 copies in 1918; and over the next decade a total of some 38,000 volumes had been sold.[75]

During the war, collections dedicated to fallen soldiers, special attention to soldier poetry, and poems memorializing the dead were not just personal remembrances or advertising gimmicks. They were also vehicles for propaganda. Battlefield death, to be sure, can be used for a variety of political purposes; in much recent war poetry as well as in traditional criticism of Great War poetry, it is a seemingly unanswerable charge *against* the justifiability of wars. In collections of Great War poetry, however, it had the opposite effect: as hundreds of thousands of British corpses piled up in Flanders, scores of poems and collections of poems declared that these deaths must be avenged. The deaths of soldiers must "mean something." Elizabeth Marsland sums up the perspective of many civilians on every side of the conflict:

> As the length of casualty lists increased, and the public at home became aware of the awesome tally of human destruction that the war was causing, the need remained strong for people to be convinced, and to convince themselves, that death on behalf of the nation was different from ordinary death, and that the sacrifice, the "royal gesture," was indeed not "in vain."[76]

Thus, a sonnet, "To the Men Who Have Died for England," an anonymous poem in Frank Foxcroft's *War Verse,* promises immortality to England's soldier-martyrs, while stressing their function as securities ensuring the continued prosecution of the war:

> Be glad, that still the spur of your bequest
>   Urges your heirs their threefold way along –
> The way of Toil that craveth not for rest,
>   Clear Honor, and stark Will to punish wrong!
> The seed ye sow'd God quicken'd with His Breath;
> The crop hath ripen'd – lo, there is no death! (*WV* 262)

This ethics of vengeance suggests that the soldiers were as useful dead as they were alive. While some poems console by adopting Christian promises of an afterlife, others offer another kind of secular immortality based on the national ideal: soldiers who die for their country become somehow uniquely incorporated into the national spirit, and therefore live on insofar as they have helped preserve the nation into futurity.[77] "To the Men Who Have Died for England" employs imagery of burying and planting to make this scheme seem plausible. Such imagery had a wide currency during the war, with the figure of the Grim Reaper being quickly supplanted, in nationalist literatures, with images of fertility and spring renewal.[78]

The propaganda of a poem such as this depends, however, not only on its success in persuading readers that patriotic death is noble or useful, but also, for American readers, on its ability to elicit sympathy for dead British soldiers and, by extension, the Allied cause they died for. Cunliffe's *Poems of the Great War,* Clarke's *Treasury of War Poetry,* and W. Reginald Wheeler's *Book of Verse of the Great War* – the most prominent of the earlier anthologies – included a balance of American and British writers, presumably both to satisfy American sensitivities about their national lit-

erature and to present American and British writers side by side, as compatriots. Insofar as *War Verse* was published in America for an American
audience, the fact that all authors except for Seeger were non-American
might at first seem to threaten both the collection's commercial and propaganda value. Yet *War Verse* would appear to have been a commercial
success; Reilly's bibliography indicates that there were as many as seven
editions of this collection, more than for any other book she lists.[79] The
crucial factor in the success of *War Verse* seems to have been its year of
publication, 1918, when the process of Anglo-American identification
was virtually complete. As opposed to postulating a possible alliance, by
1918 the anthology was simply cementing a bond established for some
months – and by 1918, a bond sanctified by the blood of American war
dead. With America's active participation in the war, *War Verse* could posit
with much greater certainty than previous collections the merging of
American and British identities. The anthology's opening poem, "America Comes In," represents a collective American voice:

> We are coming from the ranch, from the city and the mine,
> And the word has gone before us to the towns upon the Rhine;
> As the rising of the tide
> On the Old-World side,
> We are coming to the battle, to the Line.

This, despite the fact that the poem was published first in *Blackwood's* and
its pseudonymous author, "Klaxon," habitually writes from a British perspective in the other six poems in the collection with that byline.[80] While
Klaxon's speaking on behalf of the United States might have seemed pre-
sumptuous to careful American readers, the poem does make clear the
grounds for the kind of intermingling of national voices that the poem's
speaker/author embodies. The poem raises the specter of American war
casualties already suffered in the naval war so as to mobilize the same logic of revenge that energized the British war effort. First the poem describes the ocean crossing of the U.S. troops with reference to the deaths
of American civilians – "Right across the deep Atlantic where the *Lusitania* passed" – and then it raises those losses to the level of a military rallying cry:

> We are many – we are one – and we're in it overhead,
> We are coming as an Army that has seen its women dead,
> And the old Rebel Yell
> Will be loud above the shell
> When we cross the top together, seeing red. (*WV* 1–2)

Although the unity expressed in the poem is the American union of North and South, given the poem's motive of galvanizing American support for intervention, it could as well be British and American soldiers "crossing the top together." With Americans as well as Britons being killed in action, the national boundaries between the United States and the United Kingdom could be blurred – much to the satisfaction of many propagandists on both sides of the Atlantic. E. M. Walker's "To America, On Her First Sons Fallen in the Great War," also in *War Verse,* can claim identity between the United States and Britain. The poem's first stanza proclaims:

> Now you are one of us, you know our tears,
> Those tears of pride and pain so fast to flow;
> You too have sipped the first strange draught of woe;
> You too have tasted of our hopes and fears;
> Sister across the ocean, stretch your hand,
> Must we not love you more, who learn to understand? (*WV* 230)

The fellowship of death thus binds American and British identities and aims together; Walker can proclaim, "You are one of us."[81]

The same ideals of blood revenge and kinship through death (which suggest a relationship more intense than a racial bond, a *tribal* bond) are apparent throughout the American publishing industry. They are apparent not only in *War Verse,* published by the market-oriented firm of Crowell, but also in a book like the 1917 *Book of Verse of the Great War,* published by Yale University Press.[82] Reginald Wheeler's *Book of Verse* is anomalous in certain respects; chiefly, it permits space for antiwar American voices at a time when such perspectives were being vigorously suppressed in partisan books, magazines, and newspapers. But perhaps the strongest argument for patriotism that emerges in the collection is that Wheeler, in spite of his apparent pacifist sympathies, ended up including a greater number of poems favoring the Allied cause.[83] Charles Hanson Towne's sonnet "To My Country" chastises the United States for benefiting economically while not sacrificing American blood. In reply to those who would say, we shall " 'in this [Europe's] time of woe, / Profit and prosper,' " to those who would proclaim, " 'Kind, thrice kind is Fate, / Leaving our land secure, our grain to grow!' " Towne summons a nobler spirit:

> America! They blaspheme and they lie
> Who say these are the voices of your sons!

> In this foul night, when nations sink and die,
>   No thought is here save for the fallen ones
>   Who, underneath the ruin of old thrones,
>   Suffer and bleed, and tell the world good-by! (*BV* 166)

Once again, the blood of the dead hallows the war; to speak of commerce in wartime is blasphemy. As in many other poems about fallen soldiers, the dead provide a goad driving the United States toward the battlefield; rather than emphasizing responsibility to the living, these poems profess a responsibility to the dead – the need to avenge or justify those who have fallen.

British writer Katherine Tynan asserts the role of the living in the construction of military conflict, stressing that the battle lines have been drawn to protect life in the feminine domestic spaces of the homefront. Yet Tynan's poem "High Summer" just as surely regulates life on the homefront according to the sacrifices being made on the battlefront. Tynan uses the same binarism that had energized the women's peace movement in the United States – which contrasted pacific femininity with bellicose masculinity – but deploys it in order to urge the necessity of waging war. "High Summer" describes the beauties of the English countryside: four stanzas in celebration of "the sweet privet hedge and golden roses," "The lambs calling their mothers out on the lea," and "The dappled sky and the stream that sings as it passes." It also reminds the reader, "These are bought with a price, a bitter fee," as each stanza closes with the refrain, "*They die in Flanders to keep these for me.*" The lines explicitly divide the feminine world of the homefront and the masculine domain of the battlefield, openly declaring that the latter must be maintained to preserve the former:

> All doors and windows open; the South wind blowing
> Warm through the clean sweet rooms on tiptoe going,
> Where many sanctities, dear and delightsome, be,
> *They die in Flanders to keep these for me.* (*BV* 167)

The English landscape is both feminized and eroticized here, making the domestic space not only delicate, in need of protection, but also desirable, an object of possession. And through it all, the (apparently) female speaker acknowledges the male soldiers' power to protect and, simultaneously, expresses feelings of guilt for not having that power – "*They die . . . for me.*" This wartime poem links the homefront explicitly to the battlefront, in a way that presses the domestic woman to pledge fealty to the male warrior (as well as vice versa).

From an American perspective, it seems crucial that the poem's landscape is highly literary; Tynan describes an English countryside descending from the Cavalier, Neoclassical, and Romantic poets that would be familiar to middle- and upper-class Americans through anthologies at both home and school. Thus, the "defense" of England can become crucial to American readers for cultural reasons – ones made persuasive by American veneration and envy of English literature.[84] Most American writers in *Verse of the Great War,* as well as those in other, more thoroughgoing pieces of propaganda, are indeed convinced that England and France must be defended for cultural reasons. In George Edward Woodberry's "Sonnets Written in the Fall of 1914," the German invasion threatens the foundations of Western culture: "Lift up thy head, O Rheims, of ages heir / That treasured up in thee their glorious sum; / . . . Haunt with thy beauty this volcanic air / Ere yet thou close, O Flower of Christendom!" Woodberry is certain that the danger to Western culture threatens the United States as well; he warns, "Watch well, my country, that unearthly sea, / Lest when thou thinkest not, and in thy sleep, / Unapt for war, that gloom enshadow thee!" (*BV* 181). The treasure of Western culture, like the cause to wreak revenge on Germany, is sanctified by the dead not only of the war, but of ages past as well. "The hosts of thirty centuries" call out for the civilized world to defend their heritage:

> And never through the wide world yet there rang
>   A mightier summons! O Thou who from the side
> Of Athens and the loins of Caesar sprang,
>   Strike, Europe, with half the coming world allied,
> For those ideals for which, since Homer sang,
>   The hosts of thirty centuries have died.[85] (183)

Woodberry's view of the world extends outside the West only to the extent that the rest of the world, the so-called coming world (read today: "developing world") is rushing to the side of the Allies to protect the one true repository of civilization. Woodberry's argument about the value of culture, and the value of sacrificial death, is also at bottom about the value of the Caucasian race. When countless generations have already given their lives for Western culture, he seems to say, the present generation betrays those past and their sacrifices if it is unwilling to offer itself up to death as well. The generations of the Western world beckon America equally: that which destroys Europe today (nowhere is there the hint that *Europe* is destroying Europe) will presently assault the United States. America and Europe, heirs in common to Christ, Caesar, and Homer, are the main actors in this pageant of self-sacrifice; the rest of the world – the nonwhite world – consists of eager bit players. The United States is compelled to defend Europe because it shares in the plentitude of culture; it must defend what it has. With no apparent culture of its own to preserve, the rest of the world is drawn to Europe to defend what it lacks and desires.

VI

While we may admire the work of the antiwar soldier-poets who, since the end of the Great War, have come to define the war-poetry canon, it should give us pause to realize that our obsession with the front was cultivated in the anthologies of 1916, 1917, and 1918 for the purpose of creating a compelling case for U.S. intervention and then sustaining support for it. By focusing on the front, American poetry anthologies contributed to a dramatic narrowing of Americans' possible responses to the conflict. They boiled down, in fact, to two diametrically opposed choices. If Americans fought, they chose in favor of Western civilization, moral right, and self-defense – all qualities invested in the Belgian, French, and British soldiers fighting and dying on the Western Front. If they refused to fight, they chose in favor of cowardice, narrow self-interest, Hun bestiality, and the destruction of culture.

The peculiar figure of the soldier and the soldier-poet not only provided a fairly straightforward, personalized identification between white Americans and the military forces of Britain and France, but also offered, more complexly, a symbol for black integration, equality, and fraternity. In his autobiography *Dusk of Dawn,* Du Bois's reflections on the world war concentrate on the influence and the comaraderie of Joel Spingarn, who was in 1918 the chair of the NAACP, a recently commissioned major in the U.S. Army Military Intelligence Branch, and the man who persuaded Du Bois to accept an army commission with the understanding that the two would work together in army intelligence.[86] Du Bois comments:

> I do not think that any other white man ever touched me emotionally so closely as Joel Spingarn. . . . Of greatest influence on me undoubtedly was Spingarn's attitude toward the war. He was fired

with consuming patriotism, he believed in America and feared Germany. He wanted me and my people not merely as a matter of policy, but in recognition of a fact, to join wholeheartedly in the war. It was due to his advice and influence that I became during the World War nearer to feeling myself a real and full American than ever before or since.[87]

Military service – here evoked by his fraternal relationship with the commissioned officer and colleague Spingarn, elsewhere invoked by Du Bois's celebration of the black soldier – provides the conduit for Du Bois's identification with the nation and, in turn, his identity as a "real and full American." Here, in brief, is a graph of the ideological effects of the soldier and soldier-poet. That these effects worked upon black Americans as well as white testifies to their power. Of course, as Du Bois realized in retrospect, psychological projections of identity do not address material inequalities but rather conceal them. In *Dusk of Dawn* he writes of his wartime enthusiasm (and his neglect of black civil rights activism):

> I am less sure now than then of the soundness of this war attitude. I did not realize the full horror of war and its wide impotence as a method of social reform. . . . Possibly passive resistance of my twelve millions to any war activity might have saved the world for black and white. Almost certainly such a proposal on my part would have fallen flat and perhaps slaughtered the American Negro body and soul. I do not know. I am puzzled.[88]

Even as Du Bois tries to grasp, after the fact, what the possibilities for resistance might have been, he demonstrates how ideological construction produces indecision and bewilderment over the political and intellectual alternatives that, lying at the margins of that construction, are obscured by it. This is not to say that Du Bois and other black intellectuals – William Stanley Braithwaite and Major Charles Young among them – were not active collaborators in the creation of the ideals of heroic masculinity, national power, and democratic destiny that helped propel the United States into war. It has been my contention that they were.

4

Marketing Patriotism
THE FRUGAL HOUSEWIFE AND THE
CONSUMPTION OF POETRY

IN 1917, the mobilization of the American masses amounted to little more, or less, than the greatest marketing challenge to confront American capitalism till that time. Commercial and financial interests had been the strongest backers of intervention; Republicans such as Theodore Roosevelt and Major General Leonard Wood were the staunchest proponents of preparedness and war involvement.[1] Furthermore, wartime propaganda was to become the chief proving ground for the advertising strategies that after the war would encourage and guide the growth of American consumerism – which would, in turn, fuel the economic expansion of the 1920s.[2] Well-known commercial artists such as Howard Chandler Christie and James Montgomery Flagg created designs for U.S. government posters, and the wartime federal bureaucracy became, in effect, a huge vocational college for an unprecedentedly large and confident generation of commercial advertisers. Virtually every agency was involved in publicity and propaganda – not only the Committee on Public Information, but the Treasury Department, the Selective Service Board, and the Food Administration.

The publicity effort on behalf of the American mobilization was massive; it engaged Americans on all fronts at once: going forward simultaneously were campaigns for military service in the army, navy, marines, and army air corps, for the various Liberty Loans, for food and fuel conservation, and for civilian service in the Red Cross, YWCA, and Salvation Army. But while the U.S. government attempted to mobilize every sector of society at the same time, its efforts to mobilize women were especially conspicuous. Within nearly every war department there was a separate women's division, and the activities of certain federal agencies,

142

notably the U.S. Food Administration, were directed almost exclusively at women. Federal agencies engaged in an extended attempt to court the support of women, giving them a powerful symbolic function and a visible public role in the mobilization. In marked contrast was the government's attitude toward workers, who were apparently more to be shunned or bullied than assuaged. Although the government had the support of Samuel Gompers, head of the American Federation of Labor, labor generally was treated as an adversary to be alternately coaxed and cajoled into cooperation with the war effort. The labor representative on the War Industries Board was reportedly "not on the Board to represent labor but to manage it."[3] In effect, therefore, the U.S. propaganda campaign attempted to sunder those political factions that, up until 1917, had been most active in opposing the war – unskilled labor and women. This divisive strategy seems to have been at work throughout the propaganda effort, but it was especially marked in the literature of the U.S. Food Administration and of civilians who supported its food conservation programs. This literature, including hundreds of poems, is the focus of this chapter, as we trace the discourses of patriotic femininity that led a large majority of Americans to support, or at least to acquiesce to, the U.S. intervention.

We have already discussed the relationship between the American mobilization and the popular, largely genteel poetry being published in American anthologies. A broader vein of popular poetry was employed in support of the full national mobilization that began in 1917. More various than the writing featured in the anthologies – it included genteel work but also comic verse, parodies, satires, aphorisms – it can be most accurately identified not by style but by the media in which it was published, for, fittingly, the poetry of mass mobilization appeared in the same places where commercial advertisements regularly appeared, in newspapers and popular magazines and, in 1917 and 1918, alongside the various public service announcements and government pronouncements that urged loyalty to and sacrifice for the state. If we look mainly at poems in these contexts – where most poems supported the U.S. intervention – the relationship between poetry and official propaganda was dialogic rather than straightforwardly complementary. In the literature of food conservation, poems that stressed the relationship between food and the war actually preceded any government pronouncements about the subject, and these early poems were as likely as not to declare the life-giving properties of food to be antithetical to the death-dealing instruments of war. The conjunction of food and the war was developed in poetry before its use in U.S. government propaganda was foreseen, and long before the patriotic production and consumption of food became images of mass appeal. Even when Food Administration propaganda became widespread, poetry supporting food conservation programs continued to fulfill distinctive functions. Occupying a public space separate from the state and its propaganda, poetic declaration played the role of a chorus, responding to and affirming the leading voice of the government and its agents. Placed in opposition to the patriarchal bureaucracy of the state, this public space was also marked as uniquely feminine. So as food conservation propaganda targeted – and sought to manipulate – women, food conservation poetry allowed women a space, albeit a narrow one, to define their own, active relationship to the national mobilization.

I

In some of the earliest poems that find the relation of food and war significant, the sowing and reaping of grain become metaphors for the wastefulness of war. In August and September 1914, these metaphors were suggested and reinforced by the juxtaposition of fields ready for reaping and the unprecedented harvest of people gathered by the war. On September 6, 1914, the first page of the *New York Times* picture section ran the headline "Armies Supplant Reapers on Belgium's Harvest Fields"; photographs show Belgian pickets hiding behind shocks of grain as well as the "reaping and the digging of trenches going on side by side" (Figure 8).[4] Grain shocks, harvest equippage, and reapers were exceedingly commonplace figures in the photographic lexicon of August and September 1914; to the two that the *Times* selected from the Underwood offerings, the paper could have added any number of others – Belgian soldiers waiting for the advancing Germans, for example, "behind their intrenchment of sheaves" (Figure 9). The American journalist and poet John Finley juxtaposes the harvests of war and of grain in "The Road to Dieppe," a poem recounting an August 4, 1914, journey across northern France. Reprinted in George Herbert Clarke's 1917 *Treasury of War Poetry,* Finley's poem describes in halting blank verse ". . .peasant women bending in the fields, / Cradling and gleaning by the first scant light, / Their sons and husbands somewhere o'er the edge / Of these green-golden fields which they had sowed, / But will not reap – out somewhere on the march." These men would soon be among the "dead [that] lie / Like swaths of grain beneath the harvest moon."[5] Appearing in the same collection, the dirge "Harvest Moon" and elegy "Harvest Moon: 1916"

Figure 8. "Reaping and the Digging of Trenches Going on Side by Side." Photograph by Underwood and Underwood, *New York Times* September 6, 1914, picture section: 7. By permission of Underwood Photo Archives, San Francisco.

by genteel poet Josephine Preston Peabody adapt the same image to a statelier, rhymed verse.[6] What with the usual "fresh" spring offensives, the Great War also reinforced traditional associations among spring planting, death, and hoped-for resurrection. "1915," a free verse poem by James Oppenheim, highlights the irony between springtime and death: "What want we with a Spring of fragrant farmlands, / Gardens, smokes of the brush, / And healing rains?" the poem asks, adding, "Strange sowing of seed goes on: / This is the year when we sow the Earth with the flesh of young men."[7] The horrors – and the implied hope – of springtime burials and planting are central metaphors also in that monument of experimental modernist verse, *The Waste Land*.

But the connections these poems establish between war and food, whether connecting the Grim Reaper with the fall harvest or burial with the spring planting, remain relatively superficial – metaphysical, in the sense that they yoke together images whose relation is accidental. The more material connections between the harvest and the prosecution of war – between producing food and feeding military and civilian populations – were taken up by other authors. By Edith Thomas, for instance. Thomas, one of the poets included in the Association for International Conciliation's *Contemporary War Poems*, was a literary figure of impeccably genteel credentials, having published in *Scribner's*, the *Atlantic*, *Harper's*, the *Nation*, and the *Century*, and having been a reader for *Harper's*.[8] Thomas was mentioned among the "Poets of this Generation" in William Edward Simonds's 1909 *Student's History of American Literature*, and fifty

Figure 9. "Defenders of Antwerp – Belgians behind Their Intrenchment of Sheaves Defending One of the Roads Leading to Fort Waelhem." Photograph by Underwood and Underwood. By permission of
the Bettman Archive.

years later she was described as a writer of "gentle imaginative lyrics."[9]
But Thomas's status as an established genteel poet, far from ensuring that
she would refrain from commenting on the war, seems to have demanded that she hold forth as an oracle on contemporary affairs. She had at
first applied her talents to the cause of women's pacifism. "We Mourn for
Peace" appeared soon after the New York peace march that it commemorated, first in the *New York Evening Post* and soon after in *Contemporary
War Poems*. The poem was reprinted yet again in Thomas's 1915 collection, *The White Messenger*. Another antiwar poem, "The Woman's Cry,"
was also printed in this collection and found its way into W. Reginald
Wheeler's 1917 *A Book of Verse of the Great War,* where the poem's denunciations of conscription stood sharply at odds with American war
policy – and where she was lumped with the pacifists denounced by
Charlton Lewis, author of the book's foreword.

But even in 1914, while Thomas was publishing poems that supported the women's peace movement, she began writing a series of poems
concerned with the imagery, the rationale, and the logistics of American

food relief to Europe – a discourse that led her to sympathize ever more intensely with the people of France and Belgium. Whereas the harvest imagery of Finley, Peabody, Oppenheim, and Eliot is largely traditional (however experimental the poetic language of Oppenheim and Eliot), the progression of Thomas's food poetry is toward a distinctively contemporary understanding of the importance of food supply in modern warfare. The comparison between the autumn harvest fields and the war's killing fields that Finley spelled out in "The Road to Dieppe" is duplicated in Thomas's "The Harvesters (France, 1914)": " 'Look! the harvest stands unreaped / In the silent golden field! . . . // Hush! the reaper – he is reaped, / He is brother to the clod; / Not like sheaves can he be raised.' "[10] Yet Thomas's poem, by focusing on the woman left behind by the slain reaper, has in view the political economy of the farm as well as the poignancy of reaping the reapers. With male farmers and farmhands conscripted as soldiers, the poem recognizes that French women will assume the crucial work of agricultural production:

> "Woman, you your land must serve;
>   Breast the silent golden corn;
> Do not stay for words or tears
>   Till the teeming field be shorn,
> Till the clusters dark with wine
>   To the presses shall be borne.
> Him, the valiant, whom you loved,
>   Proudly shall our cross adorn."[11]

In these lines Thomas situates women in terms of their domestic and economic roles in society; they are placed centrally within the wartime economy, and therefore become tractable to the idioms of national duty and the "womanly" virtues of self-sacrifice and faithfulness.

By stressing the looming agricultural crisis in Europe, poems such as Thomas's implicitly endow American farming with heightened political importance. Just this politics of food supply was soon to be popularly disseminated by the Commission for Relief in Belgium, which was already being organized by Herbert Hoover in October 1914.[12] The campaign to supply Belgium with food was carried on with special vigor in national women's magazines, which assumed their readers would empathize with the bereft women and children of Europe. In January 1915, the *Ladies' Home Journal* launched an appeal for donations to its own relief effort, the "Queen of the Belgians Fund." Edward Bok's editorial stressed the "natural" bond tying American to European women: "Her cry is not that of a Queen, but that of a woman and a mother; and her appeal should bring forth the greatest response ever given to a woman."[13] The magazine also postulates the special call upon American women as part of the most powerful neutral country, "great, rich and generous America." Edith Thomas's poem "The House With Sealed Doors" responds to, and augments, these popular conceptions of the United States as uniquely responsible for and capable of helping neutral Belgium. Underscoring Thomas's engagement with American culture is her quotation of a *New York Times* piece in the poem's epigraph: "*A house with sealed doors, where a family of 7,000,000 sits in silence around a cheerless hearth. . . . America opened the window . . . and slipped a loaf of bread into the larder.*" Thomas's poem transforms the newspaper's approving account of the Belgian relief into an injunction to the poem's readers: "Bring food for the family robbed of its stores; / Open a window where sealed are the doors!" Appealing to American women's domestic identifications, Thomas casts the relief of Belgium as a conflict between an extended family whose "table is bare" and an autocratic state, Germany, which feeds its soldiers by Belgian granaries. In this drama, the powerful United States comes naturally, selflessly to the aid of the oppressed family:

> Merchant ships many are on the main.
> This that we send plies not for gain –
> Ship of the loaves! . . . Ye have given them lead,
> Ye lords of the "Province," but we give bread![14]

Thomas's poem is hostile toward Germany, which after conquering Belgium has apparently declared it a new "Province." But if the poem demonstrably sympathizes with the Belgians and casts blame on the Germans, it remains at least implicitly neutral and pacifist, for it offers "bread," not "lead," in reply to German aggression. Just so, as head of the Commission for Relief in Belgium from 1914 to 1916, Herbert Hoover made use of U.S. neutrality to ensure that the offices of his commission could be carried on effectively.[15] But Thomas's political commitments, like those of other genteel poets and intellectuals, continued to shift toward closer ties with Belgium, France, and England and more bellicose relations with the Central Powers.

Thomas's early identification with the women's peace movement was to be transformed into an alliance with the patriotic leagues that led the call for intervention abroad and suppression of dissent at home. By 1917, Thomas took a major role in the Vigilantes, publishing three poems in the group's 1917 anthology, *Fifes and Drums,* and contributing poems to

its syndicate service throughout the war. Like her earlier pacifist manifestation, the final steps of Thomas's wartime evolution can be traced
through the discourse of food production and distribution. One of the
poems in *Fifes and Drums,* "The War of Bread," echoes the populist
rhetoric of Thomas's earlier poems: "the war I most abhor" is "The theft
of the people's bread!"[16] But unlike the earlier poems, which see the people and the state at odds, Thomas's acceptance of the U.S. government's
authority to speak and enforce the popular will seems unqualified. "The
War of Bread" takes its cue from a presidential declaration that forms its
epigraph – "*There shall be no unwarranted manipulation of the nation's food
supply by those who handle it on the way to the consumer.*" The poet who had
formerly advocated civil disobedience to resist the war now writes:

> Arm of the law, reach forth in your might,
> And the hidden stores unbind,
> And defeat their power who, at this hour,
> Wage dastardly war on their kind! (*FD* 132–33)

Ostensibly Thomas is urging the swift prosecution of capitalist speculators in food, but effectively she endorses a Wilson administration policy
that would, by 1918, brand any who resisted its directives as traitors.[17] In
fact, during the war, the respectable middle- and upper-class businessmen
who profited from the shipping and storage of food were rarely prosecuted; the courts, police, and vigilante groups instead pursued dissenters
belonging to nationalities of suspicious (central or eastern European) origin and to radical political groups such as the Socialist Party and the Industrial Workers of the World.[18] At best, Thomas's defense of the common people is subsumed in a national crackdown that affected many of
them. At worst, her poem offers a kind of veneer, a respectability, for a
jingoist, reactionary politics.

Edith Thomas's work provides further evidence that genteel poetry
was by no means isolated from social and political change. Far from being lost in an ethereal poetic realm, her wartime poetry's signification –
and its significance as both literary and cultural texts – was largely determined by the publishing contexts and political groups through which it
entered into sociopolitical struggle. This is the case with much of the partisan poetry we have been considering here. Consequently, interpretation
of such literary texts must be accompanied by analysis of other cultural
textualities – in the case of food conservation poetry, the texts of the
Food Administration and the writing of civilian agencies that either supported or reacted against its directives. At the same time, far from sug-

gesting that such extraliterary contexts define entirely the significance of a given poem, I maintain that the interplay between poetry and culture underscores as well the agency of poetic discourses in determining other cultural textualities. So if, as I will presently suggest, the U.S. government and its propagandists seized upon the connection between food and warfare in mobilizing the American populace, they were in part borrowing from food discourses that had already been inscribed by poets such as Thomas. And even as the Food Administration worked to harness the discourses of food production and conservation to the purposes of the wartime state, it remained possible for these discourses to be used and reused by groups on the margins of state control – both those resisting the war mobilization and those demanding even greater patriotic conformity than the government demanded.

When Herbert Hoover was appointed to head the U.S. Food Administration in May 1917, the discourses of food production and conservation as well as the tropes of harvest and planting already had a considerable cultural history. These discourses, previously circulated in politics, poetry, and popular culture, had to be reckoned with and rearticulated in the rhetoric of the newly formed Administration. Charged with regulating the procurement and shipment of foodstuffs to America's European allies and its own burgeoning army, Hoover's Food Administration could readily appropriate the rhetoric of humanitarian concern that prevails in the poetry of Edith Thomas and in publicity initiated by Hoover's own Commission for Relief in Belgium. At the same time, however, the Administration had to contend with the legacy of pacifism represented, in politics, by organizations such as the Woman's Peace Party and, in popular culture, by texts such as Piantadosi and Bryan's song "I Didn't Raise My Boy to Be a Soldier." By its enormous popularity, this song had helped constitute American pacifism as a quantifiable political reality. Now the popularity of pacifism, once huge, still substantial, had to be reversed or neutralized by government propaganda. Although by 1917 most chapters of the WPP had become inactive, the chapters that did remain active, notably the New York WPP, had become radicalized, with members also participating in activist groups such as the American Union Against Militarism and allying themselves with the radicals of the *Masses* and the *New York Call*.[19] Not only socialist intellectuals but also working-class people threatened to jeopardize the efficient concentration and shipment of food for Europe. In February and March 1917, food riots erupted in New York, Philadelphia, and Boston among working-class women, who protested steeply rising prices brought about by high European demand for

American food products.[20] Hoover, who later referred to the Russian revolution as a "food riot," duly noted the social unrest.[21]

Resistance to the mobilization of American foodstuffs was reflected and articulated in food poetry that contested Thomas's and Hoover's construction of the nation's food policies as benevolent and altruistic. The New York WPP's fortnightly, *Four Lights: An Adventure in Internationalism,* worked to expose the hypocrisy and self-interest of all participants in the war, including the United States, and its contributors did not overlook the relationship between America's food policies and the progress of the war. Mary White Ovington's "Gretchen Talks to Her Doll," published on April 21, 1917, draws attention to the fact that the American food relief of Belgium and France had as its corollary a food embargo against Germany.[22] On the one hand, the poem adopts Hoover's understanding of the importance of food in the war. Anticipating the Food Administration slogan "Food Will Win the War," the poem portrays a German child who reports her mother's explanation of when the war will end: "When all of [their] children are hungry, hungrier than I am; / . . . When they all are as hungry, as hungry, / So their knees shake each time they go walking – / Then, Mother says, the war will be done, and all our foes will be conquered."[23] On the other hand, by portraying a German rather than an American household Ovington's poem undercuts the image of American benevolence purveyed in Thomas's poetry and *Ladies' Home Journal* articles. It fosters identification with the piteous German child talking to her doll – "It must be a comfort, my dear, to be stuffed full of sawdust. / You don't mind going without butter on your bread – / And such nasty bread, too" – while simultaneously it suggests the potential and actual hardships suffered by French, Belgian, English, and American children on account of strategies adopted by both sides, not just Germany. Thus, "Gretchen Talks to Her Doll" undermines the diametrical opposition between Allied and German, good and evil, that was preached by the interventionists and adopted in 1917 by the Wilson administration; rather, it suggests that both sides are evil in a war that treats children as military targets.

While the internationalists of *Four Lights* stressed the equivalence of the Triple Entente's and Central Powers' tactics of war, the socialists of the *Masses* focused on homefront inequities of food distribution, at the same time recognizing in the food riots potential common ground between middle-class women and the working classes.[24] Like Edith Thomas, the *Masses* envisaged the connections both between autumn harvest and the reaping of soldiers, and between the harvest of death and the terrible bur-

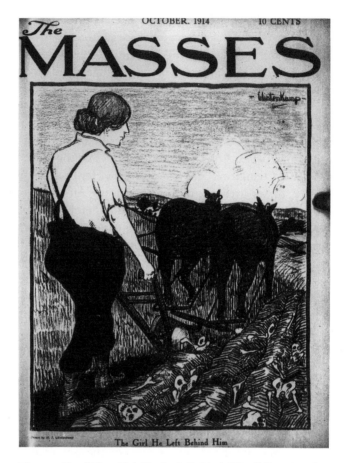

Figure 10. "The Girl He Left Behind Him." Drawing by Henry J. Glintenkamp. Cover of the *Masses* October 1914.

den placed on women. An October 1914 drawing by Henry Glintenkamp shows a woman, "The Girl He Left Behind Him," ploughing up a field of bones (Figure 10). In May 1917, Marguerite Wilkinson's poem "The Food Riots" rearticulates the protest of the bread rioters of February and April, as it sharply politicizes their demonstrations in terms of class warfare. For Americans of means, U.S. granaries and farms provided food aplenty: "And great was the harvest to nourish our pride, / Heaped high in the barns, filling train after train." This plentitude and self-satisfaction, described in long, detailed poetic lines, contrasts sharply with the poverty and the protest of the rioting women, offered in short, spare lines:

> *But poor is the people*
> *Whose women must cry,*
> *"We work, but we starve –*
> *Give us food or we die!*
> *Give milk for our babies*
> *And meat for our men*
> *And bread that our bodies*
> *May labor again!"*[25]

The class divide that Wilkinson's poem describes was part of the cultural landscape that Hoover's Food Administration had to address, as was the embryonic political activism among working-class women that her poem postulates. Food Administration literature suggests that Hoover's political strategy was, in effect, to drive a wedge between the interests of women and working-class people; while openly courting women's participation in its programs, the Food Administration rebuffed the demands of labor. For producers of food, the Administration mandated minimum prices for key foodstuffs, particularly wheat; it entered into cooperative, even "collusive," agreements with food processors and distributors that determined the rates for their services.[26] Hoover refused, however, to assert similar control over the distribution of food and warned that any government intervention in food distribution would amount to "autocracy": "If it should be proved that we can not secure a saving in our foodstuffs by voluntary effort, . . . we shall be compelled to acknowledge that democracy can not defend itself without compulsion; that is autocracy, and is a confession of failure of our political faith."[27] Hoover's "democratic" policy addressed the situations of rich and poor precisely alike, by preaching the patriotic virtue of thrift to all:

> If we save an average of a pound of flour per week for each one of us, we save 125,000,000 bushels of wheat per anum. . . . It is this multiplication of minute quantities – teaspoonfuls, slices, scraps – by millions that will save the world. Is there anyone in this land who can not deny himself or herself something? Who can not save some waste? Is not your right to life and freedom worth this service?

Of course, especially given the generally high and widely fluctuating prices of food during the war, the situations of rich and poor were hardly comparable. The one could readily give up a full pound of flour with little discomfort; the other could hardly spare a minute quantity of anything, whether a "teaspoonful, slice, or scrap." The Food Administration did little to guarantee that food would be available and affordable to Americans who had difficulty buying enough under ordinary circumstances (indeed, Administration policy ensured high food prices). In effect, poorer Americans were supposed to accept their involuntary hardship as equal to the voluntary economies of wealthier Americans, and their loyalty was open to suspicion if they would not suffer silently.

If the Food Administration could afford to ignore radical intellectuals and unionists, it could not readily do the same to women, since by Hoover's reckoning they "controlled at their tables about 80 percent of the nation's food consumption."[28] Accordingly, women's patriotic duty to conserve became fundamental to Food Administration propaganda. In *The Day's Food in War and Peace,* the Administration's targeting of a female audience is apparent in its use of inclusive gender language, rare in 1918: "Is there anyone in this land who can not deny himself or herself something?" *War Economy in Food,* published by the Food Administration in the fall of 1917, explained that wheat conservation was to be the sole means of fending off Allied starvation through the winter, all surplus beyond normal American consumption having already been exported to Europe. Given that the men were stalemated in the trenches of northern France, the crucial battleground became the kitchen table: "The question of planning meals grows daily more important, because it is more evident that food is to win or lose the war." And, consequently, the American "housewife is in an especially trying position," compelled to provide for her family's well-being and at the same time to win the war, having been effectively transformed into a front-line soldier and placed under military discipline. Women enrolled in the Food Administration "membership" were to sign a pledge card, promising "to carry out the directions and advice of the Food Administrator."[29]

II

In 1917 and 1918, Food Administration literature was largely responsible for setting the parameters of the politics and poetry of food. But Administration proclamations were by no means the only sources of symbolic production concerning food, nor even necessarily the most influential. Though Hoover sought to impose an efficient, rational order onto the war mobilization, he also preached the democratic dogma of "voluntary sacrifice," and out of necessity as well as conviction he relied heavily on volunteers to propagandize for the Administration and to enforce its regimens. In 1917 half a million volunteers went door to door to solicit Food Administration pledges; by early 1918 some 10 million households had pledged their service, and by the end of the war the number stood at 13 or 14 million.[30] Meanwhile, civilian groups not directly responsible to the Food Administration – or under its supervision – were eager to make up for the Administration's lack of enforcement apparatus; such organizations as the National Security League and the American Defense Society harried Americans into complying with codes of patriotic conduct – as defined by themselves, of course.[31] The Food Administration also received publicity assistance, in spite of the propaganda machine that was one of its primary organs. Some was simply donated for Administration use, as businesses and publishers provided "an amazing amount of free billboard, streetcar, newspaper, magazine, and retail store window advertising space . . . proclaiming that 'Food Will Win the War.' "[32] At the same time, aligned with the Security League and the Defense Society were ultrapatriotic newspapers and book publishers interested in promoting a narrow interpretation of Americanism. A chief ally in this endeavor was the Vigilantes, which functioned as a union exhorting its members to produce patriotic propaganda and a press syndicate distributing this propaganda – roughly equal measures of prose and poetry – to newspapers throughout the United States.[33]

Through a variety of tactics, the Vigilantes and like-minded groups largely succeeded in wresting the language and politics of food away from socialists and even away from the progressives who populated the Wilson administration.[34] To begin with, the Vigilantes had close ties to the preparedness movement, so while the group was formed only in November and December 1916, it could rely on a cadre of writers who had long been active in conservative politics. Just as crucially, this core of Vigilantes membership was both implacable in pursuing contributors and fierce in demanding their loyalty to the organization. An aggressive recruiting campaign in 1917 yielded 328 writers who pledged to contribute to the Vigilantes syndicate. Along with Theodore Roosevelt, who had endlessly campaigned for U.S. intervention in Europe, membership rolls included such progressives as Ray Stannard Baker, William English Walling, and Ida M. Tarbell. Besides Edith Thomas, established literary figures who contributed to the syndicate included Gertrude Atherton, Katherine Lee Bates, Robert Underwood Johnson, Lizette Woodworth Reese, Jessie B. Rittenhouse, and George Woodberry. Also on the Vigilantes roll were writers still well known today, some of whom we now consider important for the formation of modernism – Edwin Arlington Robinson, Amy Lowell, Chicago Renaissance figures Alice Corbin Henderson, Vachel Lindsay, and Edgar Lee Masters, and local colorists George Washington Cable and Hamlin Garland. Having recruited this wealth of contributors, the syndicate enforced a policy of military-style discipline, which would compel Vigilantes members to produce propaganda at the demand of the Vigilantes leadership.[35] This enforced discipline apparently drove some authors away from the group – "active contributors" numbered just 160 at the end of the war – yet of the prominent writers just listed only Rittenhouse, Lowell, Henderson, and Masters dropped membership. Robinson, Cable, Garland, and the others stuck with the Vigilantes throughout the war, and in 1918 such notables as Ring Lardner and Edwin Markham (author of the 1899 social protest poem "The Man with the Hoe") joined the group. Furthermore, even inactive members had their work appropriated by the organization. Alice Corbin Henderson's "The Planting of the Green" was distributed by the Vigilantes syndicate in June 1918, and Vachel Lindsay's "The Jazz Bird" appeared in May 1918, as did his endorsement of a patriotic summons "To the Poets of America" composed by Vigilantes founder Hermann Hagedorn.[36]

The Vigilantes' recruitment of writers throughout American literary culture made its organization and its politics seem representative of majority opinion. Just as crucial to the group's success, however, was the swiftness with which it moved to define American homefront mobilization in terms of a conservative (and repressive) politics. Enlisting the support of the publisher George H. Doran, by July 1917 the organization had produced a poetry anthology to "furnish a striking record of the emotional reactions of the American people during the fortnight preceding and the six weeks following the declaration of war" (*FD* v). This supposedly disinterested "record" paralleled the Food Administration's strategy of courting women's support, but the poetry of *Fifes and Drums* works far more explicitly than Food Administration propaganda to situate women in submissive, traditional roles. While assuming as normative an absolute divide between bellicose masculinity and pacifist femininity, Vigilantes poems characterize any man's unwillingness to go to war as the consequence of a woman's undue and unnatural influence over him. Amelia Josephine Burr's "To Our Women" tells the wife or lover of a prospective soldier, "*Woman, your clinging hands have bent his soul awry. / You knew not how to love him if he knows not how to die*" (111); it derides the mother, "*Mother, your love has crippled the soul it strove to shield. / You knew not how to give the life he knows not how to yield* (112). Theodosia Garrison's "The Girls They Left behind Them" even works to reinterpret female submission as empowerment; rather than staying at home "as of old but to weep and pray," the poem's liberated patriotic girls can declare, "this is the pride that we wear today / . . . That they loved us and left us and marched away" (116).

Vigilantes poetry articulates women's life-giving, maternal power in terms of agricultural fertility; women's power, however, is a fecundity responsive only to the state and slavishly obedient to its dictates. In "Concerning Planting" by John Curtis Underwood, a male speaker is converted by "a pure-food specialist," most likely a Food Administration volunteer, to the cause of home gardening (126).[37] The speaker adopts the banter of the specialist to "Plant, Plant, Plant" and also the sensationalist propaganda of the Bryce Report: "If you want to beat those butchers of babies in the air / You'll tell your wife's relations and the uncles of your aunt / And your seventh cousin twice removed to 'Plant, Plant, Plant!'" (127). As the poem proceeds, however, government directives affect the male speaker less dramatically than they do his wife. By assimilating pro-Allied rhetoric, she appears to demonstrate its appeal to her motherly sensibility. As the male speaker reports, "This year the flowers will have to go. My wife says that we shan't / Steal one more Belgian baby's life. So 'Plant, Plant, Plant!'" (128). The patriotic woman is stern with husband and children alike: "My kids declare they can't / Slice up their tennis court. But Ma says 'Plant, Plant, Plant!'" (128). By the end of the poem, the figure of the patriotic mother and wife, prodding her husband to ever-greater gardening exploits, has supplanted that of the food specialist whose pitch she has fully internalized.[38]

Besides the publication of *Fifes and Drums,* by the summer of 1917 the Vigilantes were operating a syndicate distributing patriotic poetry and prose editorials to newspapers throughout the country, specializing in newspapers outside the major eastern cities.[39] Throughout the rest of the war, the syndicate made itself useful to the Food Administration in a variety of ways, even as it consolidated its political influence within the U.S. war machine. During the winter of 1917–18 and again in June 1918, the syndicate ran articles and poems helping to inculcate Food Administration principles and to bolster Hoover's reputation as a national leader. Laura E. Richard's "To H.C.H." (released in January), Amelia Josephine Burr's "Hoover of Belgium," and Thornton W. Burgess's "We Want Hoover!" (both released in June) define Hoover as a peerless national leader, the savior of Belgium; they base their call for patriotic conservation on Hoover's charismatic authority.[40] Despite reservations about this kind of authoritarian politics, federal officials appreciated the syndicate's assistance; the Vigilantes even provided propaganda directly to government agencies such as the Liberty Loan publicity division, whose director wrote thanking the group for its help and congratulating it for reaching "papers all over the country from Texas to New York."[41]

But if the Vigilantes were among the most aggressive in hawking American food policy, the group was swiftly joined by popular magazines and presses eager to show their patriotism. In June 1917, the *Ladies' Home Journal* editorialized on the housewife's question "How Can I Do My 'Bit'?" answering that she must practice "efficiency and economy," must "[run] her home as a business," and "must study the food problem more closely."[42] In the same issue, Mary R. Gamble's verse play, "Aunt Columbia's Dinner Party," describes American wealth and unity as a great banquet supplied by the agricultural bounty of the various states, in which the growing of grain is central: "Three dozen States will furnish wheat, to make the best of bread; / Three dozen will bring in the corn; oh, what a wondrous spread! / . . . Oh, yes, we'll have a wondrous feast, and all the States will see / How Aunt and Uncle can depend on their big family."[43] Even as the poem articulates a definition of American power based on agriculture – as opposed to, say, military might – it develops the metaphor of an extended family that, as we have seen elsewhere, could be easily adapted to include the European Allies. Throughout the summer, editorials, articles on patriotic gardening, recipes for economical meals, and directives from Herbert Hoover filled the *Journal's* pages.[44] In the fall, food poetry reappeared, while for the first time a commercial advertisement in the *Journal* based its sales pitch on the authority of the Food Administration. The large print of an October item, "Mr. Hoover's War-Time Dishes," suggests yet another public service announcement by the *Journal's* editors; the small print reveals the piece to be an ad for the Royal Baking Powder Company.[45] Edna Randolph Worrell's "Shouting the Battle Cry of 'Feed 'Em': A Patriotic Play for Children," a series of rhymed and metered songs and speeches that appeared in November, again proclaims the power of American agriculture, and it extends the metaphor of family developed in Gamble's play to include the Triple Entente. The Farmer, a central character in the play, explains:

> The fruits of the orchard, the grains of the field,
> The roots which the earth clods unfailingly yield,
> Are grown, so to speak, on my wonderful tree,
> Which feeds all our fam-*Allies* – now do you see?[46]

By fall, patriotic food conservation poetry had turned up in the book
trade as well as in popular magazines. In October 1917, Florence McLandburgh, who under the pseudonym McLandburgh Wilson frequently contributed light verse to the *New York Times* and to popular magazines, compiled her patriotic poetry in *Little Flag on Main Street*.[47] The book
gathered nine poems describing the power of agriculture or patriotic
conserving, thereby building a sustained argument for food conservation
among other forms of patriotic service. One poem, "Company for Dinner," embraces the image of family to describe America's relationships
with Belgium, France, and England:

> Our cousins are coming to dinner,
> The larder is showing a lack,
> So pass the kick under the table
> And signal the family, "Hold back!"
>
> You, Mother, decline the potatoes,
> And Father, go light on the meat;
> And Sis, have a heart for the sugar,
> And Bub, skip the bread when you eat.
>
> There – France, have some more, let us beg you;
> John Bull, let us fill up your plate;
> And Belgium, another good helping –
> Gee folks, but to have you is great![48]

Throughout 1918, commercial presses, popular magazines, and advertisers both augmented and benefited from the authority of Hoover and
the Food Administration. Anthony Euwer's *Wings and Other War Rhymes,*
published by Moffat, Yard, and Company, unabashedly revels in the hardship caused by the food embargo of Germany in poems such as "The
Substi-teut."[49] Mary Raymond Shipman Andrews's *Crosses of War,* published by Scribner's, updates the harvest poems of 1914 in "Flower of the
Land," suggesting that now America's young men as well as Europe's are
being readied for reaping. But the book also adopts the modern view of
the saving power of food in wartime, making the case for American pro-
vision to France by contrasting a healthy American baby with a starving
French one in "The Baby and the Baby."[50] In 1918 commercial advertising similarly fed – and fed on – the Hoover hype. In January, Wesson
announced baldly, "Mr. HOOVER'S request that you cook with veg-
etable oil may give you a new interest in this advertisement of Wesson
Oil."[51] Beginning in July Crisco followed with its own advertising campaign, which employed the Food Administration seal and some of its slo-

gans.[52] Even manufacturers of wheat-related products got on the patriotic bandwagon: Golden Age Macaroni suggested that housewives prepare macaroni "To Save Meat," and the manufacturers of Swans Down advertised its Pure Wheat Bran as "The Secret of Making War Cake."[53] This genre of ad design perhaps reached its apotheosis in a Yeast Foam advertisement in the September 1918 *Journal*. Here the patriotic housewife, as per Food Administration propaganda, was pictured in military attire and attitude: saluting, dressed in a cobalt blue and ecru uniform with a Food Administration badge on the headgear (Figure 11). The uniform was not, in fact, a mere fabrication by the Yeast Foam advertiser, but was designed and sanctioned by the Food Administration itself. As an article and picture in the *Ladies' Home Journal* confirms, "Here are the official badge and uniform of members of the Food Administration of the United States. Any woman who signs the Hoover pledge is entitled to wear them."[54] The brief piece describes the uniform's colors, fabrics, and design – "blue chambray, with pointed collar and cuffs of white pique and cap of white lawn" – and an address for purchasing the official patterns from, of course, "the Food Administrator." Although ostensibly the homefront campaign to conserve was about sacrifice and altruism, the symbolism and rhetoric of texts such as the Yeast Foam ad are fundamentally about power. Not only were Food Administration propaganda and policy expressions of national power, but attempts by conservative groups such as the Vigilantes and corporations like Wesson and Crisco to manipulate the imagery of food saving were, patently, grabs for political and economic power. We may partly gauge their success both by the pervasiveness of their images of wartime America and by the parallel successes of conservatism and commercialism in the 1920s.[55]

III

The symbiotic relations between patriotic poetry, government propaganda, and commercial advertising also point to an alternative history of modernism during the war and after. The direct involvement of poets such as Robinson, Lowell, Masters, Henderson, and Lindsay in wartime politics forces us to reconsider the customary view of modernist poetry as largely independent of other poetic traditions and unflaggingly critical of American mass society. At the same time, if we take the propaganda poetry of food conservation as a significant modernist narrative, we move other writers and other cultural forces to the fore. If most current constructions of modernism present its participants as antagonistic toward,

Figure 11. "Victory bread!" Color advertisement by the Northwestern Yeast Company, *Ladies' Home Journal* September 1918: 70.

or at least critical of, the growth of commerce and mass society,[56] a history including the work of the Vigilantes and other nationalist writers reveals another substantial corpus of modern poetry – one wholeheartedly embracing the publishing networks of a national mass culture and celebrating a society newly awakened to the power of systemization and economies of scale.

The radical break with the past stipulated by virtually all conceptions of modernism is unnecessary either to explain the propaganda poetry of the war or to claim some measure of uniqueness for it. Much of this poetry can be understood as a melding of the genteel and popular traditions in American poetry: the poetry of food conservation aimed to educate, instruct, and ennoble readers, and at the same time to accommodate their tastes and preconceptions.[57] These formulations of the poetic were then combined, on a national scale, with the apparatuses of mass print communication and, often, with the party discipline of a political organization. Genteel high-mindedness, a popular desire to please readers, and commercial savvy are conjoined, for instance, in the *Ladies' Home Journal*, where the motives and strategies of propaganda poetry, articles, and advertisements are strikingly parallel. These features are perhaps best distinguished, however, in the Vigilantes: in the group's swift, syndicated distribution of editorial and poetry releases throughout the country; in its hierarchic structure, which cajoled writers to declare their patriotism and produce propaganda on demand; and in its eclectic mix of writing styles, encompassing the high diction and sentiments of Edith Thomas, the satirical humor of Don Marquis and Wallace Irwin, and the jazz experimentation of Vachel Lindsay. From its inception the group was a hybrid, bearing characteristics of genteel, popular, and mass culture. One of Hermann Hagedorn's 1916 speeches mixes the motive of the popular author, "to kindle" grass-roots enthusiasm for the war, with the high purpose of the genteel poet, "to appeal . . . to the instinctive desire latent in the heart of every normal human being with an ounce of youth left on him, to be an active defender of great causes."[58] Hagedorn initially had envisioned "the boys and girls in the schools and the men and women in the colleges" as the Vigilantes' primary audience,[59] and the syndicate's aim remained fundamentally public education, even as it broadened its scope and embraced the apparatuses of both political party and publishing house.

The propaganda poetry of the war is distinctively modern precisely because of its tendency to become immersed in the discourses of mass culture. As propagandists, whether official or unofficial, sought to represent a seamless national consensus, differences among various discourses were minimized. At the same time, however, poetry was distinct from other forms of propaganda insofar as it represented, however deceptively, the individual American voluntarily choosing to join the war effort. Although the Vigilantes relied on the apparatus of mass communication, in the individual newspapers where poems appeared a single author was listed in the byline, so that her or his personal authority stood behind the poem's patriotism. The authority of the individual poet was of course most marked when a well-known poet was printed. But the tendency to see any poet as an individualized speaker is also evident in a favorable *New York Times* review of the Vigilantes' *Fifes and Drums,* which singles out the particular excellences of several of the collection's lesser-known poets, hailing, for instance, the "fine versatility and intense manner" of Amelia Josephine Burr and the "penetrating appeal and beauty" of Theodosia Garrison.[60]

Even when a particular poet's writing was not especially proficient, the marks of amateurism did not necessarily detract from the effectiveness of the poetry as propaganda. Since poetry, more than other forms of published writing, was seen as a spontaneous production, welling up from deep and indubitable conviction, it was assumed that it could and would be written by amateurs. Many poetry critics certainly saw amateurish verse as a threat to the always shaky professional status of the poet, and the flood of poetry written by avocational poets in response to the war only sharpened these critics' chagrin. But the regular appearance and apparent popularity of such poetry in newspapers, magazines, and books suggests that it was an established mode of poetry writing.[61] Sardonic comments on Florence McLandburgh's *Little Flag on Main Street,* a collection of verses "such as appear in the corners of daily papers," contrast the reviewer's ideal of professional verse with the reality of amateurish doggerel. Quoting a poem, "What You Can Do for the Country," which includes a number of food-saving measures – "The thrifty cook can fry for it; / The thirsty can go dry for it; / . . . The farmer can grow rye for it" – the reviewer asks, "Does any one still believe that this sort of thing has any relation to poetry or even to verse?" then quips, "Any one with a rhyming dictionary could do this by the yard."[62] Yet the notion that anyone could write poetry, and many, many did, was very much at the heart of a premodernist idea of poetry. And if amateurish poems like those in *Little Flag on Main Street* do little to advance the standing of poetry as craft or profession, that very quality sets the poems apart as valuable propaganda. While advertising and illustrating, not to mention reporting,[63] had gained in professional status during the 1910s, popular versifying had lost some of the stature it had held when practiced by John Greenleaf Whittier, Henry Wadsworth Longfellow, Oliver Wendell Holmes, and James Russell Lowell.[64] Yet precisely this lack of a highly visible, authoritative figure made the poetry of the American mobilization so seemingly genuine. Compared with the elegant rendering of the patriotic housewife in the Yeast Foam ad of September 1918, the homely lines of Mable I. Clapp's "Hoover's Goin' to Get You," published in the letters section of the November 1917 *Ladies' Home Journal,* have much more the ring of homegrown, voluntary patriotism:

> Oh, gone now are the good old days of hot
> cakes thickly spread;
> And meatless, wheatless, hopeless days are
> reigning in their stead;
> And gone the days of fat rib roasts, and
> two-inch T-bone steaks,
> And doughnuts plump and golden brown,
> the kind that mother makes.
> And when it comes to pie and cake, just
> learn to cut it out,
> Or Hoover's goin' to get you if you
> Don't
> Watch
> Out![65]

Poems such as Clapp's and McLandburgh's, as indeed most of the poems by Vigilantes, give the *impression* of individuality – of idiosyncratic, common voices rising up and rallying to the cause of food conservation. In a mass mobilization intended to subjugate individual interests to the national purpose and to suppress dissenting voices, this impression was indispensable.

IV

While American radicalism was vigorously marginalized by discourses of food conservation, American femininity was valorized. Women were both icons and primary actors in the discourses of food conservation and national mobilization. Given their prominence, we must ask: how much power did women gain when their interests – and their image – became central to the power of the state and mobilization of the nation? Food Administration propagandists and their allies in the advertising industry consistently placed women in positions of subjugation. Food conservation publicists represented women as fundamentally consumers, and therefore as subject to the manipulation of the advertiser and propagandist. If on the one hand publicists recognized the power of women as consumers, duly acknowledging their control over household consumption, on the other hand they sought to curb that power by limiting women's autonomy in the marketplace (after all, an advertising campaign succeeds to the degree that it makes the consumer dependent on the authority of the advertiser and his product).[66] Conceptions of women as heavily dependent upon masculine authority and fundamentally limited in their personal freedom are evident throughout wartime propaganda: in the Food Administration's admonition to women that they must conserve food or French women and children will die; in the steady stream of recipes and advice in the women's magazines that situate women as domestic incompetents; and in the radiant, sharply saluting woman of the Yeast Foam ad whose uniform suggests she is under military discipline.

Insofar as it contributed to all of these configurations of food conservation writing, poetry – including poetry written by women – was complicit in a repressive articulation of American femininity. At the same time, poems written by women do complicate women's co-optation, even while they participate in it. Since women produced poetry much more frequently than they did work in other genres of food conservation literature and art, through poetry women became themselves the agents of patriotic expostulation rather than strictly objects of state and corporate manipulation. For instance, women were far more active in writing Vigilantes poetry than men. Men dominated the membership of the Vigilantes even as they dominated its leadership: in both 1917 and 1918 only one-fourth of the Vigilantes membership was female.[67] But of the 466 press releases that survive in the Library of Congress manuscript archives, 216 – more than 45 percent – were composed by women writers; of 276 poems released, 150 – nearly 55 percent – were by women. Women's association with the Vigilantes offered the opportunity for frequent publication and, thus, recognition for espousing America's cause. The Vigilantes collection *Fifes and Drums* consisted, its reviewer notes, of "breathless cries of song wrung mostly from the hearts of our women" – 35 of the 62 poems in the anthology.[68] Two women poets, Amelia Josephine Burr and Theodosia Garrison, were those most frequently published with the Vigilantes syndicate and were among the most prolific of any American war poets. Burr wrote four books of war poetry and published 61 individual poems in addition to a total of 24 brought into print by the Vigilantes. Garrison published 42 poems in magazines and had 30 distributed by the Vigilantes exclusively.[69]

Some of Burr's and Garrison's work is notable for its projection of women as morally and socially powerful. Acting as the defender of the starving and powerless, the speaker of Garrison's "With a Drink on the Table" makes a sardonic toast to anyone who would drink down the brewed equivalent of a war refugee's dinner:

> *Here's to grain you're using up*
> (Starving folk have prayed for it),
> *Here's to those you rob of it,*
> *Some mother's hungry brood!*[70]

Many of Florence McLandburgh's poems offer a similar view of patriotic women. In "Nemesis," the title character, a married woman, is a potent, even violent, enforcer of Food Administration policy:

> He spliced with her because she made
> Light biscuits every morn,
> But now as patriotic aid
> She grimly feeds him corn.
> Poke it down!
> Choke it down!
> Stoke it down!
> She feeds him corn![71]

The man, in contrast, is impotent; "now he finds his dream denied." At the same time, however, "Nemesis" and similar poems invent little more than another incarnation of woman as witch or, less spectacularly, wife as insufferable nag. Theodosia Garrison's "With a Drink on the Table" draws upon a conservative (and at that time nearly successful) social movement – temperance – which defined women in stridently moralistic terms; and furthermore, the poem subjugates that movement, in which women were at least prominent leaders, to the larger purposes of the male-dominated mobilization. Likewise, when patriotic poems like Worrell's "Shouting the Battle Cry of 'Feed 'Em'" assume the task of educating children, they merely assert patriotic leadership within one of the few professions for which nineteenth- and early-twentieth-century tradition suggested their usefulness.[72] In writing the bulk of the Vigilantes poetry while men, by a ratio of 2 to 1, wrote most of the prose editorials, women assumed the role of producing the ornamental, educative writing while men took on the task of delineating the group's philosophy and political strategy. To be sure, women's patriotic poetry speaks from a position of feminine authority; it constructs a space for women within a nativist and jingoist politics. Yet written in this context, their poetry is deeply compromised by its subjugation within a political movement dominated by men and driven by a logic of repression, a movement to suppress difference.

Alice Corbin Henderson's contribution to the Vigilantes syndicate, "The Planting of the Green," is emblematic of the politics and poetics of women in the war. The poem's speaker describes wartime food policies as founded on economies of scale and a politics of mass mobilization: "We are rising by ten thousands / And we're ploughin' of the ground! / We are droppin' in the corn and beans, / We are plantin' wheat for all, / We are mobilizin' turnips, too, / An' answerin' the call!"[73] Whereas the poet only alludes to the state's role regarding "The notice that's going round," she offers a female personification of the nation, "Auntie Sam," as the moving force behind homefront mobilization:

> Your Auntie Sam is makin' jam
> For all the boys to eat,
> And when she gets her dander up,
> You know she can't be beat!
> She's bossin' all the folks about,
> The farm's no home at all!
> It's just a mobilizin' camp
> For answerin' the call!

The poem places Auntie Sam herself on the front lines. Yet, paradoxically, by putting her on active duty the poem inserts Auntie Sam precisely where the Food Administration would have her – and where she must heed state authority or be shot as a traitor.

Henderson's role in the formation of experimental modernism – she cofounded *Poetry Magazine* with Harriet Monroe and is credited with discovering Carl Sandburg and Edgar Lee Masters[74] – recalls again the connection between wartime politics and the supposedly independent modernist poets. But "The Planting of the Green" also points to formal experimentation as just one site of poetic production, as it gestures to American popular poetry and song by offering wartime lyrics for the popular Irish patriotic song "The Wearing of the Green" (the IWW had its version of the song as well, "Walking on the Grass").[75] Further, placing "The Planting of the Green" and other poetry concerned with food consumption at the center of a modernist narrative foregrounds other, wider issues of American culture and politics. In terms of wartime politics, the poem's recognition that Auntie Sam's homeplace, once mobilized, ceases to be a home anymore can cut two ways. On the one hand, the Vigilantes' and the Food Administration's interpretation holds that by being transformed into a military zone, the home becomes subject to military discipline. On the other hand, the option described by the poets of the New York WPP and the *Masses* holds that by transforming domestic spaces into politically charged terrain, women are politically empowered. But to the extent that poetry describing women as consumers and conservators of food testified to women's potential for empowerment, the poetry of harvest, of agricultural fecundity, and of food conservation exhibited not only women's autonomy but also the state's power to suppress it.

By outright repression where necessary and quiet coercion wherever possible, the state and its civilian volunteers significantly limited American women's political freedom. The autonomy of women, defined and encouraged by the activism of the WPP, was circumscribed; the rapprochement between women's groups and socialist – and even progressive – politics was sharply curtailed. These transformations of political economy were fomented even as they were represented by redefinitions of food and its uses. Ultimately, conservative, repressive articulations of food production and conservation prevailed not because of any inherent superiority, but rather because the Food Administration and allies such as the Vigilantes were able to exploit more effectively modern, mass modes of cultural production. While federal agencies including the U.S. Food Administration orchestrated the systematic, scientific organization of the nation's resources, groups like the Vigilantes supplied a vast number of poems advertising the state agenda and put those poems on the editorial pages of hundreds of newspapers. This seemingly frenetic outpouring of propaganda was in fact carefully calculated: in particular, the Vigilantes' propagandizing for the Food Administration was designed to mobilize housewives – still thought to be natural pacifists – for service to the state. Such targeting of key market sectors, along with propagandists' exploitation of mass distribution and populist appeals, reveals how thoroughly *modernized* the poetry of the mobilization became.

5

Beating the Competition
THE WOMAN'S PEACE PARTY
AND THE INDUSTRIAL WORKERS
OF THE WORLD ON TRIAL

BY 1917, the battle for American cultural hegemony had
turned in favor of those political factions advocating intervention abroad,
conservatism and conformity at home. Between 1914 and 1916, advocates of intervention and supporters of neutrality had seemingly been
matched evenly. If from the beginning sympathies with the Triple Entente and with Belgium were strong among American political elites, this
partiality was counterbalanced in 1914 and 1915 by strong grass-roots opposition against any U.S. involvement in Europe. Antiwar groups such as
the Woman's Peace Party could plausibly claim to represent a pacifist majority and could very likely have organized and politicized this majority
more thoroughly than they did. Through 1916, advocates of preparedness were thwarted, if not entirely rebuffed. Congress did pass the National Defense Act and institute the Council for National Defense, but
the act provided only for an army of 165,000 to be raised over five years[1]
– a far cry from the army of 2 million the United States would attempt
to raise a year later. By signing the Defense Act into law, Wilson effectively preempted hard-line advocates of preparedness. Wilson's reelection
campaign implied the necessity of ideological preparedness – "100 percent Americanism" – but at the same time trumpeted America's and Wilson's policies of nonintervention, as "He kept us out of war" became the
campaign's motto. Wilson himself was uneasy with the campaign's emphasis on his policy of neutrality and success in avoiding the war, but the
delegates to the June 1916 Democratic National Convention had acclaimed above all else that policy and that achievement. When keynote
speaker Martin Glynn had launched into a litany of instances in which
presidents had faced international provocation with conciliation and con-

169

cession, thereby preserving peace, the delegates erupted with approval; one reporter remarked that "the effect was simply electric. He identified in their own minds the cause of pacifism with that of Americanism, and made the two identical."[2]

In analyzing how the balance of political power came to change so decisively in 1917, we must emphasize the crucial role played by the American state, without seeing it as precisely identifiable with the Wilson administration or as the final cause for the directions ultimately taken by American culture in 1917 and after. (As elsewhere in my project, Gramsci's and Althusser's assertion of the interconnection between the official state and civil society obtains here.) Certainly, it is significant that the Wilson administration chose the "crisis" of Germany's resumption of unrestricted submarine warfare as the moment to extend its and America's grasp for international power.[3] Similar crises had passed without a belligerent response; now Wilson called for a declaration of war. But the reaction that followed was complex and was by no means foreseen by Wilson or other progressives in his administration. The multifarious demands of modern warfare, once unleashed, developed their own momentum within the state: standing departments such as War and Treasury declared the need for a draft and war taxation; other departments such as Labor and Food were newly instituted to deal with the special demands of war; and, beyond any centralized control but vital to its operation, a variety of semiofficial and unofficial voluntary organizations including the Vigilantes sprang up to help implement the call to arms. The rapid transformation of American political culture is evident not only in the groups that assisted in the mobilization, but also among those groups that continued to oppose the war. In a matter of months, antiwar political organizations were far past any hope of influencing public policy; they were fighting for their survival as coherent organizations. Once able to contest pro-interventionist groups for cultural hegemony, organizations such as the WPP and Industrial Workers of the World were now thrust into a position of extreme marginality. How they reacted when marginalized is instructive. In effect, these groups' critical power was in no way diminished; indeed, their persecution at the hands of the state underscored the repressiveness and hypocrisy of the American war effort. Their political power was crippled, however – and not only by the state's power but also, ironically, by the very flexibility and ingenuity of their analysis. Under pressure from the state, the WPP and IWW revised their earlier, grandiose conceptions of political poetry, and these revisions, while sometimes constructive and intriguing, usually worked to the detriment of their political effectiveness.

I

The notable exception to the reactive, even passive, tendencies of the national WPP was the New York City branch (NY-WPP), which under the leadership of Crystal Eastman charted an unswervingly radical course. While in late 1915 and throughout 1916 the national leadership of the WPP grew increasingly cautious and inactive, the NY-WPP embraced a politics that brought the branch into close association with other radical groups and into direct confrontation with the U.S. government. Crystal Eastman served both as chair of the NY-WPP and as executive secretary of the American Union Against Militarism, a group of activists committed to opposing military preparedness through demonstrations and dissent.[4] Many other women of the NY-WPP also held membership in the Union. When in April 1917, poet, diarist, and NY-WPP member Sarah Cleghorn went to Washington, joining a protest against the impending declaration of war, she sought the American Union office for directions to the demonstration.[5] On the steps of the capitol she found Tracy Mygatt, Fannie Witherspoon, and Jessie Hughan, and later talked to Emily Greene Balch – all active leaders in the NY-WPP and other radical peace groups (2, 10).[6] Many members of the New York branch found substantial common ground with theoretical Marxists and radical unionists. Crystal Eastman's brother Max was editor of the *Masses,* which championed feminist causes among those important for revolutionary art and politics.[7] The NY-WPP activists reciprocated with keen interest in the struggles of radical labor organizations. Again, Cleghorn's journal provides a gauge. She describes in detail the extraordinary lengths the combatant governments went to in order to keep socialists within their borders from traveling to the Stockholm peace conference, and at various points in the journal she expresses sympathy for socialist publications, approval for the IWW, and contempt for industries profiting by war sales.[8] Among intellectuals, cooperation between feminist pacifists and antiwar socialists was such that the two groups virtually merged. One of the most striking issues of the NY-WPP's *Four Lights* featured artwork commissioned from Boardman Robinson, one of the illustrators on the *New York Call* staff (see Figure 12). Robinson designed a frieze of maimed, weeping, and stooped figures – as many female as male – arranged as if

A Mother to Her War-Time Baby.

Babe, little babe, that vainly pleads
    At the starved, wan breast of thy mother,
What will the terrible years to come
    Teach thy heart of that other
Who, over a blood-soaked border-line,
In just such a desolate home as thine,
    Is a babe like thee
    In his misery?

Will they place thy tiny, fluttering hands
    Closely about a gun?
Will they tell thee tales of hideous things
    His father's folk have done,
Till the dream in thine eyes shall blaze to hate,
And thy soft, warm lips red vengeance prate,
    Till an old, old spell
    Reopens hell?

Dear child, let me shield thy new, white soul
    From the lust of a mad world's keeping;
Better to see thy troubled rest
    Sink into endless sleeping
Now on my heart, than ever to know
That the man my son may some day grow
    Still justified
    Men's fraticide!   **EDNA MEAD.**

Words of Wisdom from Our Allies.

"It is no exaggeration to say that if this conflict goes on indefinitely, revolution and anarchy may well follow, and unless the collective common sense of mankind prevents it before the worst comes, great portions of the Continent of Europe will be little better than a wilderness, peopled by old men, women and children."
        Lord Loreburn, in the House of Lords,
                Nov. 8th, 1915.

"We are told we are fighting for liberty and democracy against tyranny, but gradually we have seen the very system we abominate, whose existence we detest, instituted in our midst, and in setting out to destroy it in the enemy, we are creating it at home."
        Mr. Arthur Ponsonby, in the House of
             Commons, Nov. 11th, 1915.

So Doth the Happy Patriot.

(Heard before Senate Finance Committee, May 12.)

Newspaper and Magazine Publishers: Gentlemen of the Committee, magazines have already been boosted far enough. The public will not pay more. We would have to pay this war tax ourselves. We wish to do "our bit," but some other way. We urge that magazines and newspapers be not taxed.

Druggists: As the bill is now drawn we will have to pay the tax ourselves; it cannot be passed on to the customer. Gentlemen, we insist that we are patriotic, but we recommend that this bill be changed to read, "a tax to consumers of one cent upon every twenty-fice cent purchase."

Automobile Manufacturers: The automobile business of America cannot stand up under this additional 5% tax. Is it possible, gentlemen, that you do not realize that only a very few retail dealers in the country are paying expenses!

Moving Picture Producers: And it is true also that the moving picture houses of the country are operating at a loss.

Advertisers, Coffee Roasters, Electric Railways Representatives, Insurance Companies, Piano, Jewelry, Patent Medicine Manufacturers, etc. (In effect): Gentlemen, we are patriots; we wish to do "our bit," but we want to be patriotic in our own way. We recommend that you tax someone else—not us.

Sporting Goods Manufacturers: Members of the Committee, we urge careful consideration of any additional tax on sporting goods.   **JOY YOUNG.**

"In no Sense a Conscrip

And Yet —

"Rochester, July 23.—Under circumstances which give ground for the belief that they feared forced military service in the trenches of France to fight against fellow countrymen, two young men, both holding draft numbers which were among the first drawn on Friday, committed suicide near here today."
                  N. Y. Call.

／— Italy — Bulgaria — Portugal — Roumania — United States — Cuba — Siam — San Marino — Greece —

With The Glamor Off.

(From *Current Opinion*, August, 1917.)

"Undoubtedly the days are hysterical beyond experience. Every kind of vice flourishes rampantly. War invariably breeds this season of physical excitement, and this war has been no exception. Men and women who led sober lives in 1914 have abandoned themselves in many cases to orgies which are incredible.

"Can we wonder that in Australia and Canada there is the most bitter feeling upon this question?

"'We send you,' they say, 'our very best. And how do you treat them? You turn them into this cesspool of vice and stretch out no hand to save them. There is no city so absolutely vicious as London has been since the outbreak of the war. It is to London our sons go upon their errand to save the Empire.'"

MAX PEMBERTON

in the *London Weekly Dispatch*.

"War brings out strange surprises of high living and fine temper; but it still manages to drag about with it its ancient and traditional heritage of lust. It is dogged by this black shadow, as by a curse. Something in it stirs bad blood here. We have never seen, in peace, such an England as we see today. It is an ugly revelation. And ahead lies the terror of disease such as war alone seems to provoke. No glamor can disguise these dark things."

CANON SCOTT HOLLAND

in the *Commonwealth* (England).

...ion of the Unwilling."

Also, Why These Precautions?

"Men who claim (in the physical examination of drafted men) to be unable to read the test card at a distance of 20 feet will be required to read another card at a distance of 15 feet or 10 feet. This card will be so arranged as to trap any normal visioned malingerer. Color blindness will be tested with such combinations of complementary colors that any faking will be instantly detected." *N. Y. Call*, July 24.

IF.

A Mother to her Daughter.

(After Rudyard Kipling.)

If you can lose your head when all about you
Are losing theirs and saying false is true;
If you can feel that Might alone is Mighty—
Reverse your creed in all you say and do;
If you can cast aside your private ethics,
And claim another law holds for the pack;
If you can join in race annihilation
And never pause to question or look back;

If you can call yourself a Christ disciple
Yet incense burn before the God of war;
If you can chant with saints the sixth commandment,
Then plan to kill and kill—and kill some more;
If you can keep your tender woman's spirit
And dull the charge of murder on your soul,
If you can ease your conscience with a bandage
And daily sit and dumbly roll and roll;

If you can sing "My Country first" and never
Observe that lands melt freely into one;
If you can prove mankind is not united,
Led by one hope as by one rising sun;
If you can doubt that greed of State must perish,
And God, the King, One Sovereignty unfurl,
You'll be a "loyal patriot" my darling,
And which is more—a thing of stone, my girl.

FLORENCE GUERTIN TUTTLE.

Peace Terms Mentioned at Last.

"Senator Lewis: My judgment is, that now is a time when Germany will accept the offer of peace based upon the terms: first, the restoration of Belgium; second, the restoration of the possessions which she has held of France; third, the return of the countries of Serbia, Bulgaria, and Roumania to their previous status; in consideration for that the return to Germany by the allies of those particular parts of the German country which have been taken, to wit, her colonies in Africa.

"Senator King: We are at war, and the thing to talk about is not peace but war."

Congressional Record, June 23, 1917.

in procession across the top of the middle two pages of the magazine; below are written the names of the combatant nations in order of their entry into the war.

The NY-WPP founded its periodical, *Four Lights: An Adventure in Internationalism*, in January 1917 when Woodrow Wilson declared his commitment to "peace without victory" in a speech before the Senate.[9] The periodical continued publication throughout most of 1917, long after Wilson had changed his mind and the nation was at war. Published fortnightly and edited by a different group of two or three NY-WPP members for each number, this little four-page magazine represented a fusion of the artistic and political energies of the young, radical women who dominated the New York branch. Cleghorn, Mygatt, Witherspoon, and Hughan, participants at the April antiwar demonstration, each took at least one turn as a *Four Lights* editor. Despite its modest format, the magazine deserves comparison with better-known avant-garde literary magazines such as *Blast, Others,* and *Seven Arts* that had similarly brief runs. To be sure, *Four Lights* emphasized its politics, not its art; the manifesto in the opening issue foregrounds the editors' political aims: "FOUR LIGHTS will attempt to voice the young, uncompromising woman's peace movement in America, whose aims are daring and immediate. – to stop the war in Europe, to federate the nations for organized peace at the close of the war, and meanwhile to guard democracy from the subtle dangers of militarism."[10] At the same time, *Four Lights* contributors relied heavily on brief, incisive poems to augment the news, criticism, and exhortation contained in its articles, and these poems indicate a shift in poetic assumptions as well as the political orientation of NY-WPP writers. If, for instance, the poems of Olive Tilford Dargan and Angela Morgan demonstrate that there is no necessary connection between a traditional poetics and conservative politics – indeed, I would argue that using a familiar poetic form may be politically advantageous – the poetry written for *Four Lights* nevertheless shows some correlation between a liberated feminist politics and free-verse forms. While metered and rhymed verse exhibiting the high seriousness of a genteel poetics can be found in *Four Lights,* more prominent in the magazine are free-verse poems, both in short and long lines, and verses where rhyme is employed for satiric effect rather than for poetic gravity. Although *Four Lights* was, first of all, a political forum, the literary ambitions of the authors were not inconsequential. Not only do they deserve study in the context of literary modernism, but the self-conscious modernism of the editors also contributes to their positioning of the journal as an organ of marginalized dissent (even as Kreymborg's *Others* and the imagist anthologies were positioning themselves as operating outside dominant culture).

This is not to say that genteel poetry and the "new poetry" did not mix in *Four Lights*. Compare, for example, Jessie Wallace Hughan's "For Valiant Hearts," published on February 6, 1917, with Florence Guertin Tuttle's "A Call to Arms," published on May 19. Hughan's poem resembles stylistically the elevated strains of Dargan's "Beyond War," as the speaker of the poem seeks divine assistance that she and other pacifists might be equal to the confrontation with militarist power and propaganda:

> For valiant hearts we pray, that when we hear
> The tumult of the battle coming near,
> The panic where men strike, they know not why,
> The rout where men are driven forth to die
> We may not join the serried ranks of fear.[11]

Tuttle's "A Call to Arms" likewise seeks courage for the women of the peace movement, but her poem adopts not genteel rhetoric and form but rather a pattern provided by modern newspapers, as each stanza becomes a want ad: "Wanted – Women Insurgent, those who will lead, not follow, / Not imitators of men, but standing steadfast as women." The rhetorical differences between these forms are not inconsiderable. Tuttle's prosy lines, for instance, seem much better able to accommodate the terms of twentieth-century warfare and politics, therefore enabling the poem to enter more directly into contemporary antiwar discussion. Such prosaic, contemporary terms as "trade-wars," "profiteers," and "World State" are employed in a stanza redefining patriotism in terms of international rather than national citizenship:

> Wanted – Patriot Women, whose pulses leap not at trade-wars,
> Launched by the profiteers – purveyors of love that is flag-bound,
> Women whose voices rise as National barriers crumble
> Shaping a new World State whose boundaries know no
>   horizon.[12]

More notable than any differences between these forms, however, is the fact that the *Four Lights* editors seemed to see no particular contradiction between printing both genteel and modernist poetries, which we now regard as competitive, even antagonistic. The different sets of conventions are used to express largely the same political convictions and, indeed, are sometimes intermixed in the same poem.[13] On the one hand, it seems appropriate that Mary Johnston's "The Artist," which calls for women to liberate themselves from conventional notions of femininity, should be written in free verse:

> Rich in knowledge must be the artist,
> Wealthy in wisdom and the visions of love.
> But in bonds the artist perishes!
> O woman! why are you not the supremest artist?
> Awake, Mother of the World!
> Gain Wisdom!
> Gain Freedom![14]

On the other hand, Johnston's vision of the artist mingles a modernist ideal of the artist freed from past conventions with a genteel view of the artist as wise, knowledgeable, and loving – in short, as an exemplar of moral character.

But even as *Four Lights* poetry freely mixes modernist and genteel styles of verse, the dominant perspective of *Four Lights* editors is characteristically modernist: they have come to see themselves as an embattled, select minority swimming against a tide of cultural philistinism. Such a view was, of course, historically conditioned, a consequence of the U.S. intervention and the intense patriotism whipped up in support of it. But it also was the consequence of the political and literary positions taken by *Four Lights* editors, especially in respect to their former allies in various women's organizations. Whereas in 1915 women's pacifist poetry could proclaim all women united against war, by 1917 it had become painfully clear that women were not inevitably pacifistic, for they not only went along with intervention but also mobilized their civic organizations in support of the national war effort. The reaction of those NY-WPP members who continued to oppose war was swift and scathing. Mary Johnston's "The Artist" begins with something like reproach toward women themselves as well as outrage at war: "War! / Let us stop it! / Let us begin with ourselves, / O women!" Apparently, peacemaking does not come naturally to women after all. "Let us colour and model [the world] so that it may love peace," Johnston writes, "But for that woman must be an artist. / And the artist must have her training." Even Hughan's "For Valiant Hearts" strikes a note of fiercer introspection, self-criticism, and self-definition than most earlier WPP poems. Rather than assuming certain "natural" feminine traits, Hughan is consciously concerned with defining the character of the Pacifist Woman, who is willing "To breast the current in its mad career / Of terror at the stranger" as well as to "turn deaf ear / To sacred words." Similarly, the very form of Tuttle's want ads suggests that some women lack the qualifications to be peace activists. She calls for women resistant to appeals of patriotic and religious cant: "women, heroic in mind, refusing to sanction evil / Even when evil is sanctioned both by the Church and the State." She even demands women willing to become revolutionaries for the sake of democracy:

> Wanted – Inspired Women, democracy's uplifted daughters,
> Firm in the new-born faith that sovereignty rests in the people,
> Women who would o'erthrow the Might of Kings and
> Kingdoms,
> Bowing before Ideals, checked by the sceptre of Freedom.

Writing in 1917, the poets of *Four Lights* defined not only pacifist action in the positive terms of exhortation; pacifist activism also came to be defined, haunted by a powerful negative image – that of the activist woman channeling her political energy into war work, whether out of patriotic fervor or based on the calculation that women's support for the war would win the vote. *Four Lights* poetry thereby became as interested in redefining femininity – or in defining an emergent feminism – as in reformulating antiwar activism; its politics was less concerned with negotiating among disparate activist groups, more interested in discerning a new, nonessentialist conception of woman as pacifist and activist. *Four Lights* poems and articles castigated the patriotic activities of American women as often as they criticized the policies of the U.S. government. The satirical piece "Woman's Way in War" was first printed in the issue of June 2, 1917, then reprinted in the July 28 issue after the earlier imprint was banned from the mails. While satirizing pro-war propaganda urging women to help the war effort, the article by Mary Alden Hopkins also implicitly criticizes the women who choose to "do their bit": "Women must not feel that because they work in the narrow confines of the home, they cannot help in the great work of destruction. It is a tender nursery thought . . . that this helpless floppy pink hand may some day write his mother's name in the blood of the enemy, – though of course it is too early to tell just yet which enemy it will then be." Hopkins goes on to overturn the "accusation" and "slander" that women are "essentially producers and conservers." She exhorts women to "prove that they are glad and eager to destroy joyfully all that the ages – and other women – have produced. Courage, sisters! It takes but a minute to destroy a boy into whose making have gone eighteen years of thoughtful care."[15] This savage satire presumably operates on the assumption that most people, but women especially, would be repulsed by the thought of mothers training their boys to kill. The WPP had been founded as a separate organization for women on the basis of this axiom. But for the radical women of the NY-WPP, less inclined than others to see pacifism as essentially feminine, the satire's invocation of pacifistic motherhood would function less as a moral exhortation than as a barb directed against conservative women activists: former allies who had turned their attention from the peace movement to patriotic services such as food conservation, Liberty Loan campaigns, and Red Cross fund-raising drives.[16]

For every poem in *Four Lights* that offers a more affirming view of femininity, there is at least one other that augments the criticism of Hopkins's piece. Included in the same July 28 issue as Hopkins's bloodthirsty mothers is Edna Mead's "A Mother to Her War-Time Baby," whose speaker wonders fearfully, "Will they place thy tiny, fluttering hands / Closely about a gun? / Will they tell thee tales of hideous things / *His* father's folk have done[?]" Rather than permit this "old, old spell" of nationalism to take hold of her son, the mother resolves she would rather see him "Sink into endless sleeping / Now on my heart."[17] But while Mead's poem describes the mother–son relationship tenderly, a second poem in the same issue, Florence Tuttle's "IF," portrays the relationship between mother and daughter through a cynical, satiric mode closer to that of Hopkins's article. Both Mead's and Tuttle's poems employ rhyme and meter, but whereas "A Mother to Her War-Time Baby" uses these to underscore a conventionally sentimental scene, "IF" employs these devices for grim comic effect. The poem's perfect rhymes stand in particularly grisly, ironic contrast to the compendium of betrayal, illogic, and self-deception that characterizes the "patriotic" mother's advice for being a dutiful female citizen in wartime. In the poem, a mother advises her daughter that she can be a patriot

> If you can lose your head when all about you
>   Are losing theirs and saying false is true;
> If you can feel that Might alone is Mighty –
>   Reverse your creed in all you say and do;
> If you can cast aside your private ethics,
>   And claim another law holds for the pack;
> If you can join in race annihilation
>   And never pause to question or look back.

In short, the girl should dispense with all independent thinking, personal ethics, and humane feeling. She can simply enough salve her guilt with

Red Cross work – "ease your conscience with a bandage / And daily sit and dumbly roll and roll." She can easily enough deaden her sense of international solidarity with other women, too: "you can sing 'My Country first' and never / Observe that lands melt freely into one." And then, the mother announces, "You'll be a 'loyal patriot' my darling, / And which is more – a thing of stone, my girl."[18]

Satire of this kind was directed more squarely at the women's organizations supporting intervention – in many cases the former allies or even affiliates of the WPP – than at the government itself. These attacks were not reserved only for conservative women of the social clubs, either, but were directed also at the suffragists of the National American Woman Suffrage Association (NAWSA), who by 1917 had calculated that they might finally win the vote by supporting the war effort. As far back as the April 21 issue, a *Four Lights* poem had railed against the unholy alliance between militarists and suffragists (English suffragists specifically, though the same alliance was forged by the majority of American suffrage activists). A. B. Curtis's "A Study in Evolution" criticizes most harshly the manipulation of "Mr. Asquith and the British Government," who constitute the collective speaker of the poem. Mr. Asquith and his government admit (in an unusually self-reflective mood presumably supplied by the poet): "We had no eyes to see / The patient service of the days of peace, / The steady building of each human life." The quiet contributions of women were ignored; only when women did their part in supporting the manly "clash of steel" were they appreciated. Posed against Curtis's catalog of womanly sacrifices, the government's token appreciation of "votes" looks appallingly puny:

> You have translated thus
> Yourselves to us,
> And for your service and your sacrifice,
> Your heroism, self-denial, skill,
> Endurance, strength,
> Your nimble fingers shaping things to kill,
> We grant you votes.[19]

But if Asquith and his government receive the heaviest criticism, the poem also insinuates the patriotic woman's connection to death on the battlefield: "Your nimble fingers shaping things to kill." In the terms described by the poem, the compromise cut by suffragists and the British government is much more than a politically expedient act; it marks the co-optation of women's politics and industry by men's destructive designs. If declaring their patriotism seemed a necessary compromise to many of the suffragists, to the feminists of the NY-WPP it seemed a betrayal of earlier political commitments. They sought alternatives to the calculus of political necessity used by the majority of the suffragists: they preferred to oppose the government rather than to collaborate with it, to separate instead of link the issues of suffrage and war service.

The publication of a poem such as Curtis's marks a parting of the ways between the NY-WPP and the NAWSA, the largest American suffrage organization, which had embraced war work as the vehicle for winning public support for women's suffrage. It was this transformation of women from natural pacifists to perfect patriots, accepted by the NAWSA and many former WPP members, that made it imperative for feminist pacifists to reject the essentialism of earlier thinking about women's pacifism. *Four Lights* poems such as Curtis's display this kind of increasing theoretical sophistication. "A Study in Evolution" draws attention to the nonessential character of any political position, especially promoting a nonessential understanding of political positions underwritten by gender. Even as they stipulated that femininity and masculinity did not determine pacifist or nonpacifist inclination, *Four Lights* editors also maintained that neither did nationality determine one's stand on the war. This is the theoretical and political insight encapsulated in Hopkins's "The Picket," published on October 20, 1917, the final issue of *Four Lights.* "The Picket" declares women's political independence from the policies of the wartime mobilization:

> Men tell us women
> Not to ask for suffrage now
> Lest we hinder the pursuit of war.
> Well, for my part,
> I would rather have a vote than a war any day.

Refusing to accept the devil's bargain of votes for war support, Hopkins's poem theorizes a women's political movement that is independent of the dictates of the patriarchal state: a movement for women's rights and for peace both.[20]

But as *Four Lights* editors and contributors grew more sophisticated in their analysis of pacifism and wartime politics, more sharp in their criticism of political collaborators with the state, they decreased their chances of building a significant antiwar coalition. In distancing themselves from the genteel ideologies (and poetics) of the WPP of 1915, the activists of the NY-WPP were certainly moving toward a modern conception of feminism and a modernist definition of poetry, but they were also leaving behind the open, heterogeneous ideology and pragmatic coalition politics that had carried the WPP of 1915 to substantial success. By dramatically cutting their ties with the WPP's political formula of coalition building, the *Four Lights* editors cut their ties even with moderates within their own New York branch.

It is by no means coincidental that *Four Lights* was put out of circulation not by the U.S. Post Office, as most other dissenting periodicals were, but rather by its own financial supporters and governing body. Though the *Four Lights* issues of June 2 and June 30 were banned from the mails, managing editor Margaret Lane thereafter resorted to sending out the magazine sealed in envelopes, an expensive but apparently successful strategy.[21] By September 1917 Lane was on a leave of absence because she was about to have a baby.[22] Therefore, it was acting secretary Lucile Davidson who introduced the possibility of softening the magazine's approach. She wrote of criticism of the magazine: "The accusation has been made that FOUR LIGHTS is flippant and casual, with sarcasm futile and nagging policy, ineffective although clever. Many believe that a constructive policy in the future should be dealt with in each number."[23] But just as the *Four Lights* editors debated whether to scrap the magazine's oppositional politics, another kind of verdict on the magazine came in: the contributions financing *Four Lights* virtually ceased. On October 15, 1917, Davidson wrote Fannie Witherspoon, explaining that *Four Lights* had barely enough money in the bank to pay for present expenses: "Our position is so very uncertain. Not one of the women who gave us large sums this past year, have offered to renew their pledges."[24] Apparently, the wealthier members of the NY-WPP were also more conservative politically (and perhaps literarily) than the *Four Lights* editors; the loss of their support brought the magazine to an end. With the NY-WPP facing financial hardship generally, and given criticism of *Four Lights* within the branch itself, the NY-WPP leadership board refused to divert money for continued publication of the magazine. Davidson and Lane made various attempts to resurrect the magazine, but only a single additional number appeared, in June 1919, well after the war was over.[25]

The pressure of patriotic conformity divided the NY-WPP's activist, radical leaders from other pragmatic, more politically experienced WPP leaders: while the former became marginalized (and themselves moved toward the political margin), the latter were assimilated into the national mobilization. If the activists of *Four Lights* were not accommodating enough toward their more moderate colleagues in the peace movement, those more moderate colleagues were certainly far too accommodating toward the state in giving up active war opposition altogether. The dramatic silencing of the WPP was produced not only by errors in political judgment by the New York radicals, but also by failures of political persistence among the other members. More conservative WPP members had, after all, dedicated themselves to the ideal of their own immutable pacifism. That Jane Addams should have been willing to campaign for the U.S. Food Administration[26] reflects either monumental intellectual naïveté or a disturbingly chameleon view of her political identity – in either case, she would have done well to listen to her more radical, less flexible compatriots of the NY-WPP. Although the WPP remained a solvent organization throughout the war, it did so principally by becoming a peace organization that no longer campaigned for peace; in June 1918 it even ceased to become a pacifist organization in name, as this was changed to the Woman's International League. The group adopted its current title, the Women's International League for Peace and Freedom, only after the war.[27]

II

Transformations of political allegiance such as Addams's were far from exceptional. They were common among American socialists as well as pacifists. It is in these groups, which before 1917 had been staunch war opponents, that we can see perhaps most clearly the psychological and political pressures brought to bear by mass patriotism and civic conformity. For when the political commitment of pacifists and labor radicals waned, it did so not spontaneously but under the influence of a newly persuasive – or a seemingly unstoppable – ideological and cultural matrix (which, through major press anthologies and food conservation poetry, we have already examined from within). Women's groups such as NAWSA, committed only secondarily to peace activism, made the pragmatic calculation that conservative, mass patriotism could not be deterred and chose rather to support the mobilization so as to have some chance of gaining the vote. For pacifists who chose not to be activists in 1917, their passivity was accompanied by strenuous, often acrobatic intellectual work that reconciled their pacifism with the militarist, nationalist ideologies then dominant. Jane Addams's *Peace and Bread,* for instance, appears to essentialize the connection between peace and the "staff of life" and thereby finesses the major role that U.S. food production and conservation played in the Allied war effort.[28]

Similarly, pro-war socialists did not typically renounce their loyalty to socialism, but rather explained their support for the United States in terms of revolutionary and Marxist terminology. Generally, they overlooked the capitalist economies of the United States, Great Britain, and France, stressed the class equality given lip service by these Western democracies, and railed against class injustices suddenly supposed to be peculiar to German autocracy. This kind of dichotomy between the Allies and the Central Powers became even more persuasive after the May 1917 revolution in Russia, which put a republic – albeit a tottering, fledgling one – into place. As well as being disseminated by the widely publicized pro-war statements of the socialist intelligentsia,[29] an interventionist version of socialistic thinking was popularized by the newly famous poet Carl Sandburg. Sandburg was always a relatively conservative socialist, belonging to the "gradualist" camp that dominated the Wisconsin Social-Democratic Party. Still, as we have seen, poems from his 1916 collection, *Chicago Poems,* had been unequivocal in their condemnation of the capitalist war. In "Ready to Kill" Sandburg had written:

> TEN minutes now I have been looking at this.
> I have gone by here before and wondered about it.
> This is a bronze memorial of a famous general
> Riding horseback with a flag and a sword and a revolver on him.
> I want to smash the whole thing into a pile of junk to be hauled
>   away to the scrap yard.
> I put it straight to you,
> After the farmer, the miner, the shop man, the factory hand, the
>   fireman and the teamster,
> Have all been remembered with their bronze memorials,
>
> . . . .
>
> Then maybe I will stand here
> And look easy at this general of the army holding a flag in the air,
> And riding like hell on horseback
> Ready to kill anybody that gets in the way,
> Ready to run the red blood and slush of the bowels of men all
>   over the sweet new grass of the prairie.[30]

In 1917 Sandburg, the newly acclaimed poet of industrial Chicago and the working masses, wrote "The Four Brothers," a celebration of the recent alliance between the republics of France, Britain, Russia, and the United States that was printed in newspapers across the country, reprinted in the news sheets of the pro-war American Federation of Labor, and praised by, among others, Committee on Public Information chief George Creel.[31] About a year after the publication of *Chicago Poems,* Sandburg reinvented the Great War as a constructive, progressive war. In "The Four Brothers," the "long-range guns" and the machine guns that "run a spit of metal" become the rhythm section for a triumphant martial procession:

> MAKE war songs out of these;
> Make chants that repeat and weave.
> Make rhythms up to the ragtime chatter of the machine guns;
> Make slow-booming psalms up to the boom of the big guns.
> Make a marching song of swinging arms and swinging legs,
> > Going along,
> > Going along,
> On the roads from San Antonio to Athens, from Seattle to
> > Bagdad –
> The boys and men in winding lines of khaki, the circling squares
> > of bayonet points.

Sandburg's transformation from antiwar zealot to pro-war enthusiast is thorough, and all the more ominous because the language and scenes of the earlier poems are so freely evoked in the later ones. The "huskies" who do the gritty industrial work of the world are, after all, the volunteers and conscripts who do the bloody, military work of war:

> Cowpunchers, cornhuskers, shopmen, ready in khaki;
> Ballplayers, lumberjacks, ironworkers, ready in khaki;
> A million, ten million, singing, "I am ready."
> This the sun looks on between two seaboards,
> In the land of Lincoln, in the land of Grant and Lee. (*CP* 143)

The bronze military figure in Grant Park – probably the general himself – had been an object of contempt; now Sandburg joins the erectors of the statue in celebrating Grant and identifying the heroism of the workers with that of Grant. The divide between the commanding officer and the soldiers whom he orders into battle, precisely delineated in "Ready to Kill," is here obliterated by the honoring of Civil War generals and by soldiers who say " 'I am ready to be killed.' "

Certainly, the Russian revolution was feeding socialists' hopes that a proletarian revolution was under way – that the war had after all precipitated the shake-up of old, oppressive orders.[32] The poem can proclaim,

"The czar gone to the winds on God's great dustpan, / The czar a pinch of nothing, / The last of the gibbering Romanoffs" (*CP* 145). It can reasonably hope that "The kaiser will go onto God's great dustpan – / The last of the gibbering Hohenzollerns." In keeping with his past socialist commitments, Sandburg adopts the rhetoric of international solidarity and labor's nobility: "Look! It is four brothers in joined hands together. / The people of bleeding France, / The people of bleeding Russia, / The people of Britain, the people of America" (144). Yet the identification of "the people" with their governments – "These are the four brothers, these are the four republics" – flies in the face of a socialist understanding of class division and class warfare, an understanding that Sandburg had himself earlier articulated. Sandburg's emphasis on the virtues of the working classes only underscores how he gives over his poem to the same nationalist clichés that had mobilized Europe for war in 1914. Now he dedicates the working classes – and if need be, their lives – to the service of the nation:

> I swear only reckless men, ready to throw away their lives by
>   hunger, deprivation, desperate clinging to a single purpose
>   imperturbable and undaunted, men with the primitive guts of
>   rebellion,
> Only fighters gaunt with the red brand of labor's sorrow on their
>   brows and labor's terrible pride in their blood, men with souls
>   asking danger – only these will save and keep the four big
>   brothers. (145)

From Sandburg's perspective, the republic depends for its survival on the desperation, the recklessness, and the self-denial of its workers. But these are precisely the qualities Sandburg had earlier complained any nation-state – whether ideal republic or despotic monarchy – had been able to rely upon in waging its wars. At issue, then, was the extent to which the interests of the nation in going to war could be identified with those of the working classes that fought it. As a socialist writing while the United States was neutral, Sandburg had denied such an identification. As an American writing after the government had declared war, he insisted upon it.

Sandburg's decision to proclaim his allegiance to the state – and to redefine his relationship with socialism so as to allow this – might be plausibly credited to uncertainty about his own identity as an American. As a second-generation immigrant, Sandburg, like many other new Americans in the labor movement, was particularly susceptible to the kind of 100 percent Americanism promoted by state propaganda, which not only encouraged a narrow version of patriotism but sharply questioned the loyalty of anyone who would not adhere to it.[33] Still others in the labor movement made the same kind of pragmatic calculation that NAWSA had. The American Federation of Labor was the most active and cynical collaborator. AFL chief Samuel Gompers believed the war presented an unparalleled opportunity for business and labor to cooperate – and, not incidentally, for his federation to establish itself as the dominant union in the United States. An outspoken advocate of preparedness in 1916, Gompers was appointed by Woodrow Wilson to the Advisory Commission of the Council for National Defense, a federal organization charged with making mobilization plans. Then, in March 1917, Gompers convened a special conference of the AFL; in sharp contrast to the socialists who met less than a month later, at Gompers's urging the federation leadership endorsed a resolution promising the organization's support if and when the United States went to war.[34] Furthermore, Gompers and the secretary of New York's Central Federated Union, Ernest Bohm, founded the New York-based American Alliance for Labor and Democracy, a news syndicate that distributed conservative, pro-government articles – and poems – to union newspapers throughout the country.[35]

Other organizations involved in labor politics, notably the Socialist Party of America (SPA), were fractured by internal controversy much like that which neutralized the Woman's Peace Party. The SPA, which had experienced its high-water mark of 118,000 members in 1912, continued to decline throughout the war, sinking to approximately 80,000 members in 1917.[36] U.S. entry into the war immediately threw the SPA leadership into crisis. The national convention, which gathered in St. Louis just as war was being declared in Washington, adopted an antiwar platform ratified by the membership at large by a ratio of 3 to 1.[37] But many of the most prominent socialist intellectuals outside the convention defected to the interventionist cause. John Spargo, who in St. Louis had authored a dissenting resolution supporting U.S. war involvement, was joined by Upton Sinclair, Meyer London – the one socialist in Congress – and a host of the party intelligentsia in New York, among them the journalists Charles Edward Russell and William English Walling and the historians Gustavus Myers and William James Ghent.[38] So while the St. Louis convention brought forth a majority declaration condemning the war, the party's leadership as well as its membership was sharply and destructively divided by the appeals of nationalism and political pragmatism.

III

In comparison, the IWW took a consistent stand against the war that both union leadership and membership adhered to – though, as I have argued, many IWW members expressed their lack of patriotism not by specifically denouncing the war, but by declaring the war insignificant to their concerns as workers. Although IWW literature proclaimed the Wobblies' willingness to engage, if need be, in a bloody revolution, IWW leaders seemed much more inclined toward a bloodless one. Throughout the summer of 1917, with the significant exceptions of Frank Little's campaigning in Montana and Ralph Chaplin's writing and cartooning, the IWW had avoided direct antiwar agitation since the April declaration of war, preferring to work for improved wages and working conditions in its locals.[39] Even the solidarity of the IWW was shaken, however, by the discourses of patriotism and conservatism that drove wartime politics; the IWW's agitation and the very language used by IWW agitators were fundamentally altered by the wartime state.

In the summer of 1917, it is at first striking how little the IWW's opposition to war affected its operations. To be sure, violence against the IWW intensified immediately after the U.S. declaration of war. By that time pro-war patriotism dominated all but a few labor newspapers,[40] preventing the IWW from orchestrating a national and international publicity campaign as it had in the arrest, trial, and execution of Joe Hill. Yet through the summer of 1917, the IWW generally succeeded in portraying reactionary attacks against it as additional proof of the diametrical opposition between capitalism and revolutionary unionism, as well as of the essential goodness of the latter. On July 12, 1917, in Bisbee, Arizona, two thousand citizens deputized by the town marshall rounded up twelve hundred IWW-organized miners, loaded them onto two freight trains, and deported them to a New Mexico desert (Dubofsky 386–87). The July 28, 1917, issue of *Solidarity* responded with a cartoon by Chaplin – alias "Bingo" – which paralleled the deportation of the union miners with the German deportations of Belgians (Figure 13).[41] While indeed suggesting that law and order, Bisbee style, was as autocratic and inhuman as the German subjugation of Belgium, the cartoon also configures a social and moral chasm, underscored by the column of extended bay-

Homes Broken Into, Men Robbed, Women Assaulted, Stores
Closed Down — Mob Law Rampant When Bisbee's
Corporation Thugs Deport Union Men for
Refusing to Scab.

STRIKE UNBROKEN — MINERS MORE DETERMINED TO WIN THAN EVER

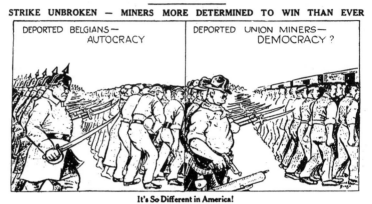

It's So Different in America!

Figure 13. "It's So Different in America!" Cartoon by Ralph Chaplin and headlines, *Solidarity* July 28, 1917: 1. By permission of the Archives of Labor and Urban Affairs, Wayne State University.

onets, between the union miners and the Bisbee deputies which was as wide as that supposed to exist between the savage "Huns" and saintly Belgians. The news column below the cartoon emphasizes further the heroism of the workers:

> This was probably one of the greatest exhibitions of solidarity ever shown. Fellow Workers made speeches in Spanish and English amidst the roaring cheers. The air was blue with curses, and we swore to stick together whatever might happen. Guns were aimed at the workers; women and young and old were shouting defiance at the human monsters who were breaking up their homes. It seemed for a few minutes as if the social revolution was on. We were defenseless, but our spirit was unbroken.[42]

If injustices of the sort perpetrated by authorities in Bisbee and other western localities had been even more widespread, the revolution might have gotten under way after all. When, in July 1917, IWW organizer Frank Little went to Butte, Montana, to agitate among the copper miners in favor of IWW organization and against America's capitalist war, he was killed by a lynching organized by the patriotic, pro-business citizens of the town (Dubofsky 391–92). In the same issue of *Solidarity* that reported Little's August 1 murder, an opinion column by Richard Brazier was hyperbolic in proclaiming, "America's Bloodless Revolution Has Started," but it could make a fairly convincing case that workers *should* begin the revolution. When warrants for IWW leaders including Brazier were issued in September, the U.S. Justice Department might have anticipated, based on Wobbly rhetoric, that the accused traitors would resist arrest and perhaps even try to initiate a general strike. Had they heeded their oft-stated distrust of capitalist "justice," IWW leaders might have comprehended better the difficulty of being acquitted of treason charges while the capital, industry, and populace of the United States were being systematically mobilized for war. Instead, recalling peacetime trials in which IWW members had been acquitted of trumped-up charges, IWW leaders placed their faith in the capitalist courts they had often denounced.[43] Almost immediately after the indictments were made, General Secretary Haywood and IWW defense lawyer George Vanderveer recommended that the accused Wobblies surrender themselves to the federal authorities, and all did (Dubofsky 408).

By arresting IWW leaders from every branch office in September 1917, the federal government largely shut down union operations: the IWW's disintegration can be directly attributed to this national crackdown, which continued through the "Red Scare" of 1919 (Dubofsky 406–7). But if the sedition trials had everything to do with naked political power, the struggle in the Chicago courtroom had virtually nothing to do with the IWW's seditious or nonseditious conduct. It was rather a contest of ideology, played out in the severely uneven terrain of federal courtrooms at the height of wartime jingoism. From the start, federal prosecutors realized the difficulty of marshaling hard evidence to convict all 101 Chicago defendants on the more than one hundred charges brought against each of them.[44] So the prosecutors aimed to convict individual IWW members by charging that the union *as a whole* was, simply by virtue of its philosophy and character, seditious (Dubofsky 435).[45] The prosecutors could present only a few alleged instances of direct IWW interference with war mobilization (and even these could rarely be tied to any of the Wobblies on trial); instead, beginning on May 9, prosecution attorneys Porter and Nebeker contemptuously recited and lectured on IWW newspaper editorials, advertisements for literature, the preamble, pamphlets, IWW songbook selections, and "Bingo" cartoons.[46] By making the IWW's literature the chief witness for the prosecution, government lawyers put up for trail the very ideological and sociopolitical underpinnings of the IWW.

Even as the state used federal courts to strip the IWW of its power, those courts also fundamentally altered the language of poetic protest and mobilization that had characterized IWW literature. On the one hand, the prosecution interpreted Wobbly propaganda as purely, merely subversive; it (predictably) ignored the ways in which the IWW's iconoclasm and its publicity were distinctively American, and (of course) it ignored the ways in which the IWW offered a specific, constructive alternative to American capitalism. On the other hand, the IWW defense accepted, virtually without contest, the binary discourse of treason–loyalty that the prosecution introduced, so that defense witnesses tried to position themselves as loyal, only moderately progressive Americans. As we have seen, the IWW was in fact a distinctively American organization, but in reframing its discourse of labor solidarity and socialist struggle in the terms of progressive reform, the IWW ceased to speak for the economically marginalized with the same distinctive socialist authority it had formerly held. Even if they had been found innocent, the IWW leaders had effectively abandoned the discourses of social revolution that had drawn in thousands of unskilled workers. Since their conviction was inevitable given the patriotic conformism of 1918, there seems to have been little reason for the IWW to give up its revolutionary rhetoric. But abandon it they did, and thus they closed dramatically the gap between proletariat and bourgeois that the union had always relied upon to define both its identity and its mission. The trial transcript shows this strikingly, as IWW members repeatedly testified to the nonviolent, nonrevolutionary, and even patriotic tendencies of their union. The defense in fact attempted to reinterpret the government's evidence to show that the IWW's theories, including its conceptions of sabotage, revolution, and class warfare, countenanced neither violence nor destruction; in effect, while the prosecution affirmed – albeit luridly – the IWW's advocacy of a radical labor agenda, the IWW defense substantially softened the radical commitments long held by the union members on trial.

The first defense witness, James Thompson, had been active as an IWW agitator in the lumber mills of the Northwest. When he took the stand on June 26, 1918, defense attorney Vanderveer immediately led him through an extensive reinterpretation of the IWW literature earlier presented by the prosecution, focusing on the ninth edition of *Songs of the Workers,* published in March 1916.[47] According to an account written by codefendant Harrison George, later one of a few Wobblies to urge IWW cooperation with the Russian communists, when Thompson testified "the marble walls of a federal court echoed with the most passionately terrible denunciation of capitalism ever heard in such dignified surroundings."[48] But the court transcript – today on file at the IWW Collection of the Reuther Library, Wayne State University – reveals Thompson in another character, not denouncing capitalism but disavowing the revolutionary ideas and tactics described in Wobbly songs. On the strength of his experience in leading meetings where IWW songs were sung and, consequently, his expertise in explaining what the songs meant, Thompson revealed that "Christians at War" "was not written by an I.W.W." and, at any rate, "it was written when the war started, or shortly after" as a response to Germany's march on Belgium – "when Germany started to walk rough-shod over the people of Belgium, and did it in the name of God."[49] Thompson thus implies that materials in *Solidarity* and *Songs of the Workers,* if written by a nonunion member, were not to be taken as authoritative even though these materials bore the IWW Publishing Bureau imprimatur. Just as remarkably, Thompson attributes to the poem a particular antipathy for the German abuse of religion – a convenient reading given the kind of Kaiser-bashing then rampant, exemplified by Sandburg's "The Four Brothers."

The publishing history of "Christians at War" and the IWW association of its author, John F. Kendrick, belie Thompson's interpretation of the poem. Whether or not Kendrick was ever an IWW member – Joyce Kornbluh says only that he may have been a Chicago newspaperman[50] – he did have at least three poems published in *Solidarity* during 1915 and 1916, so editor Ben Williams presumably regarded his perspective as consonant with the IWW's, and the parodic form of "Christians at War" indicates Kendrick's acquaintance with Wobbly song composition. When the poem first appeared in December 1915 (hardly "when the war started, or shortly after," as Thompson claimed), a footnote remarked that "the above poem was written especially for Solidarity." Furthermore, it was reprinted in the next edition of *Songs of the Workers,* in March 1916 (where it was first titled "Christians at War"), and has appeared in almost every edition since. As for Thompson's argument that the poem referred primarily to the German invasion of Belgium, certain lines might indicate this context as opposed to others: something like the "rape" of Belgium is indicated by

> Smash the doors of every home,
> Pretty maidens seize;
> Use your might and sacred right
> To treat them as you please.

But other lines could refer just as easily to the food rationing in any of the belligerent countries:

> Steal the farmers' savings,
> Take their grain and meat;
> Even though the children starve,
> The Saviour's bums must eat.

And still other lines, in the final stanza of the poem, by their reference to the "dollar-sign" definitely suggest American war profiteering and, perhaps, aggressive expansion of U.S. trade to Latin America:

> Praise The Lord whose dollar-sign
> Dupes his favored race!
> Make the foreign trash respect
> Your bullion brand of grace.[51]

What is more, Kendrick's poem was printed in *Solidarity* alongside a companion piece written by William Lloyd Garrison and reprinted in 1899, when its satire applied not only to Britain's imperial conquests but also to America's seizure of the Philippines:

> The Anglo-Saxon Christians, with Gatling gun and sword,
> In serried ranks are pushing on the gospel of the Lord.
> On Afric's soil they press the foe in war's terrific scenes,
> And merrily the hunt goes on throughout the Philippines.[52]

Between Kendrick's new poem and Garrison's old one, then, there are more references to the United States and Britain than to Germany, suggesting at least an across-the-board condemnation of capitalist, Christian wars and not, certainly, an indictment focused exclusively on Germany's war making.

The first publication in which "Christians at War" appeared need not – indeed, could not – determine its meaning in the Chicago courtroom. The interpretation supplied by Thompson is, however, precisely the point at issue, for his reading dulled the poem's critical edge, diminishing the separation it describes between the IWW and bourgeois society. Under the pressure of possible conviction, the federal court of Judge Keenesaw Mountain Landis was inculcating proper bourgeois manners in the IWW's leaders. The trial was effectively provoking a new discourse of poetry interpretation among the Wobbly defendants. Heretofore, IWW songs and verse were at the same time singular and multiple in their interpretive possibilities. They were singular insofar as they were used consistently to further the aims of the "one big union," whether published in *Solidarity,* in the "Little Red Song Book," or on broadsides; whether sung in workers' camps, recited on street corners, or read privately. But they were also always multiple in their significance: not just in the variety of contexts in which they were used and interpreted, but also in the motility of signifiers such as "sabotage," "black cat," and even "revolution," which were particularly unstable in terms of the degree of violence – or of sheer bluffing – they implied. In a sense, the IWW's reinterpretation of its verse extends the radical instability of those texts. That is certainly what seems to be demonstrated by reading a poem such as "Christians at War" as siding with the Triple Entente against the Central Powers. But once having reread the poem and others in benign, untreasonous, and even patriotic ways, the defense sought to reify those readings; for the jury, the poems were supposed to become, once and for all, patriotic declarations or just harmless scribbling. So even as the IWW defendants were introducing willful misreading, exploiting the indeterminacy of their texts – introducing the very insights about reading poetry that were guiding the modernist "revolution" in criticism and writing – they were also working (like, perhaps, some of the modernists) to maintain exclusive critical authority over their own work. Like modernists such as Pound and Eliot, they made use of the materials of history – the class war, the ideology of proletarian revolutions – and at the same time attempted to break free of their own historicity. As Pound and Eliot looked to create a transcendent art out of twentieth-century ennui, so the IWW defendants tried to disengage their verse from the historical struggle that had shaped it.

The process was repeated many times in Thompson's readings of IWW poems, even when his interpretations reflect IWW views relatively accurately. For instance, in discussing Joe Hill's "Casey Jones, the Union Scab," Thompson offers a clear expostulation on the difference between trade unions and the IWW's "one big union," but he attributes the sabotage in the poem to trade unions when it seems evident that the sabotage is done by IWWs, not least because the poem celebrates the practice. "Casey Jones," which first appeared in the 1912 edition of *Songs of the Workers,* is according to Thompson's testimony "a criticism of the craft union methods of conducting a strike."[53] He explained that the IWW, as opposed to the AFL, organized workers throughout an industry rather than within each individual craft or trade, so that in a railroad strike, for example, engineers would go on strike along with shop mechanics, instead of permitting one group to work while another was on strike. The song "Casey Jones," Thompson argued, showed the chaos resulting in an industry where the craft-union system was in force. Thompson's explication by turns quotes from and discusses the song:

> "The Workers on the S.P. line" – that is the Southern Pacific – "to strike sent out a call;

>> But Casey Jones the engineer, he wouldn't strike at all;
>> His boiler it was leaking, and its drivers on the bum,
>> And his engine and its bearings, they were all out of plumb.
>> Casey Jones kept his junk pile running;
>> Casey Jones was working double time" –

> scabbing on the shop men –

>> "Casey Jones got a wooden medal,
>> For being good and faithful on the S.P. line."

> Good and faithful to his employers – not to the strikers; instead of helping the strikers win the strike, he was helping the company break the strike, and he ought to have a wooden medal. (5165–66)

Thompson persuasively outlines the IWW position on the trade versus industrial union question; basically, he succeeds by sticking with the IWW pitch that he had undoubtedly often made in the lumber camps. His further explanation of the poem, however, is less convincing:

> "The Workers said to Casey: 'Won't you help us win this strike?'
> But Casey said; 'Let me alone, you'd better take a hike.'
> Then someone put a bunch of railroad ties across the track,
> And Casey hit the river with an awful crack."

> Now that is a craft union on strike, and they asked the engineer to strike with them, so they put a bunch of ties across the track, or some other violence. That is not the I.W.W. idea. That is a form of weakness; that is no way to stop a train. The idea that he should stick together with them, is what we preach, not that they should go and put a bunch of ties across the track. (5166)

Certainly Thompson is right in saying the Casey Jones of the poem is a craft unionist, if he belongs to a union at all. But given the history of unionism, the shop mechanics are at least as likely to be IWWs as members of another craft union. Although it is true that craft unionism would make it possible for shop mechanics to strike while engineers continued to work, in the 1910s there were few industries in which the IWW and trade unions were not both active and in competition with each other.[54] Repeatedly, IWW-affiliated workers went on strikes while AFL members in the same industry kept on working, hoping, like Casey Jones, that their loyalty would be rewarded by their employers.

Most crucially, Thompson's account of how the song was interpreted by IWW organizers and members at large is improbable ultimately because of the glee with which the poem treats Jones's death by sabotage. Thompson himself recited in court:

> "Casey Jones hit the river bottom,
> Casey Jones broke his blooming spine,
> Casey Jones was an Angeleno,
> He took a trip to heaven on the S.P. line."

> "When Casey Jones got up to heaven to the Pearly Gate,
> He said: 'I'm Casey Jones, the guy that pulled the S.P. freight.'
> 'You're just the man,' said Peter; 'our musicians went on strike;
> You can get a job a-scabbing any time you like.'" (5166)

After such rambunctiousness, a rank-and-file member of the IWW would certainly not be inclined to criticize the striking workers who had caused Casey's demise; in the context of singing this song, union organizers would hardly be likely to go into distinctions between those tactics "officially" approved by the IWW and those celebrated in the IWW songbook. Given the Wobblies' taste for raucous songs like "Casey Jones – The Union Scab," the striking musicians in heaven might well have belonged to an IWW local.

Thompson's interpretations of other selections from *Songs of the Workers,* like his reading of "Casey Jones," tried to explain away the songs' apparent approval of destructive forms of sabotage. Explicating Pat Brennan's "Harvest War Song," set to "Tipperary" (the famous marching song of the British Empire), Thompson argued that "Up goes machine" – as in the line "Up goes machine or wages, and the hours must come down" – might mean "that it was blown up or burned up" in the parlance of bosses and capitalist papers, "but in the terminology of union men . . . they mean they tie it up," either by a work slowdown or by walking off the job altogether (5170). Even if some readers of the IWW songbook might have assumed the "capitalist" idea of "Up goes the machine," Thompson argues that in 1914, when newspapers claimed the IWW was destroying threshing machines, the union had made little attempt yet to organize harvest workers – so the song could not possibly reflect the actual practices of any IWW members. (He avoids returning to his earlier testimony during which he admitted that IWW members had destroyed crops "last summer" – 1917 – when the IWW's Agricultural Workers' Organization had been a force to be reckoned with [5159].)

Thompson's reading of "Ta-ra-ra Boom-de-ay," another Joe Hill song, had to counteract even more obvious references to sabotage. Thompson begins by pointing out that the song is about an individual worker – the narrator is an "I" – and thus, since the IWW preached the collective identity of workers ("The I.W.W. says, you must learn to think in terms of 'we'" [5166]), the song does not present the tactics approved by the IWW but those resorted to by an isolated, desperate laborer. Thompson read the first stanza and chorus in court:

> "I had a job once threshing wheat, worked sixteen hours with hands and feet."

What does he mean by that, working with hands and feet? He wasn't using his head, that is what it means.

> "And when the moon was shining bright, they kept me
>   working all the night.
> One moonlight night, I hate to tell, I 'accidentally' slipped and
>   fell.
> My pitchfork went right in between some cog wheels of that
>   thresh-machine.
>   Ta-ra-ra-boom-de-ay!
>   It made a noise that way,
>   And wheels and bolts and hay
>   Went flying every way.
>   That stingy rube said, 'Well!
>   A thousand gone to hell.'
>   But I did sleep that night,
>   I needed it all right." (5167)

Thompson explains, "There is the picture, a man working his head off sixteen hours a day, and there is nobody to help him only his old pitchfork. He hasn't got any solidarity apparently, no organization, just his own individual methods, and under such conditions, why he uses the only available thing he has to stop the work." Still fed up, in the second stanza the farmhand, instructed by the farmer to grease the axles of his wagon, sabotages the job by "forgetting" to screw on the nut. When the farmer goes to town with a load of eggs, the stanza reports that "the wheel slipped off and broke his hip," and the chorus – which Thompson neglects to quote – further remarks, "His whiskers and his legs / Were full of scrambled eggs."[55] Yet there is still more excitement to come. The third stanza reports that the farmer fires the first worker, but that fellow clues in his "chum" who replaces him, and " 'Next day when threshing did commence, my chum was Johnny on the fence; / And 'pon my word, that awkward kid, he dropped his pitchfork like I did' " (5168).

The turning point of the song's narrative comes, Thompson argues, in the fourth and final stanza. Thompson recites and comments on it thus:

> "But still that rube was pretty wise, these things did open up
>   his eyes,
> He said, 'there must be something wrong; I think I work my
>   men too long.'
> He cut the hours and raised the pay, gave ham and eggs for
>   every day." –

Now here is the line you want to specially notice:

> "Now gets his men from union hall, and has no 'accidents' at all."

[H]e didn't get them from there before. (5168–69)

Thompson focuses on the farmer's realization that "there must be something wrong." By skipping some of the song's earlier passages making the farmer look ridiculous, he may even diminish the sarcasm of the phrase "that rube was pretty wise." His final comment on the poem further emphasizes the constructive initiative of the farmer: "Get the men from a union, they will use union methods; get them from individuals, and fight them individually, they will fight you individually. That is the sense of that song" (5169).

The farmer's change of heart, however, does not spring from any innate goodwill toward his hired hands, but is compelled by conditions set up by the agricultural workers in his vicinity. Thompson's assertion that the poem describes a form of sabotage initiated by an "individual" is belied by the fact that the scheme works only when a second worker joins in; rather than acting individually, the two farmhands show precisely the kind of solidarity that Thompson claims they lack. Finally, he fails to read the final refrain, for good reason:

> Ta-ra-ra-boom-de-ay!
> That rube is feeling gay;

> He learned his lesson quick,
> Just through a simple trick.
> For fixing greedy slobs,
> This is the only way,
> Ta-ra-ra-boom-de-ay![56]

Far from revealing "the sense of the song" as simply the availability of co-operative workers at the union hall, the final chorus underscores the power of workers, when united, to make the bosses meet their demands, and it indicates that the "trick" of sabotage, though simple, is the "only way" to accomplish this.

There is no clear indication that evidence supplied from *Songs of the Workers* weighed especially heavily in convicting the Chicago defendants – insofar as the jury deliberated for about an hour to convict them of more than ten thousand crimes, it appears that *all* of the prosecution's evidence was damning (Dubofsky 436). Yet from defense attorney Vanderveer's decision to have James Thompson spend part of the first day of defense testimony explicating IWW songs in depth, we might conclude that Vanderveer found especially dangerous the songs' vivid witness to the IWW's revolutionary aspirations and subversive (and potentially destructive) tactics. At any rate, Thompson's willful reinterpretation of IWW ideals and renunciation of class-war tactics – particularly sabotage – that were repugnant to bourgeois sensibilities established a pattern repeated by other defendants. When Ralph Chaplin took the stand on July 18 and 19, Vanderveer led him through testimony regarding the United Mine Workers strikes of 1911, which occurred in West Virginia while Chaplin was living there and which brought him to begin producing poems, articles, and cartoons for labor newspapers. As Vanderveer explained in justifying his line of questioning to Judge Landis:

> Now, I want to show what he did, why he did it, and in fact, that he did the identical thing before he was with this organization at all, and for the same identical reason that he did it now. Does not that answer the charge of conspiracy? . . . He was a reporter, writing editorials for the paper throughout the West Virginia strike, where the troops were employed; he wrote about the troops then just as he wrote about the troops last year, under the same aggravating circumstances.[57]

Vanderveer's aim was to create for Chaplin a coherent personal narrative that distanced him from the collective decision making and mass agitation of the IWW. In effect, he argued that the IWW as an organization was of no great consequence either in fostering Chaplin's radical social views or in empowering him to advance those views. In tracing Chaplin's development as a commercial artist, Vanderveer helped establish the defendant as an industrious, successful practitioner of a trade. By narrating Chaplin's close experience with class inequities in Mexico and West Virginia, Vanderveer portrayed for the court a sensitive man troubled by injustice. Chaplin's observation of peonage in Mexico, Vanderveer explained, "became a part of this man's artistic life in an unusual degree, and in an unusual degree was responsible for moulding his ideas and ideals, as he is essentially an idealist."[58] Chaplin became, in effect, a highly individual, independent thinker and artist: a bourgeois intellectual, as it were.

Even while such a portrayal failed to cultivate any sympathy among the jurors, it helped diminish ideological and methodological differences between the IWW and liberal reformers, thus implicitly bringing into question the justification for a union with "nothing in common" with the "employing class."[59] Chaplin's testimony occasionally verged on patriotic hyperbole – particularly striking coming from someone once committed to revolution and internationalism. Of the flag Chaplin says:

> Like everybody else, every American boy at least, I was taught that the Flag was the symbol of freedom. It was the symbol of the things that my forefathers had lived for, fought for and died for; that the Flag stood for American freedom; that this American freedom was different from the freedom in other countries, and that the Flag stood for it all. (7726)

Under cross-examination Chaplin even claimed that in 1914, while working in Montreal, he had considered joining the Canadian army: "I will tell you, Mr. Nebeker, I wanted to join the army, that is what I wanted to do, right there in Montreal, that is the way I felt about it" (7753). Chaplin, to be sure, laid aside neither his partisanship for the laboring class nor his contempt for the "profiteering gang of profiteers" who "now ruled" (7728). Yet he certainly rounded off the rough edges of his radicalism for courtroom consumption. When prosecuting attorney Nebeker asked about his tenure as editor, "Now whatever was said in Solidarity against registration, against soldiers, against the war, against the Flag, against patriotism, everything of that kind, came to your attention before it was ever printed, didn't it?" (7751–52), Chaplin wisecracked, "Well, I think it came to your attention first, because I haven't seen it there yet" (7752).

Then, to Nebeker's retort, "Oh, you never have seen anything along that line?" Chaplin repeated his denial less rambunctiously: "Nothing that impressed me the way it has you, no, indeed" (7752). The difference between Chaplin's first response and the second indicates the alteration in style that the Chicago trial induced: the obstreperous, defiant Wobbly wisecrack became a resolute affirmation of the IWW's good behavior, never before a self-image consciously cultivated by the organization.

Oppressed, disaffected workers continued to be within the IWW's reach. But while fighting its battle in the courtroom, the IWW also increasingly abandoned the apparatuses and methods that had served it well in the class war – particularly, local organizing and pragmatic, direct action for concrete benefits. Only one issue of *Solidarity* appeared after Chaplin and the rest of the IWW leaders were indicted. Replacing it was the single sheet of the *Daily Bulletin* or, when the trial was under way, the *Trial Bulletin*. Frequently compelled to appeal for donations replenishing the defense fund, the bulletins managed to sustain the IWW's rhetoric of class warfare while "the New order clash[ed] with the Old every day in the big white and gild court room."[60] Gone, however, was *Solidarity*'s commentary on international events affecting the labor movement and reportage of IWW agitation from across the United States. So while trials in Chicago and elsewhere busied the few IWW leaders not in jail and defense costs nearly bankrupted the union (Dubofsky 449), the IWW was forced to give up the publication and organization networks that had previously unified the far-flung union locals and connected the IWW with the international labor movement.

From one perspective, the disintegration of the IWW spells the success of reactionary politics in the United States. From this point of view, it appears that the wartime repression of the union was historically determined from outside, by the triumph of the kinds of nationalist, conformist, and conservative ideals that were represented and championed in the major poetry anthologies and the grass-roots poetry of the Vigilantes. These ideological forces determined the verdict even before the first evidence was presented. But from another perspective, we can also see that the IWW was broken down from within. We cannot exactly blame IWW defenders such as Chaplin and Brazier for their courtroom conduct. We must appreciate, however, the way that protocols of the courtroom – above all, the need to defend one's individual self (not, at bottom, one's party) at all costs – established a context that effectively defused the IWW members' socialist rhetoric and undermined their labor solidarity. We must note, too, how the IWW itself reinterpreted its poetic discourse of socialist revolution as a nonthreatening language of liberal reform. Brazier's and Chaplin's behavior on the witness stand testifies to the fragility of their class consciousness – and perhaps also to the state of proletarian class consciousness in the IWW generally. What is revealed seems disappointing, given their earlier commitments and proclamations: under pressure, carefully nurtured visions of revolution and the long-cherished tactic of sabotage became for them flights of poetic fancy or excesses the IWW had supposedly never really believed in.

The defendants' failure amounts to a breakdown of ideological vision and nerve. If the IWW's radicalism seemed more brazen, defiant than that of the Woman's Peace Party – for the IWW, after all, was the object of public denunciation and state suppression – there is little substantive difference between the quiet capitulation of the NY-WPP and the public cowing of the IWW defendants. Similarly, if the IWW's willful rereading (or misreading) of their own verse represents, like the poetic and intellectual work of the *Four Lights* editors, a significant step toward embracing the telos – or antitelos – of modernism, at the same time the theoretical advances in both organizations came at the expense of group solidarity. Insofar as both the IWW defendants and the WPP activists virtually abandoned attempts at coalition building and organizing, their intellectual work represents a bifurcation of their own selves, a splitting away of the intellectual from the activist. Wobbly organizers and writers, confronted with their songs and poetry in court, ingeniously reread the verses as benign and unrevolutionary, thereby demonstrating – and trying to exploit – the flexibility and openness of poetic discourse. But in doing so, they also abandoned the connection between poetic declaration and organizational purpose upon which their political success had depended. And ultimately, insofar as all defendants were convicted on all charges of sedition, the federal trial demonstrated who had final authority to reread IWW poetry as it chose: not the IWW, but the state.

6

"While This War Lasts"

READERLY RESISTANCE ON THE COLOR
LINE AND THE BREAD LINE

SOMETIME in 1917 the condition of relative flux in American politics, in which even minority political groups such as the Woman's Peace Party and Industrial Workers of the World could exercise influence, changed considerably. The federal government took control of those segments of the economy needed for war mobilization (a process that consisted largely of creating favorable opportunities in the wartime economy for investors, business owners, and property owners while barring others from interfering with those opportunities), and the publicity agencies of the federal government joined forces with magazines, newspapers, and other unofficial patriotic groups such as the Vigilantes to regulate public speech and political activity. In many cases, organizations representing marginal groups – workers, women, ethnic and race minorities – saw the rising tide of patriotic conformity, collaborated with it, saw some of their own interests appeased or advanced, and by their collaboration contributed to the cultural juggernaut repressing other collective organizations that had formerly been allies or rivals. The American Federation of Labor, led by Samuel Gompers, affiliated itself closely with the Wilson administration's war drive; by the end of the war it was the preeminent U.S. labor organization; the IWW, its smaller, more radical rival, was effectively driven out of existence. The National American Woman Suffrage Association pledged its support for the war effort, and women gained suffrage in 1920; the pacifist WPP, meanwhile, though it survived the war to become the Women's International League for Peace and Freedom, was pared down to a splinter group with no significant popular following.

Central to the federal government's suppression of antiwar organizations and dissenting politics was its censorship of the press and of public speech generally, which was enforced through the postmaster's office as well as by the courts. In 1917, with the nation being mobilized to make the world "safe for Democracy," dissident groups and presses were silenced. The physical spaces in which public debate could be carried on – printing presses, the mails, the courts – were systematically denied to those resisting the war drive. With the passage of the Espionage Act on June 15, 1917, prosecution awaited anyone who "willfully" promoted "insubordination, disloyalty, mutiny, or refusal of duty in the military or naval forces of the United States."[1] Armed with the act's provisions denying the mails to any disloyal publication, Postmaster General Albert Burleson revoked the mailing privileges of many Left publications on record as opposed to war: the *American Socialist* was targeted almost immediately, in July 1917; the *Masses,* though not affiliated with any particular socialist organization, was stopped in August; the *Milwaukee Leader,* organ of the Wisconsin socialist party, had mailing privileges suspended in September.[2] By the time Burleson's authority was expanded by the Sedition Act of May 1918, he had already silenced forty-five "unpatriotic" periodicals.[3] The amendment forbade anyone to "urge, incite or advocate any curtailment of production in this country of any thing or things, product or products, necessary or essential to the prosecution of the war,"[4] but the earlier act had already been sufficient to send IWW leaders to prison and to suppress others who might advocate resistance to the wartime state. As we have seen by the example of the New York WPP's *Four Lights,* official government suppression was not necessary in many cases; the kind of private, unofficial intolerance of dissent that was modeled and promoted by the Vigilantes, the "housekeeping magazines," and individual poets was often just as devastating in curbing "unpatriotic" speech and shutting down dissenting presses.

This political environment called for a change of tactics among dissenting groups – or, rather, a shift from a hegemonic strategy to subversive tactics. While my aim in the bulk of this study has been to illuminate a poetics and politics that engage openly in hegemonic struggle, my focus now must be on a poetics and politics of subversion. In place of a national strategy, dissenting groups were reduced to adopting local tactics of resistance.[5] In American wartime culture of 1917 and 1918, when dissenting views were largely kept out of print and dissenting presses were kept out of general circulation, dissent had to be carried on not by practices of inscription, of writing, but by practices of interpretation, of reading. As a culture becomes more repressive, Michel de Certeau argues, such subversive reading becomes more widespread, because more spaces become politicized, though this subversion becomes simultaneously less visible:

> A rationalized, expansionist, centralized, spectacular and clamorous production is confronted by an entirely different kind of production, called "consumption" and characterized by its ruses, its fragmentation (the result of the circumstances), its poaching, its clandestine nature, its tireless but quiet activity, in short by its quasi-invisibility, since it shows itself not in its own products (where would it place them?) but in an art of using those imposed on it.[6]

De Certeau's formulation presents a practical problem that is at the same time a theoretical one: How does one *write* a history of reading when reading is "quasi-invisible"? If resistance is invisible, can it hope to effect a practice that is in any way more than *local* – something more than making the best of a bad situation?

De Certeau's juxtaposition of writing with reading might suggest wholly separate paradigms, wholly disparate modes of action, and indeed his example placing television production in opposition to watching television seems to reinforce this.[7] But of course, writing and reading are interconnected; they are, as in Jacques Derrida's famous demonstration, reversible terms.[8] Consumption, by de Certeau's own account, is productive – just not in the ways that are measurable by the usual standards of quantity. Subversion is difficult to observe, but it is "quasi-invisible" rather than wholly so. What this means for writing about poetry of the Great War and, through poetry, writing about American culture of the period is that subversive "readings" of culture get written down as poems: many pieces are, quite literally, rewritings, and therefore readings, of earlier poems, songs, or newspaper clippings (many IWW songs, for example, are readings of popular, religious, or patriotic songs). Given that other poems, whether patriotic or dissenting, provide responses to (or readings of) the specific historical and cultural events comprising World War I, any of the poetry I have previously discussed might be thought of as "readerly." But more particularly, because controls on American speech and political activity were never absolute during World War I (de Certeau argues that such control is never total), dissenting readings of culture continued to be written down as poems even during 1917 and 1918. These poems are the traces of the subversive readings that persisted despite state and civilian pressures toward conformity. They are available because a few publishers, most of them small presses outside the eastern publishing establishment, continued to print dissenting work. Even more frequently, they are available because newspapers such as the *New York Call* and the

Milwaukee Leader served and gave expression to local communities whose access could not be entirely cut off by the loss of mailing privileges. These papers lost their national readerships and thereby the possibility of mobilizing mass audiences, but unlike magazines such as the *International Socialist Review*, the *Masses, Solidarity*, or the *Industrial Worker*, they did not lose their readerships altogether. Though they experienced cutbacks, they continued to be published and distributed locally throughout the war.

I insist on the interrelationship between tactics and strategies in part because, looking historically at the period from 1914 to 1918, we can clearly see political options including pacifism and socialism that offered an overall cultural strategy, that indeed contested more dominant political blocs favoring nationalism and political conservatism, but that under wartime pressures were reduced to locally dissenting tactics. The political radicalism of the 1910s, pushed underground by the war mobilization and the Red Scare of 1919, reemerged in the 1930s, often through different organizations but with some of the same leaders and much of the same political criticism. Thus, the practice of resistance, I agree with de Certeau, must be a politics of time and patience as well as one of opportunism, though I cannot fully agree with de Certeau's account, which implies that tactical practice is most often sealed off from any kind of overall strategy.[9] My argument, grounded historically, is that the political positions maintained by dissenters through World War I were held later as well. This is not to say that those political options, groups, and individuals suppressed during World War I were later to gain hegemonic power, but that many of them were able to enter into hegemonic struggle and to shape culture significantly at a later time. Thus, while there may be historical moments when the function of dissenting writers and readers becomes almost inevitably parasitic and oppositional, such moments of crisis are not by any means to be sought; the covert, subversive tactics required under these conditions are desperate, unenviable contingencies. On the contrary, subversive tactics and texts ideally function as a complement to a long-term strategy of hegemonic struggle, whether by maintaining a critical, political consciousness within individuals until political groups can be reorganized or by preserving until a more opportune time a kind of memory of suppressed political and cultural options.

I

As we have seen, since 1916 W. E. B. Du Bois, along with Major Charles Young and William Braithwaite, had begun accommodating – and themselves defining – a version of black patriotism that not only allowed for military service for blacks in time of war, but also admitted the possibility of laying aside "while this war lasts" African-Americans' "special grievances."[10] Yet while a positive view of patriotic service and even self-sacrifice emerged as the dominant perspective in the *Crisis,* the journal still occasionally offered substantial, resistant alternatives to the conservative, Anglo-American culture whose icon was the Anglo-Saxon soldier then being described by white soldier-poets. Certain poems in the *Crisis* even revised the image of the loyal black soldier so prominent in the journal's portrayal of Major Charles Young. In the *Crisis* of June 1916 – the year when Young was named the winner of the second annual Spingarn award – the black soldier-poet Lucian B. Watkins, then serving in the Philippines,[11] wrote a rejoinder to "Song of the American Eagle," a preparedness poem, replacing the earlier poem's call for national power with the struggle for racial justice. The second half of "Song of the American Dove" critiques the rhetoric of patriotic song and the symbolism of the flag:

> "Land of the free," whose flag I see!
> What boots thy boast of Liberty?
> What avails thy might, while in thy sight
> A race is robbed of its dearest right?
> Hark! I hear the yell of the hounds of hell –
> Thy sons obsessed with the lynching spell!
>
> How I long to see thy Liberty
> With e'en thy lowliest subject free:
> With none denied or crushed in pride,
> But souls ascending side by side;
> Thy streaming Stars and bleeding Bars
> Thus mean a victory more than war's!
>
> "Let freedom ring!" – 'tis well to sing,
> But let it from the mountains bring –
> Not only to the fortunate few –
> Its peace to all 'neath the "Red, White and Blue!"
> Ah! I see and sigh, 'neath the heavens high,
> While a race is hung on the trees to die![12]

Written and published when war was located "over there" and the United States was supposedly at peace, Watkins's poem goes beyond simply saying that the race struggle at home is a more important fight than war abroad. It intimates that peace itself is chimeric, only for "the fortunate few" in a country where one-tenth of the populace is at risk of being hunted by dogs and lynched.

When, in 1917, the image of the black soldier was first portrayed in the *Crisis,* it was similarly employed to emphasize the vast gulf between the freedom enjoyed by white citizens and that permitted blacks in the United States. In June, the poem "Negro Soldiers" by Roscoe C. Jamison adopted more conventional demarcations between peace and war than does Watkins's "Song of the American Dove," and its conception of military heroism was likewise more conventional – and more similar to Du Bois's. Yet by describing the heroism of black soldiers as being of a higher order, the poem also marks the racial injustice that denies blacks their rightful citizenship:

> THESE truly are the Brave,
> These men who cast aside
> Old memories, to walk the blood-stained pave
> Of Sacrifice, joining the solemn tide
> That moves away, to suffer and to die
> For Freedom – when their own is yet denied!
> O Pride! O Prejudice! When they pass by,
> Hail them, the Brave, for you now crucified![13]

The closing reference to crucifixion, a commonplace among the many English and American poems assuming white Christ figures, evokes in this poem not just the cliché of battlefield martyrdom but an ongoing history of lynching at home. Insofar as the poem describes a military parade preceding embarkation, the "blood-stained pave" suggests not just the sacrifice to be made abroad but the violence already endured at home. "Black Samson of Brandywine," published in the same issue, anonymously, is less bold in invoking racial injustice.[14] Still, it offers a black military hero, based on the legend of a "giant Negro, armed with a scythe," who "[swept] his way through the red ranks" at the Revolutionary War battle of Brandywine. This figure demands fair comparison with the Anglo-Saxon and Gallic warriors then being celebrated in poetry anthologies:

> Sing of your chiefs and your nobles,
> Saxon and Celt and Gaul,
> Breath of mine ever shall join you,
> Highly I honor them all.
> Give to them all of their glory,
> But for this noble of mine,

>Lend him a tithe of your tribute,
>   Black Samson of Brandywine.[15]

While in embracing the ideal of Charles Young the *Crisis* was giving ground politically and ideologically (and "Black Samson of Brandywine" is in fact cut from the same cloth as Young), the magazine continued to provide space to poets offering more subversive accounts of the black soldier. Printed out of context, Lucian Watkins's "These" might appear to be the most mundane of tributes to the soldier dead. When placed in its context within the *Crisis,* however, where it was published in February 1918, the poem becomes a celebration not of any soldiers, and not just of any black soldiers, but of thirteen of those executed for the murderous incident in Houston.[16] The poem is bordered by a pen-and-ink illustration featuring a troop of black soldiers marching in formation and including a headnote that specifically connects the poem to the Houston mutiny (Figure 14). It thus celebrates as heroic the executions of black soldiers who were convicted of assaulting a police station, provoked not by some act of mob violence or of murder, but by a discriminatory application of state power (the wrongful arrest of a black soldier) and by the systematic racism experienced by the black soldiers stationed at Fort Houston. Using the conventions of the patriotic heroism of soldiers, the poem pays tribute, amazingly, not to black soldiers who sacrifice themselves for the sake of the nation but to black soldiers who take up arms *against* the nation. They sacrifice their lives, but not their claim to the rights of citizens. Even in wartime, they assert their allegiance to their race over their nation, making the claim that within months Du Bois would explicitly renounce.

While my argument has repeatedly stressed the power of poetry as political utterance, in the case of Watkins's "These" we can recognize the limitations of that power as well as the potential. In addition to the immediate context provided by the headnote, the poem's publication in a journal reaching tens of thousands of African-Americans, all of whom had experienced the same kind of institutional, systematic, and casual racism against which the soldiers finally exploded, gives it the potential of mass political mobilization. Yet there was, at the time, no organizational structure working in support of the violent revolt against state power that the poem might seem to approve of. Indeed, the National Association for the Advancement of Colored People was working, in the main, to promote loyalty among African-Americans. The genre of poetry, we must note, was flexible enough to be taken either very seriously

Figure 14. "These." Poem by Lucian Watkins, illustration by staff, *Crisis* 15.4 (February 1918): 185. By permission of *The Crisis Magazine*.

or hardly seriously at all, largely depending on the circumstances of its production and consumption. In this case, for instance, it was read as something far less authoritative than an editorial statement, for if the *Crisis* had published not a poem but an editorial praising the heroism of the Houston mutineers, the journal would almost certainly have been deemed unmailable and may well have been targeted for prosecution as seditious. It was a poem's virtue, under conditions of state repression – even as it was a liability – that a poem could seem too insignificant to make the law take notice.

Subversive poetry writing – which also means subversive reading – appears in all kinds of institutional cracks where it might be overlooked. Even in an agency like the Vigilantes, which took poetry very seriously indeed, it is possible to find the foundation for subversive reading. Consider, for example, what a reader attuned to the precariousness of race relations – an NAACP member, for example – might make of Vachel Lindsay's poem "The Jazz Bird." Released by the Vigilantes press syndicate, the poem may seem to offer a version of the patriotic American singer that is indebted to African-American music and thus comprises a tribute to African-American soldiers serving in France.[17] Lindsay's poem distinguishes the "Jazz Bird" from a more usual symbol of American patriotism, the eagle; it is the eagle who proclaims, "'Son Jazz Bird, / I send you out to fight.'" The Jazz Bird in fact somewhat resembles a jazz player as it takes off: "the Jazz Bird spread his sunflower wings, / And roared with all his might," waking Americans from sea to sea, "in Oregon, / In Florida and Maine." Yet even as a tribute to African-American patriotism, the poem departs fundamentally from the norm of Anglo-Saxon virility assumed elsewhere in Vigilantes propaganda as well as in soldier poetry. Provocatively, the poem concludes with a lynching of the Kaiser and his heirs, a scene that calls forth the specter of American lynchings of blacks:

> At midnight on a haunted road
>   A star bends low and sees
> The Kaiser and his row of sons
>   Marching at their ease.
>
> Their necks are broken by the hemp,
>   They goose-step in a line,
> Their stripped bones strutting in the wind
>   Swinging as a sign
>
> That Jazz Birds come on sunflower wings
>   When loathsome tyrants rise . . .
> The Jazz Bird guards the gallows,
>   He lights it with his eyes.

If this poem decries the tyranny of Germany, it also implicitly denounces the tyranny of American white supremacy. If it pledges retribution to the German Kaiser and his princes, it seems also to promise revenge against oppressors elsewhere, not excluding the United States itself. At bottom, the images potentially undercut the kind of moral authority that the

United States not only claimed for itself in going to war, but actually made into the very basis of its war policy.

If the meeting of subversive, sufficiently subtle readers with a text like this seems to be too much a chance event, I would point out the limited claim I am making about the relationship between such a poem and its reader: I speak, most immediately, of local tactics, a local gesture or even simply an individual memory of political resistance, neither of which has to be massively organized and both of which can be inspired by a subversive rereading of any text, including patriotic propaganda. More broadly, I have also argued that these local tactics can enable the coalescing of political collectivities that might at some point act openly in hegemonic struggle. Certainly, it is difficult to trace the part that a single poem such as "The Jazz Bird" might play in this formation. Yet it is easy enough to identify readers who might, given the chance, see such a poem as indicative of injustices at home as well as in the lands ruled by imperial Germany. We might take, for example, the fifty thousand who by January 1918 were subscribers to the *Crisis*[18] or, alternatively, the 12 million African-Americans who were daily the subject of racist prejudice and discrimination. (As for the illiteracy of many blacks, it is of course not necessary to know how to read to be able to "read" a culture.)

By the summer of 1918 the *Crisis* was not the most likely place to find indications of continued dissent among African-Americans.[19] Greater evidence of ongoing subversive reading can be had in some of the metropolitan newspapers serving black communities. At one time or another, Du Bois's tilt toward patriotism was criticized by black newspapers in cities throughout the Middle West and the East, the most prominent being the *Baltimore Afro-American, Chicago Defender, Cleveland Gazette, New York News,* and *Pittsburgh Courier*.[20] The independent stance taken by these papers points to a significant body of African-American intellectuals and a significant readership that was less enthusiastic than Du Bois about the prospect of African-American soldiers dying for the cause of "democracy." It is among these intellectuals and readers that the more radical critique of militarism, imperialism, and democracy formerly broadcast by Du Bois was continued and preserved in spite of the black patriotic majority of 1917 and 1918.

Within individual newspapers, dissent could be maintained even when the editorial policy of a particular paper tended to support patriotic service. Consider, for example, an exchange of commentaries between the *Richmond Planet* and the *Oklahoma Black Dispatch* reported in the *Planet* of September 1, 1917. In the July 27 issue, the *Planet* had published a letter by Uzziah Miner, previously the editor of the *Howard University Journal*, which the Richmond Post Office ruled to be seditious, making the issue undeliverable. Miner had written:

> Personally I wish to say that I am completely disgusted with America's hypocrisy and insincerity. It has entered the war for the avowed purpose of bringing to pass a "World Democracy." I fail to see how I can conscientiously volunteer to fight for a "World Democracy" while I am denied the fruits and blessings of Democracy at home. Of course I may be called a "slacker," I may be regarded unpatriotic, I may be looked upon as disloyal, but I must say, unless President Wilson, like Colonel Theodore Roosevelt, speaks out [boldly] against the unspeakable atrocities perpetrated upon my despised and mistreated race; unless the Department of Justice brings the guilty parties in East St. Louis to a "strict accountability," for their unparalleled brutalities; unless I am assured that the glorious flag which I love so dearly will offer protection in the future for twelve million peace-loving colored inhabitants of this country; unless I am convinced that this "World Democracy" includes black men as well as white men, I shall consider myself a disgrace to my race and my country . . . because I firmly believe and maintain that Democracy, like charity, should begin at home and spread abroad.

The issue and the letter were eventually printed, however, when the *Planet* editorial staff appended its own commentary critical of Miner's letter. This, moreover, was not the last time Miner's letter appeared in print. The *Oklahoma Black Dispatch* had picked the story up, reporting on it and commenting on it as a free-speech issue – and reprinting Miner's letter to illustrate "what he said that got him into bad standing with the postal authorities." Quoting the Bill of Rights, the *Dispatch* argued that "while we fail to reach the same conclusion as he . . . [we] feel that he has a right under the Constitution of the United States to state his case." This was not the end, either, for on September 1 the *Planet* reprinted not only the *Dispatch*'s article but also the article's long quotation of Miner. It concluded by defending its editorial stance, reprinting part of its earlier rejoinder to Miner: "In the issue of July 27th we had what we feel is a fitting answer to Prof. Miner and we summed it all up in this terse expression, 'Nothing comes to the man who sulks, nothing has come to the Indian. Men can only try to chain you from without and he is truly helpless who chains himself within.'"[21]

All the while the editors of the *Planet* and of the *Dispatch* were disavowing the dissenting perspective offered in the letter, it is notable that the *Dispatch* nevertheless published the letter, while the *Planet* found reason to publish the seditious document twice over. The loyalty demanded of newspapers meant that they had to denounce seditious speech; yet standards of journalist professionalism "demanded" also that they print news of sedition along with other material, so that the distinction between the newspaper proper and a private correspondent allowed the paper to distance itself from Miner's letter even while broadcasting it.[22] Even if we assume the genuineness of the patriotic loyalty asserted by the *Planet* editorials, it is not the editorial but the letter by Miner that seems to gain reinforcement from the cartoon appearing next to the front-page article. George Johnson's cartoon pictures a black man in uniform facing the figure of President Wilson; the African-American figure asks, "In this big world's *democracy* have you considered the black?" and the external caption challenges, "How speakest thou?"[23] Thus, the visual text, like the newspaper's editorial, proclaims its willingness to support black military service and patriotism – besides the black man being in uniform, an American flag appears prominently in the illustration's center – but meanwhile the verbal text echoes Miner's demand that "World Democracy" be extended to blacks and, like Miner, it addresses that demand directly to Woodrow Wilson. By equivocation such as this, the employment of multiple and apparently contradictory perspectives, black newspapers – and newspapers allied with political and other ethnic minorities – continued to print dissenting matter. Unlike critical practice under the New Criticism, this equivocation was not an end in itself, but was rather the political tactic necessary to avoid legal prosecution.

Poems in the *Richmond Planet* reflect this strategy again and again. Patriotic verses appeared regularly, indicating readers' and the editors' support for the war effort. On the front page of its July 14, 1917, edition, the *Planet* published Robert Dangerfield Crawley's "Ethiopia's War Song." The poem suggests unanimity of response among African-Americans, even a kind of essential racial response to the battle call, and at any rate claims that any who do not respond with enthusiasm to the mobilization are traitors:

> The call each Ethiopian heart
> With War's fierce rapture fills
> The cry that in the traitor's veins
> The coward current chills –

> Let it ring up from the valleys,
> And roll along the hills![24]

But the *Planet* also continued to publish poems demanding justice at home for African-Americans. Since poems in the *Planet* and most other newspapers were submitted by readers of the paper rather than by newspaper staff, it was possible for the editors to disclaim responsibility for the personal views presented in these poems even while proceeding with publication. On March 30, 1918, for example, at a time when the government was supposed to have curbed dissenting opinion and put dissenting periodicals out of business, the *Planet* published the Rev. E. D. Caffee's "Now or Never," which, while it does not resist the war effort per se, diverts attention from military mobilization to a political mobilization that he urges black Americans to undertake to win their own interests:

> The Woman Suffrage Bill
> Passed Argument to Law!
> Democracy didst give its will
> To void an ugly flaw.
>   Daylight Saving Bill has passed,
> And Labor Laws – all anti-caste!
>
> While brand new epoch rules
> Get on Law's Statute Book,
> Negroes should not be fools,
> To stand around and look!
> It's now or never for our race,
> To win or ever lose our case![25]

Caffee's political urgency, his exhortation that African-Americans act immediately, stands in marked contrast to Du Bois's advice in "Close Ranks": "Let us, while this war lasts, forget our special grievances."[26]

Lucian Watkins, regularly featured in the pages of the *Richmond Planet*, provided poetry that saw the war for democracy in domestic as well as international terms. Indeed, if in seeking a military post Du Bois somehow felt it incumbent upon him to proclaim absolute loyalty, even to disavow his political and racial identity as secondary to a national identity, the soldier-poet Watkins never saw as incompatible his identities of soldier and patriot, black man and dissenter. "The Negro Soldiers of America: What We Are Fighting For," published on March 2, 1918, declares allegiance to the "war for democracy," but only in the poem's first stanza (which, interestingly, focuses on fighting not for the United States but for France):

> We fight – and for DEMOCRACY
> Lord, we are glad of this sweet chance
> To brave whatever hells there be
> Beside the bleeding heart of France![27]

The remaining seven stanzas of the poem relate the fight for democracy to the fight at home in Tennessee. "We fight that Liberty may reign / From Berlin unto Tennessee," Watkins writes:

> To Tennessee where last we saw
> Infernal brands of death applied
> To men – our men, within the law,
> But "lawless" as they moaned and died.
>
> .   .   .   .
>
> In Tennessee – where Wrong is Might
> With Hate and Horror on the throne.
> Where GOD'S DEMOCRACY of LIGHT
> AND LOVE, it seems, has never shone.
>
> In Tennessee – and all her kin
> Of sister criminals, year by year,
> Who've lost the consciousness of sin,
> The tenderness that is a tear.
>
> We fight – and for DEMOCRACY
> We'll dare Atlantic's tragic foam,
> Go "over the top" – Lord, let us see
> PEACE AND ITS HAPPINESS AT HOME!

For the Anglo-Saxon soldier-poet and the elite white reader, the dichotomy of homefront and battlefront constitutes an opposition between safety and danger: the war waged in Europe was therefore a struggle to defend a safe home from a perceived threat, which is to say that it was also a struggle to keep intact the symbolic boundary between a homefront where all is well and a battlefront that is "hell." For the African-American soldier-poet and the working-class black reader, there was no such easy separation between a safe and a dangerous zone. All the oppositions of democracy versus autocracy, mercy versus brutality, lightness versus darkness upon which America's justification of war rested were radical-

ly undercut by the daily experience of African-Americans on the supposedly safe homefront. Even as he wrote from a position of experience
and authority as a soldier-poet, the injustice and danger of the American
homefront continued to be Watkins's theme in his *Planet* poems. "'No
Man's Land'" was published in the October 19, 1918, issue, just three
weeks before the Armistice:

> Between contending storms of strife
> A blasted world is void of life;
> There only Death may move or stand –
> The warriors call it "NO MAN'S LAND!"
>
> And yet wherever love is not,
> Wherever murderous hate is hot
> And Liberty belies her name –
> That place is "NO MAN'S LAND" the same![28]

The second stanza might, in another context, describe a kind of generalized, sentimental patriotism; in the *Planet,* addressing an audience that
knew intimately both murderous hate and liberty belied, the stanza constitutes a historically specific indictment of American culture. If the majority of African-Americans were behind the war effort, as seems to be
indicated by blacks' high participation in wartime programs and widespread, if qualified, support from the black press,[29] the evidence of local
newspapers such as the *Richmond Planet* argues that African-American
service was offered on very different grounds than the service of white
Americans, and especially white middle- and upper-class men. For
whites, support for the war was premised on the retention and even the
expansion of cultural and political power. For blacks, support was offered
much more conditionally. Most African-Americans, though they supported the war effort, were wary of promises that the nation would now
finally fulfill its promises of equal rights and opportunity for blacks. For
a significant percentage of blacks, support was sharply qualified by the
understanding that demands for racial justice at home could never be secondary to justice abroad and that these demands would continue to be
made during and in spite of the war. This writing about, and reading of,
U.S. involvement in the war did not produce a mass movement against
the war. But the culturally critical and politically astute attitudes that underlay, and consistently qualified, African-American readings of the Great
War milieu are indicated by the surge in popularity the NAACP experienced when, after the war, W. E. B. Du Bois traveled to France and re-

ported scathingly on the racist treatment of black soldiers in the U.S. Army. The series of articles Du Bois published, "The Black Man in the Revolution of 1914–1918" (March 1919), "Documents of the War" (May 1919), and "An Essay Toward a History of the Black Man in the Great War" (June 1919),[30] led the *Crisis* to a circulation topping a hundred thousand – a figure considerably larger than the *Atlantic's* circulation for the same period and roughly the same as *Harper's*.[31] It was the peak of *Crisis* circulation.[32]

II

That thousands of Americans resisted the logic and rhetoric, if not the policies, of the wartime mobilization seems clear. Besides the tens of thousands of readers who subscribed to the *Crisis* before 1917, or who responded to Du Bois's renewed criticism of racism in 1919, or who read the black newspapers that remained critical of the mobilization during 1917 and 1918, we must also allow for thousands of citizens and activists who, having been mobilized by the Woman's Peace Party, the Industrial Workers of the World, and the Socialist Party of America, were not likely to be transformed suddenly into patriotic zealots and warmongers just because the government declared war and demanded patriotic conformity. The WPP had counted 40,000 members at its peak. The IWW's leaders were imprisoned from September 1917 onward, but IWW membership had swelled from 40,000 in 1916 to 100,000 in 1917.[33] The SPA had been in decline since approximately 1912, yet membership remained around 80,000 in 1917 and 1918, and rose again to 100,000 in 1919. We need also to account for the dissent of various European ethnic groups that, like African-Americans, had historical and cultural reasons to resist the war mobilization.[34] George Sylvester Viereck's *Fatherland,* which served up pro-German, anti-British propaganda of outrageous bile, nevertheless maintained a circulation of some 65,000 readers through 1917.[35] If we judge the number of subversive readers by the circulation of these dissenting periodicals and the membership of dissenting organizations, we can tally perhaps half a million – out of an American population of more than 100 million, less than one-half of 1 percent. Of course, measured this way, the number would also be lowered by individuals holding multiple memberships. Yet if we consider that these half a million represented additional readers of similar political persuasion or ethnic identification, they can also indicate a far larger number than half a million. A hundred thousand bought the *Crisis* in June 1919, but there were 12 million African-Americans at the time of World War I. Just 65,000 readers subscribed to the *Fatherland,* but the second largest ethnicity in the United States was German, outdistanced only by English, and the third largest was Irish. By 1917, the NAWSA had approximately 2 million members.[36] While the group's official policy eschewed pacifism in favor of suffrage activism, many members, perhaps a majority, were nevertheless sympathetic with the criticism of masculine authority and war that the WPP enunciated.[37] If the IWW and Socialist Party could count by 1918 fewer than 200,000 members between them, it bears mentioning that in 1920 nearly 1 million Americans cast their ballots for Socialist presidential candidate Eugene Debs, who ran his campaign from the prison cell where he was serving his ten-year sentence for sedition.[38] More Americans voted for Debs in 1920 than in 1912, the height of the Socialists' organizational strength.[39]

As with the African-American presses, it is possible to see resistant readings of American wartime culture in poetry writing that appeared in various, often marginal sites of publication and circulation. The state was not ineffective in keeping dissenting readers and writers from forming political blocs, but it politicized so many spaces, private as well as public, that it expanded the possible discourses in which dissent could be articulated. Whereas in African-American periodicals the process of rereading patriotic culture is clearest in treatments of the soldier-poet, in working-class publications the process is perhaps clearest in the handling of the U.S. Food Administration's conservation rhetoric. The basic tactic is apparent in the July 1917 *Masses,* where a collage poem under the title "Why the Poor Should Be Patriotic" places in ironic counterpoint a list of high food prices and one of Hoover's food conservation platitudes:

> BREAD fifteen cents a loaf.
>   Potatoes one dollar and forty cents a peck.
> Coal ten dollars a ton.
> HOOVER SAYS WE MUST DENY OURSELVES, TO FEED
>   ALLIES.
>   – *Newspaper Headline.*[40]

The piece offers a devastatingly concise critique of the democratic pretensions of Hoover's Food Administration: Hoover claims that Americans must practice voluntary self-sacrifice; with high prices for basic needs, the poem suggests, the poor already practice self-sacrifice involuntarily.

The poem indicates, at the same time, the kind of mass, patriotic propaganda that was then in the process of overwhelming its criticism. The very presence of the capitalized, anonymous headline in the poem suggests that the poem's socialist interpretation of food conservation is under assault in the mainstream press. The ubiquity of state power is either a central theme or an underlying anxiety in one poem, article, and illustration after another that address the Food Administration's programs. At the same time, the persistence of the Left's denunciation of Hoover is just as remarkable as the suppression of that denunciation. The *Masses'* unceasing condemnation of the war led to its being banned from the mails from August 1917 onward; given that this national journal had a relatively small circulation, the postal restrictions effectively ended its run. But for other Left periodicals, particularly socialist newspapers in metropolitan areas, being barred from the mail, though it put a crimp on revenue and severely limited the socialists' possibilities for concerted national organization, did not necessarily cut them off from their constituency, nor did it prevent them from maintaining fairly large readerships. Editors still had to beware the Espionage and Sedition acts, but the day-to-day power of the Post Office to censor was limited.

Beginning in September 1917, the *New York Call* ran a verse-editorial titled "The Sayings of Patsy," which appeared in the "Women's Sphere" segment of the Sunday magazine section and regularly addressed the absurdities of food conservation propaganda. Written by Bernice Evans, the two- and three-word unrhymed columns of "The Sayings of Patsy" simultaneously invite comparison with modernist vers libre and with popular comic verse. All installments were illustrated with stick-figure drawings of Patsy and other characters from the poems. One of the "Sayings," published on September 30, 1917, repeatedly plays on the disparity between the middle-class standards assumed by "ladies' magazines" and the lower-class existence of many Americans (Figure 15). While denouncing U.S. wartime policies, Evans's speaker acknowledges the pervasiveness of Food Administration propaganda in "all the / Housekeeping magazines."[41] This uneasiness pervades the poems: the recognition that "sayings" such as those offered by Patsy would be unlikely to diminish the impact of mass propaganda churned out by patriotic newspapers and magazines. But if Bernice Evans marks the cultural marginality of her position, her concerns about the power of patriotic periodicals can be read as an inside joke to socialist readers as well as a recognition of socialist disempowerment. For example, in the October 14, 1917, "Sayings," Evans remarks, "It seems that / Almost any / Dinky little / Editor / Can hoodoo us."[42] If the "us" means Americans generally – which means

The Sayings of Patsy, as Recorded By Bernice Evans

SAYS PATSY:

You can't pick up
A magazine
These days
Without reading
A column about
The American sin
Of extravagance,
And feeding
The allies
Out of our
Garbage cans
(Which, I think,
Is rather rough
On the allies).
Some people
Are certainly
Funny.
It flatters them
To death
To be told
That they can
Feed the allies,
When really

They know
Perfectly well
That they've never
Managed to feed
Their own children
Enough.
And all the
Housekeeping magazines
Tell us
To show our
Patriotism
By serving
Meatless meals
And wheatless meals
And eggless meals
and desertless meals
And almost
No meals
At all.
They tell us
How to utilize
Leftovers—
Although
It's perfectly obvious
That you can't have
Left over
Something you never had
To begin with—
How to
Reduce the meat bill
With such economical dishes
As molded lobster,
Jellied veal,
And salad
Made of cubes

Of cold roast chicken
Which (presumably)
We are to find
In the refrigerator—
To our intense
Astonishment,
I assure you.
They say
Hereafter
Patriotic Americans
Will eat only
Three course dinners—
Which is welcome news
To some of us.
If these thrift-crazy folks
Would go after
The food speculators
Half so vigorously
As after the
Poor housewives
It would be
More to the point
Than telling us
How to make salad
Of cubes of things
Of which
Our refrigerators
Don't contain even
The cube root.

PATSY.

Figure 15. "The Sayings of Patsy." Illustrated poem by Bernice Evans, *New York Call* September 30, 1917, magazine section: 13. From the copy in the Peace Poems.

mostly nonreaders of the *Call* – the statement may be taken straightforwardly, but of course poems actually address those who do read them, not those who do not; so the actual "us," the socialist reader and writers of the *Call,* are not hoodwinked as long as they take the poem's warning to heart. In response to editorial prohibitions against hoarding food, Evans wryly comments that "we," the working classes, "never stop / To figure out / How many / Carloads / We could buy / Out of / Twelve dollars / A week / After the rent / Is paid." But of course the implication is that the working classes *do* know how many carloads of food can be bought and hoarded with their weekly pay: none at all. So at the same time that the poem highlights the delusions of the common reader it winks at the self-consciousness of its actual working-class audience. Furthermore, for a series of poems that imply they will soon be buried by the patriotic hyperbole broadcast by the larger number of publications, "The Sayings of Patsy" were remarkable for not being silenced. Patsy ran in the Sunday magazine section for six straight weeks beginning September 23, 1917; after a one-week hiatus, she returned for three more installments in November. There were two "Sayings of Patsy" in December, another in January, and a final one in March 1918. In all, installments of the "Sayings" appeared in Sunday editions thirteen times. During a period when the Post Office was restricting mailing rights – in December the *Call* notified subscribers that delays in delivery were the postmaster's fault, not the newspaper's[43] – the "Sayings of Patsy" continued to decry patriotic loyalty. The March 17 column began thus:

> Says Patsy:
> A lot of folks
> Would oodles rather
> Have an arm
> Amputated
> Than an idea.
> They'd rather
> Chant in chorus
> "My country,
> Right or wrong,"
> Than use their brains
> To make their country
> Really right.
> They'd rather
> Endure all the
> Meatless days,
> And wheatless days,
> And heatless days,
> Than to give up
> Their thinkless days.

Bernice Evans was far from being the only poet in the *Call* who attacked Food Administration policies or who used the struggle over bread as symbolic of working people's struggle to gain control over the economic system that was starving them both materially and politically. Willard Parker's poem "America's 'Man with the Hoe'" appeared in the same issue as an interview with Edwin Markham, the populist poet of the original, and hugely popular, poem. The interview quotes Markham as saying, "If the hoe-man truly understood war he would refuse to fight his master's battles";[44] the poem by Parker urges the "Man with the Hoe" to feed the world's starving, but not to budge from the harvest fields to go to war.[45] Lola Ridge's "Bread," appearing on October 19, commemorates the "Women's demonstration against the high cost of living. N.Y. City Hall, December, 1916." Other "food poems" printed in the *Call* include "Patriotism," which describes a working-class man whose patriotism comes easy, since he cannot afford either the meat or the wheat bread he is supposed to conserve ("also shoes and gloves and coats"), and "Hic Jacet Henry Dubb," a memorial to a working person who proves so patriotic in his enforced abstinence from food, drink, and heating coal that he dies (cutting wasteful consumption still further).[46] "To Herbert Hoover," published on November 10, 1917, above the pseudonym "Foy," is perhaps the most outrageous of the food conservation poems, for while almost all other such poems emphasize the hardship of working people in getting sustenance under American capitalism, this poem imagines a scene in which an unemployed person, finding a dollar dropped by a wealthy food speculator, purposely binges on all the foods he is supposed to conserve. The binge is triggered by two recognitions: the speaker's observation that the particular capitalist from whom he has sought employment relentlessly hoards wealth and his discovery that the man's wealth derives from an economic sector in which common citizens are forbidden to hoard or to overconsume – "The sign on the door read: '*Commission Merchant, / Grain and Foodstuffs.*'"[47] The speaker responds with a fig for Herbert Hoover:

> Today it is cold and dismal.
> I don't care.
> Last night I ate steak, and onions, and potatoes,
> Coffee, and milk, and sugar, some pie
> And a bottle of beer.
>
> This morning I ate pancakes, and coffee, and bread, and butter.
> (A quarter pound of butter used at one breakfast! ! !)
>
> While it rains I shall rest and play love songs on my violin to my
>   wife . . .
> Tomorrow I shall look for a job again.

The poem relishes two activities expressly forbidden in government propaganda: binging and slacking. Of course, even if the poem were read as advocating wastefulness, the action of the unemployed man is hardly threatening, simply because his poverty, after all, sharply reduces how much he can squander. The practice of the individual, circumscribed by the limitations of his position within capitalism and driven to distraction by Herbert Hoover, is materially self-destructive even as it is psychologically satisfying; it keeps resistance alive, but through a gesture that has effects only within the worker's immediate locale. The *Call*, similarly limited in its ability to formulate effective resistance and to broadcast dissent, nevertheless continued to publish throughout the war. Because of close and constant censorship of the paper, some editions of the *Call* could be distributed only if many of the day's stories were deleted. But on these days the paper persisted in its subversive defiance by printing blank columns where the unpatriotic news and commentary had originally been laid out and thereby testifying to how much information the censors were keeping from common citizens.[48]

For some of the same apparent reasons as in the black press, poems printed in regional newspapers seem to have had more latitude for proclaiming, or implying, dissent than did editorials and news stories. In part, this meant that individual poems simply never could constitute a threat to the propaganda and legal juggernaut directed by the state and supported by the most vocal and influential bloc of American citizens. Furthermore, it was difficult to hold the periodicals accountable for materials furnished as often as not by their "readers," who sometimes used pseudonyms or published anonymously. So newspaper poetry could, and often did, dissent when a newspaper otherwise proclaimed its 100 percent loyalty. The *Detroit Labor News,* published by the Detroit Federation of Labor, an affiliate of Gompers's AFL, gives ample editorial evidence of conformity to patriotic dogma. "Frank D. Walsh Writes Vigorously on the Duty of Foreign-Born Americans," an opinion piece featured on the editorial page of December 28, 1917, condemns a soapbox speaker representing the "Friends of Irish Freedom" encountered recently on a New York street: "I say to those men today, and to all men of like kind, that the part of manfulness and the part of bravery, if they hold such thoughts, is to take a gun and join the army of the autocrat as the open enemy of America."[49] A similar piece by Chester M. Wright, publicity director for the AFL's national syndicate for patriotic labor literature, was printed on February 1, 1918. The headline is sufficient to indicate its gist: "An Age Is Dying! An Age Is Being Born! / Samuel Gompers Says: 'This WAS a War; Now It Is a CRUSADE for Freedom,' and He Puts the Story of an Epoch in a Sentence."[50] On the same page, however, is a poem that only gives lip service to the crusade against autocracy, figured in the Kaiser. What occupies all but one line of "O, You Hoover!" and what really rais-

es the anonymous author's hackles are Hoover's and the government's restrictions on consumption:

> My Tuesdays are meatless,
> My Wednesdays are wheatless;
>   I am getting more eatless each day.
> . . . .
> The barrooms are treatless,
> My coffee is sweetless;
>   Each day I get poorer and wiser;
> My stockings are feetless,
> My trousers are seatless,
>   My! how I do hate the Kaiser![51]

Such a poem enunciates no political alternative but passive resistance. It
does not even entirely displace resentment for the Kaiser. Yet it does
make wartime deprivations instituted by the American state more immediate and irritating than anything the Kaiser has done to the speaker,
and thereby the poem undercuts the assumption that Hollenzollern autocracy was qualitatively different from and more threatening than the
U.S. variety.

On the one hand, when potentially subversive poems were published
in newspapers otherwise pledging loyalty to the war mobilization, we can
well imagine that their subversion would be either missed entirely or pre-
emptively dismissed by patriotic readers. On the other hand, readers inclined to subversiveness might be expected to detect even the faintest
scent of resistance, in spite of the place of publication or even the author's apparent intention. For instance, there is little to suggest that the
Roanoke Times, a newspaper serving a southwest Virginia city with a population in 1918 of twenty thousand, would have served as a focal point
for civilian resistance against the state. Indeed, the paper regularly printed patriotic editorials, and conspicuous in the newspaper's pages are full-
size public service announcements broadcasting the government's latest
directives; sometimes these were sponsored by advertisers, other times
they were donated by the newspaper itself. Yet James Montague's "A Petition" not only ridicules the Food Administration by suggesting it will
next control the distribution of prunes, but complains about high prices
for more common edibles such as apples, eggs, and meat:

> (To Uncle Sam, who threatens to take over and administer the
>   prune supply.)

Uncle, spare that prune!
   Touch not its wrinkled brow:
To us it's been a priceless boon
   And we'll defend it now.
When breakfast food would pall,
   And has allured us not,
A half dozen prunes was all
   The breakfast that we got!

When apples soared too high
   We scorned to eat them dried,
But filled with fine fat prunes our pie,
   And feasted, satisfied.
When steaks rose like balloons
   And eggs began to soar,
We hoisted in a pound of prunes
   And asked for nothing more.

   . . . .

So, Uncle, stay your hand,
   Take over wheat and meat,
Exert control throughout the land
   Of everything to eat.
Conserve both bread and cake,
   Let pie not be immune,
But for a hungering public's sake
   Pray spare the humble prune![52]

To the reader convinced of the patriotic truth spoken by the Committee on Public Information and the Food Administration, the poem might seem only a good-natured recognition of the small inconveniences demanded by patriotic conservation. But a "disloyal" reader might well accept the satire of the poem as more serious. The poem's speaker sees state control over prune consumption as both absurd and possible, suggesting that Montague (and his subversive readers) might see the state's control of any and all private spaces as similarly outrageous and possible.

III

Food conservation poems published in socialist papers such as the *New York Call* suggest self-conscious, intentional criticism, and therefore a kind of subversive compact between writer and reader. The relationship between the (perhaps) dissenting writer and the subversive reader is less certain in such spaces as the *Detroit Labor News* and the *Roanoke Times,* which apart from occasional resistance were largely – and, as editorial policy, explicitly – supportive of the war mobilization. While we here venture into the realm of chance readings – the subversive reader meeting up with just the right text – it is clear that even ostensibly patriotic literature could also, by revealing unwittingly the gaps in militarist, nationalist discourses, facilitate the activities of subversive readers. The propaganda of the state itself cannot escape this kind of willful, subversive rereading or misreading. While the nondiscursivity of poetry can contribute to certain ambiguous, potentially subversive effects, other genres of patriotic literature, widely varying in their poeticism and discursivity, are open to the same kinds of effects. Accompanying the U.S. Food Administration's 1918 pamphlet, *The Day's Food in War and Peace,* for instance, were "Lantern Slides," which provided a visual complement to the pamphlet's lessons. The pamphlet included captions for the slides, presumably to be read at public gatherings while the slides were projected. Here it is the discipline not of rhyme but of descriptive accuracy – of verbal description corresponding, to some degree anyway, to the visual images – that helps provide an opportunity for subversive reading. The captions are driven, as it were, by an imagist poetics as opposed to a genteel one. Indeed, arranged as they are together on a single page, they form a kind of "found" imagist poem, the new technology of lantern slides providing the stimulus for a spare, provocative verbal artifact:

> The Reaper – French Women Harvesting Grain in Reconquered District of Somme.
> French Women Threshing.
> Poverty Forces a Mother to Dispose of Six Children.
> A Crippled Hero of France Still Doing His Bit.
> German Prisoners at Work in England.
> A Belgian Schoolhouse is used as a Center for the Allotment of Wheat.
> Women and Children of Brittany, France, Praying Before the Statue of Christ for a Plentiful Supply of Sardines.
> If Each Person Saved Each Week.
> Not What We Give but What We Share.
> Save the Grains and Share the Bushels.[53]

The last three captions enunciate the rationale of national food conservation: small economies by individuals, accumulated en masse, would amount to enough to save the European Allies. Furthermore, these economies need not be painful sacrifices – Americans are not "giving" their food away, but "sharing" it. But what to the loyal reader might appear reasonable requests for patriotic compliance might to another reader look very much like unwarranted, intrusive state control, and this possibility is amplified by the more poetic, imagistic lines that precede the closing.

Such a reader might note, for instance, the number and variety of public and private spaces that the Food Administration attempts to bring under its purview: French farms, French Veterans' hospitals, prisoner of war camps for Germans, Belgian schoolhouses. To begin with, surely the "German Prisoners at Work in England," contributing unwillingly to the destruction of their country, is for unbiased observers, let alone for a sympathetic German-American reader, a sad and degrading scene. But perhaps most distinctive and disturbing is the captions' focus on French *women*. In the Food Administration literature, this emphasis on Allied women overseas is of course used to evoke American women's sympathy and support for food conservation programs in the United States: "The American woman has the clear choice between assuming for herself at the most one hour's work per day or deliberately imposing this upon her French sister. There is no escape from this situation; the American woman must choose; she must assume this burden or place it upon the shoulders of the woman who is probably bearing the hardest load ever imposed upon woman in the history of the world."[54] But is such rhetoric an unassailable claim on American women's loyalty or a particularly obvious attempt at psychological coercion, as the state attempts to blame American women for the plight of their French counterparts and thereby impose its moral and political authority over them? When the pamphlet concludes, "There is no escape from this situation," one reader might take this as an inviolable injunction to obey, but another would see in it the brute imperative of a totalitarian state.

Also ominous is the first caption – "The Reaper – French Women Harvesting Grain in Reconquered District of Somme" – an image that suggests not just French women harvesting grain but also the Grim Reaper and the harvest of death. The correlation of "The Reaper" with individual reapers recalls those poems of 1914 and 1915 that make this connection explicitly, including Finley's "The Road to Dieppe," Josephine Preston Peabody's "Harvest Moon" poems, even Edith Thomas's "The Harvesters." The analogies of planting and harvesting to killing were never more applicable to the American situation than in 1917. With two of the nation's primary contributions to the war effort being shiploads of grain and of men, associations among grain, harvesting, and the reaper of death are fairly prevalent. But with the grim metaphor of harvest now applying so directly to masses of American rather than British or French men, pro-war poets used it more obliquely. The metaphor of harvest, by connecting U.S. agriculture so closely with the mobilization that would put young American men in the field of fire, came too close to revealing citizens' complicity in the destruction of their own sons, fathers, and lovers. American soldiers, like American agriculture, might be boundless, but patriotic poets typically avoided the further parallel between the two – that the soldiers, like the fields of grain, would be cut down. In "The Substi-Teut," Anthony Euwer revels in the success of the Allies' embargo of the Germans, who have been forced to seek out substitutes in producing even the most basic foods and clothes. (By implication, the Allies face no such necessity because of the abundance of American food.) The "most resourceful Substi-Teut" is forced to make do with "a humbug host / Of Very-nears and Foods-almost": "each stray 'scrap of paper' goes / Into the making of your clothes" and "Your masses live on wheatless-wheat – / Or die on expurgated meat." What Germany needs most, however, is "A substitute for mortal clay. . . . To make more fodder for our guns / And substitute your slaughtered sons."[55] The poem is taunting and cocksure; its battle cry, heartening to patriotic Americans, is based less on confidence in the Allied cause than on ridicule of the German war effort. For a less patriotic and more critical reader, however, the comparisons between food and cannon fodder begun in the poem might become more worrisome. Food and human flesh are both necessary for the prosecution of war, but they are not precisely alike: wheat can be substituted for, human bodies cannot. This the poem applies, triumphantly, to the German predicament. That the same formula might apply to American soldiers is a possibility Euwer ignores, though we can guess it was considered by resistant readers – or by doughboys who met the machine gun, mortar, and artillery fire even of dwindling German troops.[56]

What value does this nearly invisible dissent then have? To begin with, we must acknowledge the ways in which both consciously and unconsciously subversive textualities might keep alive, or even stir up, in their readers the disposition to dissent and to resist. Moreover, the Food Administration had redefined private household activities as crucial to the war effort, so that farm workers, cooks, and eaters could individually, even privately, resist the war effort. Thus, in small measure anyway, subversive readers of government propaganda could resist the state within their own homes; subversion could be manifested materially for anyone who had an excess to waste by the sly dumping of table scraps, baking of wheat bread, and outright gorging. It remains true, at the same time, that the agencies that could have channeled this dissent into visible, concrete political action were discredited by wartime propaganda, were actively suppressed by the government, or for various reasons themselves collaborated with the war mobilization. As long as the government acted coercively, suppressing political and cultural difference alike, it may be possible to see a common, subversive interest pulling together African-Americans, German-Americans, Irish-Americans, socialists, IWWs, large segments of the working classes, pacifists, and even perhaps women as a group. We should not, however, mistake this kind of common ground, created when a coercive state marginalizes numerous groups on the basis of minority race, ethnicity, gender, class, and politics, for a working oppositional coalition.[57] We have seen, for example, a species of German-American racism represented in the *Fatherland* that was partly responsible for black Americans' receptivity to the jingoist, military expansionism of Theodore Roosevelt. Racism could not be overcome simply because African-Americans and German-Americans shared marginal status during the Great War. Likewise, I have explored how the ties forged between socialism and women's pacifism were tentative and never widely embraced among either the middle- and upper-class women dominating the peace movement or the working-class people committed to socialism. The hurdles of gender and class prejudices could not be cleared simply because the state coerced and suppressed both women and working-class people during the war. So while the state may have helped create multiple antagonists by its war policies, these were kept from forming a political bloc in part because the state limited free speech and, more centrally, because the various parts of that potential bloc were mutually antagonistic. Is it possible that state coercion can form the basis for a unified opposition? Of course. But this did not happen in wartime America; and American political economy during the war suggests that such a unified opposition cannot be created solely by negative pressure from outside, but must be knit together by activist political work from the inside. The tools for constructive political work might be preserved and even forged in wartime, but they must also be wielded when the opportune moment for activism arises, not just cherished or contemplated.

Two additional generalizations may be offered here. First, politically ripe moments can be *made* as well as simply seized; at no point is history simply given. Second, the opportune time for activism may come just as readily in war as in peace, as the Russian revolutions of 1917 make clear. But to say that history is made, and that revolution can happen at all kinds of historical junctures, is not to suggest that history is made by everyone, equally, all the time: its making is the subject of hegemonic struggle, and at certain times a dominant bloc may hold all the key positions. For the moment, in 1917 and 1918, pacifists, socialists, and civil rights activists had lost virtually all positions gained during the period of neutrality. They were constantly giving ground rather than gaining it. Dissenters were left with little more to do than to wait and read.

Conclusion

HISTORY AND POETRY IN THE AGE
OF IRONY

By focusing on political poetry – poems written on behalf of or purposely used by political organizations to promote their agendas – I have chosen in this study to privilege work that has seldom received anything but derogatory and passing attention in other critical studies. By examining poetry engaged in a specific set of political struggles, which took place at a particular historical juncture and had definite losers and winners, I have dwelled on poetry that is commonly thought of as "ephemeral" and therefore of no interest to later readers. But in valorizing that work, I think we can recognize the emergence of a uniquely constructive poetics and politically engaged literary practice, a practice that at its best combines political commitment with historical timing: that both makes a long-term commitment to a particular political struggle and displays the instinct to act decisively at the historically opportune moment. Such a conception of literary practice suggests that individual poets wishing to engage in politics must eschew the romantic, Shelleyan model of the poet as "unacknowledged legislator." This individualistic conception of the poet, which seems to persist in numerous contemporary studies of individual authors' "political" significance, has little relevance to (indeed, is virtually discredited by) a history of those writers who were most influential in World War I–era ideological and political formation. The myth of a writer's individuality was certainly useful to, say, the Vigilantes, as they promoted a notion of individual American citizens voluntarily responding to the national mobilization, but the Vigilantes themselves recognized the importance of collective organization and group discipline and dramatically exploited these in contributing to political change.

A partisan poetics emphasizes the necessity of operating within, and upon, historical contingencies. If a political group would strive for hegemonic power, it must act when those historical circumstances become favorable to its programs. For marginal groups, there is the additional imperative to act quickly and decisively, for such favorable conditions are unlikely to persist. The struggle for hegemony, the war of position, must and *can* be waged by even those groups that lack privilege and occupy positions of relatively little political and social power. At times between 1914 and 1917 American women and unskilled laborers, in spite of emerging from marginalized positions, were able to offer political alternatives embraced by mass audiences, to call upon majority opinion, and even to influence national policy. Marginality does not always imply powerlessness in hegemonic struggles; for a marginalized group to gain ground does, however, demand perfect timing. The opportunities for pacifist and radical mobilization during the world war were not many and passed rapidly. The proponents of reaction and militarism had more chances, backed as they were by the economic and political capital of the most privileged classes of society, though they too had to formulate the right kind of popular discourse, seize the right moment of patriotic fervor to propagate it, and mobilize the mechanisms of mass culture. Given the ultimate failure of pacifist and revolutionary movements in World War I America, I will conclude by highlighting not only the opportunities for dissenting poetry and politics illustrated in Great War–era work, but also the dangers illustrated therein – and perhaps, too, the challenge it provides for our own contemporary practice.

I

The politics and poetry of the war demonstrate both the importance and the difficulty of coalition building as a process within hegemonic struggle. Antonio Gramsci sees that form of hegemonic struggle he calls the "war of position" as the simultaneous contestation of all sites of cultural production and political power: the state is effectively in control of all the important hegemonic structures, but the proletariat can hope to wrest control by contesting all of them simultaneously and thereby overwhelming state power. In certain respects Gramsci's version of hegemonic war of position fits the American experience of the Great War incisively, for faced with the possibility of pacifist and revolutionary resistance from within, the state sought to "organise permanently the 'impossibility' of internal disintegration" through a far-reaching wartime bureaucracy and a still more expansive mobilization of patriotism in the civil sphere. Those groups that continued to offer organized resistance to the war mobilization, particularly the Industrial Workers of the World and the Socialist Party, were met with the legal and military power of "a more 'interventionist' government, which [took] the offensive more openly against the oppositionists."[1]

Yet Gramsci's formulation, though it emphasizes the "enormous sacrifices by infinite masses of people" demanded by the war of position,[2] seems to suppose too readily a dualistic conflict: a primary struggle between capitalist and proletariat that, though it may suit the Italian context which was foremost to Gramsci, does not entirely fit the American context during the Great War. Certainly, my argument, and to some extent the organization of my materials into patriotic and dissenting groups, has suggested a dualistic struggle within culture and politics. I have likewise argued that, at certain promising junctures, individuals and splinter groups within working-class and women's movements sought to form coalitions between these two most prominent antiwar movements. Still further, when interventionist groups insisted on a binary logic that defined patriotism as complete conformity to state authority and labeled as treason all other options, the wartime mobilization did create the conditions for a dualistic struggle. I would also argue, however, that the struggle to prevent military intervention and to promote democratic political change was lost well before the state organized its repressive apparatus most fully, in 1918. In short, the comparisons between political and military struggle that Gramsci offers must, as he himself points out, "always be taken *cum grano salis* . . . as stimuli to thought."[3] Most glaringly, American politics and culture in the key period of 1914–17 was defined not by the kind of dualistic conflict described by Gramsci, but by multiple struggles involving gender, race, and ethnicity as well as social class. Conservative political forces held all the key political positions not just because they began with all the strategic advantages, but also because they were best able to organize a coalition, or a hegemonic formation, involving key players in all of these struggles. Not only did the progressive reformers who populated the Wilson administration opt for intervention; so too did the majority of "ordinary," middle-class Americans who felt no particular economic or practical relationship with the European conflict but who could be mobilized on the basis of cultural, moral, racial, and ultimately personal identifications. Also brought into the national war effort – and, to various degrees, persuaded to suspend the pursuit, or defense, of their own political rights – were the larger share of distinct ethnic groups, including German-Americans and African-Americans who could be threatened by loss of social status. Likewise, the support of key factions within organized labor and women's groups was gained by quid pro quo economic and political concessions. In comparison with this impressive network of coalition building, in which ideological consistency was never more important than pragmatic and political advantage, war dissenters were all too likely to let theoretical and ideological differences among themselves obstruct their view of those interests that, if not common, were not mutually incompatible and therefore offered some basis for concerted political opposition. The model of class warfare enunciated by the IWW – the closest American parallel to Gramsci's perspective – was widely applicable to American society, and especially to the particular industrial struggles in which the union was involved, but its rigorous application to all social conflict did not make allowance for the situation of middle- and upper-class pacifist women whose opposition to the militarist, patriarchal state was no less fervent than Wobblies' opposition to the capitalist state. The majority of women in the peace movement, meanwhile, did not recognize the connection between their denunciation of military violence and radicals' condemnation of capitalist violence, and their aversion to confrontational politics – combative, ungenteel tactics in politics and poetry both – made a recognition of common interest and shared political agendas impossible. Meanwhile, both groups largely overlooked potential alliances with the African-American community. If, at the time of the East St. Louis riot, there lay a germ of full-scale war resistance in Du Bois's and the black press's criticism of the Wilson administration's weak response, that perspective never led to a wartime alliance with socialists – both because it was white working-class people who were mainly responsible for the riot and because the Socialist Party was inclined to explain the workers' attacks against blacks in terms of capitalist exploitation instead of racism.[4]

I would argue, then, that my study of the formation of a conservative hegemony in American society and the corresponding marginalization of progressive and minority groups, while it does not particularly undercut the importance of ideologies in shaping national policies and social movements, nevertheless foregrounds a consideration of political action alongside ideological formation. I have argued that a "nonmodern" poem that seems, to later readers, to offer an unpersuasive ideological position or an amateurish artistry can, if contextualized rightly and offered up to the right audience, transform poetry into political action. For approximately the same reasons, the most rough-and-ready ideological conception can, if positioned rightly in a particular social and cultural formation, be more politically effective than the most nuanced analysis of that ideology, or alternative to it.

II

Of course, these generalizations do not yet tell us what is most important of all: what forms of practice and analysis will be politically and rhetorically most effective at a given historical moment. Here the example of American poetry and politics from the Great War is both instructive and cautionary. I have suggested, in discussing subversive poetries of the period 1917 and 1918, that the value of such work typically lies not in its immediate power of resistance but in its role within a longer-term hegemonic struggle. This seems to be precisely the relationship between the Left's discourses that resist wartime food conservation and later discourses that reconfigure that resistance and its rhetoric in terms of proletarian power. Postwar poetry that reflects on state control over food offers additional proof of the existence – and perseverance – of subversive readers during a period when they were marginalized. The wartime discourse about food conservation – and resistance to it – provided connections between material waste and rhetorical subversion that became a resource for new, constructive political discourses. If, during the war, the opposition of radicals and the quiet resistance of unpatriotic consumers could claim, at best, only to have slowed the mobilization and deployment of the U.S. Army, after the war these dissenters could use poetry of harvesting, cooking, and consuming to recall the hypocrisy of American war rhetoric and the menace of state control. Poetry of this kind could once again become an instrument of open protest. Written after the war, Covington Hall's "War Lord's Harvest" uses the metaphor of reaping to apply to all the soldiers killed in the fighting: "the harvest is ten million boys in Europe lying dead." The poem not only portrays the harvest of death as the ultimate end of soldiers; it also extends the metaphor to expose those ultimately responsible – the politicians who betray the people they lead by the lies "they sow . . . the woeful crop of lies." Hall catalogs the abuses of these politicians as follows: "They sow it in the parliament and in the justice hall; / They sow it in the souls of men, of mother and of child. / . . . They sow it unto worldwide war, to Hate and Famine's tread."[5] Thus, in a few lines, he offers the dissenter's perspective of America's repressive wartime laws, its propaganda machine, and its food policy both at home and abroad.

It took the Great Depression for radical political groups to wield anything like the influence of the IWW and the Socialist Party before U.S. intervention in World War I. But when in the 1930s the American Left renewed its strength, its apologists could appeal to the repression dealt them during the Great War, and its writers could draws upon the war's poetics of bread and harvest. "Remember," a poem from Henry George Weiss's 1935 collection, *Lenin Lives,* recalls the deadly harvest that enlisted the working class: "When the bosses go to war / they arm Labor / with poison gas, / machineguns, / aeroplanes, / rifles, / tanks." The poem then bids workers to "remember" what little thanks they got for their sacrifice:

> Let Labor remember
> that when they asked for bread
> they were vagrants,
> that when they demonstrated
> against starvation
> they were Reds,
> that when they talked of rights
> they had no rights.[6]

For Weiss as well as the earlier writers of the war, bread becomes at once a material and symbolic resource. Its absence means starvation; to deprive people of it, the most basic of necessities, is the greatest outrage. But because bread is so basic, it also becomes, like Hoover's "wheat loaf," a "positive symbol . . . in the imagination of enormous populations."[7] So when Weiss appeals to his audience to join in forming a new state, a proletarian dictatorship, he not only draws attention to the lack of bread in the United States during the 1930s, but also draws upon bread as a positive symbol of physical and political sufficiency: "Let Labor remember," Weiss writes, "that Communism is bread, / Communism plenty, / Communism workers' rule."[8] For this synthesis between symbolic and material domains, melding bread poetry with "bread politics," Weiss could find many predecessors in the literature of the Great War. And there were many in his left-wing audience for whom the experience of wartime political repression was all too fresh a memory.

This kind of negotiation between historically situated texts and later political struggles is, however, a process fraught with instability and risk. Since history can never precisely return to the same set of political and social conditions, a set of discourses developed under earlier circumstances may become irrelevant when applied under other, later conditions, no matter how similar. At the same time, insofar as certain histor-

ical struggles of nationality, class, race, and gender are virtually perpetual, the strategies of hegemonic struggle and tactics of resistance that
proved politically dangerous at one historical moment are likely to remain so. The Left politics practiced by Covington Hall and Henry George
Weiss continued to seem threatening to dominant American culture and
accordingly were suppressed in the 1930s as they were in 1917 and 1918.

The women's peace movement, especially influential in 1915, was be-
deviled in 1940 by a second world war that was at the same time too
much and too little like the first one. Naval blockades and the war of food
were again employed as strategies on both sides but as of 1940 were not
equally prominent on both. Sarah Norcliffe Cleghorn, one of the young
radicals of the New York branch of the Woman's Peace Party during
World War I, was in 1940 an activist in the WPP's successor, the Women's
International League for Peace and Freedom. Her poem "Come, Fifty
Million Men and Women," published in December 1940 in the pacifist
journal *Fellowship,* described with greater accuracy the Allied food embargo of World War I than the (then inconsequential) British embargo of
World War II. The poem begins with the same premise enunciated by
Hoover's Food Administration, underscoring the power held by millions
of households acting in concert, while, like the Great War poems of Edith
Thomas and Mary White Ovington, Cleghorn shows how this power can
be used to bring disaster upon the households of the "enemy":

> Yet now, as our crops come rolling home,
> What is this that the war lords say?
> "Starving the helpless is tactics of war;
> *America, keep your food away."*
>
> Shall we take orders like to these,
> And help make Europe's childhood die?
> Or shall we folk of the Western world,
> With our mighty harvests, ask them WHY?

Cleghorn's poem declares that the standards obtaining in one's own home
ought to apply as well to policies affecting the homes of so-called enemies. Cleghorn asks in the final stanza, shall we "boldly call on the lords
of war / To help our ships for the starving through?" For an answer she
suggests, *"Ask your children at supper tonight, /* Mothers and fathers, which
to do."[9]

But Cleghorn's application of the food embargo of 1914–18 to that
of 1940 is problematic historically and especially politically. In Decem-

ber 1940, with the Battle of Britain being reported in Edward Murrow's daily radio broadcasts, Cleghorn's appeal, which substitutes the binary logic of friend–enemy with a logic of equivalence between American and German households, turned out to be far less plausible than the very similar appeal of "I Didn't Raise My Boy to Be a Soldier" and of WPP productions in 1915. The methodical ravaging of French and Belgian harvest fields in the first war, the thoroughly reported occupation of Belgium, the inconclusive trench warfare being waged on the Western Front, and the equally vague and unconvincing reasons given by the Central Powers and Triple Entente for continuing the war – these factors contributed both to a focus on the war of food and to the possibility of seeing the warring parties as being equally at fault. A year into World War II, circumstances could not bolster a similarly neutral view; with the occupation of France, the bombing of English cities, and the German submarine blockade of England, it seemed that only England was threatened by the heinous modern warfare against civilians. Ultimately, the closest similarity between Cleghorn's pacifist activism of World War I and that of World War II was its effect on her literary career. Cleghorn's *Portraits and Protests,* a collection of her pacifist verse about the first war, appeared in 1917, just in time to alienate the greater share of the audience she had won by her fiction writing.[10] So too, "Come, Fifty Million Men and Women" appeared just when American animosity toward Germany was growing fierce, and the poem reappeared in her collection *Poems of Peace and Freedom* in 1945, when wartime censorship was eased but Americans, enthralled with their military power, were hardly likely to respond favorably.

III

The historical dilemma faced by Cleghorn is finally the one confronting this study. How can the genteel, popular, and demotic poetry of the 1910s be used to speak to the cultural and political struggles of the present, given that the dynamics of history and of poetry are undeniably and irreducibly different in the 1990s than they were eighty years ago? In spite of the ongoing and important political projects of contemporary poets, printed poetry seems no longer positioned, as it was during World War I, as a mode of political and social authority. Since poetry no longer has access to a national audience and poets are no longer looked to as national prophets, I do not presume that this study can re-create, by its summoning the milieu of the 1910s, the linkage of poetic utterance and political conviction that then widely obtained. Similarly, in the literary academy of the 1990s – in spite of its professed eclecticism and political consciousness – few literary or cultural critics have seen the kind of partisan-political poetry I have discussed as having any vital relation whatsoever to contemporary criticism. The American poetries of World War I, whether they engage in political struggles of hegemony or of subversion, do not necessarily stand in a constructive relationship with the present moment. In fact, there is a striking analog between the status of subversive poetry in wartime and the standing of the various popular, genteel, and demotic poetries of the war in relation to the present literary-critical discourses of modernism. The poetry of the war has, in literary-critical terms, been the excess literary production that has had to be stripped away to expose and maintain the monument of poetic modernism, much as subversive poetry was suppressed to keep intact the illusion of national unity in time of war. If the key project of postwar resistant poetries was to bring subversive wartime poetry into a tangible, productive relationship with present hegemonic struggles, accordingly the key aim of this study is to bring the excess poetry of modernism – nonmodernist modern poetry – into a critical and constructive relation with the literary debates and political struggles of the present.

While poetry (printed poetry, anyway) cannot reposition itself as a political oracle for the 1990s, the literary academy, though still a fundamentally conservative institution, has shown since the 1960s a greater willingness to speak out on political issues. The multicultural studies and classrooms of the 1990s do represent a raising both of political consciousness and of intellectual rigor in the literary academy. But still – and this is perhaps most crucial – there remains a chasm between critics' commitment to politicize their readings of literary texts and their willingness to study (and therefore also to encourage the production of) literary texts that are themselves consciously fashioned to political ends. The difference between these two fields of study comprises, it seems to me, a continuing reluctance among scholars to engage in scholarship that is genuinely committed to political discussion (in both the wide and narrow senses). Always there is the reluctance to engage in textual discussions that dispense with considerations of "literary" or "aesthetic" merit as primary (though perhaps unacknowledged) categories and instead foreground the categories of cultural and political signification (which perforce does consider aesthetics, but secondarily and contextually).[11]

At bottom the American literary academy continues to be dominated by modes of thought enunciated by the modernists and their pedagogical heirs, the New Critics. Central to these modes is their deployment of irony. My study closes with a few reflections on this powerful, captivating, and yet potentially narcotic mode of literary reasoning. Its persistent influence in literary studies, I maintain, goes some distance toward explaining both the current popularity of subversion and resistance as literary tropes and the continuing reluctance of the U.S. literary studies academy to attempt something like fully engaged, committed political action.

The seductions of irony as a critical mode are evident in a book as simultaneously traditional and forward-looking as Paul Fussell's *The Great War and Modern Memory* (which features such canonical warhorses as Siegfried Sassoon, Wilfred Owen, Edmund Blunden, and Herbert Read, but at the same time analyzes cultural artifacts such as recruiting posters and military form letters). On the one hand, even if we reject Fussell's claim that the Great War established a modern tendency toward ironic observation, it seems clear that ironic modes have since the 1910s become indispensable to the work of producing and interpreting American literature. The compulsion to read with a sense of the disparity between expectation and result has certainly been at work in my study of Great War poetry, as I have argued that the patriotic and egalitarian ideals supposedly guiding the U.S. intervention actually contributed to divisiveness and repression in wartime politics. Certainly, too, I have often focused on texts that respond to the tensions and ironies of U.S. history, particularly in devoting considerable space to poetry written by women, blacks, and political radicals. This project would have been very different without its free employment of irony; I made little attempt to squelch it, whether in interpreting individual poems or their historical situations.

On the other hand, Fussell's unremitting focus on irony conceals as well as it discloses. As we have seen, by his privileging of a certain kind of irony, Fussell's work occludes our view of a considerable variety of literature written by women and noncombatants. Just as important, the ironic mode conceals not only forms of literary production but, with this, other possible modes of critical reading. Fussell's summation of his argument is worth quoting once more, with attention to the way it precludes attention to styles of reading other than the ironic, as he asserts "that there seems to be *one dominating* form of modern understanding; that it is *essentially* ironic; and that it *originates largely* in the application of mind and memory to the events of the Great War" (emphasis mine).[12] Of course, Fussell cannot mean that irony is ascendant throughout twentieth-century culture. Such a view would simply fly in the face of the overwhelming evidence that monologic, unironic nationalist and militarist ideologies have dominated twentieth-century history and to this day remain pervasive in movies, sports jargon, occasional verse, and public policy.[13] It would disregard, as well, the power wielded by twentieth-century discourses of "hard" and behavioral science, statistical economics, corporate management, and industrial efficiency.[14] He seems to mean, quite the contrary, that the ubiquity of these uncomplicated, deadly discourses in modern mass culture is what makes the ironic viewpoint necessary and vital in twentieth-century high literature and literary criticism. Dominant, mass culture is what twentieth-century high literature is ironic about. But while I would not deny the productive power of a critical antagonism such as this, it also suggests that "ironic" understanding is by definition reactive and dissenting: irony depends upon its monologic and univocal other (whose paradigm is the military command, immediately understood and obeyed unhesitatingly and unthinkingly) and simultaneously collaborates in constructing that other as culturally dominant. From this perspective, irony might be practically defined as that attitude taken by a dissenter or dissenters of a particular cultural system who have nevertheless resigned themselves to that system and may, in the case of the New Critics in the academy, be profiting from the very cultural formations they putatively oppose.

The problem is not simply that New Critics (or poststructuralists) have been in collaboration with the dominant culture they criticize; all members of a society are in some way collaborators in its production. The problem lies rather in our cultivating a critical mode that so problematizes any historical or political problem as to render impossible either coherent action or a consistent praxis dedicated to changing the shape of dominant culture. This is the point at which an initial critical choice – the preference of protesting soldier poetry over patriotic verse, for example – can later serve to delimit the range of conceivable critical stances. Even as the soldier-poet can debunk the war system but is singularly unable to extricate himself from it, the ironic critic can criticize the social system but can do nothing in particular to design a constructive social alternative. As a way out of this cycle, I would suggest, one must begin not only by deconstructing the collaboration of high literary texts with social ideologies and politics, but also by recovering the texts previously dismissed as unimportant because not suitably ironic. Throughout this study, I have argued against a monologic conception of modern American literary history; instead, I have worked to show that American poetry of the 1910s was far more diverse than our literary histories acknowledge and – what is perhaps more crucial – that the poetries of this period did cul-

tural work as important as the experimental modernist writing that has
absorbed academics' attention almost exclusively. The grandiose aspirations and cadences of genteel war poetry, the poetic application of feminine ideals to women's movements (as well as the interrogation of those
ideals), the deployment of poetry in the mobilization of America's citizenry and industry (and the resistance to this mobilization among
women, socialists, and African-Americans), the ribald parody of "capitalist" literary modes in the poetry and songs of the Industrial Workers of
the World – these all move beyond the customary parameters of modernism. They both expand the range of styles included in modern American poetry and broaden our understanding of the social contexts in
which, and audiences for whom, poetry was written, read, and acted upon.
Especially insofar as we have repressed these alternative contexts, our collective forgetfulness of poets affiliated with the Woman's Peace Party, the
Industrial Workers of the World, the Vigilantes, the National Association
for the Advancement of Colored People, and even the genteel publishing establishment in the 1910s has had political as well as literary consequences. Even aside from the possibility that our cultural absentminded-
ness will help to marginalize potentially valuable forms of politics, our
forgetting (or dismissing) poetry inseparably linked to specific political
movements encourages us to imagine a separation of our professional
identities from our political ones. This, in a sense, is the final consequence
of asserting irony to be both the predominant and the *preferred* mode of
understanding – a critical distance that undermines all politics.

The pose of ironic detachment and disinterestedness that irony nur-
tures has other important effects; for the notion that the critic can somehow stand apart from society reinforces an illusion long cherished by
literati and literary critics: the illusion of radical individual freedom,
which suggests that literary texts and literary figures provide access to
realms of unfettered personal and political opportunity. So there are further reasons that the literary scholar may have difficulty with the intellectual work this book has attempted: to participants in a discipline that
persistently constitutes itself as an inquiry into "imaginative" or political
possibility, it may appear unseemly or irrelevant to be interested in, and
to strive for, an interpretation of poetry that connects its meaning so
closely with the specific history and politics of consciously organized political groups. The sharp sense of historical contingency provided by such
a reading, however, seems to me precisely what is needed in literary studies if our most critically subtle and culturally astute interpretation is ever
to become politically powerful. It may seem, at first, that a poem's close

identification with the aims and ideals of a particular political group restricts its potential for defining new kinds of politics. After all, if a poem can be paraphrased in terms already laid out in the agenda of some group, why bother with the poem at all? But such a question denies the productive, dialogic relationship that can exist between poems and the social collectivities that call them into their service. It is also marked by the lingering conviction, shared by many literary academics, that literature worthy of study must be produced by an inimitable, solitary genius. As it turns out, there are two sides to the situation of the poet who is committed to a given politics and a duly instituted group. On the one hand, there is the difficulty of sticking by one's commitment, and there is the risk associated with identifying with a group that may be swept away by historical contingencies beyond its control. On the other hand, the potential leverage of consciously working within and working through a collective organization is far greater than the potential for an individual writer speaking his or her mind. The kinds of poetry we have examined are not just historically determined – which all textualities are, after all – but historically timely. The poets of the Vigilantes, IWW, NAACP, and WPP do not just appear to sacrifice their artistic individuality to the determined constraints of given social and political identities; they seize upon the possibilities for social change that lie in self-consciously constituted collectives.

I should not want to propose commitment to a collective idea – the degree to which a poem or poet adheres to a collectivist or, as I have called it, partisan poetics – to be the unquestioned, ultimate measure of a poem's value. Within the historical scope of this study, such a measure might demand adulation for the jingoism of the Vigilantes, scorn for the internationalism of the WPP – a judgment I, for one, am not prepared to make. Yet this reservation by no means implies that we should devalue the poetics of partisanship or dismiss it as unsuitable for study. At the very least, if we distrust the politics of the Vigilantes, for instance, it hardly makes sense to ignore their collectivist, historically timely work as trivial. Still more important, if the literary academy is to reshape its role in society, interrogating its status as a privileged but largely powerless enclave, then literature scholars would do well to investigate past literary work that was able to establish wider connections with American political and cultural life.

We should certainly guard against uncritical idealization of the political-literary communities or the political poetry of the United States during the Great War. And yet our ironic habits of reading, deeply ingrained by the New Criticism and even amplified by most American variants of deconstruction, would seem ample to keep us from overenthusiasm. At this moment, it seems to me that the literary academy has to rethink literary criticism and analysis in ways that allow for more intense political partisanship and commitment. This theorization, I argue, can be promoted by the kind of recovery of American war poetry begun here. In its various forms, American poetry of the Great War draws upon premodernist traditions of collective production and group solidarity while simultaneously confronting the historical contingencies that gave rise to, among other phenomena, literary modernism. At the cusp of the "modernist revolution," as we have come to call it (and fashion it for ourselves), these poetries confront problems and propose solutions that are at the same time familiar and strange to us. On balance, the problems – militarism, nationalism, racial and class divisiveness, patriarchy – are probably more familiar, though the concrete instances of these, exhibited and confronted by poetry of the Great War, provide us with new materials for examining their historical mooring. In comparison, the poetic solutions offered by the poems of the Great War appear stranger, even bizarre. But they are not removed from our cultural agendas in the ways we have imagined when dismissing these premodernist (or extramodernist) poetries as "genteel." That is, we have not disregarded them for the politically noble reasons that, for example, David Perkins presumes: "For subject matter Genteel poetry articulated generalized attitudes, and in its Romantic spiritual elevation it did not grapple with experience . . . with characters and actions, with society and politics, least of all with the contemporary milieu."[15] On the contrary, I have argued that we neglect American poetry of the war not because its production and reception were hopelessly removed from political life, but because they were so closely and self-consciously involved in political and ideological formation and transformation. The kind of rapprochement between poetry and politics we see here is threatening, but it is precisely the threat we need.

Notes

Introduction

1. According to Wendy Chmielewski, curator of the Swarthmore College Peace Collection, the Peace Poems Subject File includes clippings received and organized by the staff of the Peace Collection since the 1930s. It consists of miscellaneous poetry written by authors unknown or authors otherwise not included in the collection (Chmielewski, personal interview, Mar. 26, 1992). Given that most of the poetry in the Peace Poems file predates World War II, it is tempting to visualize the period from the 1910s through the 1930s as a kind of forgotten heyday of pacifist verse.

2. In my limited survey of newspapers, I found Vigilantes poems in papers as dispersed and various as the *Atlanta Constitution, Los Angeles Times, Colorado Springs Gazette, Portland Oregonian, Richmond Times-Dispatch, Virginian-Pilot and Norfolk Landmark,* and *Roanoke Times.*

3. W. Reginald Wheeler, ed., *A Book of Verse of the Great War* (New Haven, CT: Yale UP, 1917); Lyman P. Powell, *The Spirit of Democracy* (New York: Rand McNally, 1918); L. C. McCollum, *History and Rhymes of the Lost Battalion* (1919; n.p.: n.p., 1929).

4. "Writing Poems on War," *New York Times* Aug. 8, 1918: 8.

5. Ernst Lissauer, "A Chant of Hate against England," trans. Barbara Henderson, *New York Times* Oct. 15, 1914: 12.

6. Beatrice M. Barry, "Answering the 'Hassgesang,'" *New York Times* Oct. 16, 1914: 10.

7. Rosalie M. Moynahan, "Another Chant of Hate," *New York Times* Oct. 17, 1914: 10.

8. Beatrice Barry, "The Crucial Moment," *New York Times* Oct. 20, 1914: 12; McLandburgh Wilson, "Motherhood's Chant," ibid. Oct. 21, 1914: 10; *Contemporary War Poems*, special bulletin of International Conciliation series

(New York: American Association for International Coalition, Dec. 1914); Frank L. Stanton, "'The Song of Hate,'" *Atlanta Constitution* May 30, 1915: 2F; Charles J. O'Neill, "Ireland's Chant of Hate," *Fatherland* Apr. 21, 1915: 8; Jules de Marthold, "France's Hymn of Hate," trans. Barbara Henderson, *New York Times* July 4, 1915, mag. sect.: 1; Harry McClintock, "Hymn of Hate," *Solidarity* Jan. 1, 1916: 2.

9. "To Hate or Not to Hate," editorial, *New York Call* Feb. 10, 1918: 6.

10. Max J. Herzberg, "An Old-New 'Song of Hate,'" translation of Georg Herwegh's "Ein Lied des Hasses," *New York Times* June 11, 1918: 10.

11. In its run from 1914 to 1929, the *Little Review* never gained a circulation higher than 1,000, argues Frank Luther Mott, *A History of American Magazines*, 5 vols. (Boston: Houghton Mifflin, 1968) 5: 171. *Poetry* had between 2,000 and 3,000 subscribers during the war, according to James A. Hart, "American Poetry of the First World War (1914–1920): A Survey and Checklist," diss., Duke U, 1964, xiii. Hart is hereafter cited parenthetically in the text.

12. William Archer, Introduction to *Letters and Diary of Alan Seeger* (New York: Scribner's, 1918) xxiv, xliv.

13. Manufacturing-record for *Poems* by Alan Seeger, box 21, Manufacturing Records: Editions Published 1902–1955, Charles Scribner's Sons Archive, Princeton University Rare Books and Special Collections, cited with permission of the Princeton University Libraries.

14. Manufacturing records for the Thomas Y. Crowell Company are not extant. But Catherine W. Reilly's bibliography indicates that the seventh edition as well as the first was published in 1918 (*English Poetry of the First World War: A Bibliography* [New York: St. Martin's, 1978] 12). Some of the "editions" were almost certainly simple reprints. Still, if we assume print runs of comparable sizes, this rate of production would roughly match that of Seeger's *Poems* in the preceding year.

15. Jane LeCompte, communications manager, Houghton Mifflin company, letter, Dec. 19, 1994.

16. Joyce Kilmer, "The White Ships and the Red," *New York Times* May 16, 1915, mag. sect.: 1. Kilmer was a staff writer for the *Times*, a well-known poet and literary critic in the 1910s, and known to schoolchildren for decades after by his poem "Trees." "The White Ships and the Red," a poem written on assignment, was reprinted repeatedly: "a poem so wonderfully effective that it was at once reprinted all over the country and in Europe" (Robert Cortes Holliday, "Memoir," in *Joyce Kilmer*, 2 vols. [New York: Doran, 1918] 1: 63). At age thirty Kilmer volunteered within weeks of the U.S. intervention (79), was elevated to the rank of sergeant (90), and was killed in France on July 30, 1918 (96).

17. "Lusitania Disaster Provides Inspiration to Many Poets," *New York Times* May 16, 1915, sect. 7: 1.

18. Nicolas Slonimsky, *Music Since 1900*, 4th ed. (New York: Scribner's, 1971) 249.

19. The manufacturing record from Charles Scribner's indicates that 3,300 copies of the book were in the bindery on January 18, 1916; 547 copies were still there when, on June 28, 1916, 300 sets of pages were ordered destroyed to reduce inventory (manufacturing record for *The Book of the Homeless* by Edith Wharton, box 26, Manufacturing Records: Published Editions 1902–1955, Charles Scribner's Sons Archive, Princeton University Rare Books and Special Collections, cited with permission of the Princeton University Libraries).

20. Statistics on national school attendance, though fragmentary, show that among Americans growing up in the United States after 1870 – those sixty and younger when the nation entered the Great War – a clear majority spent at least some time in public schools. Approximately 57% of school-age children were enrolled in 1870, 69% in 1890, and 80% in 1910 (Edward H. Reisner, *Nationalism and Education Since 1789: A Social and Political History of Modern Education* [New York: Macmillan, 1920] 464; Larry Cuban, *How Teachers Taught: Constancy and Change in American Classrooms, 1890–1980* [New York: Longman, 1984] 18; Patricia Albjerg Graham, *Community and Class in American Education, 1865–1918* [New York: Wiley, 1974] 15).

21. Arthur Fairchild's "The Teaching of Poetry in the High School" (*University of Missouri Bulletin* 15.8 [Mar. 13, 1914]) singles out poetry – particularly the "great poetry" taught in schools – as the discourse uniquely suited to effecting the schools' aims of moral education and socialization. The study of poetry, according to Fairchild, "sets standards of action to which man, in his daily life, consistently fails to attain. The pleasure of poetry is refined and elevated" (90). He proposes reading Wordsworth to "break away from the narrow and conventional ideas that dominate [one's] every-day actions," for Wordsworth exemplifies the poet whose "view differs from that of the average man," being "free from considerations of self-interest, immediate service, use, and ownership" (92–93). In Fairchild's view, the poet speaks from a disinterested, indisputable position of moral and philosophical authority, whereas common readers, or "average men," trapped in a web of quotidian concerns, must confess their shortcomings and strive to model themselves (though always imperfectly) after the poet's superior example.

22. The sociopolitical aims of poetry education, circa 1900–20, reflected a general expansion of the schools' attempts to inculcate in students a moderate, patriotic ideal of citizenship and to direct them into the vocations where they might be useful to industry. Joel H. Spring, *The American School, 1642–1900: Varieties of Historical Interpretation of the Foundations and Development of American Education,* 2nd ed. (New York: Longman, 1900), describes both the expansion of the schools' socializing function, especially in urban,

predominantly immigrant communities (162–72), and the development of vocational training programs in junior high and high schools (196–220). Of one key teacher-education text, William Bagley's *Classroom Management,* "reprinted 30 times between 1907 and 1927," Spring writes that its author believed "the primary role of the school is to build good industrial habits of the type needed on the assembly line" (183). See also Spring, *Education and the Rise of the Corporate State* (Boston: Beacon, 1972).

23. Burton Egbert Stevenson, ed., *The Home Book of Verse, American and English, 1580–1920,* 5th ed. (New York: Holt, 1922).

24. Quoted in Russel Nye, *The Unembarrassed Muse: The Popular Arts in America* (New York: Dial, 1970) 94. My point here follows Nye's distinction between "great" and "popular" poetry, which he argues, with reference to the statements of numerous anthology editors, was perfectly clear to nineteenth- and early-twentieth-century readers. Indeed, Burton Stevenson professes this kind of division, announcing in his introduction to *Home Book of Verse,* "The attempt is made in this collection to bring together the best short poems in the English language from the time of Spenser to the present day, together with a body of verse which, if not great poetry, has at least the distinction of wide popularity" (xi). What Nye neglects to mention, however, is that for Stevenson and other anthologists the social function of "great poetry" and "popular poetry" alike was moral, spiritual, and almost exclusively *personal* improvement.

25. Katherine Devereux Blake, ["O say can you see, you who glory in war,"] Peace Poems Subject File, Swarthmore College Peace Collection, box 1, folder B. This verse is printed on a postcard-size broadside along with Francis Scott Key's 1814 stanza and another pacifist stanza written by Blake in 1929. A footnote reports that the "President of the Board of Education" endorsed Blake's 1914 version for New York City schools and that "it was sung in schools in places all over the United States until we entered the war."

26. "International Peace Day to Be Observed," *New York Call* May 18, 1917: 2.

27. Robert L. Tyler, *Rebels of the Woods: The I.W.W. in the Pacific Northwest* (Eugene: U of Oregon P, 1967), 32, 68.

28. *Songs of the Workers on the Road, in the Jungles and in the Shops,* 8th ed. (Cleveland: IWW Publishing Bureau, Dec. 1914) 28.

29. Tyler, *Rebels of the Woods,* 73–75.

30. "War Poem Read to the Senate," *New York Times* May 19, 1918, mag. sect.: 5.

31. Nick Salvatore, *Eugene V. Debs: Citizen and Socialist* (Urbana: U of Illinois P, 1982) 291, 294.

32. Quoted in ibid. 296.

33. Mary Thomas Raymond, "History of a Poem: 'The Volunteer's Mother' Has Helped in Recruiting," *New York Times,* Jan. 27, 1918, sect. 2: 4. All quotations of Raymond are from this source.

34. Sarah Fenton Dunn, "The Volunteer's Mother," *New York Times* July 3, 1917: 8.
35. Raymond, "History of a Poem."
36. Antonio Gramsci, *Selections from the Prison Notebooks,* ed. and trans. Quintin Hoare and Geoffrey Nowell Smith (New York: International Publishers, 1971) 18.
37. The slogan "He kept us out of the war" was extracted from a plank of the Democratic platform and used at Democratic rallies without Woodrow Wilson's full endorsement; nevertheless, it became the keynote of his campaign (Arthur Walworth, *Woodrow Wilson,* 2nd ed. [Boston: Houghton Mifflin, 1965] book 2, 54). Wilson's peace policy was apparently the key to his electoral victory, since he lost all states in the Northeast except for New Hampshire – the region most inclined toward preparedness and intervention – and won all states in the Midwest except for Minnesota – the area generally conceded to be most pacifistic (August Heckscher, *Woodrow Wilson* [New York: Scribner's, 1991] 415–16).
38. Woodrow Wilson, *War Message to the Senate and House of Representatives in Congress Assembled* (Boston: Graphic Arts, 1917) 10.
39. David Kennedy, *Over Here: The First World War and American Society* (New York: Oxford UP, 1980) 37–38.
40. Ernest R. May, *The World War and American Isolation, 1914–1917* (1959; Chicago: Quadrangle Books, 1966) 426–27.
41. Ibid. 425.
42. Richard Hofstadter's anthology, *The Progressive Movement, 1900–1915* (Englewood Cliffs, NJ: Prentice-Hall, 1963), provides some indication of the range of activists and social reform movements gathered under the umbrella of progressivism.
43. "Reasonable preparedness" was Woodrow Wilson's rhetorical formulation in late 1915 (quoted in Kennedy, *Over Here* 32). It was, in effect, Wilson's concession to the gathering strength of the pro-preparedness movement and was used to lobby for legislation passed in mid-1916 to augment the navy and army.
44. Neil A. Wynn, *From Progressivism to Prosperity: World War I and American Society* (New York: Holmes & Meier, 1986) 3–4.
45. Frederick C. Luebke, *Germans in the New World: Essays in the History of Immigration* (Urbana: U of Illinois P, 1990) 81.
46. Wynn, *From Progressivism to Prosperity* 42.
47. Austin J. App, "The Germans," in *The Immigrants' Influence on Wilson's Peace Policies,* ed. Joseph P. O'Grady (Lexington: U of Kentucky P, 1967) 31.
48. See Robert Debs Heinl, Jr., and Nancy Gordon Heinl, *Written in Blood: The Story of the Haitian People, 1492–1971* (Boston: Houghton Mifflin, 1978), on the U.S. invasion, occupation, and constant (and increasingly troubled) counterinsurgency campaigns in Haiti beginning on July 28, 1915. The Per-

shing expedition into Mexico, which pursued the rebel Pancho Villa after his forces crossed the border and attacked the town of Columbus, New Mexico, began on March 15, 1916, and lasted until February 5, 1917. See Linda B. Hall and Don M. Coerver, *Revolution on the Border: The United States and Mexico, 1910–1920* (Albuquerque: U of New Mexico P, 1988) 57–77, for a compact account of the punitive expedition.

49. Malcolm Bradbury and James MacFarlane, eds., *Modernism, 1890–1930* (1976; New York: Penguin, 1991), connect the war explicitly with the emergence of modernist art, as they include "the destruction of civilization and reason in the First World War" among a few historical events that precipitated the movement (27). They locate the war precisely between the "two peaks" of modernist activity, "the years immediately preceding, and the years immediately following" (36).

50. Cary Nelson, *Repression and Recovery: Modern American Poetry and the Politics of Cultural Memory* (Madison: U of Wisconsin P, 1989), 22–23.

51. Frank Lentricchia, *Modernist Quartet* (New York: Cambridge UP, 1994) 2.

52. Here my study joins company with those of others doing work on modern American poetry, and for that matter of critics of modern American writing in other genres. Important studies of American political literature both precede and succeed the period under consideration here, with which this book might be thought to link up to provide an extended – though also multifaceted and discontinuous – history of American political literature. These studies share certain convictions regarding the relations between the political and the aesthetic, maintaining the general theoretical principle that the two are never simply antithetical, indeed arguing that the political and the aesthetic are necessarily interconnected and demonstrating just this contention through concrete historical evidence: Robert H. Walker, *The Poet and the Gilded Age: Social Themes in Late Nineteenth-Century American Verse* (Philadelphia: U of Pennsylvania P, 1963), finds that roughly 30% of all books of poetry published between 1890 and 1901 commented on explicitly American social problems and controversies; Aaron Kramer, *The Prophetic Tradition in American Poetry, 1835–1900* (Rutherford, NJ: Fairleigh Dickinson UP, 1968), follows the "prophetic tradition" from the Mexican-American War through the Spanish-American War; Melba Joyce Boyd, *Discarded Legacy: Politics and Poetics in the Life of Frances E. W. Harper, 1825–1911* (Detroit: Wayne State UP, 1994), recovers the work of an important nineteenth-century black poet and political activist; Alan Filreis, *Modernism from Right to Left: Wallace Stevens, the Thirties, and Literary Radicalism* (New York: Cambridge UP, 1994), documents the participation of the preeminent modernist experimenter, Wallace Stevens, in social and political debates of the 1930s; and Alan M. Wald, *The Revolutionary Imagination: The Poetry and Politics of John Wheelwright and Sherry Mangan* (Chapel Hill: U of North Carolina P, 1983), provides an in-depth examination of radical poets Wheel-

wright and Mangan, stressing the connections between biography and political praxis. Revisionist studies of fiction include Jane Tompkins, *Sensational Designs: The Cultural Work of American Fiction, 1790–1860* (New York: Oxford UP, 1985), and Barbara Foley, *Radical Representations: Politics and Form in U.S. Proletarian Fiction, 1929–1941* (Durham, NC: Duke UP, 1993).

53. Lentricchia, *Modernist Quartet* ix.

54. Here again, Nelson in *Repression and Recovery* provides a valuable counterpoint to Lentricchia. He describes critics of canonical writers and literary historians as operating in "shameless collaboration" with one another (54) and calls for them to establish semiautonomous critical discourses that compete with and contest one another (53–54). In this dialectic, I would count myself among the literary historians: those who, according to Nelson, "would consider it their responsibility to write sympathetically about, on behalf of, much of the literature they encountered."

55. I follow Barbara Herrnstein Smith and Jane Tompkins in arguing for the cultural construction of literary aesthetics: literary excellence is not an immutable essence or an abstraction, but rather is always defined by the particular literary works we find valuable, whatever texts we choose to read and call important, and these choices are informed by contingencies that are highly variable across history, cultures, and even individual communities. See especially Smith, "Contingencies of Value," in *Canons,* ed. Robert von Hallberg (Chicago: U of Chicago P, 1984) 15–16, and Tompkins, *Sensational Designs* 186–87, 193–94. My imagined question (in fact asked of me in various forms while my study was under way) is a paraphrase from Tompkins's chapter 7 in *Sensational Designs,* "'But Is It Any Good?' The Institutionalization of Literary Value." My answer paraphrases Robert Dale Parker's, also discussing Herrnstein Smith, in "Material Choices: American Fictions, the Classroom, and the Post-Canon," *American Literary History* 5.1 (Spring 1993): 96. Other important contributions on the subject of the canon and the cultural construction of aesthetics include Alan Golding, "A History of American Poetry Anthologies," in *Canons,* ed. von Hallberg 279–307; Lillian S. Robinson's "Treason Our Text: Feminist Challenges to the Literary Canon," *Tulsa Studies in Women's Literature* 2.1 (Spring 1983): 83–98; and Paul Lauter, *Canons and Contexts* (New York: Oxford UP, 1991).

56. Mary Louise Pratt, *Toward a Speech Act Theory of Literary Discourse* (Bloomington: Indiana UP, 1977) 80–81.

57. Though I use the terminology adapted from John Searle by Mary Louise Pratt, my application of it is somewhat distinct, for while Pratt uses the terms to construct a general theory of literary discourse as comprising the whole range of speech-acts, my argument asserts that certain forms of literary discourse foreground representation and expression as primary functions, while others foreground direction, commitment, or declaration. I do not

mean to argue that literary texts cannot or do not work as directives, commissives, and declarations, but I do mean to suggest that they are not usually and primarily *read* in these ways.

58. I allude here to Stanley Fish's discussion of "serious" and "fictional discourse" in "How to Do Things with Austin and Searle" (*Is There a Text in This Class? The Authority of Interpretive Communities* [Cambridge, MA: Harvard UP, 1980]). Fish admits Searle's distinction between these two kinds of discourse in practical terms, while denying that the distinction has any essential value: the distinction "is one between two systems of discourse conventions (two stories) which certainly can be differentiated, but not on a scale of reality" (239). My own approach follows Fish both in emphasizing that the "fictional discourse" of poetry might represent "reality" as much, and as well, as a journalistic report and in examining how the conventions that differentiate the serious from the fictional are "in fact" used in particular historical and political arguments.

59. My emphasis is on the British soldier-poets because it is their poetry and, symbolically, the figure of the soldier-poet that have dominated discussions of modern war poetry and, to a significant extent, modern war literature generally. Especially notable among books subscribing to the soldier-poet school of criticism are Bernard Bergonzi, *Heroes' Twilight: A Study of the Literature of the Great War* (London: Constable, 1965); Richard Eberhart and Selden Rodman, eds., *War and the Poet: An Anthology of Poetry Expressing Man's Attitudes to War from Ancient Times to the Present* (New York: Delvin-Adair, 1945); John H. Johnston, *English Poetry of the First World War: A Study in the Evolution of Lyric and Narrative Form* (Princeton, NJ: Princeton UP, 1964); Arthur E. Lane, *An Adequate Response: The War Poetry of Wilfred Owen and Siegfried Sassoon* (Detroit: Wayne State UP, 1972); Jon Silkin, *Out of Battle: The Poetry of the Great War* (London: Oxford UP, 1972); and Peter Vansittart, ed., *Voices from the Great War* (New York: Watts, 1984). Studies and anthologies of American Great War literature – many of them tangibly haunted by the absence of an American canon comparable in literariness to the British soldier-poetry canon – include William Allan Brooks, ed., *The Soldiers' Collection of Poems and Ballads* (1941; Miami: Granger, 1976); Stanley Cooperman, *World War I and the American Novel* (Baltimore: Johns Hopkins UP, 1967); Alfred E. Cornebise, ed., *Doughboy Doggerel: Verse of the American Expeditionary Force, 1918–1919* (Athens: Ohio UP, 1985); Thomas C. Leonard, *Above the Battle: War-Making in America from Appomattox to Versailles* (New York: Oxford UP, 1978); and Jeffrey Walsh, *American War Literature, 1914 to Vietnam* (New York: St. Martin's, 1982). Recent studies oriented less exclusively toward battlefield representation are Samuel Hynes, *A War Imagined: The First World War and English Culture* (New York: Macmillan, 1991), which focuses on British wartime culture, civilian as well as military; and Timothy Sweet, *Traces of War: Poetry, Photography, and the Crisis of the Union*

(Baltimore: Johns Hopkins UP, 1990), which discusses photography, poetry, and culture in the U.S. Civil War.

60. Such a dichotomy was supported by the accounts of the soldier-poets themselves. Siegfried Sassoon wrote, "The man who had really endured the War at its worst was everlastingly differentiated from everyone except his fellow soldiers" (*The Memoirs of George Sherston,* 3 vols. [New York: Literary Guild of America, 1937] 2: 280). Among the many poems by soldier-poets that exemplify this view, see Sassoon's "Glory of Women" (*Counter-Attack and Other Poems* [New York: Dutton, 1918] 32) and Wilfred Owen's "Dulce et Decorum Est" and "S.I.W." (*The Complete Poems and Fragments,* 2 vols., ed. Jon Stallworthy [New York: Norton, 1983] 1: 140, 160–61). In his introduction to Owen's *Collected Poems,* C. Day Lewis emphasizes that to understand Owen's poetry we must recognize "how great was the gulf between the fighting man and the civilian at home, and between the front-line soldier and the brass-hat" (*The Collected Poems of Wilfred Owen,* ed. C. Day Lewis [1931; New York: New Directions, 1965] 22). Lewis continues, "To the soldier, those on the other side of the barbed wire were fellow sufferers; he felt less hostility towards them than towards the men and women who were profiting by the war, sheltered from it, or willfully ignorant of its realities."

61. Paul Fussell, *The Great War and Modern Memory* (New York: Oxford UP, 1975) 87.

62. Ibid. 35.

63. For a specific rebuttal of Fussell's views on war poetry by women, see Susan Schweik, *A Gulf So Deeply Cut: American Women Poets and the Second World War* (Madison: U of Wisconsin P, 1991) 293–94. Important sources for women writers of World War I include Catherine W. Reilly, *English Poetry of the First World War,* and Reilly, ed., *Scars upon My Heart: Women's Poetry and Verse of the First World War* (1981; London: Virago, 1982); Margaret Randolph Higonnet et al., eds., *Behind the Lines: Gender and the Two World Wars* (New Haven, CT: Yale UP, 1987); and Helen M. Cooper, Adrienne Auslander Munich, and Susan Merrill Squier, eds., *Arms and the Woman: War, Gender, and Literary Representation* (Chapel Hill: U of North Carolina P, 1989). In *English Poetry* Reilly calculates that of the 2,225 British writers who published poetry in single-author books or anthologies, 417 were members of the armed forces while 532 were women (xix).

64. Writing about poetry of World War II, Schweik argues that "the total war was being fought, as the Great War had already to a lesser extent been fought, not by armies but by populations"; she therefore underscores "the active presence of women *as subjects* in the action and the discourse of the war" (*A Gulf So Deeply Cut* 4).

65. See Cooper, Munich, and Squier, *Arms and the Woman* xiii–xv and 9–17; also see Miriam Cooke and Angela Woollacott, eds., *Gendering War Talk* (Princeton, NJ: Princeton UP, 1993); Cynthia Enloe, *The Morning After: Sexual Pol-*

itics at the End of the Cold War (Berkeley: U of California P, 1993); Sandra M. Gilbert, "Soldier's Heart: Literary Men, Literary Women, and the Great War," in *Speaking of Gender,* ed. Elaine Showalter (New York: Routledge, 1989) 282–309; and Nosheen Khan, *Women's Poetry of the First World War* (Lexington: U of Kentucky P, 1988). For a history of American women workers in World War I, see Maurine Greenwald, *Women, War, and Work: The Impact of World War I on Women Workers in the United States* (1980; Ithaca, NY: Cornell UP, 1990).

66. Jane Marcus, "Corpus/Corps/Corpse: Writing the Body in/at War," afterword to *Not So Quiet . . . Stepdaughters of War* by Helen Zenna Smith (New York: Feminist Press, 1989) 242.

67. Schweik, *A Gulf So Deeply Cut* 7.

68. Jon Silkin, ed., *The Penguin Book of First World War Poetry* (London: Allen Lane, 1979) 29.

69. A few of Owen's poems were published in the hospital magazine that he edited, *The Hydra* (*Poems of Wilfred Owen,* ed. Edmund Blunden [1931; London: Chatto & Windus, 1961] 27), but only four were published in national publications during the war, and only one of those, "Futility," which appeared in the *Nation,* referred explicitly to the war (*Complete Poems* xviii).

70. The engagement for which Owen won the Military Cross he describes thus to his mother: "I lost all my earthly faculties, and fought like an angel. . . . With [a boy lance-corporal] who stuck to me and shadowed me like your prayers I captured a German Machine Gun and scores of prisoners. . . . My nerves are in perfect order" (*Collected Letters,* ed. Harold Owen and John Bell [New York: Oxford UP, 1967] 581).

71. Sassoon, *Memoirs* 2: 319–22. Of the autobiographical content of Sassoon's *Memoirs of George Sherston,* Samuel Hynes remarks that "the man who lives Sassoon's life is called George Sherston, Robert Graves is David Cromlech," and Hynes attests to the factual accuracy of the book's descriptions of "the fighting, the medals, the Protest, Dottyville [the psychiatric hospital], the return to the Western Front and the final wound all there" (*A War Imagined* 436).

72. Sassoon, *Memoirs* 3: 232–33, 241.

73. Elizabeth A. Marsland, *The Nation's Cause: French, English, and German Poetry of the First World War* (New York: Routledge, 1991) 167. Cf. Marsland's chapter 6, "A Few Alone: Readers, Non-Readers, and Protest."

74. See Marcus, "Corpus/Corps/Corpse" 259; and Marcus, *Suffrage and the Pankhursts* (New York: Routledge, 1987).

75. Louis Althusser, "Ideology and Ideological State Apparatuses (Notes towards an Investigation)," *Lenin and Philosophy and Other Essays* (New York: Monthly Review P, 1971) 133. Hereafter cited in the text parenthetically.

76. Before Althusser, this distinction between two kinds of superstructural levels was described by Antonio Gramsci: "the one that can be called 'civil so-

ciety,' that is the ensemble of organisms commonly called 'private,' and that of 'political society' or 'the State.' These two levels correspond on the one hand to the function of 'hegemony' which the dominant group exercises throughout society and on the other hand to that of 'direct domination' or command exercised through the State and 'juridical' government" (*Prison Notebooks* 12). Hereafter the *Prison Notebooks* are cited parenthetically in the text.

77. Cf. Catherine Belsey, "Constructing the Subject: Deconstructing the Text," in *Feminist Criticism and Social Change: Sex, Class and Race in Literature and Culture,* ed. Judith Newton and Deborah Rosenfelt (New York: Methuen, 1985) 45–64. If the determinism of ideology over subject is as absolute as Althusser appears to suggest, the kind of ideological criticism that Belsey outlines for "Althusserian" deconstruction would be virtually impossible, simply because the kind of critical self-consciousness achieved by the deconstructor would never be possible: "To deconstruct the text . . . is to open it, to release the possible positions of its intelligibility, including those which reveal the partiality (in both senses) of the ideology inscribed in the text" (58). The success of Belsey's deconstruction suggests, I believe, that the relationship between ideology and subjectivity should be considered less as a box of mirrors and more as dialectic with partially distinguishable, autonomous terms.

78. For a further consideration of Gramsci's place in Marxist cultural analysis, see Stuart Hall, "Cultural Studies: Two Paradigms," in *Media, Culture and Society: A Critical Reader,* ed. Richard Collins et al. (Beverly Hills, CA: Sage, 1986) 33–48.

Chapter 1

1. "Protesting Women March in Mourning," *New York Times* Aug. 30, 1914: 11.

2. The "Preamble and Platform" of the WPP stated demands establishing a fairly radical, oppositional stance: a peace convention of neutral nations, limitation of U.S. armaments, opposition to militarism in America, peace education, popular control over U.S. foreign policy, and rectification of economic inequalities ("Woman's Peace Party Preamble and Platform Adopted at Washington, January 10, 1915," Records of the Woman's Peace Party, Swarthmore College Peace Collection, Scholarly Resources microfilm edition [cited hereafter as WPP Records], reel 3, box 3, folder 4). Barbara J. Steinson, *American Women's Activism in World War I* (New York: Garland, 1982), argues that the January 1915 inaugural platform comprised "the most comprehensive peace plan yet adopted by an American peace group" and thereby put the WPP "in the vanguard of the American peace movement" (36, 37). Useful for an overview of the American peace movement during

World War I are C. Roland Marchand, *The American Peace Movement and Social Reform, 1898–1918* (Princeton, NJ: Princeton UP, 1972), and Charles Chatfield, *For Peace and Justice: Pacifism in America, 1914–1941* (Knoxville: U of Tennessee P, 1971). The definitive accounts of the WPP are provided by Steinson and Marie Louise Degen, *The History of the Woman's Peace Party*, Johns Hopkins University Studies in Historical and Political Science 57.3 (Baltimore: Johns Hopkins UP, 1939). Hereafter Steinson and Degen will be cited parenthetically in the text.

3. Jane Addams, *Newer Ideals of Peace* (New York: Macmillan, 1907); Charlotte Perkins Gilman, *The Man-Made World: Or, Our Andocentric Culture* (1911; New York: Source Book, 1970); Olive Schreiner, *Woman and Labour* (London: Unwin, 1911).

4. See Stanton's "'Address Delivered at Seneca Falls,' July 19, 1848," and Anthony's "'Constitutional Argument,' 1872" (*The Elizabeth Cady Stanton–Susan B. Anthony Reader: Correspondence, Writings, Speeches*, ed. Ellen Carol Dubois [Boston: Northeastern UP, 1992] docs. 1 and 13).

5. Olive Tilford Dargan, "Beyond War," Peace Poems Subject File, Swarthmore College Peace Collection [cited hereafter as Peace Poems], box 1, folder D. The poem appeared as "This War," in *Scribner's* 57.1 (Jan. 1915): 89–91; it was later published in W. Reginald Wheeler, ed., *A Book of Verse of the Great War* (New Haven, CT: Yale UP, 1917) 40–45.

6. Dargan was born in 1869 in Kentucky and lived until 1968. In her career she wrote and published in three genres. During her early adult years in New York City, she concentrated on drama and poetry, publishing four books of plays and three of poems between 1904 and 1922. After 1915, when her husband died and she moved back to Kentucky, she began to concentrate more on fiction; she became widely known for both her local-color sketches about Appalachian mountain people and her proletarian fiction protesting their plight, written under the pseudonym Fielding Burke. Her novels and story collections number seven, published between 1925 and 1962 (Lina Mainiero, ed., *American Women Writers*, 5 vols. (New York: Ungar, 1979) vol. 1).

7. Jane Addams, Emily G. Balch, and Alice Hamilton, *Women at the Hague: The International Congress of Women and Its Results* (New York: Macmillan, 1916) 65–66.

8. See e.g., James E. B. Breslin's account of modernist poetics in *From Modern to Contemporary: American Poetry, 1945–1965* (Chicago: U of Chicago P, 1984). Modernist poetry, Breslin explains, held as exemplary "a language that swiftly shifts tone or attitude, thickens texture with allusion and ambiguity in an effort to examine subjects from several sides without selecting any one as final" (18).

9. "The Women's Manifestation," *New York Times* Aug. 30, 1914: 14.

10. Marguerite Merington, "The Call to the Colors," *New York Times* Aug. 10,

1914: 6; Clara Davidson, "The Cry of the Women," ibid. Aug. 15, 1914: 8; Edith Thomas, "Princes and War," ibid. Aug. 20, 1914: 10; and Caroline Russell Bispham, "Peace and War," ibid. Aug. 22, 1914: 6.

11. Rudyard Kipling, "For All We Have and Are," *New York Times* Sept. 3, 1914: 1.

12. "A Poem That Expresses British Feeling," *New York Times* Sept. 3, 1914: 6.

13. No written policy on the distribution of broadsides is extant. While it is impossible to say what individuals did with broadsides when they received them, it is fairly clear that the WPP adopted the policy of sending materials only to people or organizations who requested them, and then it often charged a fee. The distribution policy for sheet music of Ewer's "Five Souls" is indicative: "Copies may be ordered through the National Headquarters – twenty-seven cents, postpaid" (WPP Arts Committee, "The Woman's Peace Party," WPP Records, reel 3, box 3, folder 4).

14. "Woman's Peace Party Preamble and Platform." The "Preamble" actually identifies five avenues for pacifist propaganda, and in all of these party members employed poetry to some degree: "Holding nation-wide mass meetings," "Stimulation of a Peace Propaganda throughout existing organizations," "Promotion of a Peace Educational Program for our Schools and Colleges," and "Formation of Committees for Publicity and Press Work," as well as "Encouragement of Artists, Musicians and Writers to productions promoting peace."

15. Florence Wilkinson, "The Fighters," WPP Arts Committee, "The Woman's Peace Party," WPP Records, reel 3, box 3, folder 4.

16. Mina Packard, "Woman's Armaments," Peace Poems, box 1, folder P.

17. Here I dispute C. Roland Marchand's contention that party ideology was old-fashioned in its assumptions about male and female character, whereas the methods of the peace parties exhibited "new departures in style," including "the tactic of appealing for popular support through public demonstrations" (*American Peace Movement* 183). As we shall see, the poems used by the WPP Arts Committee in public programs articulated a conservative brand of pacifism. However, in poems reprinted or commissioned by the committee and distributed by mail individually, WPP poets tended to idealize a far more radical ideology of protest and matriarchal power. A poem like Packard's may assume that the sexes are essentially different, but it dramatically overturns traditional conceptions of men's and women's spheres, putting women in charge of national and international politics for a change.

18. "WPP Platform and Preamble."

19. The nineteenth-century development of a "maternal model" for education is covered by Joel H. Spring, *The American School, 1642–1990: Varieties of Historical Interpretation of the Foundations and Development of American Education,* 2nd ed. (New York: Longman, 1990), esp. "Organizing the American School: The Nineteenth-Century Schoolmarm." Spring emphasizes that

"the proper role for women was to connect with the public sphere by nurturing moral character in the family and the school" (126).

20. "WPP Platform and Preamble."

21. WPP Arts Committee and Chicago Peace Society, "Suggestions and Bibliography for Program for Peace Day, 1915," WPP Records, reel 3, box 3, folder 4.

22. "Peace Day: May 18, 1915," WPP Records, reel 3, box 3, folder 4.

23. Ibid.

24. *Newer Ideals of Peace* was first published in 1907, so of course it would not speak to conditions during the war. It was selected over some more recent writing by Addams perhaps because it offered a greater cultural status than a more immediate, ephemeral piece. *Newer Ideals,* Marie Degen reports, "established Miss Addams as a spokesman [*sic*] of the American peace movement" (18).

25. Since the publication of his "Man with the Hoe" in 1899, Markham's work was identified with social protest and progressive change (David Perkins, *A History of Modern Poetry,* 2 vols. [Cambridge, MA: Harvard UP, 1976], 1: 115–16). Whether or not the poem expressed the ideals of women's pacifism, Markham's name and reputation were such that it would have been only natural to seek out a poem by him for a peace program.

26. "Peace Day: May 18, 1915."

27. "Meeting for Constructive Peace," WPP Records, reel 3, box 4, folder 8.

28. Kipling's "Recessional" fits more readily into True Worthy White's "Patriotic Celebration Program," *Atlanta Constitution* June 24, 1917, mag. sect.: 1. Designed for the Georgia Federation of Women's Clubs, White's program concludes with Kipling's "Recessional." Like the WPP's program, it includes "America"; other poems suggested are Sir Walter Scott's "Breathes There a Man," James Russell Lowell's "The Fatherland," and Henry Wadsworth Longfellow's "The Ship of State."

29. Addams, Balch, and Hamilton, *Women at the Hague* 109.

30. Al Piantadosi (composer) and Alfred Bryan (lyricist), "I Didn't Raise My Boy to Be a Soldier" (New York: Leo Feist, 1915).

31. "Our 'Ignoble, Rancid' Popular Song," *Literary Digest* Aug. 21, 1915: 350.

32. Gerald G. Lively, " 'Twas You Who Raised Your Boy to Be a Soldier," *San Francisco Bulletin* June 5, 1915: 20.

33. "Roosevelt Calls Woman's Peace Movement 'Silly,' " *Philadelphia Public Ledger* Apr. 17, 1915: 2. Degen quotes several long passages from Roosevelt's castigation of women's pacifism, which was first published as a letter in the *Chicago Herald* and was reprinted by papers nationwide (70–72).

34. Nicolas Slonimsky, *Music Since 1900,* 4th ed. (New York: Scribner's, 1971) 249.

35. "M.O.R.C.," *Detroit Saturday Night* n.d.: n.p. Available in Peace Poems, box 3, misc. folder 2.

36. "I Did Not Raise My Boy to Be a Soldier," *Sydney Journal* Aug. 25, 1916. Available in Peace Poems, box 2, folder P.
37. While the Wilson administration knew that contraband had been carried on the *Lusitania,* it chose to cast blame almost exclusively on Germany rather than taking Britain to task for its shipment of military supplies on a passenger liner (Daniel M. Smith, *The Great Departure: The United States, 1914–1920* [New York: Wiley, 1965] 54–56). The administration's handling of the *Lusitania* crisis therefore did nothing to mitigate the anti-German feelings aroused by initial reports of the sinking.
38. "Roosevelt Calls Woman's Peace Movement 'Silly.'"
39. The prewar peace societies dominated by men had been unhelpful almost from the start. The Carnegie Endowment, perhaps the richest and most influential of these groups, had financed the WPP production of *The Trojan Women,* and the Carnegie-supported American Association for International Conciliation published *Contemporary War Poems* (largely antiwar poems) in December 1914. Yet while the monthly publications of the organization provided a forum where pacifist and anti-interventionist ideas could be disseminated, its overall stance toward the war was noncommittal. The association members presented themselves as impartial observers of the war and as disinterested scholars of pacifist ideas. So that "facts" about the war's causes would be available, the association published the documents of each warring nation that justified its cause – the German White Book, the French Yellow Book, etc. – but the association took no particular stand on the legitimacy of the various warring nations' claims. The organization eventually gave space to proponents of intervention, printing, for instance, a debate between the hawkish Taft and dovish Bryan over a *Proposal for a League to Enforce Peace* (New York: American Association for International Conciliation, Sept. 1916), which proposed a British-French-American alliance to bring about world peace by force – a plan that in effect advocated U.S. intervention.
40. Crystal Eastman, letter to New York City WPP members, Mar. 3, 1917, WPP Records, reel 4, box 5, folder 2.
41. Based on membership rolls for the Chicago WPP branch, Washington State WPP, and Washington, D.C., WPP (WPP Records, reel 3, box 4, folders 2, 9, and 11). Whether these figures are for 1915, 1916, or 1917 – the membership rolls are, unfortunately, undated – they suggest that the number of women committed to the WPP was probably never large.
42. The publication of sheet music seems to have been carefully coordinated with the Fuller Sisters' tour, and the song is consistently advertised as being "sung by the Fuller Sisters." "The Woman's Peace Party" list puts the recital first, mentioning later that "Clayton Summy Co. has published the song with music as sung by the Fuller Sisters for the Woman's Peace Party." "The Woman's Peace Party Lists for Distribution" features the piece under sepa-

rate headings as both a song and a performance, while "Suggestions and Bibliography for Program for Peace Day, 1915" lists it as a song but is careful to note, "as sung by the Fuller Sisters of Dorsetshire, England."
43. WPP Arts Committee, "Woman's Peace Party."
44. W. N. Ewer, "Five Souls," arrangement by Frances Frothingham (Chicago: Clayton F. Summy, 1915). After its initial publication in the *Nation* and its arrangement by Frothingham, the poem was reprinted in the United States in *Literary Digest,* May 27, 1915; in Wheeler, *Book of Verse* 46–47; and elsewhere. The extant versions I have examined differ only in punctuation, which in my quotation reproduces the Clayton Summy song printed in March 1915.
45. WPP Arts Committee, "Woman's Peace Party."
46. Peace Poems, box 1, folder E–G. The small printed card located in the Swarthmore Peace Collection containing the additional stanza is not dated. But the same stanza, differing slightly in punctuation and typography only, appears in the *New York Call,* which notes that it was "written by an English schoolgirl, 14 years old" and originally appeared in "the Advocate of Peace, July 1916" (*New York Call* June 13, 1917: 8). Just below, the *Call* published yet another stanza fitting Ewer's pattern, Ellen Winsor's "The American Conscript, 1917," which gave the song a further proletarian twist:

> My Country gave the cry; it needed me,
> But sent me to the European strife;
> I gave my blood and took another's life,
>   'Twas thus, they said, I'd set the whole world free.
> I spent my life in poverty and woe;
> I died to please my Masters, now I know.

Yet a third version was performed in the program for the "Presentation of the World Peace Prize to Rosika Schwimmer," in New York on December 4, 1921 (Peace Poems, box 3, misc. folder 2). In this case the sixth stanza is credited to "Rev. H. W. Pinkham – unflinching pacifist" in a note written on the reverse of a typescript draft (Peace Poems, box 1, folder E–G). The new stanza portrays a young man who ostensibly sailed along with Schwimmer on Henry Ford's Peace Ship and later was killed when drafted as an American soldier:

> I was a student from the Empire State
> I joined the Peace Ship; sailed to stop the War!
> Statesmen and merchants scorned the word we bore.
> Next year they sent me out to meet my fate.
>
> I gave my life for freedom, this I know
> For those who bade me fight had told me so.

The repeated use of "Five Souls" for functions related to the WPP – Schwimmer was an honorary member – seems to confirm its strong association with the party as well as its popularity among WPP members. Its appearance in the *Call* suggests a wider popularity for the song among various dissenting groups.

47. Marchand, *American Peace Movement* 214–15. See also the NAWSA's own official account of its wartime activities, which provided a separate chapter entitled "War Service of Organized Suffragists" (*History of Woman Suffrage,* 6 vols. [1922; New York: Arno, 1969] vol. 5 by Ida Husted Harper, 720–40).

48. Shelly is described by one newspaper clipping in the Swarthmore collection as "the youngest delegate" to the Hague convention ("Angela Morgan Tells of War Suffering in Berlin," *Chicago Examiner* July 12, 1915 [available in Papers of Angela Morgan, Swarthmore College Peace Collection [cited hereafter as SCPC]). She was twenty-seven in 1915, according to Barbara Steinson (75). Steinson's *American Women's Activism* mentions that in 1910 Shelly earned a B.A. in German language and literature, was later employed as a teacher of those subjects, traveled in Germany twice between 1910 and 1914, and became engaged to a German journalist (who was later a soldier) (75–76). Steinson's book goes on to trace Shelly's wartime peace activism in some detail, as well as discussing her "physical breakdowns" in 1917 and 1918 and her postwar activities (279–81). Louis Lochner's considerable participation in the peace movement are documented in Marchand, *American Peace Movement,* and in Chatfield, *For Peace and Justice.* Already in 1903–4 while in college, Lochner had helped found the Association of Cosmopolitan Clubs, a confederation of college organizations dedicated to international understanding (Marchand, *American Peace Movement* 37; Chatfield, *For Peace and Justice* 16). Angela Morgan's activities in the peace movement receive much slighter treatment. In Steinson's account, Morgan is placed with Shelly among the younger, more radical generation of female peace activists; she appears, however, to be more a loyal confidant and supporter of Shelly than a leader of the movement in her own right (75–77).

49. See Marchand, *American Peace Activism* 181n.

50. Addams characteristically shied away from the tactics of political confrontation and press publicity; one biographer describes her as the "quiet administrator" of the peace movement (Allen F. Davis, *American Heroine: The Life and Legend of Jane Addams* [New York: Oxford UP, 1973] 236).

51. Steinson, *American Women's Activism* 77. The conflict between women peace activists reaching maturity in the 1870s and 1880s and those coming of age in the twentieth century is a prominent theme in Steinson's book (see 394–95). The dispute between Jane Addams and Rebecca Shelly over the Detroit peace rally is taken by Steinson as symptomatic of a generational divide within the peace movement (77).

52. "400 Societies Urged to Join Peace Move Launched at Meet," Detroit newspaper clipping, Nov. 6, 1915, Papers of Angela Morgan, SCPC.

53. "Ferris Indorses Plan for Great Assembly," Detroit newspaper clipping, Nov. 5, 1915, Papers of Angela Morgan, SCPC.

54. Morgan's first book publication, *The Hour Has Struck (A War Poem) and Other Poems* (New York: Lewis, 1914), established her as a commentator on the war as early as the fall of 1914. In press reports of the trip through Germany that she and Shelly made, she is typically described as "the Poet" as well as a "Peace Delegate," and her comments are reported at greater length than Shelly's. See "Angela Morgan Tells of War Suffering in Berlin"; "Finds Germany Practical," *New York Times* July 12, 1915: 14; and "Angela Morgan, the Poet, Returns from Germany," *Lewiston Journal* Sept. 18, 1915, mag. sect.: 12 (all available in Papers of Angela Morgan, SCPC).

55. "Mme. Schwimmer to Help Make Peace," *Detroit Free Press* Nov. 6, 1915: 3.

56. "400 Societies Urged."

57. "Pacifists Will Meet on Street," *Detroit Times* Nov. 6, 1915: n.p., Papers of Angela Morgan, SCPC.

58. Ibid.

59. "400 Societies Urged."

60. *Utterance and Other Poems* (New York: Baker & Taylor, 1916) 44–45. Hereafter cited parenthetically in the text as *U.*

61. Morgan, *The Hour Has Struck* 13–14.

62. "Angela Morgan Tells."

63. "Pacifists Will Meet on Street."

64. Addams declares unequivocally in *Peace and Bread in Time of War* (New York: Macmillan, 1922), "The newspapers were, of course, closed to us so far as seriously advocating such a conference [of neutrals] was concerned, although they were only too ready to seize upon any pretext which might make the effort appear absurd" (27). But this opinion, expressed after the war, was most likely colored by reflection on the patriotic frenzy that would seize the United States in 1917 and 1918 (as well as the Ford Peace Ship debacle). Furthermore, given Addams's differences with Shelly, it is hardly surprising that she would not recognize the potential for capitalizing on press coverage, which Shelly's Detroit rally had in fact demonstrated.

65. The blame for the WPP's inaction must be shared by all the WPP's leaders, not just Addams. In fact, in 1916, when the national WPP fell silent even during the U.S. confrontation with Mexico, other leaders must bear the greater share of responsibility, since for most of the year Jane Addams was convalescing from a kidney ailment (Steinson, *American Women's Activism* 154–55).

66. *Who Was Who,* 5 vols. (Chicago: Marquis Who's Who, 1942–73) vol. 3.

Chapter 2

1. Harry McClintock, "Hymn of Hate," *Solidarity* Jan. 1, 1916: 2. Joyce Kornbluh, ed., *Rebel Voices: An I.W.W. Anthology* (Ann Arbor: U of Michigan P, 1964), reports that McClintock participated in an IWW band organized in

Portland around 1908 to compete with Salvation Army bands. Between 1925 and 1955 he performed on the radio, mostly for San Francisco stations. McClintock's dates are 1883–1957 (29).

2. The poem's author is actually indicated by an alias, "Bingo," in *Solidarity*. In the transcript of the Chicago IWW trial, the printer for IWW publications in Chicago identified that alias, the signature on numerous Wobbly cartoons, as the pen name of "Fellow Worker Chaplin" (*United States v. Haywood, et al.*, May 3, 1918, IWW Collection, box 103, folder 7, p. 258, Archives of Labor and Urban Affairs, Wayne State University [cited hereafter as ALUA-WSU]).

3. Ralph Chaplin, "Harvest Song 1915," *Solidarity* Apr. 3, 1915: 4.

4. Cf. Dick Hebdige, *Subculture: The Meaning of Style* (New York: Methuen, 1979), whose semiotic approach to style might address in several ways the relationship of the IWW's songs and poetry with the discourses of dominant culture. Like the youth subcultures that are Hebdige's focus, the IWW appropriated the poetic modes in use in the general culture – appropriations that to some extent included the mimicry and parody for which they are famous – but inflected those languages with their own style, which aimed to offend, outrage, and bewilder those outside Wobbly subculture. However, when Hebdige generalizes that "the challenge to hegemony which subcultures represent is not issued directly by them" (17), I would argue that the IWW provides an example of a subculture that was quite self-consciously organized and explicitly proclaimed as a challenge to dominant American culture.

5. See "Sabotage: What It Means and Why," Baskette Collection, box 107, folder A, Rare Book and Special Collections Library, University of Illinois at Urbana-Champaign. Probably printed by the IWW, this 3″ × 5″ leaflet explains the origin of sabotage in a way that portrays its application as a fairly guileless reaction to oppressive working conditions:

> SABOTAGE comes from "sabot" meaning shoe, wooden shoe.
>
> During a labor trouble in France some years ago, one of the dissatisfied workmen employed in a factory where machinery of a delicate character was necessary to the turning out of the product, took off his shoe and tossed it into the whirring wheels, putting the engine out of business. Since then the acts of men who believe in using similar methods have been called "sabotage's." . . .
>
> SABOTAGE is very popular with certain classes, but never with the man who owns the machine.

For Chaplin's account of the origin of "sabotage" and the term's applications in the United States – which, he argues, were unlike the French usage, non-destructive – see Ralph Chaplin, *Wobbly: The Rough-and-Tumble Story of an American Radical* (Chicago: U of Chicago P, 1948) 206–7.

6. The most comprehensive history of the IWW is Melvin Dubofsky, *We Shall Be All: A History of the Industrial Workers of the World* (Chicago: Quadrangle Books, 1969). Hereafter cited parenthetically in the text. Also of interest are Paul F. Brissenden, *The IWW: A Study of American Syndicalism* (1919; New York: Russell & Russell, 1957); and Philip S. Foner, *American Socialism and Black Americans: From the Age of Jackson to World War II,* Contributions in African-American and African Studies 33 (Westport, CT: Greenwood, 1977).

7. The first six editions of *Songs of the Workers* were published in Washington State, either by union locals in Spokane or Seattle or by the western organ of the IWW, *Industrial Worker* (also based in Spokane). These are not dated. However, because both the fourth and fifth editions contain the poem "John Golden and the Lawrence Strike," they must date to sometime after January 1912, when the Lawrence, Massachusetts, textile strike began. Considering that the seventh edition, published at the IWW Publishing Bureau in Cleveland, appeared in June 1914, the fifth edition was probably published in late 1912 or early 1913, and the sixth sometime in the latter half of 1913.

8. Born in Sweden in 1879, Joel Hagglund emigrated to the United States in 1902; in America he adopted the name Joe Hill. Around 1910 he joined the IWW, and in 1911 and 1912 his songs first appeared in *Solidarity* and *Songs of the Workers.* In 1914 he was arrested in Utah on charges of murder, and in 1915 he was convicted and executed – but not before becoming an international celebrity as a martyr for the cause of labor (Mari Jo Buhle, Paul Buhle, and Dan Georgakas, eds., *Encyclopedia of the American Left* [New York: Garland, 1990]).

9. *Songs of the Workers on the Road, in the Jungles and in the Shops,* [5th ed.] (Spokane, WA: Industrial Worker, [ca. 1912–13]) 5.

10. The collaboration of local and state militias, district and municipal courts, and business leaders against the IWW and affiliated unions is a refrain of Dubofsky, *We Shall Be All.* Well-publicized strikes in which IWW-affiliated workers were killed by police, militia, or company detectives include the Lawrence textile strike of 1912 (248–49), the Paterson, New Jersey, textile strike of 1913 (278), and the Wheatland, California, agricultural strike of 1913 (296). In these cases, no law enforcement officers were brought to trial.

11. This is the basic critique of Ben Williams, then editor of *Solidarity,* as expressed in several fall 1914 editorials (quoted in ibid. 351–52).

12. Ralph Chaplin, "Slaves, to the Slaughter!" *Solidarity* Aug. 29, 1914: 2.

13. "'When Block Meets Block,'" *Solidarity* Sept. 5, 1914: 2.

14. Ernest Riebe, "When Block Meets Block," cartoon, *Solidarity* Sept. 5, 1914: 1. Riebe is one of the Wobbly cartoonists featured in Kornbluh, *Rebel Voices,* with examples of his work appearing on pages 5, 171, 231, 234, 254, and

258. His cartoons were published in both *Solidarity* and *Industrial Worker*, particularly between 1912 and 1914. Specific biographical information on Riebe and many other Wobblies is difficult to locate. All we know is that they published their work in *Solidarity*, that they were affiliated with the IWW, and therefore that they probably held low-paying, often temporary jobs. Even for an IWW poet as well known as Joe Hill, we can gather surprisingly little concrete information on certain portions of his life. About Hill's life between 1902 and 1908, biographers can say only that he spent time in Philadelphia, Pittsburgh, Cleveland, Chicago, the Dakotas, Spokane, and Portland and that he held jobs, at one time or another, as a porter, longshoreman, and harvest hand ("Joe Hill," in *Encyclopedia,* ed. Buhle, Buhle, and Georgakas).

15. Charles Ashleigh, "The Anti-Militarist," *Solidarity* Oct. 31, 1914: 1. Robert L. Tyler describes Ashleigh as "an English hobo-intellectual and poet" and notes that he wrote a letter of protest to the *Masses* over the Everett incident (February 1917) (*Rebels in the Woods* [Eugene: U Oregon P, 1967] 77). Kornbluh adds that Ashleigh came to the United States in 1910, was among the IWWs arrested and sent to Leavenworth Prison in 1917, and was deported in 1920 as an enemy alien (*Rebel Voices* 79).

16. Albert Bushnell Hart, *The War in Europe* (New York: D. Appleton, 1914) 252–53.

17. Ibid. 11, 216.

18. Clarence W. Barron, *The Audacious War* (Boston: Houghton Mifflin, 1915).

19. Newell Dwight Hillis, *Studies of the Great War: What Each Nation Has at Stake* (New York: Revell, 1915) 259, 22.

20. C. Roland Marchand, *American Peace Movement and Social Reform, 1898–1918* (Princeton, NJ: Princeton UP, 1972) 38. For further discussion of the mostly conservative prewar peace organizations, see Marchand's chapters 2–4, "Courts, Judges, and the Rule of Law," "Businessmen and Practicality," and "Peace through Research."

21. *Contemporary War Poems,* International Conciliation Special Bulletin (New York: American Association for International Conciliation, Dec. 1914) 24. Hereafter cited parenthetically in the text as *CW.* Morley (1890–1957), author of some fifty-five books, also worked as an editor at Doubleday, Page, and Co. (1913–17), the *Ladies' Home Journal* (1917–18), *New York Evening Post* (1920–24), and *Saturday Review of Literature* (1924–40) (*Who Was Who in America,* 6 vols. [Chicago: Marquis Who's Who, 1942–73] vol. 3).

22. Widdemer's later response to the U.S. intervention gives further evidence that her feelings about the laboring masses were equivocal. Although she was not a frequent contributor to the Vigilantes, an article she did contribute reveals limited sympathy indeed with the immigrant masses who populated the working class ("Fool Tolerance," Dec. 12 release, Vigilantes Press Releases

ca. Nov.–Dec. 1917, Hermann Hagedorn Collection, Library of Congress Manuscript Division). A sampling:

> [American hospitality] has extended itself not only to the well-bred lecturing visitor but to the immigrants. We have said, in effect, for generations: "Welcome! We are sure you are going to be good Americans. We won't be rude enough to tell you that there are some of your old-world characteristics we don't like. If you wish to speak your mind, why, speech is free, and you had a hard time over in the Old Country you praise so desperately."
>
> We have trusted, as a whole, to their good sense and honor and courtesy. . . . But we have been acting polite hosts too long. There is such a thing as fool tolerance.

Widdemer (1890?–1978) worked as a teacher and novelist as well as a poet. While "God and the Strong Ones" and *The Factories and Other Poems* (1917) reveal some early enthusiasm for social activism, early popular success with *The Rose-Garden Husband* (1915) (coupled with the pressures of wartime patriotism) seems to have eventually moved her career in a more conventional direction, as she wrote children's books, romantic and historical novels, and the professional advice books *Do You Want to Write?* (1937) and *Basic Principles of Fiction Writing* (1953) (Ann Evory, ed., *Contemporary Authors,* New Revision Series [Detroit: Gale Research, 1981] vol. 4).

23. Margaret Widdemer, "God and the Strong Ones," *Masses* Nov. 1914: 3.
24. Cf. Louis Althusser, "Ideology and Ideological State Apparatuses," *Lenin and Philosophy and Other Essays* (New York: Monthly Review P, 1971) 127–86.
25. Charles W. Wood, "King of the Magical Pump," *Masses* Dec. 1914: 3.
26. Penelope Niven, *Carl Sandburg: A Biography* (New York: Scribner's, 1991) 285.
27. Carl Sandburg, *The Complete Poems of Carl Sandburg* (New York: Harcourt Brace Jovanovich, 1969) 28–29.
28. Ibid. 42.
29. See Dubofsky, *We Shall Be All* (esp. 350–52), for a summary of the IWW's general position on national wars and its specific stance on World War I. Foner, *American Socialism,* includes separate chapters on wartime IWW organizing in the lumber and mining industries.
30. Citing figures from party records, David Shannon documents a membership drop of approximately 10% from 1916 to 1918: 83,138 in 1916; 80,126 in 1917; and 74,519 in 1918 (*The Socialist Party of America* [New York: Macmillan, 1955] 121). Daniel Bell's figure of 81,000 for 1918 would suggest a slighter decline ("The Background and Development of Marxian Socialism in the United States," in *Socialism and American Life,* 2 vols., ed. Donald Drew Egbert and Stow Persons [Princeton, NJ: Princeton UP, 1952] 1: 291). Bell, however, argues that the Socialist Party of America waned in political in-

fluence because its membership consisted increasingly of recent immigrants in a period of intense xenophobia; membership in Socialist Party foreign language federations grew from approximately 16,000 in 1912 (13% of total union membership) to 24,000 in 1918 (30%) – and ballooned to 57,000 in 1919 (57% of union membership).

31. Dubofsky points out that the IWW did not organize a defense campaign for Hill until three months after his arrest, and then largely in response to Utah newspapers which emphasized Hill's Wobbly connections (*We Shall Be All* 309). Hill had done only limited work as an organizer, and he was known in the IWW almost exclusively for his songs, so that Dubofsky concludes, "Joe Hill arrived in Utah an insignificant migrant worker; when his corpse departed the state two years later, he was internationally proclaimed as a martyr to labor's cause" (312). Writing in Buhle, Buhle, and Georgakas's *Encyclopedia,* Franklin Rosemont places a higher priority on the "Little Red Song Book" in the IWW's operation and, thereby, sees Hill as "one of the better known Wobblies" by mid-1913, when he had far more of his compositions in the songbook than any other author. Indeed, though Hill did not belong to the leadership of the union as Ralph Chaplin did, the visibility of his poems and songs in *Solidarity* and *Songs of the Workers* must have ensured that, at the time of his arrest, he was far more important to the union than Dubofsky estimates.

32. "The Last Letters of Joe Hill," *Industrial Pioneer* Dec. 1923: 53.

33. According to the *Industrial Pioneer,* not only Haywood but a number of organizations supporting Hill received this "famous farewell wire," which the *Pioneer* quotes in a version slightly different from Dubofsky's: "Goodbye, Forget me. Don't mourn, Organize" (ibid. 56).

34. "In Memoriam Joe Hill," memorial service program, Chicago, Nov. 25, 1915, IWW archive, Joe Hill subject file, Labadie Collection, Department of Rare Books and Special Collections, University of Michigan, Ann Arbor. Also printed in *Songs of the Workers on the Road, in the Jungles and in the Shops,* 9th ed. (Cleveland: IWW Publishing Bureau, Mar. 1916) 1; in *Songs of the Workers to Fan the Flames of Discontent,* 34th ed. (Chicago: IWW, 1973) 10–11 (with music); and in most editions of the songbook between.

35. Chaplin, *Wobbly* 207.

36. *United States v. Haywood, et al.,* July 19, 1918, IWW Collection, box 112, folder 7, p. 7702, ALUA-WSU. Hereafter cited parenthetically in the text according to page number in the transcript.

37. Richard Brazier, an IWW member who wrote Wobbly songs and helped compile the first "Little Red Song Book," remarked that the union's songs were a primary means of inciting interest and raising a crowd: "What first attracted me to the I.W.W. was its songs and the gusto with which its members sang them. Such singing, I thought, was good propaganda, since it had originally attracted me and many others as well; and also useful, since it held

the crowd for Wobbly speakers who followed" (quoted in Salvatore Salerno, *Red November, Black November: Culture and Community in the Industrial Workers of the World* [Albany: State U of New York P, 1989] 28).

38. John Patrick Finnegan, *Against the Specter of a Dragon: The Campaign for American Military Preparedness, 1914–1917* (Westport, CT: Greenwood, 1974) 154.
39. Ralph Chaplin, "Preparedness," *Solidarity* June 24, 1916: 2.
40. Victor L. Basinet, "A Song of Preparedness," *Solidarity* July 22, 1916: 2.
41. Alan Golding, "A History of American Poetry Anthologies," in *Canons,* ed. Robert von Hallberg (Chicago: U of Chicago P, 1984) 280–81.
42. Ben Williams, the editor of *Solidarity* from 1909 through 1916, inserted poems throughout the columns of the newspaper, apparently using them more or less as filler. Ralph Chaplin, who edited the paper from March to September 1917 (when he and other union leaders were arrested), usually included one poem in each issue, allotting it a distinguished though conventional placement on the right side of the editorial page.
43. Salerno, *Red November* 130. For an extended examination of the relationship between American evangelicalism and the IWW, see Donald E. Winters, *The Soul of the Wobblies: The IWW, Religion, and American Culture in the Progressive Era, 1905–1917,* Contributions in American Studies 81 (Westport, CT: Greenwood, 1985).
44. "Young Man," stickerette in Tony Bubka, "Time to Organize! The IWW Stickeretts" [*sic*], *American West* 5 (Jan. 1968): 25.
45. Quoted in ibid. 25.
46. "The Deadly Parallel," *Solidarity* Mar. 24, 1917: 1.
47. Ralph Chaplin, "Were You Drafted?" *Solidarity* July 28, 1917: 8.
48. Ibid.
49. See Alfred E. Cornebise, *War as Advertised: The Four Minute Men and America's Crusade, 1917–1918* (Philadelphia: American Philosophical Society, 1984); and "Art as Ammunition: Posters, World War I, and the Virginia Home Front," *Virginia Cavalcade* 41.4 (Spring 1992): 158–65. For examples of patriotic songs published with accompanying government directives, see George W. Meyer (composer), Grant Clarke and Howard E. Rogers (lyricists), "If He Can Fight Like He Can Love, Good Night Germany!" (New York: Leo Feist, 1918), which admonishes on its back cover, "Food Will Win the War / Don't Waste It / Save Food – Save Money – Save Lives"; and Jean Schwartz (composer), Sam M. Lewis and Joe Young (lyricists), "Hello Central! Give Me No Man's Land" (New York: Waterson Berlin & Snyder, 1918), which includes along the inside spine a lesson in patriotic food conservation and the slogan, "Do Your Bit / Help Win the War."
50. "One Half Million Free Advertisements Boosting the I.W.W.: Stickerettes Designed by Ralph H. Chaplin," *Solidarity* Nov. 20, 1915: 4. Twelve stickerette designs are reproduced in Bubka, "Time to Organize." Otherwise,

stickerettes are extant only in a few special collections, notably the IWW Collection, box 142, folder 7, ALUA-WSU; the Baskette Collection, box 71, folder F, Rare Book and Special Collections Library, University of Illinois at Urbana-Champaign; and the Washington State Historical Society Library, Tacoma.

51. Aside from special collections, "The Scissorbill's Prayer" can be found reproduced in the original *Solidarity* advertisement ("One Half Million") and on the inside back cover of *Songs of the Workers,* 9th ed. Chaplin defines a scissorbill "as a potential scab" and testifies that, though he designed the stickerette, a fellow Wobbly authored the verse (*U.S. v. Haywood,* July 19, 7701).

52. *Songs of the Workers,* 9th ed., inside back cover.

53. Tyler records a specific instance of this sort of stickerette harassment against Donald McRae, the sheriff in command at the Everett massacre. In the weeks preceding the massacre, McRae's "property was decorated with IWW propaganda stickers" (*Rebels of the Woods* 69).

54. Reproductions of the stickerettes "Beware: Sabotage" and "Slow Down" can be seen in Bubka, "Time to Organize" 22, 26. The originals can be found in the library of the Washington State Historical Society.

55. Quoted in Bubka, "Time to Organize" 26.

56. *United States v. Haywood, et al.,* May 3, 1918, IWW Collection, box 103, folder 7, ALUA-WSU.

57. "Shorty," "Stick 'Em Up: Song for Stickerette Day, 1917," *Solidarity* Apr. 28, 1917: 2.

Chapter 3

1. For an account of America's convoluted course from neutrality to intervention focusing on diplomacy and popular politics, see H. C. Peterson, *Propaganda for War: The Campaign against American Neutrality, 1914–1917* (1939; Port Washington, NY: Kennikat, 1968).

2. *Contemporary War Poems,* International Conciliation Special Bulletin (New York: American Association for International Conciliation, Dec. 1914) 4–5. Cited hereafter parenthetically in the text as *CW.*

3. Born in 1879 in New York City, Erskine was a professor of English. Besides writing the introduction to *Contemporary Poems,* during the war he published *The Moral Obligation to Be Intelligent and Other Essays* (1915) and the poetry collection *The Shadowed Hour* (1917), and coedited the three-volume *Cambridge History of American Literature* (1917–19) (Albert Nelson Marquis, ed., *Who's Who in America,* vol. 11 [Chicago: A. N. Marquis, 1920]).

4. George Steunenberg, "Effusions of Uncle Sam's Soldier-Poet, Capt. Steunenberg, Famous in the Army, to Be Published at Last in Book Form," *New York Times* Oct. 25, 1914, sect. 7: 2.

5. Ibid.

6. By 1920 MacKaye had published twenty-eight plays, including comedies, tragedies, "civic dramas," masques, and an opera (Marquis, ed., *Who's Who*).

7. Percy MacKaye, "The Battle Cry of Alliance," *New York Times* May 6, 1917, sect. 6: 3. For bibliographies of war poetry published by MacKaye and Clinton Scollard, see James A. Hart, "American Poetry of the First World War (1914–1920): A Survey and Checklist," diss., Duke U, 1964.

8. Edith M. Thomas, *The White Messenger and Other War Poems* (Boston: Richard G. Badger, 1915).

9. Marquis, ed., *Who's Who*.

10. The period between 1914 and 1919 marked the NAACP's emergence as a national political organization; founded in 1909 and composed of just 329 dues-paying members in 1912, the organization grew to 3,000 in 1914 and to 9,500 in 1916; by the end of 1918 membership had mushroomed to more than 44,000 (*Crisis* 11.5 [Mar. 1916]: 255; 17.6 [Apr. 1919]: 284–85). During the same period, moreover, the circulation of the *Crisis* ran ahead of NAACP membership. In 1912, the magazine already had a paid circulation of 22,000 (13.5 [Mar. 1917]: 218). The issue of March 1915, containing the sixth annual NAACP report, had a print run of 43,000 copies (11.5: 244); on average, the magazine sold 32,156 copies per number in 1915 and 37,625 in 1916 (13.5: 218). The April 1918 number, which advertised the NAACP's drive for 50,000 members, was printed in 100,000 copies (15.6 [Apr. 1918]: 267).

11. Using a figure obtained from the *American Newspaper Annual and Directory*, Hart lists the circulation of the *International Socialist Review* at 25,424 for 1915 ("American Poetry" xiii).

12. W. E. B. Du Bois, "Editorial: World War and the Color Line," *Crisis* 9.1 (Nov. 1914): 28, 29.

13. "'Out of Africa Have I Called My Son!'" illustration, *Crisis* 9.1 (Nov. 1914): 26–27.

14. "The Paradox," photograph, *Crisis* 9.2 (Dec. 1914): 68.

15. Paul Thiriat, *The Desperate Attempt of General von Kluck to Break the Allied Line on the Marne*, illustration, *Crisis* 9.3 (Jan. 1915): 130–31.

16. Quoted in Raymond Cook, *Thomas Dixon* (New York: Twayne, 1974) 170.

17. Hanns Heinz Ewers, "We and the World," trans. Simon Lieban, *Fatherland* Sept. 23, 1914: 9.

18. S. Helmholz Junker, "Germany: Defender of Civilization against the Barbarian Host," cartoon, *Fatherland* 1.7 (Sept. 23, 1914): 11.

19. Frank Harris, *England or Germany – Which?* (New York: Wilmarth, 1915) 186–87.

20. Henry Labouchere, "Where Is the Flag of England?" *Fatherland* Nov. 4, 1914: 9.

21. One very different context in which the poem was in fact printed was one of the IWW's postwar publications, *The One Big Union Monthly* Jan. 1921: 62.

22. Frederick H. Martens, "A White Man's War," *Fatherland* Oct. 21, 1914: 4; "Recruits of English Culture," cartoon, *Fatherland* Oct. 21, 1914: 9.

23. "Advertise in the Fatherland / It Is Read Cover to Cover," *Fatherland* Oct. 14, 1914: 8–9. Though this figure was probably exaggerated by counting several likely readers per issue sold, the *Fatherland* nevertheless did achieve a considerable circulation, estimated at 65,000 by the *American Newspaper Annual and Directory* (quoted in Hart, "American Poetry" xiii) and claimed by the *Fatherland's* advertising director to be 73,056 in February 1915, within six months of the magazine's first issue ("What Our Circulation Statement Shows: Advertising Talk – No. 6," *Fatherland* Feb. 17, 1915: 13).

24. David Perkins, *A History of Modern Poetry: From the 1890s to the High Modernist Mode,* vol. 1 of *A History of Modern Poetry,* 2 vols. (Cambridge, MA: Harvard UP, 1976) 401.

25. William Stanley Beaumont Braithwaite was born in 1878 in Boston. He was a regular contributor of literary criticism to the *Boston Transcript* and of verse and essays to *Forum, Century, Lippincott's, Scribner's,* and the *Atlantic Monthly.* In addition to his many anthologies, his book publications include *Lyrics of Life and Love* (1904), *The House of Falling Leaves* (1908, poetry), *The Poetic Year for 1916* (literary criticism), and *The Story of the Great War* (1919) (Marquis, ed., *Who's Who*).

26. William Stanley Braithwaite, ed., *Anthology of Magazine Verse for 1915* (New York: Gomme, 1916).

27. Hugo Münsterberg, *The War and America* (New York: Appleton, 1914); Münsterberg, *The Peace and America* (New York: Appleton, 1915).

28. H. G. Wells, *The War That Will End War* (New York: Duffield, 1914).

29. Viscount Bryce et al., *Evidence and Documents Laid Before the Committee on Alleged German Outrages* (New York: Macmillan, [1915]). James Buitenhuis explains that, early in the war especially, the British ministry attempted to make its pro-Allied propaganda appear spontaneous by publishing through private presses such as Macmillan. Its aim, accomplished with considerable success, was to make "it appear that pro-Allied propaganda emanated largely from the spontaneous overflow of generous emotions by Americans themselves on behalf of the Allied cause, which soon became identified with the cause of civilization itself" (*The Great War of Words: British, American, and Canadian Propaganda and Fiction, 1914–1933* [Vancouver: U of British Columbia P, 1987] 55).

30. Albert Bushnell Hart, *The War in Europe* (New York: Appleton, 1914); Newell Dwight Hillis, *Studies of the Great War: What Each Nation Has at Stake* (New York: Revell, 1915); Clarence W. Barron, *The Audacious War* (Boston:

Houghton Mifflin, 1915); Edward S. Van Zile, *The Game of Empires: A Warning to America* (New York: Moffat, Yard, 1915); Robert Herrick, *The World Decision* (Boston: Houghton Mifflin, 1916).

31. Herrick, *The World Decision* 238.

32. William Stanley Braithwaite, ed., *Anthology of Magazine Verse for 1916* (New York: Gomme, 1916) xiii.

33. Ibid. xiii.

34. "War Will Probably Benefit World's Literature, Declares Prof. Brander Matthews of Columbia," *New York Times* Sept. 13, 1914, sect. 6: 2.

35. Perkins, *A History of Modern Poetry* 401.

36. W. E. B. Du Bois, "Editorial: To Our Young Poets," *Crisis* 9.5 (Mar. 1915): 236; William Stanley Braithwaite, "Democracy and Art," *Crisis* 10.4 (Aug. 1915): 186–87. Whatever Braithwaite's appeal to later readers, his work clearly manifested high culture in the *Crisis*. Two poems in the April 1915 issue, "Scintilla" and "Laughing It Out" (*Crisis* 9.6 [Apr. 1915]: 309), receive special treatment in terms of layout: an illustrated border in pen and ink represents a burial vault, a memorial obelisk, a formal garden, and, as backdrop, a moonlit seashore.

37. J. W. Cunliffe, *Poems of the Great War* (New York: Macmillan, 1916) v. Hereafter cited parenthetically in the text as *GW*. Cunliffe was a transplanted Englishman, born in Lancashire in 1865. He was a university professor first in Canada and later in the United States, holding the positions of professor of English and associate director of the School of Journalism at Columbia during the war. He was also the first vice-president of the Modern Language Association (Marquis, ed., *Who's Who*).

38. James Sait hints at the variety of forces – commercial, personal, and incidental – that conspired during the Great War to bring American presses steadily under the Allied sphere of influence ("Charles Scribner's Sons and the Great War," *Princeton University Library Chronicle* 48.2 [Winter 1987]: 152–80). Using documents on Scribner's from the Princeton University archives, Sait argues that the press strove before U.S. intervention to observe a strict neutrality, believing that this stance would make its publications salable to the widest possible audience. But financial expediency was worn down, over time, by the editors' own predisposition toward the Allies over Germany. And, at the same time, commercial considerations dictated continued publication of Edith Wharton's work, which was "sought after competitively" by other publishers and advocated the cause of France vigorously (179).

39. Edith Wharton, ed., *The Book of the Homeless* (New York: Scribner's, 1916) v. *The Book of the Homeless* seems to represent a genre among American publishers. A similar anthology was *The Anzac Book: Written and Illustrated in Gallipoli by the Men of Anzac* (New York: Funk & Wagnalls, 1916). Like Wharton's collection, the book mixed poetry, prose, and illustration, included

color reproductions, and was published for the benefit of a charitable agency, "Patriotic Funds connected with the A.N.Z.A.C." (Australian and New Zealand Army Corps).

40. Wharton, *Book of the Homeless* x. Roosevelt was a powerful advocate of intervention throughout the war. In *Great War of Words* Buitenhuis describes his contributions to pro-Allied publications in the United States as substantial, including, besides the preface to *The Book of the Homeless,* a collection of newspaper articles titled *America and the World War* (57) and a preface to Mrs. Humphrey Ward's *Towards the Goal* (59). Roosevelt campaigned tirelessly for American support of the Allies, writing to numerous correspondents on the subject, making many pro-Allied speeches, and offering to raise an army division to be commanded in France by himself. Buitenhuis characterizes Roosevelt's talent for pro-war advocacy as an "ability to see all sides of the question from a single point of view" (57).

41. Wharton, *The Book of the Homeless* xvi. R. W. B. Lewis's *Edith Wharton: A Biography* (New York: Harper & Row, 1975) describes the production and the contents of *The Book of the Homeless* (379–80) as well as offering the most complete account available of Wharton's activities in Europe during the war (339–415).

42. Manufacturing record for *The Book of the Homeless* by Edith Wharton, box 26, Manufacturing Records: Editions Published 1902–1955, Charles Scribner's Sons Archive, Princeton University Rare Books and Special Collections, cited with permission of the Princeton University Libraries.

43. W. E. B. Du Bois, "Editorial: Hayti," *Crisis* 10.5 (Sept. 1915): 232.

44. W. E. B. Du Bois, "Editorial: Hayti," *Crisis* 10.6 (Oct. 1915): 291. Du Bois's charges were largely justified; of the conditions laid down by U.S. Admiral Caperton, Robert and Nancy Heinl comment, "The U.S. would allow Haiti to hold a free election subject to the one condition that the election hypothecate to Washington the freedom of Haiti" (*Written in Blood: The Story of the Haitian People, 1492–1971* [Boston: Houghton Mifflin, 1978] 416).

45. "Major Charles Young, U.S.A.," *Crisis* 11.3 (Jan. 1916): 130.

46. W. E. B. Du Bois, "Editorial: Young," *Crisis* 11.5 (Mar. 1916): 240–42.

47. "NAACP: Soldiers," *Crisis* 11.6 (Apr. 1916): 310.

48. John S. D. Eisenhower, *Intervention! The United States and the Mexican Revolution, 1913–1917* (New York: Norton, 1993) 294–97; Herbert Molloy Mason, Jr., *The Great Pursuit* (New York: Random House, 1970) 210–11.

49. W. E. B. Du Bois, "Editorial: Carrizal," *Crisis* 12.4 (Aug. 1916): 165.

50. Charles T. Dazey, "At Carrizal," *New York Times* June 30, 1916: 10.

51. Mason writes that the troops had to approach the town of Carrizal across a "flat grassy plain devoid of cover," where they faced some 120 Mexican soldiers holding positions in a cottonwood grove, an orchard, and an irrigation ditch (*The Great Pursuit* 209–10).

52. "The Looking Glass: The Negro's Capacity," *Crisis* 11.6 (Apr. 1916): 300–1.

53. "Horizon: Military," *Crisis* 12.4 (Aug. 1916): 194; "Men of the Month," *Crisis* 12.6 (Oct. 1916): 278–81.
54. "The Looking Glass: Eaves," *Crisis* 12.1 (May 1916): 22.
55. Charles Young, "The Outer Pocket: From Mexico," *Crisis* 12.4 (Aug. 1916): 192.
56. "Men of the Month," *Crisis* 12.6 (Oct. 1916): 281; W. E. B. Du Bois, "Editorial: Preparedness," *Crisis* 11.5 (Mar. 1916): 242–43.
57. W. E. B. Du Bois, "Editorial: To the Rescue," *Crisis* 10.6 (May 1916): 31.
58. "NAACP: Soldiers," *Crisis* 12.1 (May 1916): 40.
59. W. E. B. Du Bois, "Editorial: The Perpetual Dilemma," *Crisis* 13.6 (Apr. 1917): 271.
60. "The Looking Glass: Loyalty," *Crisis* 14.1 (May 1917): 22.
61. David Levering Lewis, *W. E. B. Du Bois: Biography of a Race, 1868–1919* (New York: Henry Holt, 1993) 537.
62. Ibid. 541–42.
63. W. E. B. Du Bois, "Editorial: Close Ranks," *Crisis* 16.3 (July 1918): 111.
64. Lewis, *Du Bois* 555.
65. Quoted in ibid. 552.
66. The notion of black masculinity affirmed by Du Bois, and symbolized by the black soldier, may well be seen as an instance of what bell hooks calls the "reinscription" of white domination through the black male's embrace of "patriarchal masculinity, phallocentrism, and sexism" (*Black Looks: Race and Representation* [Boston: South End, 1992] 98).
67. Some of the other elegies in *Poems of the Great War* are Philip Byard Clayton's "They Held Their Ground," Lord Crewe's "A Harrow Grave in Flanders," Gerald H. Crow's "When They Have Made an End," Violet Gillespie's "The Dead," Edmund John's "In Memoriam (To Field Marshall Lord Roberts)," (Major) Sydney Oswald's "The Dead Soldier," Andrew John (Viscount) Stuart's "Sailor, What of the Debt We Owe You?" Frank Taylor's "England's Dead," and Iolo Aneurin Williams's "From a Flemish Grave Yard."
68. The "United Kingdom" selections in *Poems of the Great War* include a few of the poems familiar to us through the canon of war poets established by postwar anthologies: the four cited by Brooke, Grenfell, Hardy, and Sorley, plus Lawrence Binyon's "For the Fallen," appear in Jon Stallworthy, ed., *The Oxford Book of War Poetry* (Oxford: Oxford UP, 1984); those by Brooke, Grenfell, and Sorley also appear in Jon Silkin, *The Penguin Book of First World War Poetry* (London: Allen Lane, 1979).
69. Edward Bolland Osborn, ed., *The Muse in Arms: A Collection of War Poems, for the Most Part Written in the Field of Action* (New York: Frederick A. Stokes, 1918).
70. George Herbert Clarke, ed., *A Treasury of War Poetry: British and American Poems of the World War, 1914–1917*, [1st series] (Boston: Houghton Mifflin,

1917); Clarke, ed., *A Treasury of War Poetry: British and American Poems of the World War, 1914–1919,* 2nd series (Boston: Houghton Mifflin, 1919).

71. Frank Foxcroft, ed., *War Verse* (New York: Crowell, 1918) v. Hereafter cited parenthetically in the text as *WV.* Born in 1850 in Boston, Foxcroft was a journalist whose career included editorial work at the *Boston Journal, Youth's Companion,* and *Living Age* and articles in the *Atlantic Monthly, Nineteenth Century,* and *Contemporary Review.* By 1911 he seems to have retired from his work as magazine editor, freeing him for projects such as editing the seven editions of *War Verse,* which appeared in 1918 (Marquis, ed., *Who's Who*).

72. Stallworthy writes that poems in the heroic mode, written by Brooke, Sorley, and other soldier-poets early in the war, "illustrate the hypnotic power of a long tradition; the tragic outcome of educating a generation to face not the future but the past. By the end of 1915, Brooke, Sorley, and many lesser public-school poets were dead" (*Oxford Book of War Poetry* xxvii–xxviii).

73. The *Chicago Tribune* from June 1917 provides some evidence of Seeger's popularity. The edition of the 24th listed his *Poems* as one of the best-sellers at Chicago-area bookstores; that of the 21st ran "I Have a Rendezvous with Death" with the following comment: "We supposed that everybody had read Seeger's frequently quoted poem . . . but almost every day some inconstant reader inquires for it. So, to save postage, we'll reprint it" (6). As anecdotal evidence of Seeger's reputation, I can cite marginalia from my used copy of Cunliffe's *Poems of the Great War.* Under Seeger's "I Have a Rendezvous with Death" appears a note that calls the poem "One of the 3 best in this volume," referring to Winifred M. Lett's "The Spires of Oxford" and Rupert Brooke's "The Soldier" as the other two.

74. Herbert Adams Gibbons, ed., *Songs from the Trenches: The Soul of the A.E.F.* (New York: Harper & Brothers, 1918) v; Clarence Edward Andrews, ed., *From the Front: Trench Poetry* (New York: Appleton, 1918). Later poetry anthologies have also collected work exclusively by writers killed in the war. See, e.g., Frederick Ziv, ed., *The Valiant Muse: An Anthology of Poems by Poets Killed in the World War* (1936; Freeport, NY: Books for Libraries, 1971); and Tim Cross, ed., *The Lost Voices of World War I: An International Anthology of Writers, Poets, and Playwrights* (London: Bloomsbury, 1988).

75. Manufacturing record for *Poems* by Alan Seeger, box 21, Manufacturing Records: Editions Published 1902–1955, Charles Scribner's Sons Archive, Princeton University Rare Books and Special Collections, cited with permission of the Princeton University Libraries.

76. Elizabeth A. Marsland, *The Nation's Cause: French, English and German Poetry of the First World War* (New York: Routledge, 1991) 106.

77. See ibid. (chapter 3), "We Serve You Best: The Promoting of Mass Heroism," on the various schemes offered to justify and idealize the deaths of soldiers. Marsland argues, for instance, that "the English patriotic poets cele-

brate heroic death as frequently as the French, but with an emphasis on immortality rather than martyrdom" (83).

78. See Chapter 4, this volume, for an in-depth discussion of tropes of planting and harvesting, as well as those of baking, eating, and conserving.

79. Catherine W. Reilly, *English Poetry of the First World War: A Bibliography* (New York: St. Martin's, 1978) 12. See Introduction, note 14, on the seven "editions."

80. The place of initial publication is listed below the poem along with its author. Reilly in fact identifies "Klaxon" as the pseudonym for the British writer John Graham Bower (ibid.).

81. Even before the U.S. declaration of war there were poems anticipating the fellowship of British and American war dead and using the British martyrs as a goad for American soldiers. Reprinted from the Digby, Nova Scotia, *Courier,* Frances Fenwick Williams's "Recruiting Song of the Dead" (*New York Times* Mar. 25, 1917, mag. sect.: 11) implicitly connects the legacy of American war dead with the British dead by its dedication to the American Legion. Expecting the imminent intervention of the United States, the poem concludes:

> And now you prove to us, brothers, that we have not died in vain!
> At the mouth of the belching cannon, 'mid the roar of the great
>   hell-gun,
> We bid you to share our glory, we charge you to meet the Hun,
> To meet the Hun as we met him in the face of death and of hell,
> To show the Hun, as we showed him, that the Breed of the Bull dies
>   well!

82. W. Reginald Wheeler, ed., *A Book of Verse of the Great War* (New Haven, CT: Yale UP, 1917). Hereafter cited parenthetically in the text as *BV.* Wheeler (1889–1963) was further removed from the nationalistic pressures of wartime America than perhaps any other editor of an American war-poetry anthology. He received a bachelor of arts degree from Yale in 1911 and a bachelor of divinity degree from Auburn (New York) Theological Seminary; from 1915 to 1919 he worked as a Presbyterian missionary in China. It was by correspondence from China that he edited *A Book of Verse of the Great War* (1917); later he also published *China and the World War* (1919) (*Who Was Who in America,* vols. 1–5 [Chicago: Marquis Who's Who, 1942–73] vol. 4).

83. Wheeler sent in his completed work with a preface dated a month before U.S. intervention – March 1, 1917 (*Book of Verse* xv). Wheeler's inclusion of a significant number of pacifist poems was apparently regarded as unfortunate – and especially untimely – by Yale University Press, which added a long foreword by Charlton M. Lewis arguing for the superiority of the patriotic poetry over the pacifist verse.

84. My suggestion here, and indeed my general argument about how English-language literature facilitated American identification with Britain, finds support in Mark Sullivan, *American Finding Herself,* vol. 2 of *Our Times: The United States, 1900–1925,* 6 vols. (New York: Scribner's, 1927). Writing of the influence of the McGuffey's readers, ubiquitous in American school-rooms from the 1850s through the 1910s, Sullivan notes: "One can readily believe that millions of Americans must have been moved subconsciously by the feeling, not always identified by themselves, that they were one with the race of Shakespeare and Milton. Every little prairie schoolhouse in America was an outpost of English literature, hardly less potent to inspire recruits when the time came than the British drum-beat itself. Had American school children been brought up on Goethe and Heine, as they were on Shakespeare and Milton, is it certain America's role in the Great War would have been the same?" (48).

85. Given Woodberry's predilection for the sonnet and his elevated diction, it may not be surprising to learn that he was an admirer of Rupert Brooke; he was editor of Brooke's *Collected Poems* (1915). Woodberry, born in Beverly, Massachusetts, in 1855, was a professor of comparative literature at Columbia University from 1891 to 1904 (Marquis, ed., *Who's Who*).

86. Lewis, *Du Bois* 52–53.

87. W. E. B. Du Bois, *Dusk of Dawn: An Essay Toward an Autobiography of a Race Concept* (New York: Harcourt, Brace, 1940) 255–56.

88. Ibid. 255.

Chapter 4

1. John Patrick Finnegan, *Against the Specter of a Dragon* (Westport, CT: Greenwood, 1974) 31, 58, 92.

2. James R. Mock and Cedric Larson, historians of the Committee on Public Information, approvingly describe the CPI as "a gargantuan advertising agency the like of which the country had never known, and the breathtaking scope of its activities was not to be equalled until the rise of totalitarian dictatorships after the war" (*Words That Won the War: The Story of the Committee on Public Information, 1917–1919* [Princeton, NJ: Princeton UP, 1939] 4). While C. Roland Marchand focuses on the development of advertising in the 1920s and 1930s, he also emphasizes the importance of wartime propaganda in developing advertising techniques, public acceptance of advertising, and professional confidence among advertisers themselves (*Advertising the American Dream: Making Way for Modernity, 1920–1940* [Berkeley: U of California P, 1985] 5–6). See also William J. Breen, *Uncle Sam at Home: Civilian Mobilization, Wartime Federalism, and the Council of National Defense, 1917–1919,* Contributions in American Studies 70 (Westport, CT: Greenwood, 1984); and Stephen Vaughn, *Holding Fast the Inner Lines: Democracy,*

Nationalism, and the Committee on Public Information (Chapel Hill: North Carolina UP, 1980).

3. Quoted in Mock and Larson, *Words That Won* 190. The remark was made by Grosvenor Clarkson, director of the Council for National Defense. While Mock and Larson try to discount Clarkson's statement by noting it was made after the war, their only examples of voluntary labor cooperation relate to Samuel Gompers's American Federation of Labor and its offshoot, the American Alliance for Labor and Democracy, which they call "a field organization of the CPI charged with the special responsibility of keeping labor industrious, patriotic, and quiet" (190–91).

4. "Armies Supplant Reapers on Belgium's Harvest Fields," *New York Times* Sept. 6, 1914, picture sect.: 1, 7.

5. John Finley, "The Road to Dieppe," in *A Treasury of War Poetry: British and American Poems of the World War, 1914–1917,* ed. George Herbert Clarke (Boston: Houghton Mifflin, 1917) 114, 113.

6. Josephine Preston Peabody, "Harvest Moon" and "Harvest Moon: 1916," ibid. 243–45.

7. James Oppenheim, "1915," in *A Book of Verse of the Great War,* ed. W. R. Wheeler (New Haven, CT: Yale UP, 1917) 117–18.

8. *Dictionary of American Biography,* vol. 18 (New York: Scribner's 1936).

9. William Simonds, *A Student's History of American Literature* (Boston: Houghton Mifflin, 1909) 330; Max Herzberg et al., eds., *The Reader's Encyclopedia of American Literature* (New York: Crowell, 1962).

10. Edith M. Thomas, *The White Messenger and Other War Poems* (Boston: Badger, 1915) 69.

11. Ibid. 69.

12. George H. Nash, *The Humanitarian, 1914–1917,* vol. 2 of *The Life of Herbert Hoover,* 2 vols. (New York: Norton, 1988) 30.

13. Edward Bok, "'For God's Sake Send Food: Thousands of Little Ones Are Starving,'" *Ladies' Home Journal* Jan. 1915: 1.

14. Thomas, *White Messenger* 44–45.

15. Eugene Lyons, *Herbert Hoover: A Biography* (Garden City, NY: Doubleday, 1964) 87.

16. The Vigilantes, *Fifes and Drums* (New York: Doran, [1917]) 132. Hereafter cited parenthetically in the text as *FD.*

17. See H. C. Peterson and Gilbert Fite, *Opponents of War, 1917–1918* (Madison: U of Wisconsin P, 1957), for a detailed description of the Espionage Act, passed on June 15, 1917, and the Sedition Act, passed on May 16, 1918 (esp. 17 and 215). Conspicuously, neither act aimed to ensure fair distribution of scarce products *within* the United States, and both focused on unpatriotic speech rather than putatively unpatriotic acts such as war profiteering.

18. Peterson and Fite, *Opponents of War,* chronicle the diverse groups that were

persecuted for their war opposition or lukewarm support, among them the Industrial Workers of the World; the Socialist Party of America; the Non-Partisan League, an association of small-scale farmers primarily in the Dakotas; nonorganized Oklahoma sharecroppers; the People's Council of America for Peace and Democracy, a pacifist group that lobbied for a negotiated end to the war; and "hyphenated" Americans of German, Austrian, Polish, Finnish, and Russian extraction. Christopher Gibbs, *The Great Silent Majority: Missouri's Resistance to World War I* (Columbia: U of Missouri P, 1988), finds a similar lack of war enthusiasm in middle America (see, e.g., 134).

19. For instance, Crystal Eastman, whose brother Max was editor of the *Masses,* served both as chair of the New York WPP and as executive secretary of the American Union Against Militarism. Also, Anne Herendeen was an active member of the New York WPP and was married to Hiram Moderwell, the editor of the *New York Call* in 1917 ("Who's Who Among the Editors of Four Lights," *Four Lights* 1.14 [July 28, 1917] supplement).

20. See William Freiburger, "War Prosperity and Hunger: The New York Food Riots of 1917," *Labor History* 25.2 (Spring 1984): 217–39. For accounts of earlier European food riots led by women (disturbances with which Hoover was doubtless acquainted), see Paul R. Hanson, "The 'Vie Chere' Riots of 1911: Traditional Protests in Modern Garb," *Journal of Social History* 21.3 (Spring 1988): 463–81; and Temma Kaplan, "Female Consciousness and Collective Action: The Case of Barcelona, 1910–1918," *Signs* 7.3 (1982): 545–66. Janet Lyon of the University of Illinois at Urbana-Champaign first acquainted me with the food riots as well as these sources.

21. David Burner, *Herbert Hoover: A Public Life* (New York: Knopf, 1979) 96.

22. Born to a wealthy New York family, Ovington was active in the settlement house movement in New York. In 1909, she was one of the founders of the National Association for the Advancement of Colored People and served as its chair in the 1920s and 1930s (Lina Mainiero, ed., *American Women Writers,* 5 vols. [New York: Ungar, 1979] Vol. 3). During the war she was a member of the WPP.

23. Mary White Ovington, "Gretchen Talks to Her Doll," *Four Lights* Apr. 21, 1917: 2–3.

24. To be sure, rapprochement between working-class and women's concerns was not central to – or even necessarily compatible with – the agendas of either the major labor organizations or women's groups, whose members were mostly middle or upper class. Nevertheless, two conjunctions between labor and women's politics emerged under the pressure of the war. First was the spontaneous leadership of working-class women in the urban bread riots of early 1917. Second was the intellectual synthesis of feminism and socialism that is reflected in the poetry discussed in this chapter and in the concrete allegiances between editors of the *New York Call,* the *Masses,* and *Four Lights.* For further discussion of the (largely unrealized) potential for a syn-

thesis of American women's and workers' movements during the war, see my "Women's Ways in War: The Poetry and Politics of the Woman's Peace Party, 1915–1917," *Modern Fiction Studies* 38.3 (Autumn 1992): 687–714.

25. Marguerite Wilkinson, "The Food Riots," *Masses* May 1917: 33.

26. David Kennedy, *Over Here: The First World War and American Society* (New York: Oxford UP, 1980) 119–20.

27. U.S. Food Administration, *The Day's Food in War and Peace,* ([Washington, DC: Government Printing Office,] 1918) 13.

28. Herbert Hoover, *An American Epic: Famine in Forty-Five Nations; Organization Behind the Front: 1914–1922,* vol. 2 of *An American Epic,* 2 vols. (Chicago: Henry Regnery, 1960) 57.

29. U.S. Food Administration, *War Economy in Food with Suggestions and Recipes for Substitutions in the Planning of Meals* ([Washington, DC: Government Publishing Office,] 1917) 6, 9, 4.

30. U.S. Food Administration, *Day's Food* 5; Hoover, *American Epic* 58.

31. For discussion of the American Defense Society and the National Security League, see respectively Peterson and Fite, *Opponents of War* 18, and Kennedy, *Over Here* 31.

32. Hoover, *American Epic* 59.

33. Hermann Hagedorn, one of the Vigilantes' founding members, praises the efforts of the National Security League and American Defense Society at an early organizational meeting, in November or December 1916 (Speech to "Gentlemen," Vigilantes Organization Memos and Drafts, [ca.] 1916, Hermann Hagedorn Collection, Library of Congress Manuscript Division [hereafter cited as Hagedorn Collection]). John Carver Edwards notes that Hagedorn was in fact on the publicity committee of the American Defense Society, along with Vigilantes Julian Street, Cleveland Moffett, and Hamlin Garland (*Patriots in Pinstripe* [Washington, DC: UP of America, 1982] 46). The $30,000 that initially funded the Vigilantes was supplied by prominent backers of the National Security League, and thereafter the Vigilantes were regularly assisted by Theodore Roosevelt in getting further financial support. According to Edwards, the Vigilantes syndicate sent releases to more than 2,000 newspapers and also had its materials distributed to 12,000 tabloids through the Associated Press (47).

34. The erosion or outright abandonment of ideals such as civil rights, freedom of speech, and due process among progressives in the Wilson administration is described by John A. Thompson, *Reformers and War: American Progressive Publicists and the First World War* (New York: Cambridge UP, 1987) esp. 177–233. The ferocity with which dissent was typically squelched in wartime America is covered thoroughly by Peterson and Fite, *Opponents of War,* and Kennedy, *Over Here*. See Kennedy's chapters 1 and 2, "The War for the American Mind" and "The Political Economy of War: the Home Front."

35. Meetings of the Executive Committee, Oct. 8, [1917,] and Oct. 22, 1917, the Vigilantes Minutes, 1917, Hagedorn Collection.

36. A list of contributors was printed on the reverse side of the Vigilantes' official letterhead. The paper used for a letter dated December 22, 1917, lists 328 contributors; a letter dated November 23, 1918, after the stricter rules are adopted, lists 160 contributors (Charles J. Rosebault, letter to Hermann Hagedorn, Dec. 22, 1917; and Vigilantes Executive Committee, letter to the Vigilantes, Nov. 23, 1918, both in Vigilantes Bulletins, 1917–18, Hagedorn Collection). One supposed member whose status I would regard with some suspicion is Edwin Markham. It seems more likely than not that his name was included on the Vigilantes' rolls without his full consent, given the syndicate's rather liberal appropriation of the work and authority of well-known writers (the cases of Vachel Lindsay and Alice Corbin Henderson, just mentioned), the fact that none of his work appears to have been actually published by the Vigilantes, and an interview that Markham gave to the *New York Call* in which he declared opposition to U.S. war involvement (Frederick A. Blossom, "The Man with the Hoe and the Man with the Gun," *New York Call* Aug. 26, 1917: 8).

37. "War gardens" were grown not only at homes but also at schools and were organized by state and city committees as well as the federal government: "About 3,000,000 gardens were planted aside from the increased acreage planted by farmers. Vegetables estimated to be worth $350,000,000 were raised" (U.S. Food Administration, *Food and the War: A Textbook for College Classes* [Boston: Houghton Mifflin, 1918] 204–5).

38. Four other poems from *Fifes and Drums* make specific reference to food conservation: Faith Baldwin's "They Also Serve – " (122–23), Amelia Josephine Burr's "His Job" (124–25), John Kemble's "Spades Are Trumps!" (130–31), and Edith Thomas's "The War of Bread" (132–33).

39. The Hermann Hagedorn Collection at the Library of Congress Manuscript Division contains many Vigilantes releases dating from October 30, 1917, through the end of the war (though even from that date the collection is by no means complete). The syndicate service was started up well before then, however. I located Vigilantes poems from June 1917 in three of the five mainstream newspapers I surveyed systematically: the *Atlanta Constitution* (Hermann Hagedorn's "The Song Time" on June 30), *Boston Globe* (Thornton Burgess's "His Bit" on June 14) and *Los Angeles Times* (Amelia Josephine Burr's "Taken for Granted" on June 30).

40. Laura E. Richards, "To H. C. H.," Jan. 24 release, Vigilantes Press Releases, ca. January–March 1918; Amelia Josephine Burr, "Hoover of Belgium," June 3 release, Vigilantes Press Releases, ca. June 1918; and Thornton W. Burgess, "We Want Hoover!" June 5 release, Vigilantes Press Releases, ca. June 1918, all in the Hagedorn Collection. Richards (1850–1943) had by 1916 written, co-written, or edited fifty-eight volumes; her latest, *The Life of Julia Ward*

Howe, having won the first Pulitzer Prize for biography, she lent considerable distinction to the Vigilantes (Mainiero, ed., *American Women Writers,* vol. 3). By 1916, Burgess (1874–?) was well started in his long career in children's literature, having begun his long-running syndicated column of bedtime stories in 1910 and published six volumes of animal stories (Herzberg, ed., *Reader's Encyclopedia*).

41. Meetings of the Executive Committee, Oct. 8 and 29 [1917], the Vigilantes Minutes, 1917, Hagedorn Collection. Long after the war, George Creel, head of the Committee on Public Information, remarked that the Security League and the Defense Society, allies of the Vigilantes, were "easily the most active and obnoxious [of the civilian patriotic organizations]. At all times their patriotism was a thing of screams, violence, and extremes, and their savage intolerances had the burn of acid" (quoted in Peterson and Fite, *Opponents of War* 18; brackets mine). On April 5, 1917, Creel, Ray Stannard Baker, and Walter Lippman, soon to be appointed to positions in the Wilson administration, attended a meeting of the Vigilantes. None were impressed; Baker in particular criticized the group's "simplistic propaganda" (Thompson, *Reformers* 184). Yet the Wilson administration did little to deter the activities of the Vigilantes or any of the other ultraconservative groups; indeed, it came to rely on them insofar as they supported administration programs and, further, because their activities made the administration's repression seem moderate in comparison. In spite of his criticism, Ray Stannard Baker was among the contributors honored by the organization at the end of both 1917 and 1918 (Rosebault, letter to H. Hagedorn; Vigilantes Executive, letter to the Vigilantes).

42. "How Can I Do My 'Bit'? An Editorial Answer to the American Housewife," *Ladies' Home Journal* June 1917: 26.

43. Mary R. Gamble, "Aunt Columbia's Dinner Party: A Patriotic Play by Mary R. Gamble That Shows Us What We Have," *Ladies' Home Journal* June 1917: 28.

44. The *Journal* averaged four opinion pieces or features focusing on food economy in the July through October issues, including several written by Herbert Hoover.

45. Royal Baking Powder, "Mr. Hoover's War-Time Dishes," *Ladies' Home Journal* Oct. 1917: 61.

46. Edna Randolph Worrell, "Shouting the Battle Cry of 'Feed 'Em': A Patriotic Play for Children," *Ladies' Home Journal* Nov. 1917: 40.

47. Alice Kahler Marshall, *Pen Names of Women Writers from 1600 to the Present* (Camp Hill, PA: published by the author, 1985), identifies Wilson as the pseudonym for Florence McLandburgh and gives 1850 as the year of her birth. McLandburgh Wilson was the author of "Motherhood's Chant" (which was printed in both the *New York Times* and *Contemporary War Poems* [42]) and appeared regularly in the *New York Times* and *New York Times Magazine.*

48. McLandburgh Wilson [Florence McLandburgh], *The Little Flag on Main Street* (New York: Macmillan, 1917) 123.
49. Anthony Euwer, *Wings and Other War Rhymes* (New York: Moffat, Yard, 1918) 69–70.
50. Mary Raymond Shipman Andrews, *Crosses of War* (New York: Scribner's, 1918) 8–9, 10–15.
51. Wesson Oil, "Mr. Hoover's Request," *Ladies' Home Journal* Jan. 1918: 69.
52. The ads in the Crisco campaign ran in the *Ladies' Home Journal* in July, October, and November 1918. Additional Wesson Oil ads appeared in February, March, and December of the same year.
53. Golden Age Macaroni, "Serve Macaroni to Save Meat," *Ladies' Home Journal* Mar. 1918: 109; Ingleheart Brothers, "The Secret of Making War Cake," *Ladies' Home Journal* Sept. 1918: 63.
54. Dudley Harmon, "How You Will Know Her," *Ladies' Home Journal* Sept. 1917: 1.
55. See Neil A. Wynn, *From Progressivism to Prosperity: World War I and American Society* (New York: Holmes & Meier, 1986).
56. Frank Lentricchia, "On the Ideologies of Poetic Modernism, 1890–1913: The Example of Henry James," in *Reconstructing American Literary History,* Harvard English Studies 13, ed. Sacvan Bercovitch (Cambridge, MA: Harvard UP, 1986) 244–45; Richard H. Brodhead, "Literature and Culture," in *Columbia Literary History of the United States,* ed. Emory Elliott (New York: Columbia UP, 1988) 713–14.
57. Generally speaking, genteel aims to instruct and inculturate can be distinguished from popular motives to entertain and establish rapport. These aims can be seen, in turn, as projections of two distinct kinds of literary culture. Richard Brodhead contrasts a cosmopolitan, New England elite who came to prominence around the middle of the nineteenth century with a commercial, professional class of publishers and writers who gained power after 1885 through mass-circulation magazines ("Literature and Culture" 471, 475). But while these groups and their impulses were always in tension – and sometimes in open conflict with each other – Brodhead also speaks of "the emergence, at the beginning of this century, of publishing institutions that work to join the appreciation of the literary with the commercial cultivation of mass markets, instead of treating these interests as antithetical" (478). In *The Unembarrassed Muse: The Popular Arts in America* (New York: Dial, 1970), Russel Nye's formulation of nineteenth-century traditions of American popular poetry consistently combines the motives to delight and to instruct, suggesting that "people read poetry for amusement, exhortation, and edification" (100) and remarking that poetry occupied secure niches both as household entertainment and as public oracle (100–1). Contrary to Nye, who believes that poetry largely forfeited those functions by slipping into benign sentimentality (119) – I argue that these functions for popular

poetry were both maintained into the 1910s and sharpened by wartime politics.

58. Hermann Hagedorn, speech to "Gentlemen." For a comparative study of Hagedorn, Hugo Münsterberg, and George Sylvester Viereck – perhaps the three German-Americans most outspoken about the war and, also, figures provocatively different in their approach to the crisis – see Phyllis Keller, *States of Belonging: German-American Intellectuals and the First World War* (Cambridge, MA: Harvard UP, 1979).

59. Hermann Hagedorn, letter to Woodrow Wilson, Vigilantes Organization Memos and Drafts, [ca.] 1916, Hagedorn Collection.

60. Review of *Fifes and Drums* by the Vigilantes, "Some Recent Books of Verse," *New York Times Book Review* Aug. 5, 1917: 287.

61. As Elizabeth Marsland notes, the events of World War I called forth a remarkable volume of poetry in all combatant nations, most of it written by amateur poets and people "who became poets for the occasion" (*Nation's Cause* [New York: Routledge, 1991] 1).

62. Review of *Little Flag on Main Street* by McLandburgh Wilson, *New York Times Book Review* Feb. 3, 1918: 39.

63. C. Roland Marchand, *Advertising the American Dream: Making Way for Modernity, 1920–1940* (Berkeley: U of California P, 1985); Christopher Wilson, *The Labor of Words: Literary Professionalism in the Progressive Era* (Athens: U of Georgia P, 1985).

64. Frank Lentricchia, *Modernist Quartet* (New York: Cambridge UP, 1994) 2.

65. Mable I. Clapp, "Hoover's Goin' to Get You," *Ladies' Home Journal* Nov. 1917: 146.

66. Stuart Ewen, arguing that advertising played a key role in cultivating an American consumer culture in the 1920s, suggests that central to the advertiser's task was the formation of a public consciousness dependent on nonessential products (*Captains of Consciousness: Advertising and the Social Roots of the Consumer Culture* [New York: McGraw-Hill, 1976] 38–39). Marchand describes the gender politics that prevailed in commercial advertising: partly because almost all professional advertisers were men, partly because studies showed women were the principal shoppers in most households (66), the advertiser was constructed as a male figure of science and reason, the consumer as a female figure of whimsy and illogic (see 52–87).

67. Rosebault, letter to Hermann Hagedorn, Dec. 22, 1917; Vigilantes Executive Committee, letter to the Vigilantes, Nov. 23, 1918.

68. Review of *Fifes and Drums.*

69. Burr and Garrison must have published their war poetry even more frequently than these figures show. James A. Hart, "American Poetry of the First World War (1914–1920): A Survey and Checklist," diss., Duke U, 1964, upon which my tally of magazine publications is based, covers a limited

(though large) sample of periodicals, and his survey even of the *New York Times* is incomplete. Besides the fact that the Vigilantes files at the Library of Congress are not comprehensive, it is virtually impossible to track down the number of newspapers that picked up even the poems which are extant in the files. Born in 1878, Amelia Josephine Burr published one book of poems before the war (*The Roadside Fire*, 1912), and she made a career of writing poetry and novels (W. J. Burke and Will D. Howe, eds., *American Authors and Books: 1640–1940* [New York: Gramercy, 1943]). Theodosia Garrison, who contributed more work to the Vigilantes than any other writer, was otherwise less frequently published than Burr and appears in none of the literary dictionaries and encyclopedias that I have consulted. She did, however, have a poem published in *Scribner's* before the war ("The Mother," 56 [1914]: 162), so she had some literary recognition before turning her attention to patriotic verse.

70. Theodosia Garrison, "With a Drink on the Table," June 10 release, Vigilantes Press Releases, ca. June 1918, Hagedorn Collection.
71. Wilson, *Little Flag,* 12.
72. On the nineteenth-century development of a "maternal model" for education, see Joel Spring, *The American School, 1642–1900: Varieties of Historical Interpretation of the Foundations and Development of American Education,* 2nd ed. (New York: Longman, 1990), esp. chapter 5, "Organizing the American School: The Nineteenth-Century Schoolmarm."
73. Alice Corbin [Henderson], "The Planting of the Green," June 3 release, Vigilantes Press Releases, ca. June 1918, Hagedorn Collection.
74. Herzberg, ed., *Reader's Encyclopedia.*
75. *Songs of the Workers,* 9th ed. (Cleveland: IWW Publishing Bureau, Mar. 1916) 50.

Chapter 5

1. John Patrick Finnegan, *Against the Specter of a Dragon* (Westport, CT: Greenwood, 1974) 154.
2. Quoted in August Heckscher, *Woodrow Wilson* (New York: Scribner's, 1991) 400; see also 398–401; Arthur Walworth, *Woodrow Wilson,* 2nd ed. (Boston: Houghton Mifflin, 1965) book 2, 52–54.
3. In the Introduction I have already described how Wilson chose to go to war to assert his notion of America's international status: "[to exert] the influence to which her power and virtue entitled her" and "[to avoid sacrificing] America's prestige and moral reputation" (quoted in Ernest May, *The World War and American Isolation, 1914–1917* [1959; Chicago: Quadrangle, 1966] 425). Daniel M. Smith, *The Great Departure: The United States, 1914–1920* (New York: Wiley, 1965), emphasizes how U.S. intervention marked the beginning of a further-reaching, more active foreign policy, in effect demon-

strating the importance of national self-interest and aggrandizement as motives for intervention (81; also chapter 6, "The Moral Leader of the World").

4. C. Roland Marchand, *The American Peace Movement and Social Reform, 1898–1918* (Princeton, NJ: Princeton UP, 1972), provides a useful overview of the organization, methods, and activities of the American Union Against Militarism. See especially Marchand's discussion of the American Union's formation and early success in discrediting official accounts of the U.S. dispute with Mexico in June–July 1916 (240–44).

5. Sarah N. Cleghorn, "War Journal of a Pacifist, 1917," typescript, Society of Friends Historical Collection, Swarthmore College, p. 1.

6. Ibid. 2, 10. According to Barbara Steinson, *American Women's Activism in World War I* (New York: Garland, 1982), Hughan came to particular prominence in the party when, in 1918, she led opposition to changing the group's name from the Woman's Peace Party to the Woman's International League (the change was adopted) (297). In Marchand, *American Peace Movement,* she is listed among eight "youthful radicals" who by 1917 had emerged as "the active leaders of the New York branch" (207). Mygatt and Witherspoon collaborated in various pacifist activities, especially in assisting draft resisters; they were cofounders of the Anti-Enlistment League (265) and of the Legal First Aid Bureau, part of the Civil Liberties Bureau, an organization soon to become the American Civil Liberties Union (284). Balch was, after Jane Addams, perhaps the best-known public figure who retained active membership in the WPP throughout the war. Her commitment to internationalism and pacifism, which during the war led to her dismissal from her position as professor of sociology and economics at Wellesley College, and after it involved various leadership positions in the Women's International League for Peace and Freedom, is documented most thoroughly in Mercedes Randall, *Improper Bostonian: Emily Greene Balch* (New York: Twayne, 1964).

7. See, for instance, the cluster of feminist pieces in the November 1914 *Masses:* Cornelia Barns's "Patriotism for Women," a cartoon ridiculing the belligerent nations' policy of encouraging men to marry before enlisting in the army (7); Mabel Dodge's "The Secret of War," an essay discussing men's natural predilection for and women's aversion to war (8–9); and Elizabeth Waddell's "Them and Their Wives," a poem portraying the spouses of "Emperors, War Lords and Czars" as "Firm anti-suffragist wives" (20). The *Masses* of November 1915 was dedicated to "Woman's Citizenship."

8. Cleghorn, "War Journal," Preface, 5, 90–91, 84, 107, 134.

9. Quoted in August Heckscher, *Woodrow Wilson* (New York: Scribner's 1991) 424.

10. Anne Herendeen, Edna Kenton, and Zoe Beckley, manifesto, *Four Lights* 1.1 (Jan. 27, 1917): 1.

11. Jessie Wallace Hughan, "For Valiant Hearts," *Four Lights* 1.2 (Feb. 6, 1917): 1.

12. Florence Guertin Tuttle, "A Call to Arms," *Four Lights* 1.9 (May 19, 1917):

1. On the 1916 letterhead for the NY-WPP, Tuttle is listed as one of three "Vice-Chairmen," so she was clearly active in party politics along with writing poetry for *Four Lights* ("Woman's Peace Party of New York City," official letterhead including officer lists, [1916], Records of the Woman's Peace Party, Swarthmore College Peace Collection [cited hereafter as SCPC], Scholarly Resources microfilm edition, reel 4, box 5, folder 3). For contributors to *Four Lights* who, like Tuttle, were active in the peace movement but did not necessarily distinguish themselves as leaders, it is difficult to locate much biographical information. One source of some use is "Who's Who Among the Editors of Four Lights," *Four Lights* 1.14 (July 28, 1917) supplement, which was compiled for the U.S. Justice Department to rebut its suspicions about the national origins of the editors. Tuttle's autobiographical note, like those of many of the other editors, reveals a blue-blooded (as well as all-American) lineage: "My mother was a descendant of Patrick Henry. I have always felt that I inherited my radical views from this one of the world's great rebels. My husband is descended from Mayflower ancestry."

13. See on this point Cary Nelson, *Repression and Recovery* (Madison: U of Wisconsin P, 1989) esp. 22–23. Nelson argues that the binary, oppositional model of literary history governing discussions of modernism frequently blocks the recognition "that traditional forms continued to do vital cultural work" throughout what we regard as the modern period (23).

14. Mary Johnston, "The Artist," *Four Lights* 1.3 (Feb. 24, 1917): 3.

15. Mary Alden Hopkins, "Woman's Way in War," *Four Lights* 1.14 (July 28, 1917): 4. Hopkins's autobiographical piece in the "Who's Who" supplement reveals much the same sarcastic wit as "Woman's Way in War" (the supplement and the July 28 issue were, incidentally, delivered together). She writes that "the ancestor with whom I feel the most sympathy at present is the one who was hanged as a witch by the Salem judges." She concludes her statement thus: "I have no more spiritual kinship with Germany than physical, and but slight acquaintance. Once, when I crossed the upper Rhine from Switzerland for a picnic on a German Island, a German soldier stuck his august nose into my knapsack to make sure that I carried no contraband. Dignified as was his action, it did not impress me with that passion for German militarism which is somewhat illogically assumed to be the ruling motive of all of us who believe that war is evil."

16. See Steinson, *American Women's Activism* chapters 4 and 7, "Relief For Europe and Defense for America" and "The Women's Relief, Preparedness, and Suffrage Movements Go to War," for an overview of the activities of women's organizations in support of U.S. preparedness and intervention.

17. Edna Mead, "A Mother to Her War-Time Baby," *Four Lights* 1.14 (July 28, 1917): 2.

18. Florence Tuttle, "IF: A Mother to Her Daughter," *Four Lights* 1.14 (July 28, 1917): 3.

19. A. B. Curtis, "A Study in Evolution: From Mr. Asquith and the British Government," *Four Lights* 1.7 (Apr. 21, 1917): 2.
20. Mary Alden Hopkins, "The Picket," *Four Lights* 1.20 (Oct. 20, 1917): 2. Hopkins's poem refers, as a matter of fact, to suffrage picketing by the National Woman's Party, a group founded in June 1916 that was more radical and much smaller than NAWSA. From January through November 1917 the group picketed the White House daily, demanding that Woodrow Wilson throw his support behind the federal suffrage amendment. In June the Washington, D.C., police began arresting the pickets for "obstruction of traffic," and in July they were sentenced to considerable prison terms ranging from sixty days to seven months. When conditions at the Occoquan Work House in Virginia became known in the press – NWP members were locked in solitary confinement, beaten, and brutally force-fed when they staged hunger strikes – Wilson ordered the prisoners released, and by January he came out in support of the amendment. Just how pivotal the NWP was in winning this victory is debated: NAWSA's version of events, which hardly mentions the NWP, is contained in Ida Husted Harper, ed., *After Seventy Years Came the Victory*, vol. 5, 1900–1920, of *History of Woman Suffrage*, 6 vols. (1922; New York: Arno, 1969). The NWP's side is told by Inez Haynes Irwin, *The Story of the Woman's Party* (1921; New York: Krause, 1971). A perspective stressing the interplay between the groups and redressing past neglect of the NWP's importance is provided in Christine A. Lunardini, *From Equal Suffrage to Equal Rights: Alice Paul and the National Woman's Party, 1910–1928* (New York: New York UP, 1986); see esp. chapters 7 and 8, "The Home-Front War: 'A Poor Business'" and "Politics, Prison, and Resolution."

    The Suffragist, the NWP's weekly organ, provides a nearly day-by-day account of the picketing and jail experiences of organization members; like most periodicals of the period, it regularly published poetry. For accounts of the function of poetry in the daily lives of the Occoquan prisoners, see "Over the Top," *Suffragist* Nov. 10, 1917: 4, and "Woman's Party Song, Composed in Prison by the Suffrage Pickets: Shout the Revolution of Women" (quoted in Irwin, *Story* 262).

    Clearly, the story of the NWP is an important chapter in the narrative of World War I homefront politics. Hopkins's "The Picket" performs a certain rhetorical sleight of hand when it suggests that the picketers protested both for suffrage and against the war; when Wilson supported the suffrage amendment, the picketing was halted, and throughout 1917 part of the NWP's argument in favor of suffrage had involved the civic contributions women were making to the war effort. Still, the NWP and the NY-WPP share striking similarities: both were younger, more assertive organizations that were largely spurned by the larger, more conservative organizations, NAWSA and the national WPP, from which they had emerged as dissident groups.

21. Margaret Lane, letter to Board Members, NY-WPP, July 14, 1917, Records of the Woman's Peace Party, SCPC, Scholarly Resources microfilm edition (hereafter cited as WPP Records), reel 4, box 5, folder 5. Margaret Lane was a prominent figure in the peace movement. In addition to being the managing editor of *Four Lights,* she was secretary of the NY-WPP and of the Committee for Democratic Control, described by Marchand as "an additional publicity arm of the American Union Against Militarism" (*American Peace Movement* 249). Her husband, Winthrop D. Lane, belonged to the committee and the American Union, Marchand also reports.

22. Lucile Davidson, letter to Florence Tuttle, Sept. 8, 1917, WPP Records, reel 4, box 5, folder 13.

23. Lucile Davidson, letter to Anne Herendeen, Sept. 6, 1917, WPP Records, reel 4, box 5, folder 13.

24. Lucile Davidson, letter to Fannie M. Witherspoon, Oct. 15, 1917, WPP Records, reel 4, box 5, folder 13.

25. Margaret Lane, letter to Miss Case, Dec. 12, 1917, WPP Records, reel 4, box 5, folder 13. Lane replied to Case's inquiry about *Four Lights,* "The Board has decided to discontinue it but the editors are asking that a referendum to the members be conducted." There is no evidence that such a referendum was ever taken.

26. Neil A. Wynn, *From Progressivism to Prosperity* (New York: Holmes & Meier, 1986) 44.

27. Steinson, *American Women's Activism* 297–98.

28. Jane Addams's involvement in the Food Administration is altogether avoided in her *Peace and Bread in Time of War* (New York: Macmillan, 1922). The book expresses Addams's wish that the United States would sustain all countries, regardless of alliance, by its food production: "Would she not still feel her inadequacy unless she was able to embody in a permanent organization the cosmopolitanism which is the essence of her spirit? We feared she would not be content when she was obliged to organize food supplies solely for one group of nations, for the United States owed too much to all the nations of the earth whose sons had developed her raw prairies into fertile fields, to allow the women and children of any of them to starve" (115–16). As it happened, Addams's "fear" was entirely groundless. The United States was perfectly happy to organize food supplies for the Allies alone and to permit the women and children of the Central Powers to starve; but this Addams does not discuss.

29. David Shannon, *The Socialist Party of America* (New York: Macmillan, 1955) 8–9, 99–100.

30. Carl Sandburg, *Complete Poems* (New York: Harcourt Brace Jovanovich, 1969) 28–29. Cited hereafter parenthetically in the text as *CP.*

31. Penelope Niven, *Carl Sandburg: A Biography* (New York: Scribner's, 1991) 300.

32. See James Weinstein, *The Decline of Socialism in America, 1912–1925* (New York: Monthly Review P, 1967) 178–181, for examples of the widespread enthusiasm with which the Socialist Party greeted the Russian revolution.

33. This is the interpretation stressed by Niven, who attributes Sandburg's support of the government to a "deep affection for the United States so often ingrained in first-generation citizens" (Sandburg's parents had immigrated separately from Sweden, met and married in Galesburg, Illinois) (*Carl Sandburg* 296). Another line of inquiry, worked out more fully in my "Taming the Socialist: Carl Sandburg's *Chicago Poems* and Its Critics," *American Literature* 63 (1991): 89–103, is that Sandburg's developing aspirations as a modernist poet kept him from adopting politically controversial positions – and, indeed, made him wary of any poetry with a propagandistic edge.

34. David M. Kennedy, *Over Here* (New York: Oxford UP, 1980) 27–28.

35. Frank L. Grubbs, *The Struggle for Labor Loyalty: Gompers, the AF of L, and the Pacifists, 1917–1920* (Durham, NC: Duke UP, 1968) 39–40. Grubbs indicates that the American Alliance was organized by late July 1917. The quantity of Alliance press releases extant is small relative to the quantity that must have been printed. Some releases can be found in the national Archives, Washington, D.C.: "Articles and Editorials for Use in Newspapers and Periodicals, Issued under the Name of the American Alliance for Labor and Democracy," July–Nov. 1918, Record Group 63, entry 58. A smaller number, including releases from March and April 1918 as well as a release celebrating the anniversary of the armistice, can be found at the Rare Book and Special Collections Library, the University of Illinois at Urbana-Champaign.

36. See Chapter 2, note 30, this volume, for a summary of the various estimates of Socialist Party membership during the war.

37. Shannon, *Socialist Party* 97.

38. Ibid. 8–9, 99–100.

39. The decision to refrain from active war opposition was not made without dissent among the leading organizers of the IWW. Melvin Dubofsky mentions Richard Brazier, along with Frank Little and Ralph Chaplin, as Wobblies who chafed under the official policy and who, at some point, spoke out directly against U.S. intervention or the draft. See Dubofsky's *We Shall Be All: A History of the Industrial Workers of the World* (Chicago: Quadrangle Books, 1969) esp. 353–58, for a description of the IWW's internal debate about how to address the war crisis. Dubofsky is cited hereafter parenthetically in the text.

40. See H. C. Peterson and Gilbert Fite, *Opponents of War* (Madison: U of Wisconsin P, 1957), esp. chapter 9, "Purging the Movies and the Press."

41. "Bingo" [Ralph Chaplin], "It's So Different in America!" cartoon, *Solidarity* July 28, 1917: 1.

42. "The Blot on Democracy," *Solidarity* July 28, 1917: 1.
43. As recently as May 5, 1917, IWW members had been acquitted in Washington State of murder charges. They were among the IWW organizers who had been on the *Verona* when the boat was attacked by the Everett deputies. Dubofsky writes that the jailings and trial outcome yielded a bonanza of favorable publicity for the union (*We Shall Be All* 342–43).
44. According to Dubofsky, 166 IWW members were indicted in September 1917 (408); 113 were charged in April 1918 (the lower number being the result of severances and dropped charges); 101 were convicted in August 1918 (the balance being dismissed from the case near its outset) (ibid. 435).
45. Dubofsky provides an overview of the Chicago trial (ibid. 433–37). For a more detailed account consult Harrison George, *The I.W.W. Trial: Story of the Greatest Trial in Labor's History by One of the Defendants* (n.d.; New York: Arno, 1969). George embellishes the testimony with a class-war interpretation of the courthouse scene. (The book was published soon after the trial in the hope of fueling public – or at least Wobbly – outrage over the proceedings.) Also of interest is Art Young and John Reed, "The Social Revolution in Court," *Liberator* Sept. 1918: 20–28. The complete trial transcript is stored in the IWW Collection of the Archives of Labor and Urban Affairs, Wayne State University, Detroit.
46. "I.W.W. Trial in Chicago," *Trial Bulletin* 25 (May 9, 1918).
47. Although not specifically identified in the trial, the pagination used in the testimony to refer to particular poems matches that of the ninth edition. More recent editions of the songbook also contain a majority of the songs discussed below; the *Songs of the Workers to Fan the Flames of Discontent,* 34th ed. (Chicago: IWW, 1973), for example, includes "Christians at War," "Casey Jones – Union Scab," and "Harvest War Song." Since my discussion primarily follows Thompson's in-court interpretation of the songs, I refer in most cases to the trial manuscript.
48. George, *I.W.W. Trial* 71.
49. *United States v. Haywood, et al.,* June 26, 1918, IWW Collection, box 109, folder 2, p. 5161, Archives of Labor and Urban Affairs, Wayne State University (cited hereafter as ALUA-WSU).
50. Joyce Kornbluh, ed., *Rebel Voices* (Ann Arbor: U of Michigan P, 1964) 326.
51. John F. Kendrick, ["Onward, Christian Soldiers!"] *Solidarity* Dec. 4, 1915: 2.
52. William Lloyd Garrison, ["The Anglo-Saxon Christians, with Gatling gun and sword,"] *Solidarity* Dec. 4, 1915: 2.
53. *United States. v. Haywood, et al.,* June 26, 1918, 5164. Subsequent references to Thompson's June 26 testimony are made parenthetically in the text, referenced by page number in the trial transcript.
54. Dubofsky's depiction of the 1917 struggles between the IWW and AFL in the copper and timber industries indicates the kind of conflict and uneasy

coexistence that virtually all IWW members would have been familiar with (*We Shall Be All*, chapter 14, "The Class War at Home and Abroad").

55. *Songs of the Workers on the Road, in the Jungles and in the Shops*, 9th ed. (Cleveland: IWW Publishing Bureau, Mar. 1916) 17.

56. Ibid. 18.

57. *United States v. Haywood, et al.*, July 18, 1918, IWW Collection, box 112, folder 4, p. 7515, ALUA-WSU.

58. *United States v. Haywood, et al.*, July 19, 1918, IWW Collection, box 112, folder 7, p. 7676, ALUA-WSU. Subsequent references to Chaplin's July 19 testimony are made parenthetically in the text, referenced by page number in the trial transcript.

59. "Preamble of the Industrial Workers of the World," *Songs of the Workers*, 34th Ed., inside cover. (Printed widely in IWW newspapers, songbooks, and pamphlets.)

60. "I.W.W. Trial at Chicago," *Daily Bulletin* 16 (Chicago: IWW Publishing Bureau, Apr. 20, 1918). The complete series of the IWW *Daily Bulletin* and *Trial Bulletin* are contained in the IWW Collection, box 123, ALUA-WSU.

Chapter 6

1. Quoted in H. C. Peterson and Gilbert Fite, *Opponents of War, 1917–1918* (Madison: U of Wisconsin P, 1957) 17.

2. Ibid. 47. See also William L. O'Neill, ed., *Echoes of Revolt: The Masses, 1911–1917* (Chicago: Quadrangle Books, 1966). O'Neill describes in detail the legal proceedings that brought an end to the *Masses* (297–300). According to the *Masses* editors, the U.S. Post Office "construed the Espionage Act as giving it power to exclude from the mails anything which might interfere with the successful conduct of the war" (297).

3. Neil A. Wynn, *From Progressivism to Prosperity: World War I and American Society* (New York: Holmes & Meier, 1986) 50.

4. Quoted in Peterson and Fite, *Opponents of War* 215.

5. Describing how resistant practices remain possible even within institutional and ideological structures, Michel de Certeau's *The Practice of Everyday Life*, trans. Steven Rendall (Berkeley: U of California P, 1984) suggests as models the relation between reading and writing, speech-acts and discourse (20), consumption and production (30–31), renters and owners (33), time and space (35), walkers and city planners (92–93). "To read," de Certeau says, "is to wander through an imposed system (that of the text, analogous to the constructed order of a city or of a supermarket)," but also, "The reader takes neither the position of the author nor an author's position. He invents in texts something different from what they 'intended.' . . . He combines their fragments and creates something un-known in the space organized by their capacity for allowing an indefinite plurality of meanings" (169).

6. Ibid. 31. Also see 40 for de Certeau's account of how expanded surveillance increases the potential for subversion.

7. Ibid. 31.

8. Jacques Derrida, *Of Grammatology,* trans. Gayatri Chakravorty Spivak (Baltimore: Johns Hopkins UP, 1974). See, e.g., part I, chapter 2, "Linguistics and Grammatology."

9. De Certeau writes, "The space of a tactic is the space of the other. . . . It does not, therefore, have the options of planning general strategy and viewing the adversary as a whole within a distinct, visible, and objectifiable space. It operates in isolated actions, blow by blow. It takes advantage of 'opportunities' and depends on them, being without any base where it could stockpile its winnings, build up its own position, and plan raids. What it wins it cannot keep" (*Practice of Everyday Life* 37).

10. W. E. B. Du Bois, "Editorial: Close Ranks," *Crisis* 16.3 (July 1918): 111.

11. In a diary of his trip home from the Philippines published in the *Richmond Planet,* Watkins remarks that he had been stationed there for "the past four years" (Watkins, "Back to God's Country," *Richmond Planet* Oct. 20, 1917: 1).

12. Lucian Watkins, "Song of the American Dove," *Crisis* 12.2 (June 1916): 86.

13. Roscoe C. Jamison, "Negro Soldiers," *Crisis* 14.2 (June 1917): 249.

14. The author of "Black Samson of Brandywine" is identified as Paul Dunbar by Abby Arthur Johnson and Ronald Maberry Johnson, *Propaganda and Aesthetics: The Literary Politics of African-American Magazines in the Twentieth Century* (Amherst: U of Massachusetts P, 1991) 41.

15. "Black Samson of Brandywine," *Crisis* 14.2 (June 1917): 255.

16. Lucian Watkins, "These," *Crisis* 15.4 (Feb. 1918): 185.

17. Vachel Lindsay, "The Jazz Bird," Vigilantes Press Releases, ca. May 1918, Hermann Hagedorn file, Library of Congress Manuscript Division. In March and April 1918, the months before the release of Lindsay's poem, four African-American infantry regiments were incorporated into the French army; elements of these units served at the front longer than any others in the American Expeditionary Force (Edward M. Coffman, *The War to End All Wars: The American Military Experience in World War I* [Madison: U of Wisconsin P, 1968] 232–33).

18. David Levering Lewis, *W. E. B. Du Bois: Biography of a Race, 1868–1919* (New York: Holt, 1993) 544.

19. See Allen Tucker, "The 367th Infantry," *New York Times* June 12, 1918: 12. Reprinted in *Crisis* 16.4 (August 1918): 227. Published in the *Crisis* the month after Du Bois's "Close Ranks" editorial had been published, the poem celebrates black soldiery much as Du Bois had throughout the war; it lacks, however, the sense, until recently shared by Du Bois and virtually all other contributors, that the United States had not yet lived up to its democratic bargain with black Americans.

20. Lewis reports that the *Chicago Defender, Cleveland Gazette,* and *Baltimore Afro-American* all criticized Du Bois's endorsement of an officers' training camp for blacks that was to be segregated (*Du Bois* 529); the *Pittsburgh Courier,* the *New York News,* and the newly formed magazine the *Messenger* are particularly cited as representing the majority of black periodicals that denounced Du Bois's "Close Ranks" editorial (556).

21. "The Right of Free Speech," *Richmond Planet* Sept. 1, 1917: 1.

22. Reporting in the August 11 edition regarding the fracas with the Post Office over the July 27 issue, the *Planet* editors argued: "He [Mr. Miner] did not advise any one else to take this position [of not volunteering for armed service]. How then could it be alleged that the *Planet,* whose editorial management is not responsible for views expressed by its correspondents be punished for something done by a citizen of the United States and who under the greatest stretch of application could be held only personally for the expressions contained therein? He spoke in the people's forum, so to speak" ("Constitutional Guarantees Not Suspended," *Richmond Planet* Aug. 11, 1917: 1).

23. George Ben Johnson, "How Speakest Thou?" cartoon, *Richmond Planet* Sept. 1, 1917: 1.

24. Robert Dangerfield Crawley, "Ethiopia's War Song," *Richmond Planet* July 14, 1917: 1.

25. E. D. Caffee, "Now or Never," *Richmond Planet* Mar. 20, 1918: 8.

26. W. E. B. Du Bois, "Editorial: Close Ranks."

27. Lucian Watkins, "The Negro Soldiers of America: What We Are Fighting For," *Richmond Planet* Mar. 2, 1918: 1.

28. Lucian B. Watkins, "'No Man's Land,'" *Richmond Planet* Oct. 19, 1918: 1.

29. Wynn, *Progressivism to Prosperity* 174–75.

30. W. E. B. Du Bois, "The Black Man in the Revolution of 1914–1918," *Crisis* 17.5 (Mar. 1919): 218–23; "Documents of the War," *Crisis* 18.1 (May 1919): 16–21; and "An Essay Toward a History of the Black Man in the Great War," *Crisis* 18.2 (June 1919): 63–87.

31. James Hart lists the 1918 circulation of the *Atlantic* as 69,947 and *Harper's* as 100,039 ("American Poetry of the First World War [1914–1920]: A Survey and Checklist," diss., Duke U, 1964, xiii).

32. Langston Hughes, *Fight for Freedom: The Story of the NAACP* (New York: Norton, 1962) 25.

33. Melvin Dubofsky, *We Shall Be All: A History of the Industrial Workers of the World* (Chicago: Quadrangle Books, 1969) 316, 349.

34. Patterns of latent ethnic resistance to the war may be linked to regional variations in war enthusiasm. Christopher Gibbs claims that feelings against the war were widespread, arguing that there was a notable "lack of enthusiasm for the war in the Midwest, the South, and the Northwest, indeed, everywhere outside the metropolitan Northeast" (*The Great Silent Majority: Mis-*

souri's Resistance to World War I [Columbia: U of Missouri P, 1988] vii). Gibbs allows that the programs of the Food Administration did produce the surplus needed to supply the Allies with food, but he claims that this was never accompanied by wholehearted patriotic support for the war. Indeed, "The government set people against each other by rewarding big producers at the expense of consumers and small producers, by setting retailers against their customers, by encouraging people to spy on each other, by threatening, bribing, coercing people to work for the war" (134).

35. Hart, "American Poetry" xiii.
36. Wynn, *Progressivism to Prosperity* 135.
37. Mari Jo Buhle and Paul Buhle write of the National American Woman Suffrage Association, "By 1917, NAWSA took a patriotic stand for national victory, even while claiming that when women were free, wars would cease" (*The Concise History of Woman Suffrage: Selections from the Classic Work of Stanton, Anthony, Gage, and Harper* [Urbana: U of Illinois P, 1978] 39).
38. Nick Salvatore, *Eugene V. Debs: Citizen and Socialist* (Urbana: U of Illinois P, 1982) 325, 296.
39. Salvatore notes that while Debs garnered a larger vote in 1920 than in 1912, the percentage of overall votes slipped from 6% in the earlier election to 3% in the later (ibid. 325). Although the decline in percentage does indicate an ebbing of the Socialist Party's national political ambitions, my argument here emphasizes rather the persistence of radical views in spite of the loss of organizational coherence and power. That nearly a million people would cast their votes for a convicted seditionist serving prison time, even after all the government propaganda of 1917–19, precisely underscores this point.
40. "Why the Poor Should Be Patriotic," *Masses* 9.9 (July 1917): 37.
41. Bernice Evans, "The Sayings of Patsy, as Recorded by Bernice Evans," *New York Call,* Sept. 30, 1917, mag. sect.: 13.
42. Bernice Evans, "The Sayings of Patsy, as Recorded by Bernice Evans," *New York Call,* Oct. 14, 1917, mag. sect.: 13.
43. "Subscribers – Please Read," *New York Call* Dec. 27, 1917: 3.
44. Frederick A. Blossom, "The Man with the Hoe and the Man with the Gun," *New York Call* Aug. 26, 1917: 8.
45. Willard Parker, "America's 'Man With the Hoe,'" *New York Call* Aug. 27, 1917: 8.
46. Lola Ridge, "Bread," *New York Call* Oct. 19, 1917: 10; Sadie Amter, "Patriotism," ibid. Dec. 19, 1917: 6; "Hic Jacet Henry Dubb," ibid. Jan. 10, 1917: 6.
47. "Foy," "To Herbert Hoover," *New York Call* Nov. 10, 1917: 10.
48. Walter Goldwater, *Radical Periodicals in America, 1890–1950* (New Haven, CT: Yale U Library, 1966) 30.
49. Frank D. Walsh, "Frank D. Walsh Writes Vigorously on the Duty of Foreign-Born Americans," *Detroit Labor News* Dec. 28, 1917: 4.

50. Chester M. Wright, "An Age Is Dying! An Age Is Being Born!" *Detroit Labor News* Feb. 1, 1918: 4.
51. "O, You Hoover!" *Detroit Labor News* Feb. 1, 1918: 4.
52. James J. Montague, "A Petition," *Roanoke Times* May 10, 1918: 6. Montague was not the only American who made light of the (apparently) short supply of prunes. Mark Sullivan's *Over Here, 1914–1915,* vol. 5 of *Our Times: The United States, 1900–1925* (New York: Scribner's, 1933), reprints a cartoon from *Life* magazine of February 21, 1918, showing six policemen searching the dining room of "the citizen who was suspected of having more than his share of prunes" (421).
53. U.S. Food Administration, *The Day's Food in War and Peace* ([Washington, DC: Government Publishing Office,] 1918) 18.
54. Ibid. 35.
55. Anthony Euwer, *Wings and Other War Rhymes* (New York: Moffat, Yard, 1918) 69–70.
56. Euwer's oversight was not unusual. Military strategists on both sides came to believe that American soldiers would tip the balance in favor of the Allies because they provided a limitless pool of substitutes. German Field Marshall Hindenburg announced in September 1918, "Unlike the enemy, we had no fresh reserves to throw in. . . . Instead of an inexhaustible America, we had only weary allies who were themselves on the point of collapse" (quoted in Coffman, *War to End All Wars* 298). Coffman echoes Hindenburg's analysis when he describes an earlier period of military deployment: "In July 1918 the flood of American reinforcements made the crucial difference: Allied forces were steadily growing, while the Germans had to merely fight on with what they had" (247).
57. Cf. Ernesto Laclau and Chantal Mouffe, *Hegemony and Socialist Strategy: Towards a Radical Democratic Politics,* trans. Winston Moore and Paul Cammack (London: Verso, 1985). Two passages from their conclusion demand special attention. First, on the importance of constructing a hegemonic strategy as opposed to concentrating on locally resistant tactics, Laclau and Mouffe write: "No hegemonic project can be based exclusively on a democratic logic, but must also consist of a set of proposals for the positive organization of the social. If the demands of a subordinated group are presented purely as negative demands subversive of a certain order, without being linked to any viable project for the reconstruction of specific areas of society, their capacity to act hegemonically will be excluded from the outset" (189). Second, on the kind of difficult, conflicted negotiations that must take place for such a hegemonic strategy to be articulated by various subordinated groups, they conclude: "The de-centering and autonomy of the different discourses and struggles, the multiplication of antagonisms and the construction of a plurality of spaces within which they can affirm themselves and develop, are the conditions *sine qua non* of the possibility that the different compo-

nents of the classical ideal of socialism [the abolition of capitalist relations of production] – which should, no doubt, be extended and reformulated – can be achieved. And as we have argued abundantly in these pages, this plurality of spaces does not deny, but rather requires, the overdetermination of its effects at certain levels and the consequent hegemonic articulation between them" (192).

Conclusion

1. Antonio Gramsci, *Selections from the Prison Notebooks*, ed. and trans. Quintin Hoare and Geoffrey Nowell Smith (New York: International Publishers, 1971) 238–39.
2. Ibid. 238.
3. Ibid. 231.
4. On the relationship (and lack thereof) between white socialists and African-Americans during the war, see Philip S. Foner, *American Socialism and Black Americans*, Contributions in African-American and African Studies 33 (Westport, CT: Greenwood, 1977). The *Messenger*, founded in November 1917, was the one black periodical in the United States that declared itself socialist (271–72). The rest of the black press tended to adopt the attitude taken by Du Bois, who had quit the Socialist Party in 1912 over its silence on race issues (218) and was scornful about the *Messenger*'s argument that class antagonism, not racism, was the main factor in the East St. Louis riot (David Levering Lewis, *W. E. B. Du Bois: Biography of a Race, 1868–1919* [New York: Holt, 1993] 540). That in later years Du Bois became an avowed socialist and renounced his U.S. citizenship suggests that a wartime alliance with socialism might have been more congenial ideologically than Du Bois's support for the national mobilization.
5. Covington Hall, *Battle Hymns of Toil* (Oklahoma City: Leader Press, [1946])
6. Earlier publication dates of "The War Lord's Harvest," or of any poem in this collection, are difficult to determine. The poems, the editor says, are the "best among the hundreds" that Hall wrote during the "forty years" of his writing career (ii, i). Hall's use of "Unknown Soldiers' graves" appears to refer to the tombs of the "unknown soldier" that were commissioned by Britain, France, and the United States soon after the war; thus, the poem was almost certainly written after the war had ended. Since the collection seems to be arranged in chronological order of composition, it is probable, judging from the early position of the poem, that it was written and published within a few years of the war's end. Covington Hall was, according to Kornbluh, "one of the most prolific of the IWW writers" (*Rebel Voices* [Ann Arbor: U of Michigan P, 1964] 259). He was also active in the Non-Partisan League.
6. Henry George Weiss, *Lenin Lives* (Holt, MN: Hagglund, 1935) 16–17. Weiss's dates are 1898–1946.

7. Jane Addams, *Peace and Bread in Time of War* (New York: Macmillan, 1922) 84.

8. Weiss, *Lenin Lives* 17.

9. Sarah Cleghorn, "Come, Fifty Million Men and Women!" *Fellowship of Reconciliation* 6.10 (Dec. 1940): 153. Also published in *Poems of Peace and Freedom* (Fulton, NY: Morrill, 1945) 47. See Cary Nelson, *Repression and Recovery* (Madison: U of Wisconsin P, 1989), for further discussion and bibliography of Henry George Weiss, Covington Hall, and Cleghorn. It was *Repression and Recovery* that first alerted me to the work of these writers.

10. Lina Mainiero, ed., *American Women Writers,* 5 vols. (New York: Ungar, 1979) vol. 1. Though Cleghorn (1876–1959) was a successful novelist before the war, after it she was "unable to sell her writing because of its strong pacifist bias."

11. In an article in *Callaloo,* "Image and Action: Critics of the Academy" (16.2 [1993]: 293–302), Patricia Meyer Spacks, president of the Modern Language Association as I write in 1994, is particularly keen to stress that literature teachers who take the political to be primary are in a minority: "A minority of those currently professing literature refuse, as they say, to 'privilege' the literary over the nonliterary, works that have pleased many and pleased long over comic books and advertisements. . . . Still, many of us (a *great* many) continue to believe in the power and the importance of works that have endured – as well as, perhaps, in the power and the importance of certain texts that have more or less disappeared from view. . . . In short, today's strong college teachers often use new ways of thinking to supplement, not to displace, old ones" (297).

    Politicized teaching *would* seem to be marginalized, given the way that Spacks appeals freely (and quite unreflectively) to the primacy of literary value and to a characterization of the political minority strikingly similar to that of the p.c. bashers she deplores earlier in the article. It seems somewhat disingenuous, therefore, to describe the *majority* of professionals in literary study as embattled and overwhelmed: "Liberal and conservative opponents [of the politicized minority], a fragmented company, often feel alienated and angry but vulnerable, fearing that their voices, defending the past and sometimes the permanent, will sound outmoded, irrelevant, despite their support of truth and virtue" (297).

12. Paul Fussell, *The Great War and Modern Memory* (New York: Oxford UP, 1975) 35.

13. Poems like "Watch Over Us" (*Roanoke Times and World News* Jan. 28, 1991: A4), composed by Marine Sgt. Charles S. Cox – a soldier-poet for our time – are enabled by a whole series of cultural agencies more powerful than English literature courses. Three of the poem's eight stanzas read as follows:

    > From the West
    > From the East

We've merged upon
The Middle East.
To meet an enemy
Face to face,
Who's challenged the rights
Of the human race.

Led by a madman
Who they believe is right,
Are they a match for us
Can they put up a good fight?
They've taken innocent people
Against their will,
They hold them hostage
With threats to kill.

Army, Navy
Air Force, Marines,
We've joined together
With other countries
To restore a country
And set it free
In the name of justice
And liberty.

Published in newspapers in Roanoke, Virginia, and Kansas City, Missouri, the poem not only demonstrates familiarity with Armed Forces advertisements ("Army, Navy / Air Force, Marines") and with the pledge of allegiance ("liberty and justice" transposed to fit the rhyme). It also sets forth conceptions of "rights of the human race," of besieged peoples appealing to the United States as savior, and of war as a sporting event in which the opponent is looked to for a "good fight." The poem's spectacular conventionality of sentiment and poetics may make it seem unsuitable for serious literary study; at the same time, its very conventionality – the fact that it could be written by virtually anyone – is testament to the pervasiveness of its ideology.

14. For critiques of these forms of instrumental reason that duly appreciate their pervasiveness and power, see Michel de Certeau's *Practice of Everyday Life* (trans. Steven Rendall [Berkeley: U of California P, 1984]) esp. chapters 10 and 13, "The Scriptural Economy" and "Believing and Making People Believe"; and Jacques Derrida, "The Principle of Reason: The University in the Eyes of Its Pupils," *Diacritics* 13.3 (Fall 1983): 3–20.

15. David Perkins, *A Story of Modern Poetry: From the 1890s to the High Modernist Mode,* vol. 1 of *A History of Modern Poetry,* 2 vols. (Cambridge, MA: Harvard UP, 1976) 297–98.

Index

All titles set off by quotation marks are poems unless otherwise indicated by a parenthetical note (e.g., cartoon, essay, stickerette).

The following titles are out of print: